Handbook of the Collections

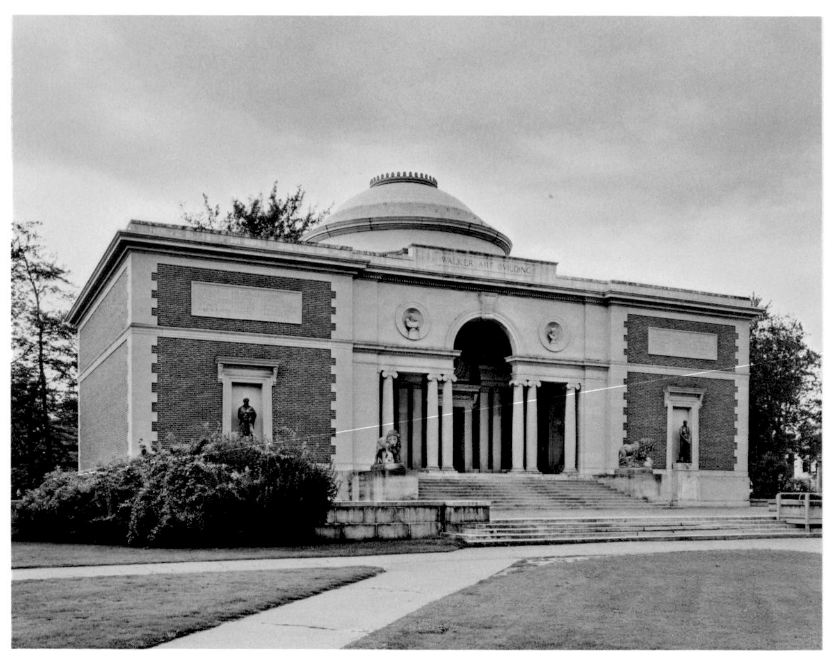

Walker Art Building
McKim, Mead & White, architects
1892-1894

Bowdoin College Museum of Art

HANDBOOK
of the
COLLECTIONS

Edited by
MARGARET R. BURKE

BRUNSWICK, MAINE
1981

*This project is supported by a grant
from the National Endowment for the Arts
in Washington, D.C., a federal agency.*

ISBN: 0–916606–01–5

Library of Congress Catalog Card Number: 81–66892

To the memory of John H. Halford,
of the Class of 1907

Table of Contents

Acknowledgements

———

A museum of art cannot continue to grow without the generosity of special patrons whose support serves to encourage overall programming and the expansion of physical facilities and collections. Appropriately, the Bowdoin College Museum of Art *Handbook of the Collections* is dedicated to one such person, John H. Halford '07, who gave in many ways to the Museum of Art over a period of more than fifty years. We are particularly grateful to James M. Fawcett III '58, who made the publication of the *Handbook* possible; his donation, matched by the National Endowment for the Arts, guaranteed realization of the project. In addition, essential financial support for staff members concerned with the *Handbook* has come in part from the Institute of Museum Services, a federal agency, and the Maine State Commission on the Arts and the Humanities.

The issuing of the *Handbook* also is an occasion to acknowledge the efforts of former directors who were concerned with the early stages of its publication: Marvin S. Sadik, Richard V. West, and R. Peter Mooz, who established the current format of the text. Professor Philip C. Beam, a former director and curator of the Winslow Homer Collection, author of two earlier handbooks and of the section on the Homer Collection in this publication, has been a stimulating, thoughtful consultant throughout.

Other members of the museum's staff have participated in varying phases of the *Handbook*'s preparation. Margaret R. Burke, curator of collections and editor of the *Handbook* from 1976 to 1980, was responsible for much of the organization, wrote many of the entries, and brought the text to completion. Laura Harrington '77, curatorial intern in 1977-1978, did research for the checklists and drafted a number of introductory sections. The steady contribution as writer and editorial assistant of Kerry A. O'Brien '78, curatorial assistant at the time of final editing, lent momentum to the entire project. David P. Becker '70, formerly museum registrar, aided in assembling the checklists of prints and drawings. We wish in addition to express our appreciation to Suzanne K. Bergeron, Kenneth G. Daniel, Russell J. Moore, Brenda M. Pelletier, Peter J. Simmons '78, and Roxlyn C. Yanok.

The *Handbook* is enriched by the work of scholars outside the museum who evaluated collections, wrote chapter introductions and entries, compiled checklists, and answered innumerable technical questions. For sharing their time and knowledge, we are indebted to Fred C. Albertson, James D. Burke, Richard Hsiao, Evan M. Maurer, Deborah Del Gais Muller, Erik O. Nielsen, Andrea S. Norris, Eva Ray, Michael Richman '65, Robert F. Trent, Zdenka Volavka, and Stephen Wilkinson.

Members of the Volunteers Association of the Bowdoin College Museum helped with the proofreading of the text and eased the responsibilities of the professional staff, freeing time for concentration on the *Handbook*. Mary E. Tiffany '78, an art history major, helped during the organizational stages of the manuscript, and Barbara Schuster and Marie S. Bengtsson '81 of the College staff aided with secretarial work. John McKee of Bowdoin's Department of Art designed the book, took most of the recent photographs, and offered support and encouragement to all concerned. Joseph Nicoletti did the cover drawing, based on architectural ornamentation of the Walker Art Building. Members of the College's editorial office, Edward Born '57, Peter H. Vaughn, Rachel D. Dutch, and Susan L. Ransom, contributed invaluable expertise.

Another patron, without whom no project of the Bowdoin College Museum of Art could be concluded, must be cited and thanked—the College itself, students, administration, faculty, staff, and Governing Boards—whose endorsement of the museum has assured its steady growth over the years. We particularly wish to acknowledge Presidents Roger Howell, Jr. '58 and Willard F. Enteman, Dean Alfred H. Fuchs, and Vice President for Development C. Warren Ring, during whose terms of office the *Handbook* was written, and whose recognition of the excellence of the museum and its essential role in the cultural life of campus, community, and state has given impetus to the institution's development. In particular, William Curtis Pierce '28, chairman for twelve years of the Governing Boards' committee concerned with the Museum of Art, deserves special recognition for his untiring efforts on behalf of the museum.

The completion of the *Handbook* is a long-awaited event. Many of the collections little known outside of the College will, for the first time, become available to a larger public through the illustrated catalogue and checklists. We can think of no more appropriate way to recognize and express gratitude to those who have faithfully supported the Bowdoin College Museum of Art in the past and whose continuing interest remains essential for its future.

Katharine J. Watson
Director

Preface

This *Handbook* represents a major step in the museum's goal of generating public as well as scholarly interest in its extensive collections through publication. Thus the format of the *Handbook* is designed to serve as a general guide to individual objects and to provide sufficient information on particularly significant works of art to stimulate research. The *Handbook* is divided into eight sections, each representing a specific area of the museum's holdings. Every section includes a brief historical introduction, essays on and illustrations of major works of art, and a selective checklist. In most cases, an art historian with a specialization in a particular area served as a section or checklist author. Individual contributions are indicated by the author's initials listed in the following key. At this time, the editor would like to express appreciation to everyone who has contributed to this extensive project and particularly to the art historical consultants, who have awaited the publication of the *Handbook* with patience.

Margaret R. Burke
Editor

Editorial Key

Alumni of Bowdoin College named in this *Handbook* are distinguished by class numerals directly following their names. The names of nineteenth-century alumni are followed by the four digits of their classes' years of graduation (1863), those of twentieth-century alumni by an apostrophe and two digits ('42). Recipients of honorary degrees have an h before their numerals (h '22), alumni of the Maine Medical School an M (M 1889).

Initials following chapter introductions and entries and preceding the lists of notes at the end of each chapter acknowledge authorship of those sections according to the following key:

Fred C. Albertson	[F.C.A.]
Philip C. Beam	[P.C.B.]
David P. Becker	[D.P.B.]
James D. Burke	[J.D.B.]
Margaret R. Burke	[M.R.B.]
Laura Harrington	[L.H.]
Richard Hsiao	[R.H.]
Evan M. Maurer	[E.M.M.]
Deborah Del Gais Muller	[D. DEL G. M.]
Erik O. Nielsen	[E.O.N.]
Andrea S. Norris	[A.S.N.]
Kerry A. O'Brien	[K.A.O.]
Eva Ray	[E.R.]
Michael Richman	[M.R.]
Robert F. Trent	[R.F.T.]
Zdenka Volavka	[Z.V.]
Katharine J. Watson	[K.J.W.]
Richard V. West	[R.V.W.]
Stephen Wilkinson	[S.W.]

Measurements throughout are in inches, with their metric equivalents following in parentheses. Height always precedes width; depth, where it is appropriate, always follows width. Diameter measurements are labelled where they occur.

Where it is impossible to determine an exact date, the closest approximations are written together and punctuated with a slash (1861/2).

✠   This symbol placed to the left of an entry in the "Selected Works from the Collection" at the end of each chapter indicates that the work is more fully described in an individual entry within the chapter itself.

History of the Collections

The collections of art at Bowdoin College are among the earliest formed in America. The Honorable James Bowdoin III, the son of the Governor James Bowdoin II of Massachusetts for whom the College was named, was the institution's first and chief benefactor and patron of the arts. A man of broad intellectual interests, the younger Bowdoin studied and traveled in Europe and served from 1805 to 1808 as a United States minister plenipotentiary to Spain during the presidency of Thomas Jefferson. During his European travels and perhaps in America as well, he acquired an extensive art collection, a most unusual activity for an American at this early date. Upon his death in 1811, Bowdoin bequeathed to the College much valuable property, among which were two portfolios of drawings and seventy paintings. Valued by the appraisers at $7.75, the 142 drawings were uncatalogued and locked undisturbed in the library until 1881, when they were inventoried by F. W. Hall. In 1885 Professor Henry Johnson, the first director of the Bowdoin Museum, incorporated this inventory into a descriptive catalogue of the Bowdoin drawings which clearly outlined the significance of Bowdoin's gift. Included were works by Beccafumi, Brueghel the Elder, Cambiaso, Koninck, Maratta, Petri, Poccetti, Quillard, Ricci, Vanni, Vellert, and Weenix.

The paintings bequeathed by James Bowdoin III remained in the custody of his widow until 1813 when the agent for the College received them in Boston. A "true and accurate" manuscript catalogue of the works given to the executors upon the receipt of the bequest in that year is now preserved in the Special Collections Department of the Hawthorne-Longfellow Library. As was commonly the case at that time, the paintings, mostly oil on canvas, were largely copies after old masters, although several originals were acquired, including Gilbert Stuart's portraits of *Thomas Jefferson* and *James Madison*. In 1826 the widow of the benefactor, herself a Bowdoin by birth, added a series of family portraits to the collection, including the *Portrait of James Bowdoin III and His Sister Elizabeth* by Joseph Blackburn, the *Portrait of James Bowdoin II* by John Smibert, and several portraits of Bowdoin family members by Robert Feke.

As the collection grew in size and significance, the College became increasingly involved with its preservation and exhibition. The paintings were originally housed in Massachusetts Hall, the first College building, which had been completed in 1802; according to Louis Clinton Hatch's *The History of Bowdoin College,* the Governing Boards in 1826 appointed a committee for "removing the pictures now in closets and placing them in situations where they will be removed from injury." Despite such precautions, the works had deteriorated considerably by 1847, when the College commissioned D. Chase and G. Haworth of Boston to preserve them. Although $200 had been appropriated from the College's limited budget to finance the endeavor, the actual cost of restoration far exceeded this sum; several paintings considered to be of insufficient quality for exhibition were sold to meet this unforeseen expense.

The College's exhibition facilities continued to be extremely limited. In 1848 a visiting committee reported that the paintings were standing on benches in the room used for medical lectures, exposed to injury by their necessary removal from place to place during the year. In 1850, however, President Leonard Woods received from his cousin and close friend Theophilus Wheeler Walker of Boston the sum of $1,000 to be applied toward the completion of the College chapel then being designed by Richard Upjohn. Since Mr. Walker had long been devoted to the art interests of the College, the Governing Boards voted to include in the chapel an art gallery dedicated to the memory of Sophia Wheeler Walker, the donor's mother. Thus, the College's first formal art museum was established on the second floor of the chapel.

During the second half of the nineteenth century, the collections continued to expand. In addition to several further important gifts from members of the Bowdoin family, the College received in 1852 a collection of twenty-five paintings and seven engravings from Colonel William Boyd 1810. In 1860 five large Assyrian reliefs from the palace of Ashurnazirpal II were given by Dr. Henri B. Haskell M 1855 and were exhibited at the north end of the chapel.

Interest in the College's art holdings continued to grow. In 1870 Professor Jotham B. Sewall, then curator, prepared the first publication relating to the art collection, a descriptive catalogue of the paintings, which considerably elaborated upon the 1813 manuscript describing the Bowdoin bequest. In 1880 a collection of plaster sculptures from antique models was begun to stimulate student support for the arts and aid in the teaching of classics. In 1875 the College again arranged for the cleaning of many of the paintings, which were further restored in 1887-1888 by Harold Fletcher of Boston. Some members of the College community, however, disagreed with the artistic emphasis developing at Bowdoin. A letter to the *Orient* of 1883 stated: "It seems decidedly foolish to stow away in a room seldom visited a collection of paintings worth thousands of dollars, and at the same time be suffering for the common necessities of life.... If these pictures are worth as much as claimed, they ought to be exchanged for a decent telescope and observatory.... There are lots of things we need, and we don't need the fossilized, antiquated collection of brown paint."

Nonetheless, the act which most solidified the College's future artistic commitment occurred in 1891 when Harriet and Sophia Walker offered to fund the construction of a separate museum building in memory of their uncle Theophilus Wheeler Walker. The Walker sisters commissioned Charles Follen McKim of the noted architectural firm of McKim, Mead & White to design a building "that shall not only be appropriate as a memorial, but will also show the purpose for which it is to be used." McKim selected a symmetrical design which drew heavily upon Italian Renaissance prototypes. The original building was a modified Greek cross plan with a central domed sculpture hall surrounded by three galleries dedicated to James Bowdoin III, George William Boyd, and Sophia Wheeler Walker. As part of the overall decorative scheme for the building, Mc-

Kim commissioned four leading American painters—Kenyon Cox, John La Farge, Abbott Thayer, and Elihu Vedder —to execute murals for the tympana under the central dome. The four cities which most profoundly influenced the development of Western art, Athens, Florence, Rome, and Venice, were selected as a theme. Additionally, McKim employed the noted sculptor Daniel Chester French to execute a bronze relief of Theophilus Wheeler Walker to adorn the building's Walker Gallery. The close collaboration of such significant artistic figures resulted in a magnificently unified monument, one of the few remaining structures in America in which the architectural and decorative ideals of the late nineteenth century are so fully realized.

Named the Walker Art Building, the museum was dedicated on June 7, 1894; a further discussion of the museum building and its decorative scheme is found in "The Walker Art Building Murals," *Occasional Papers I,* a 1972 museum publication by Richard V. West.

General publication of the collections began in 1895 when Professor Henry Johnson, the first director of the museum, compiled the initial *Descriptive Catalogue of the Bowdoin College Art Collections,* which underwent revisions in 1903 and 1906. *The Descriptive Catalogue of the Art Collections of Bowdoin College* published by Professor Henry Andrews, director, in 1930, and *An Illustrated Handbook of the Bowdoin College Museum of Fine Arts* compiled by Professor Philip C. Beam, director, in 1950, further recorded the expansion of the museum's collections in the twentieth century.

Renovation and an underground addition designed by the firm of Edward Larabee Barnes doubled the museum's size in 1975-1976 while preserving the architectural integrity of the building. Galleries for permanent collections and temporary exhibitions and space for storage and offices were considerably expanded, complementing the facilities at the newly constructed Visual Arts Center. As the crowning achievement of its career, the Bowdoin College Museum of Art, together with its affiliate the Peary-MacMillan Arctic Museum, received professional accreditation in 1979 from the American Association of Museums.   [M.R.B.]

The Collections

———

ANCIENT MEDITERRANEAN ART

In a 1929 eulogy honoring Mr. Edward Perry Warren h '26, the noted authority Sir John D. Beazley commented upon Warren's gifts to Bowdoin College: "A coin, a gem, a vase, a statuette, would speak of Greece in the heart of Maine; and sooner or later there would be a student whose spirit would require them. There was no hurry: an acorn in the forest." The man of whom Beazley spoke had served as the prime collector of antiquities for the Museum of Fine Arts in Boston from 1894 to 1904 and remained actively engaged in the acquisition of ancient artifacts throughout his later years until his death in 1928.

Warren's influence on taste in classical art can be seen today in museums in this country and throughout Europe by the collections he formed either as purchasing agent or through outright personal donations. Among the beneficiaries of his generosity were Harvard University, the University of Chicago, the University of Leipzig, and Oxford University. Bowdoin College, the only undergraduate institution among the major recipients, received nearly 600 objects which form the basis of the museum's collection of ancient art. In 1908 the first of his gifts arrived at Bowdoin; since the College had no funds for the purchase of antiquities, these gifts were an extremely important addition to the existing collections. Every year thereafter Warren donated a number of pieces to Bowdoin, resulting in a small but significant collection in which every major class of artifact is represented. Today the antiquities collection of the Bowdoin College Museum of Art contains over 1,200 Assyrian, Egyptian, Greek, Roman, and Byzantine objects and forms one of the most comprehensive compilations of ancient art in any small college museum in North America.

The classical collection of vases and vase fragments, given to the College primarily by Warren, consists of more than one hundred pieces representing Attic, Corinthian, South

Italian, Etruscan, and Arretine cultures, among others. They range in date from the Late Bronze Age, circa 1350 B.C., to the end of the Roman Republic, first century B.C. In particular, they clearly illustrate the development of Attic painted pottery from the Late Geometric period, circa 750 B.C., to the Late Classical Red-Figure period, circa 425-400 B.C.

The Greek and Roman sculpture and relief work basically are comprised of pieces from two significant collections; in addition to works contributed by Warren, a second major donor, Mr. Dana Estes h 1898 of Boston, gave to the College in 1902 a large portion of the Lawrence-Cesnola Collection from Cyprus, material which he had acquired in the last decade of the nineteenth century.

Important as they are, however, the Warren and Estes gifts were not the first antiquities to come to the College. Five large Assyrian mural reliefs dating to the ninth century B.C., which decorated the palace at Nimrud of King Ashurnazirpal II, were given to the College in 1860 by Dr. Henri B. Haskell M 1855. Unfortunately, no suitable building existed in which to display these large gypsum slabs, so the pieces were placed in a small gallery set aside in the chapel. Their presence on the campus accentuated the need for a special building to house the growing number of art treasures, a project carried out by the Misses Harriet and Sophia Walker.   [E.O.N.]

ASSYRIAN, KALAKH

Winged Genius, ca. 885-860 B.C.

   Gypsum, $90\frac{9}{16}$ x $58\frac{13}{16}$ x $6\frac{7}{16}$ (230.0 x 149.3 x 16.3 cm)
   Gift of Dr. Henri B. Haskell M 1855. 1860.2

During the thirteenth century B.C., the Assyrians gained control over Mesopotamia, a land which had been dominated by various rulers for centuries. At first the new state consisted of a small triangle bounded by the Tigris and Great Zab rivers, in what is today northern Iraq. Under Ashurnazirpal II and his successors, the Assyrian kingdom quickly developed into a power which for a short time subdued even Egypt. Her star descended as quickly as it rose,

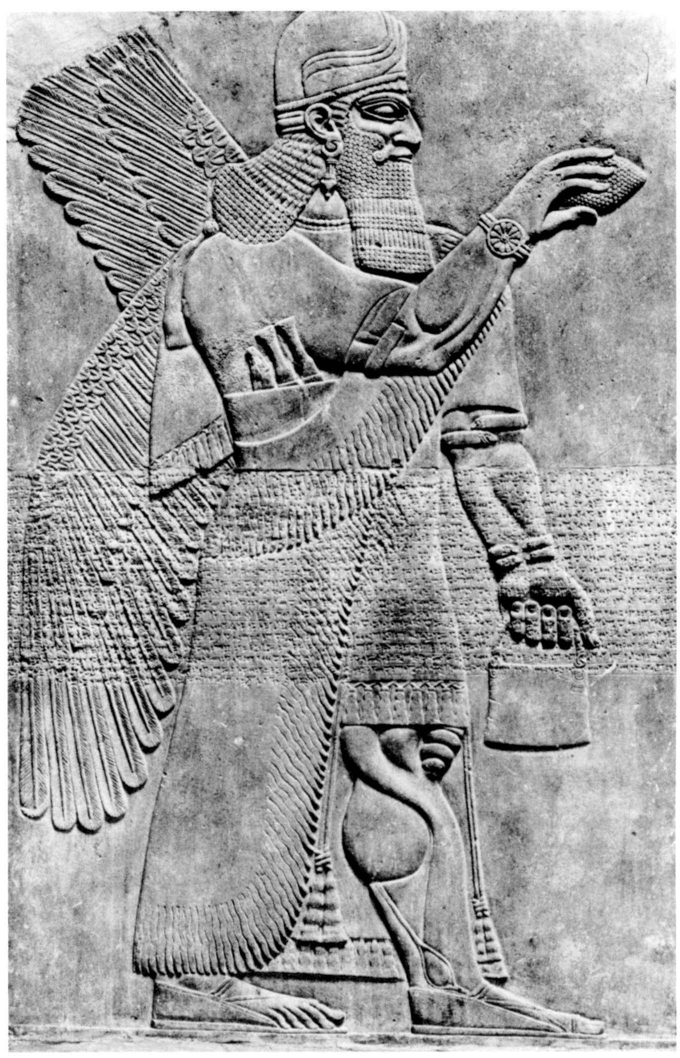

however, and in 612 B.C. Nineveh and Nimrud (Kalakh) were destroyed by the Medes. Her cities lay in ruins under rubble until their discovery in the nineteenth century by the British archaeologist Sir A. H. Layard. Despite the damage inflicted by the conquerors, enough remains of the palaces and the sculpture to suggest the power of Assyrian art.

From the ruins of his great city, Ashurnazirpal II may be judged as one of the most powerful and imaginative rulers who occupied the throne. In the first year of his reign he began the construction of a new capital at Nimrud, a city with a circuit wall of nearly five miles enclosing a town of approximately 884 acres. Within the protection of the walls stood the great North-West Palace, covering an area of approximately six acres. It was there for the greater part of the ninth century that the power of Assyria resided.

The mud brick walls of the palace were adorned with tall gypsum slabs carved in bas-relief which depicted the various exploits of the king and proclaimed his greatness. Here pictorial and literary propaganda went hand in hand, for inscribed across the face of the stone were accounts of all the ruler's accomplishments and a recitation of his royal lineage.

The large gypsum slab of the winged genius in the collection of the Bowdoin College Museum of Art is part of a larger composition which was perhaps similar to one from Throne Room B in the North-West Palace and now in the British Museum. There the king is represented on either side of the sacred tree receiving authority and kingship from the god Ashur. At each end, standing behind the dual representations of the king, is a winged genius (the one to the left is almost identical to the example illustrated here), the king's protector. The scene was intended to impress upon those present that Ashurnazirpal was king by divine right. His invincibility is reinforced by the presence of the protectors.

The two genii in the Bowdoin example are engaged in what is generally known as the "cone smearing ceremony." The fruit plucked from the sacred tree is endowed with mystical power which gives life and strength to the king when he is anointed. These divine bodyguards wear the triple-horned mitre; three handles, one carved in the shape of a horse's head, protrude from the sashes about their waists. A second relief in Bowdoin's collection (1860.5) suggests that the plain handles belong to daggers while the horse's head forms part of a whisk used in some ceremony performed by the king.

Considerable attention has been given to the details of costume. On his left forearm the genius wears heavy bracelets terminating in intricately shaped rams' heads. In contrast to the deeper carving of the outline of the body, a faintly incised elaborate border composed of panels filled with various motifs is still apparent; among the carvings are rosettes, concentric squares, and a kneeling horse or lion in the zone beneath the dagger handles. [E.O.N.]

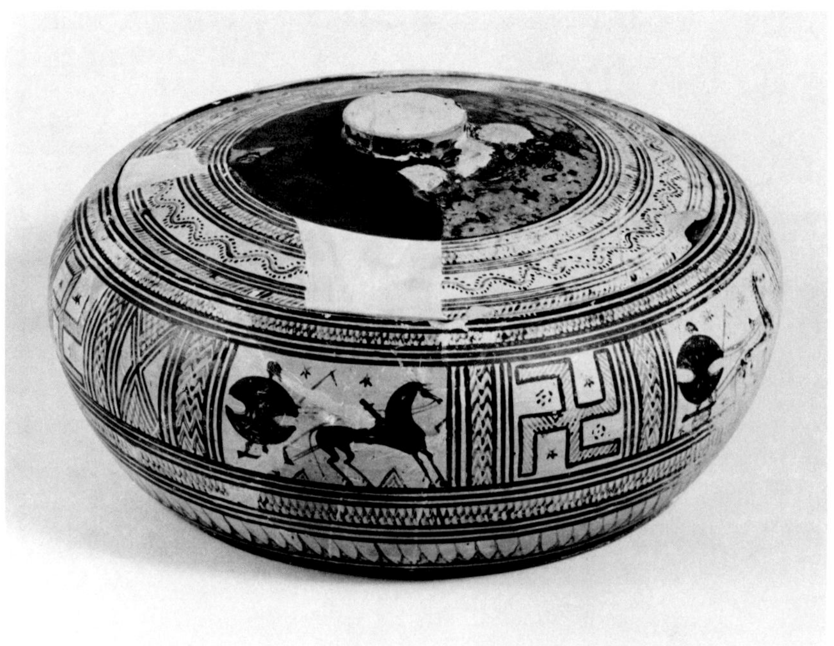

GREEK

Pyxis, ca. 750-735 B.C., Attic Geometric
  Terra cotta, $5\frac{7}{16}$ x $11\frac{3}{8}$ (diam.) (13.8 x 28.9 cm)
  Gift of Mr. Edward Perry Warren h '26. 1913.6

The Geometric period in Greece, circa 900-700 B.C., was a time of reawakening on the mainland after the collapse of the Bronze Age and the destruction of the great palaces at Mycenae, Tiryns, and Pylos. The period takes its name from the predominance of geometric patterns used to decorate the surface of vessels. Among the more popular designs were the meander, the zig-zag, the hatched triangle, and the swastika. The Geometric style appears to have been the invention of Attic potters, and it was in Athens that it reached its fullest development. Toward the middle stages of the period, the first figured scenes began to appear in Attic art. The earliest figured motifs were small animals painted in silhouette, placed on vessels in inconspicuous areas by the handles. By the Late Geometric period entire panels were devoted to elaborate funeral scenes, and the fascination and admiration of Athenian vase painters for the horse and chariot were readily apparent.

The large pyxis in the Warren Collection probably served as a jewelry box and was intended to hold the gold rings and necklaces of a wealthy Athenian lady. The purely abstract designs characteristic of the early period have been replaced by panels depicting warriors with muscular legs. Each warrior stands behind a large Dipylon shield grasping a riding crop or whip to control the powerful horses pulling the chariots. The lid, now restored, preserves two holes for thongs which were used to suspend the pyxis from the ceiling, out of the reach of little children. Three scars near the central knob attest to the existence of three horses, which served as handles and originally crowned the lid. As is customary with such forms, the underside of the pyxis, which would have been visible in its suspended state, is decorated with circular designs. The inner circle is occupied by the popular octofoil with small rosettes separating the leaves. The outer ring preserves a border formed by widely spaced swastikas. Both the shape and decoration of the pyxis suggest a date in the early stages of the Late Geometric period, circa 750-735 B.C. This particular shape of jewelry box became less popular and was not commonly used after the last quarter of the eighth century.   [E.O.N.]

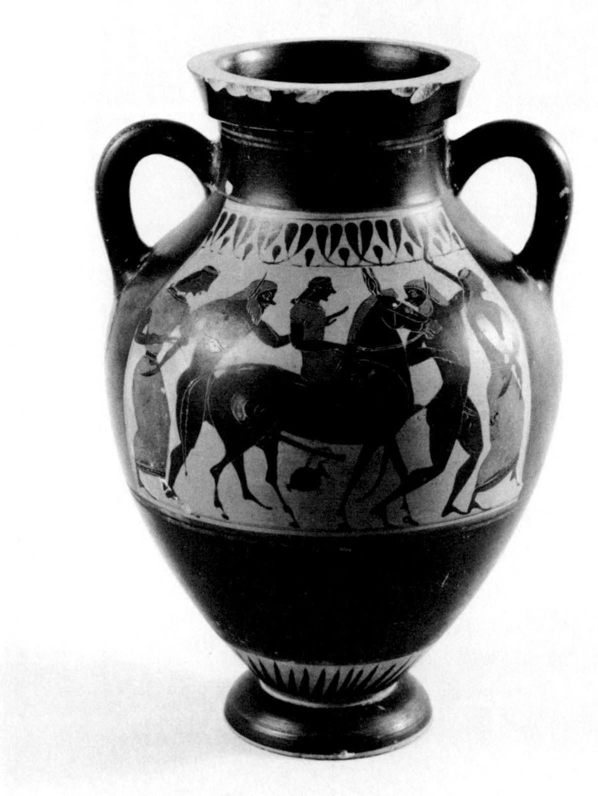

PAINTER OF BERLIN 1686, GREEK
Amphora, ca. 550 B.C., Attic Black-Figure
  Terra cotta, 12½ x 8¼ (diam.) (31.8 x 21.0 cm)
  Gift of Mr. Edward Perry Warren h '26. 1915.44

By the end of the eighth century B.C., vase patterning in the
Geometric style was losing ground perceptibly to a new interest in figured compositions. The chariot scenes were
changing into more than repetitive patterns, and the
Athenian interest in narrative gradually began to develop.
While the artists of her rival Corinth worked in the miniature style concentrating on heavily patterned animal friezes,
Athenian vase painters experimented with narrative compositions generally painted in a larger format. By the first

quarter of the sixth century B.C. the black-figure technique, begun in Corinth, had fully emerged in Athens, which became the center in Greece for painted pottery. The pre-eminence of Athenian potters was in part the result of the rich clay beds in Attica, which proved to be the finest on the mainland. The high iron content of the clay accounted for the deep metallic black while the orange tonalities of Athenian vases were produced by the addition of yellow ochre.

The term "black-figure" refers to the vase painting technique of executing figures in black silhouette upon the pale red ground which was the natural color of the clay. The silhouettes were rendered in a slip made of the same clay from which the pot was thrown. Outlines and details of anatomy or facial features were generally incised. Additional colors, most commonly deep red and white, were frequently used for garments and highlights. The overall black on red color scheme was produced not by pigmentation but by a complicated two-stage oxidation-reduction firing which the Athenian potters had perfected. The lustrous black surface was not the result of a glaze but of the careful burnishing of the clay which produced the shiny metallic effect.

With the refinement of this decorative manner, potters developed a new shape, the panel amphora, which allowed the black-figure technique to be shown to its best advantage. On such an amphora a large reserved panel was set between the handles on each side of the vessel. The upper portion of the panel was often bordered with a palmette chain or miniature figured frieze, derived from the Corinthian miniature style. Rays emanating from the base of the vessel were also commonly utilized.

The panel amphora in the Warren Collection belongs to the early Attic Black-Figure period and has been attributed to the Painter of Berlin 1686. This anonymous artist is identified by his name-piece in the Staatliche Museum in Berlin. A contemporary of the master painter Exekias, he was a capable artist whose works date to the middle and third quarter of the sixth century B.C. Though his figures do not show the care or technical excellence of yet another master, Amasis, he does share the latter's sense of humor and love of boisterous satyrs, as exhibited on this piece. His choice of scenes is common for the period. One side depicts a young man on a donkey escorted by satyrs and maenads and suggests the return of Hephaistos to Olympus. The artist's lack of expertise is perhaps most noticeable in the treatment of the young man and the donkey; here the careless manner in which incision and silhouette fail to coincide creates an overall impression of haste. On the reverse panel Dionysus, wearing a crown of ivy leaves and holding a heavily laden grapevine in one hand, stands among attendant satyrs and maenads. In his left hand the god of wine grasps a rhyton, an ample sized drinking cup made from a bull's horn. As on the obverse, whites and reds have been added to enhance the appearance of the garments. Small red dot rosettes can still be seen, carefully painted on the cloaks of Dionysus and the maenad on the left.   [E.O.N.]

PAN PAINTER, GREEK

Amphora, ca. 460 B.C., Attic Red-Figure
   Terra cotta, $12\frac{3}{16}$ x $7\frac{11}{16}$ (diam.) (31.0 x 19.6 cm)
   Gift of Mr. Edward Perry Warren h '26. 1913.30

By the last quarter of the sixth century B.C., Athenian vase painters had realized the potential of the black-figure technique and were becoming acutely aware of its limitations. As their technical skills progressed, artists became more interested in depicting the human torso, although the technique with which they worked was in many ways restrictive. While the silhouette was an adequate compositional device, it created problems with interior details of anatomy. Heavy patterning of cloaks and armor could be successfully rendered through incision, but the technique proved to be inadequate for subtle and varying lines needed to portray ribs, muscles, and sinews in the human body. Incision allowed for no variation in the intensity of the lines; all had to be of equal thickness. As a result a new technique, red-figure, was devised about 530 B.C. Attributed to the painter Andocides, a pupil of Exekias's, this invention reversed the color scheme of black-figure decoration; the background was now painted with a black slip while the figures were reserved. Upon firing in the kiln, the latter appeared in the color of the red clay ground. The great advantage of this technique was that interior details of anatomy need not, in fact could not, effectively be incised, but instead were painted with a slip. Thus, the artist could control the thickness of each line and the intensity of color by simply diluting or thickening the slip. An interest in drapery and anatomy which exploited this new technique could now develop.

The fineness and uniformity of the interior lines found in the better examples of Athenian red-figure pottery suggest that the artists often applied the slip not with a brush but with a type of instrument akin in principle to a pastry bag. A porcupine quill attached to an animal intestine filled with the slip was possibly used. As the intestine was squeezed, a thin, controlled stream of color poured forth from the quill, resulting in the finely raised, uniform interior lines found on many examples.

The first thirty years of this new technique was a period of exuberant experimentation for vase painters. Athletic contests and gymnasium scenes rose in popularity, allowing artists to show their skill at depicting the human torso. By the end of the first decade of the fifth century B.C., Athenian red-figure vase painting was approaching its zenith. The technical skill exhibited in the controlled relief lines and diluted slips was to be unequalled. The difficulties presented by the male and female torso were being mastered.

The amphora in the museum collection is the work of the Pan Painter, a prolific artist with a distinctive style. One of the finer vase painters of the early Classical red-figure manner, his period of activity ranges from circa 480 to 450 B.C.; over two hundred pieces have been attributed to him by the noted authority Sir John D. Beazley. Since his actual name is unknown, the artist is identified by his name-piece, a large bell krater at the Museum of Fine Arts in Boston, on which the goat-god Pan is depicted pursuing a young shepherd. The extremely competent draughtsmanship of the Pan Painter is evident on the Bowdoin example, and the surety of his fine lines attests to his technical skill. The drapery

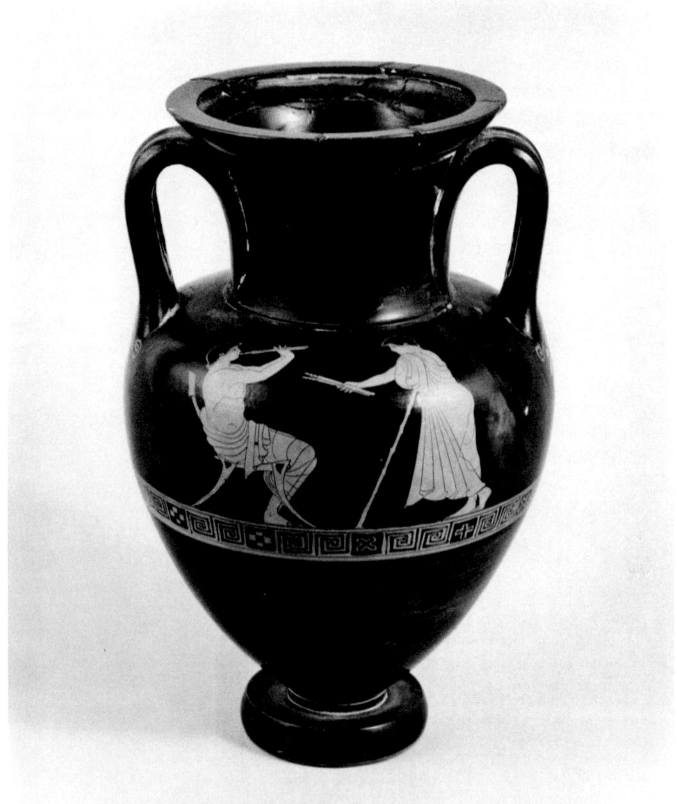

flows smoothly over the figure, and in several places limbs can be seen distinctly through the fabric. The pointed and symmetrical folds of drapery have been considered an affectation, a mannered archaism harkening back to an earlier period.

On one side two youths are engaged in a musical lesson or contest. One seated in an elegant chair vigorously plays the double flute, while his companion stands to one side leaning on a staff and gesturing encouragement or advice with a flute in his hand. The relaxed pose of the youth on the right was evidently popular with the Pan Painter, for an identical figure decorates the side of a skyphos by the same artist in the Berlin Museum. On the reverse side a young man holding a staff turns his head back and strides to the right. As is common with the red-figure style, the artist has eliminated the panel so popular in the earlier technique of black-figure painting. The figures are unrestricted and scenes flow freely across the entire vessel. Beneath the scene is a border of meander and cross forming a ground on which the figures stand. Below each handle the artist has carefully painted a small inverted palmette. The form, a Nolan amphora, is named after Nola, the Italian site where many were found. It is a type of two-handled vessel for carrying water or wine that was common in the first half of the fifth century B.C. and shortly thereafter. Relatively few examples have been preserved.   [E.O.N.]

NIOBID PAINTER, GREEK

Hydria, ca. 460-450 B.C., Attic Red-Figure

Terra cotta, $15\frac{15}{16}$ x $12\frac{1}{4}$ (diam.) (40.4 x 31.1 cm)

Gift of Mr. Edward Perry Warren h '26. 1908.3

By the second quarter of the fifth century B.C., Athens was recovering from the Persian invasion of Xerxes. The city, as head of the Delian League and governed by Kimon, was rising in power. During this time the mainland came under the influence of wall painters who worked on a grandiose scale. Although the works of such artists as Polygnotus of Thasos and Mikon of Athens are entirely lost today, they are nevertheless known to us to some extent through literary descriptions and allusions. From such travelers as Pausanias it is quite clear that their work was often characterized by numerous figures placed on varying levels. Moods and emotional states were often portrayed by postures, and their themes were epic in nature.

As is only natural, the influence of the monumental painters can be seen quite strongly in the works of certain Attic vase painters of the period. Among the first to reflect the techniques of the great wall paintings of Polygnotus and his contemporaries was the Niobid Painter, who flourished from circa 480 to 450 B.C. He is identified by his name-piece, a calyx krater in the Louvre, depicting the death of the chil-

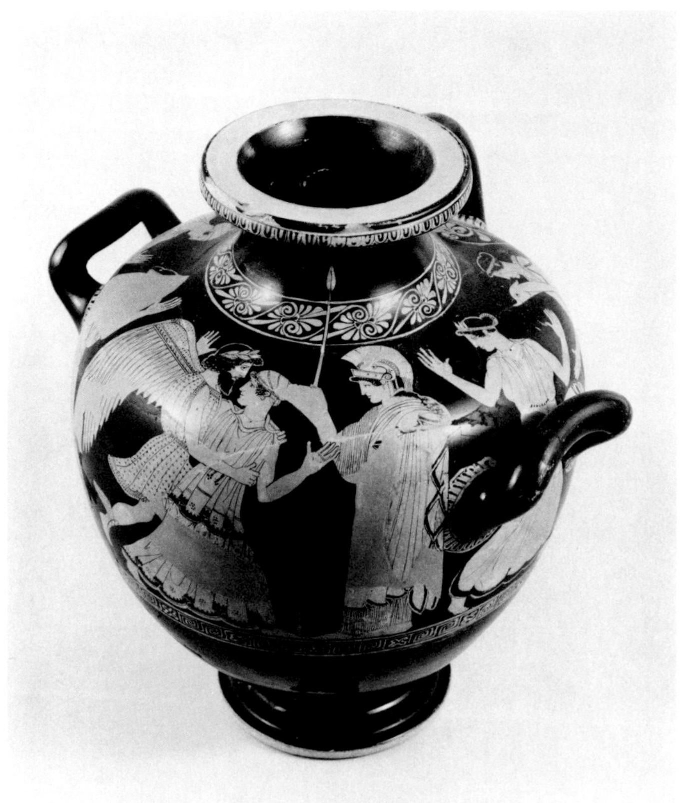

dren of Niobe. Nearly ninety vases are attributed to this artist, who preferred large shapes, such as the volute and calyx kraters, on which to paint his subjects. Much in the spirit of contemporary wall paintings, the figures of the Niobid Painter float uninterruptedly across the entire surface of the vessel. The artist is a portrayer of epic themes. His style has often been described as cold or detached, an impression which is reinforced by his preference for dark relief lines used to define facial features and the folds of garments, areas where one might expect to find the diluted softer tones which were popular with his contemporaries.

The large hydria in the Warren Collection is a fine example of his work. Particularly noticeable on this piece is the preponderance of straight lines, of verticals rather than horizontals in anatomical detail as well as drapery, which give his figures a stiff, wooden quality. The large field of decoration extends around the entire vessel and is devoted to the depiction of the rape of Oreithyia. The major figures are carefully placed in the center of the composition between the two horizontal handles. Boreas, the winged North Wind, who has tired of wooing in vain the Athenian princess Oreithyia, has swept down from the sky and is about to carry her off. In his effort to steal away the struggling maiden, the young sky god strains with open mouth. Interestingly, the Roman writer Pliny relates that Polygnotus was the monumental painter who introduced this format of depicting the mouth as open. To the left of Oreithyia stands the watchful Athena, protectress of Athens. The main group is flanked by confused women running for help in various directions, their arms raised in anguish and consternation. Behind Athena are two young women, one holding a dolphin! The significance of this representation is uncertain, though it may be the artist's attempt to present the location of the struggle; one source describes the action as taking place on the banks of the river Illissus where the princess was dancing with companions. Behind Boreas, two women run toward an old man leaning on a sceptre, probably Erechtheus, king of Athens and father of Oreithyia.

The scene was a popular one among Attic red-figure vase painters, appearing no fewer than forty-three times. Its popularity at this particular time may be due to the aid Boreas was felt to have given the Athenians in their naval victory over the Persians at Salamis. The depiction of his "marriage" to Oreithyia celebrates his status as brother-in-law to all Athenians. Among the works of the Niobid Painter the subject occurs four times, once on a pelike and three times on hydrias.

The hydria or water pitcher is one of the few vessels whose ancient name is known. The vessel is identified by its three handles, two horizontal ones for lifting and carrying and a vertical one at the back for pouring.   [E.O.N.]

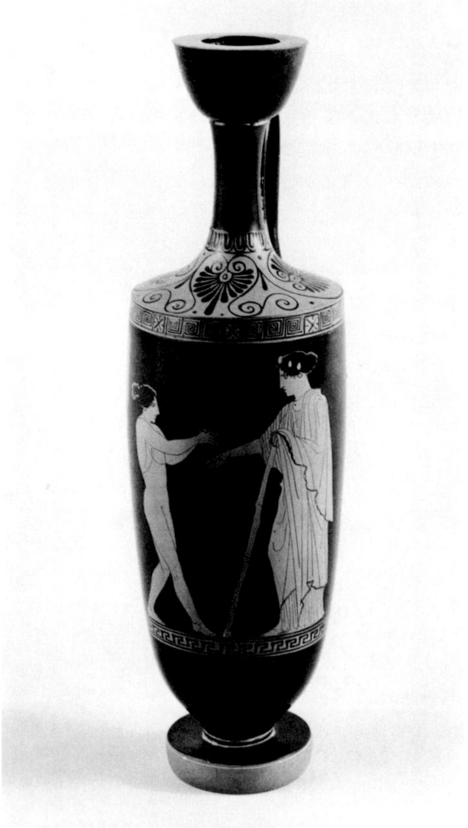

PHIALE PAINTER, GREEK
Lekythos, ca. 430 B.C., Attic Red-Figure
> Terra cotta, 14⅞ x 4³⁄₁₆ (diam.) (37.7 x 10.7 cm)
> Gift of Mr. Edward Perry Warren h '26. 1913.11

After the middle of the fifth century B.C., a quieter strain can
be seen in Attic vase painting, which is particularly evident
in the decoration of the lekythos. This vessel appears to have
been originally designed as a perfume flask, a purpose suggested by the long neck and small bore of the mouth, which
facilitated judicious pouring of the scented liquid. As the
shape became popular and the size of the vessel increased,
possibly to accommodate the decoration, the lekythos was
usually constructed with a smaller container inside to hold

the true amount of oil; thus the size of the outer vessel bore little relation to the actual amount of precious liquid within. As the shape gained in popularity, its function became more specific; by the middle of the fifth century the lekythos was the predominant shape used in burial ceremonies. On it, artists employed another decorative technique, the white-ground, which was eminently suited to its funereal nature. As befits its function, the scenes appearing on the funerary lekythos were often more somber and reflective than those found on other shapes.

The great popularity of this vessel, both in the white-ground and red-figure style, was primarily due to the Achilles Painter and his followers. The Achilles Painter's outstanding pupil, the Phiale Painter, is considered a major artist during the third quarter of the fifth century B.C., and over 150 works are attributed to him. Like those of his master, the works of the Phiale Painter were not confined to the red-figure style. His name is derived from a phiale or libation bowl at the Museum of Fine Arts in Boston, on which he depicted a visit to a school of music. Since his works frequently illustrate women in motion, the Phiale Painter has been described as an artist who introduced a more lively and human spirit into the Periklean serenity of the works of his master.

The lekythos by the Phiale Painter in the Warren Collection dates to the end of the third quarter of the fifth century B.C. To the left a young nude girl performs a dance step under the watchful tutelage of her teacher, who gestures instructions with her raised hand. The pupil, her arms extended and her weight lightly carried on her toes, appears about to begin a pirouette. Her eyes look straight ahead in studied concentration. As is common with so many teachers in antiquity, the instructress is shown leaning on a large staff, suggesting that discipline was an integral part of instruction.

The cursory treatment of the drapery is characteristic of much of the Phiale Painter's work and suggests that the artist was more concerned with evoking a certain mood than with displaying his technical skill as a draughtsman.

Both the simplicity of the composition and the soft lines used to give definition to the young girl's torso enhance the quiet intimacy of the scene. [E.O.N.]

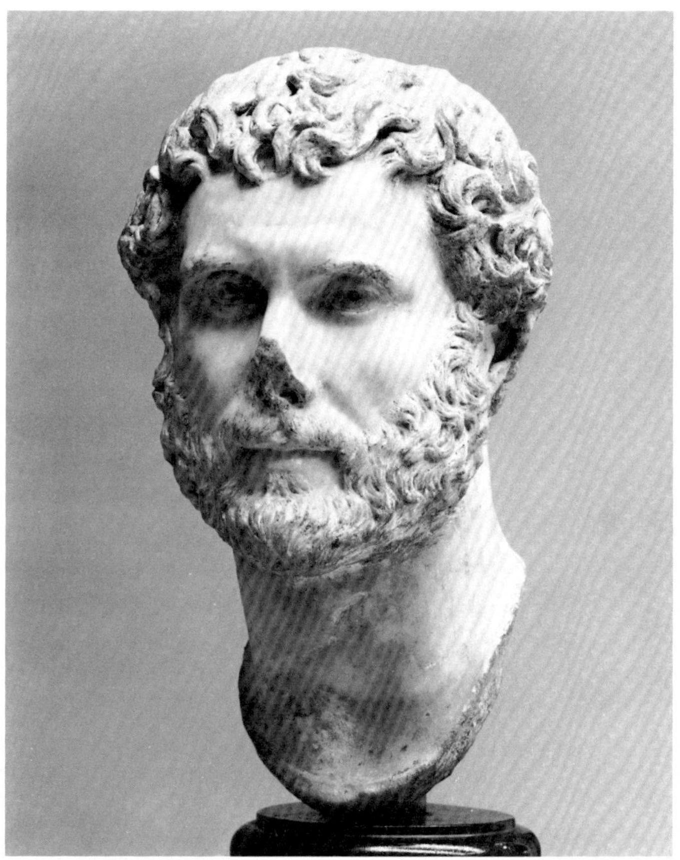

ITALIAN, ROME

Head of Antoninus Pius, ca. A.D. 140-150

Marble, $15\frac{1}{4}$ x $8\frac{3}{16}$ x $8\frac{11}{16}$ (38.7 x 20.8 x 22.1 cm)

Gift of Mr. Edward Perry Warren h '26. 1906.1

The period between the accession of Nerva in A.D. 96 and the death of Marcus Aurelius in A.D. 180 marked the high point of the Roman Empire and the *Pax Romana,* a time of unparalleled peace and economic prosperity for the ancient

Mediterranean world. The peaceful status of the empire was ensured by the stabilization of imperial accession through the adoption of a successor by the reigning emperor from outside his immediate family. Antoninus Pius, depicted in this fine marble portrait purchased by Mr. Edward Perry Warren h '26 in Rome, was an obscure nephew of the Emperor Hadrian and came into prominence only when he was adopted and designated his uncle's heir in A.D. 138. The tranquil yet majestic expression of Antoninus Pius reflects an uneventful rule of twenty-three years during which the emperor was compelled to leave the vicinity of Rome only once.

The mechanism of centralized authority for the entire Roman Empire rested in the personage of the emperor himself. Marble imperial portraits served primarily a political, rather than an ornamental, function. Since the emperor could not personally preside over every official ceremony throughout the empire, his portrait served as a symbolic representation of his presence. The Bowdoin *Head of Antoninus Pius* was originally inserted into a marble bust or statue, which would have concealed the thickened band visible at the base of the neck. This bust or statue probably once stood in a basilica, theater, or any one of numerous public buildings found in a Roman town. The erection of the emperor's portrait in every city of the empire necessitated some official control over the creation and the dissemination of these portraits to ensure an immediately recognizable likeness. Images of the imperial family were therefore not free-hand creations of artists working in Rome or in the provinces but a series of replicas copied mechanically from a standard model. The Bowdoin head belongs to a group of some twenty-five portraits of Antoninus Pius, all of which bear the characteristic pincer-like motif in the arrangement of the curls above the forehead. The group is called the "Formia Type" by modern scholars after its name-piece from Formia, Italy, now displayed in the Museo Nazionale in Rome. Many portraits following the facial traits of the Formia Type have been found in Rome and also in the regions of Gaul (France), North Africa, and Greece; this indicates that the official model was available to provincial artists as well as to those in Rome. Although the sculptor of the Bowdoin head has taken some liberties in the arrangement of the coiffure when compared to the other examples of the Formia Type, his dependence on the official model is clearly visible. Since the model originated early in the reign of Antoninus Pius, the Bowdoin head may be safely placed within the decade A.D. 140-150.

The Bowdoin *Head of Antoninus Pius* is one of the finest examples of Roman portraiture from the second century A.D.; its excellent state of preservation reveals superior technical and artistic craftsmanship. The use of a drill to define the curls of the hair with deep circular cavities joined by linear channels is best illustrated in those locks above the forehead; these same curls are outlined further by deep undercutting with a chisel. A small hole in the inside corner of each eye has been rendered by a drill; the technique of undercutting has also been employed to emphasize the transition between the upper eyelid and brow. The dark, shadowlike effect of these areas contrasts sharply with the gentle contours of other facial features and the velvet-smooth finish of the flesh, created by polishing the marble. This presents the viewer with a striking alternation of light and dark, termed "chiaroscuro," which is typical of Antonine portraiture from the workshops of Rome and is found in its primary stages on the Bowdoin head. A second technical feature which continues the play of light and shadow is the plastic rendering of the iris and pupil, the former being an incised three-quarters circle and the latter a bean-shaped cavity. This technique was first applied on portraits executed in Rome circa A.D. 130 and remained a standard feature of Roman portraiture thereafter. The effect of light and shadow would have been even more dramatic when the head was painted. The patches of red found in the curls of the Bowdoin head above the sideburns on the left side may be remnants of the original paint.   [F.C.A.]

SELECTED WORKS FROM THE COLLECTION

[K.A.O.]

Bronzes

Greek (ca. 725 B.C.): *Horse.* Bronze, $3\frac{13}{16}$ x $3\frac{7}{16}$ x $1\frac{3}{16}$ (9.6 x 8.7 x 3.0 cm). Gift of Mr. Edward Perry Warren h '26. 1927.14

Italian (ca. 700-500 B.C.): *Fibula.* Bronze, $3\frac{1}{16}$ x $1\frac{3}{4}$ x $1\frac{3}{16}$ (7.8 x 4.4 x 3.0 cm). Gift of Mr. Edward Perry Warren h '26. 1913.34

Italian (ca. 700-500 B.C.): *Fibula.* Bronze, $2\frac{3}{4}$ x 10 x $1\frac{1}{4}$ (7.0 x 25.5 x 3.2 cm). Gift of Mr. Edward Perry Warren h '26. 1930.83

Italian (7th century B.C.): *Amuletic Horse Trapping.* Bronze, $2\frac{3}{4}$ x $4\frac{7}{16}$ x $1\frac{3}{4}$ (7.0 x 11.2 x 4.5 cm). Gift of Mr. Edward Perry Warren h '26. 1915.27

Greek (ca. 620-600 B.C.): *Griffin's Head.* Bronze, $6\frac{1}{8}$ x $2\frac{3}{8}$ (diam.) (15.5 x 6.0 cm). Gift of Mr. Edward Perry Warren h '26. 1923.16

Greek (ca. 600-400 B.C.): *Ladle.* Bronze, $14\frac{3}{4}$ x $3\frac{9}{16}$ (diam.) (37.4 x 9.0 cm). Gift of Mr. Edward Perry Warren h '26. 1927.8

Etruscan (500-480 B.C.): *Right Arm and Hand Holding a Lotus Blossom.* Bronze, $5\frac{1}{8}$ x $1\frac{7}{16}$ (diam.) (13.0 x 3.6 cm). Gift of Mr. Edward Perry Warren h '26. 1913.24

Greek (ca. 500-300 B.C.): *Jar.* Bronze, $4\frac{15}{16}$ x $3\frac{15}{16}$ (diam.) (12.5 x 9.9 cm). Gift of Mr. Edward Perry Warren h '26. 1923.15

Greek (5th century B.C.): *Strigil.* Bronze, $11\frac{3}{8}$ x $\frac{13}{16}$ (28.9 x 2.1 cm). Gift of Mr. Edward Perry Warren h '26. 1913.23

Greek (ca. 480-450 B.C.): *Statuette of a Youth.* Bronze, $3\frac{1}{2}$ x $1\frac{1}{4}$ x 1 (8.9 x 3.2 x 2.5 cm). Gift of Mr. Edward Perry Warren h '26. 1923.49

Greek (ca. 470-460 B.C.): *Back Handle of a Hydria.* Bronze, $6\frac{5}{16}$ x 2 (diam.) (16.0 x 5.1 cm). Gift of Mr. Edward Perry Warren h '26. 1915.26

Greek (ca. 470-450 B.C.): *Standing Woman.* Bronze, $3\frac{9}{16}$ x $1\frac{3}{16}$ x $\frac{11}{16}$ (9.1 x 2.9 x 1.7 cm). Gift of Mr. Edward Perry Warren h '26. 1913.33

Greek (ca. 400-200 B.C.): *Cerberus Squatting.* Bronze, $2\frac{1}{8}$ x $1\frac{11}{16}$ x $1\frac{3}{4}$ (5.4 x 4.3 x 4.5 cm). Gift of Mr. Edward Perry Warren h '26. 1923.45

Greek (ca. 350-250 B.C.): *Mina Weight.* Bronze, $2\frac{5}{8}$ x $2\frac{13}{16}$ x $\frac{5}{8}$ (6.7 x 7.1 x 1.6 cm). Gift of Mr. Edward Perry Warren h '26. 1923.14

Greek (ca. 250 B.C.): *Poseidon.* Bronze, $2\frac{5}{8}$ x $1\frac{1}{4}$ x 1 (6.6 x 3.2 x 2.5 cm). Gift of Mr. Edward Perry Warren h '26. 1915.60

Italian (1st century B.C.): *Priapus.* Bronze, $4\frac{5}{16}$ x $1\frac{7}{8}$ x $\frac{13}{16}$ (11.0 x 4.8 x 2.0 cm). Gift of Mr. Edward Perry Warren h '26. 1915.37

Greco-Roman (1st century A.D.): *Dancing Satyr.* Bronze, $8\frac{7}{16}$ x $4\frac{5}{8}$ x $2\frac{1}{2}$ (21.4 x 11.8 x 6.3 cm). Gift of Mr. Edward Perry Warren h '26. 1930.215

Italian (1st century A.D.): *Fibula.* Bronze, $2\frac{1}{16}$ x $\frac{5}{16}$ x $\frac{5}{16}$ (5.2 x 0.8 x 0.8 cm). Bequest of Mrs. Helen Johnson Chase. 1958.31

Roman (1st century A.D.): *Belt Buckle.* Bronze, $1\frac{3}{4}$ x $\frac{13}{16}$ x $\frac{1}{2}$ (4.5 x 2.0 x 1.3 cm). Bequest of Mrs. Helen Johnson Chase. 1958.23

Roman (1st century A.D.): *Hinge.* Bronze, $1\frac{3}{8}$ x $1\frac{1}{8}$ x $\frac{1}{16}$ (3.5 x 2.9 x 0.2 cm). Bequest of Mrs. Helen Johnson Chase. 1958.35

Roman (1st century A.D.): *Inkstand.* Bronze, $1\frac{3}{4}$ x $1\frac{5}{16}$ (diam.) (4.5 x 3.3 cm). Bequest of Mrs. Helen Johnson Chase. 1958.45.1

Roman (1st century A.D.): *Key.* Bronze, $2\frac{1}{2}$ x $1\frac{3}{16}$ x $\frac{3}{8}$ (6.3 x 3.0 x 0.9 cm). Bequest of Mrs. Helen Johnson Chase. 1958.20

Roman (1st century A.D.): *Needle.* Bronze, 7 x $\frac{1}{4}$ (diam.) (17.8 x 0.6 cm). Bequest of Mrs. Helen Johnson Chase. 1958.25.2

Roman (1st century A.D.): *Spatula.* Bronze, $5\frac{3}{16}$ x $\frac{1}{2}$ x $\frac{1}{16}$ (13.2 x 1.2 x 0.2 cm). Gift of Mr. Edward Perry Warren h '26. 1930.30

Roman (1st century A.D.): *Spoon.* Bronze, 6 x $1\frac{1}{2}$ (diam.) (15.2 x 3.8 cm). Bequest of Mrs. Helen Johnson Chase. 1958.19

Roman (1st century A.D.): *Spoon Probe.* Bronze, $1\frac{11}{16}$ x $\frac{1}{2}$ x $\frac{5}{16}$ (4.3 x 1.2 x 0.8 cm). Gift of Mr. Edward Perry Warren h '26. 1930.28

Roman (1st century A.D.): *Tweezers.* Bronze, $3\frac{1}{16}$ x $\frac{13}{16}$ x $\frac{1}{4}$ (7.7 x 2.0 x 0.6 cm). Bequest of Mrs. Helen Johnson Chase. 1958.30

Roman (1st century A.D. or later): *Bell.* Bronze, $2\frac{1}{2}$ x $1\frac{1}{2}$ (diam.) (6.4 x 3.8 cm). Gift of Mr. Edward Perry Warren h '26. 1930.18

Roman (1st century A.D. or later): *Thimble.* Bronze, $1\frac{1}{4}$ x $\frac{7}{8}$ (diam.) (3.1 x 2.3 cm). Gift of Mr. Edward Perry Warren h '26. 1930.20

Roman (1st or 2nd century A.D.): *Lion's Head.* Bronze, $2\frac{1}{8}$ x $6\frac{5}{8}$ (diam.) (5.4 x 16.8 cm). Gift of Mr. George Warren Hammond h '00 and Mrs. Hammond. 1898.18

Roman (1st or 2nd century A.D.): *Phallus Amulet.* Bronze, $\frac{13}{16}$ x $1\frac{9}{16}$ x $\frac{11}{16}$ (2.0 x 3.9 x 1.8 cm). Gift of Mr. Edward Perry Warren h '26. 1930.27

Roman (1st or 2nd century A.D.): *Rider and Pony.* Bronze, $3\frac{1}{2}$ x $3\frac{1}{8}$ x $1\frac{7}{16}$ (8.9 x 7.9 x 3.6 cm). Bequest of Mrs. Helen Johnson Chase. 1958.36

Roman (1st or 2nd century A.D.): *Silenus Herm.* Bronze, $5\frac{3}{16}$ x $\frac{7}{8}$ x $\frac{5}{8}$

(13.2 x 2.2 x 1.6 cm). Gift of Mr. Edward Perry Warren h '26. 1923.38

Roman (1st or 2nd century A.D.): *Utensil Ring.* Bronze, $\frac{7}{16}$ x $5\frac{1}{16}$ (diam.) (1.1 x 12.8 cm). Gift of Mr. Edward Perry Warren h '26. 1927.7

Roman (3rd or 4th century A.D.): *Lamp.* Bronze, $4\frac{1}{16}$ x $2\frac{1}{16}$ x $\frac{7}{8}$ (10.3 x 5.3 x 2.3 cm). Gift of Mr. Edward Perry Warren h '26. 1930.23

Pottery and Vase Painting

Greek, Mycenae (ca. 1350-1300 B.C.): *Kylix.* Terra cotta, $6\frac{5}{8}$ x $6\frac{1}{8}$ (diam.) (16.8 x 15.6 cm). Gift of Mr. Edward Perry Warren h '26. 1908.4

Greek, Mycenae (ca. 1350-1300 B.C.): *Kylix.* Terra cotta, $6\frac{3}{16}$ x $9\frac{5}{16}$ (diam.) (15.7 x 23.6 cm). Gift of the Honorable Karl L. Rankin h '60. 1977.13.1

Cypriote (ca. 1300-1200 B.C.): *Tall-necked Jug.* Terra cotta, $7\frac{3}{8}$ x $3\frac{13}{16}$ (diam.) (18.7 x 9.6 cm). Gift of Mr. Dana Estes h 1898. 1902.36

Cypriote (ca. 1200-1050 B.C.): *Globular Bottle.* Terra cotta, $5\frac{1}{4}$ x $3\frac{3}{4}$ (diam.) (13.4 x 9.5 cm). Gift of Mr. Dana Estes h 1898. 1902.35

Cypriote (ca. 1200-1050 B.C.): *Stirrup Vase.* Terra cotta, $4\frac{1}{2}$ x $4\frac{1}{8}$ (diam.) (11.5 x 10.5 cm). Gift of Mr. Dana Estes h 1898. 1902.17

Greek, Attica (8th century B.C.): *Oenochoë.* Terra cotta, $2\frac{3}{8}$ x $2\frac{15}{16}$ (diam.) (6.0 x 7.4 cm). Gift of Mr. Edward Perry Warren h '26. 1915.30

Greek, Attica (8th century B.C.): *Vase in the Form of a Pomegranate.* Terra cotta, $4\frac{1}{8}$ x $3\frac{9}{16}$ (diam.) (10.5 x 9.1 cm). Gift of Mr. Edward Perry Warren h '26. 1915.15

⌘Greek (ca. 750-735 B.C.): *Pyxis.* Terra cotta, $5\frac{7}{16}$ x $11\frac{3}{8}$ (diam.) (13.8 x 28.9 cm). Gift of Mr. Edward Perry Warren h '26. 1913.6

Greek, Attica (late 8th century B.C.): *Mug.* Terra cotta, $3\frac{1}{2}$ x $2\frac{3}{4}$ (diam.) (9.0 x 7.0 cm). Gift of Mr. Edward Perry Warren h '26. 1915.31

Greek, Attica (late 8th century B.C.): *Trefoil Oenochoë.* Terra cotta, $9\frac{15}{16}$ x $5\frac{11}{16}$ (diam.) (23.7 x 14.5 cm). Gift of Mr. Edward Perry Warren h '26. 1915.42

Greek (ca. 650-640 B.C.): *Black-Figure Pointed Aryballos.* Terra cotta, $2\frac{5}{8}$ x $1\frac{9}{16}$ (diam.) (6.7 x 3.9 cm). Gift of Mr. Edward Perry Warren h '26. 1915.35

Dolphin Painter, Greek, Corinth (ca. 625-600 B.C.): *Black-Figure Alabastron.* Terra cotta, 3 x $1\frac{9}{16}$ (diam.) (7.6 x 4.0 cm). Gift of Mr. Edward Perry Warren h '26. 1928.3

Greek, Corinth (ca. 625-600 B.C.): *Black-Figure Alabastron.* Terra cotta, $2\frac{15}{16}$ x $1\frac{1}{2}$ (diam.) (7.4 x 3.8 cm). Gift of Mr. Edward Perry Warren h '26. 1915.28

Greek, Corinth (ca. 625-600 B.C.): *Black-Figure Pyxis.* Terra cotta, $4\frac{1}{2}$ x $4\frac{15}{16}$ (diam.) (11.4 x 12.6 cm). Gift of the Honorable Karl L. Rankin h '60 and Mrs. Rankin. 1966.52

Greek, Corinth (ca. 625-600 B.C.): *Fragment of a Black-Figure Vase.* Terra cotta, $4\frac{15}{16}$ x $4\frac{1}{8}$ (12.5 x 10.5 cm). Gift of Mr. Edward Perry Warren h '26. 1913.16

Greek, Corinth (ca. 600-575 B.C.): *Black-Figure Ring Alabastron.* Terra cotta, $2\frac{3}{8}$ x 2 x $\frac{15}{16}$ (6.1 x 5.0 x 2.3 cm). Gift of Mr. Edward Perry Warren h '26. 1930.6

Greek, Corinth (ca. 600-575 B.C.): *Black-Figure Round Aryballos.* Terra cotta, $2\frac{3}{8}$ x $2\frac{5}{16}$ (diam.) (6.0 x 5.8 cm). Gift of Mr. Edward Perry Warren h '26. 1927.15

Greek, Attica (ca. 575-550 B.C.): *Black-Figure Neck Amphora.* Terra cotta, $3\frac{7}{8}$ x $4\frac{7}{16}$ (diam.) (9.8 x 11.3 cm). Gift of Mr. Edward Perry Warren h '26. 1913.10

Greek, Attica (ca. 575-550 B.C.): *Three Fragments of a Black-Figure Neck Amphora.* Terra cotta, $4\frac{3}{4}$ x $8\frac{1}{4}$ x $\frac{3}{16}$ (12.0 x 21.0 x 0.5 cm); $5\frac{1}{2}$ x $7\frac{5}{16}$ x $\frac{3}{16}$ (14.0 x 18.5 x 0.4 cm); $5\frac{1}{8}$ x $4\frac{3}{4}$ x $\frac{1}{8}$ (13.0 x 12.0 x 0.3 cm). Gift of Mr. Edward Perry Warren h '26. 1913.25.1-.3

Greek, Corinth (ca. 575-500 B.C.): *Black-Figure Round Aryballos.* Terra cotta, $2\frac{7}{8}$ x $3\frac{1}{8}$ (diam.) (7.3 x 7.9 cm). Gift of the Honorable Karl L. Rankin h '60. 1977.13

Greek, Attica (ca. 570-525 B.C.): *Black-Figure Little Master Lip Cup.* Terra cotta, $4\frac{1}{16}$ x $5\frac{1}{2}$ (diam.) (10.3 x 14.0 cm). Gift of Mr. Edward Perry Warren h '26. 1930.4

✠Painter of Berlin 1686, Greek (ca. 550 B.C.): *Amphora.* Terra cotta, $12\frac{1}{2}$ x $8\frac{1}{4}$ (diam.) (31.8 x 21.0 cm). Gift of Mr. Edward Perry Warren h '26. 1915.44

Greek, Attica (ca. 550-530 B.C.): *Black-Figure Little Master Band Cup.* Terra cotta, $4\frac{1}{16}$ x $5\frac{1}{2}$ (10.3 x 14.0 cm). Gift of Mr. Edward Perry Warren h '26. 1915.45

Greek, Attica (ca. 530-520 B.C.): *Black-Figure Eye Cup.* Terra cotta, $4\frac{7}{16}$ x 11 (diam.) (11.2 x 28.0 cm). Gift of Mr. Edward Perry Warren h '26. 1913.7

Greek, Attica (ca. 530-520 B.C.): *Fragment of a Black-Figure Stemless Cup.* Terra cotta, $2\frac{1}{8}$ x 2 x $\frac{9}{16}$ (5.4 x 5.1 x 1.5 cm). Gift of Mr. Edward Perry Warren h '26. 1927.10

Bowdoin Eye Painter, Greek, Attica (ca. 525 B.C.): *Red-Figure Eye*

Cup. Terra cotta, $5\frac{3}{8}$ x $13\frac{1}{16}$ (diam.) (13.6 x 33.2 cm). Gift of Mr. Edward Perry Warren h '26. 1913.2

OLTOS, Greek, Attica (ca. 525-520 B.C.): *Fragment of a Red-Figure Cup.* Terra cotta, $1\frac{1}{8}$ x $2\frac{5}{16}$ x $\frac{1}{8}$ (2.9 x 5.8 x 0.3 cm). Gift of Mr. Edward Perry Warren h '26. 1913.14

Greek, Attica (ca. 525-500 B.C.): *Fragment of a Black-Figure Vase.* Terra cotta, $1\frac{3}{8}$ x $2\frac{9}{16}$ x $\frac{5}{16}$ (3.5 x 6.5 x 0.8 cm). Gift of Mr. Edward Perry Warren h '26. 1930.36

Euergides Painter, Greek, Attica (ca. 520-510 B.C.): *Fragment of a Red-Figure Cup.* Terra cotta, $1\frac{5}{16}$ x 2 x $\frac{1}{8}$ (3.4 x 5.0 x 0.3 cm). Gift of Mr. Edward Perry Warren h '26. 1913.15

In the manner of SKYTHES, Greek, Attica (ca. 520-510 B.C.): *Fragment of a Red-Figure Cup.* Terra cotta, $1\frac{13}{16}$ x $2\frac{1}{2}$ x $\frac{3}{8}$ (4.6 x 6.3 x 0.4 cm). Gift of Mr. Edward Perry Warren h '26. 1913.17.2

Greek, Attica (ca. 520-450 B.C.): *Black-glazed Unfigured Psykter.* Terra cotta, $8\frac{11}{16}$ x $7\frac{1}{8}$ (diam.) (22.1 x 18.1 cm). Gift of Mr. Edward Perry Warren h '26. 1915.43

Painter of London B343, Greek, Attica (late 6th century B.C.): *Fragment of a Black-Figure Neck Amphora.* Terra cotta, $4\frac{3}{8}$ x $5\frac{1}{8}$ x $\frac{5}{16}$ (11.1 x 13.0 x 0.6 cm). Gift of Mr. Edward Perry Warren h' 26. 1913.13

Greek, Attica (late 6th century B.C.): *Fragment of a Black-Figure Vase.* Terra cotta, $1\frac{9}{16}$ x $2\frac{15}{16}$ x $\frac{3}{16}$ (4.0 x 7.5 x 0.4 cm). Gift of Mr. Edward Perry Warren h '26. 1930.38

Greek, Attica (ca. 510-490 B.C.): *Black-Figure One-handled Kantharos.* Terra cotta, $10\frac{13}{16}$ x $8\frac{1}{16}$ (diam.) (27.4 x 20.5 cm). Gift of Mr. Edward Perry Warren h '26. 1915.43

Greek (early 5th century B.C.): *Rhyton in the Form of a Ram's Head.* Terra cotta, 4 x $2\frac{11}{16}$ (diam.) (10.1 x 6.8 cm). Gift of Mr. Edward Perry Warren h '26. 1923.23

Greek, Attica (ca. 500-475 B.C.): *Black-Figure Lekythos.* Terra cotta, $5\frac{1}{4}$ x 2 (diam.) (13.4 x 5.0 cm). Gift of Mr. Edward Perry Warren h '26. 1930.11

Bowdoin Painter, Greek, Attica (ca. 490 B.C.): *Red-Figure Lekythos.* Terra cotta, $7\frac{7}{8}$ x $2\frac{13}{16}$ (diam.) (19.9 x 7.2 cm). Gift of Mr. Edward Perry Warren h '26. 1920.1

Workshop of the Painter of Athens 581, Greek, Attica (ca. 490 B.C.): *Black-Figure Lekythos.* Terra cotta, $7\frac{11}{16}$ x $3\frac{13}{16}$ (diam.) (19.5 x 9.7 cm). Gift of Mr. Edward Perry Warren h '26. 1913.4

Panaitios Painter, Greek, Attica (ca. 490 B.C.): *Fragment of a Red-Figure Cup.* Terra cotta, $5\frac{13}{16}$ x $7\frac{1}{4}$ x $\frac{3}{16}$ (14.7 x 18.4 x 0.4 cm). Gift of Mr. Edward Perry Warren h '26. 1930.1

MAKRON, Greek, Attica (ca. 490-480 B.C.): *Red-Figure Askos.* Terra cotta, $2\frac{7}{16}$ x $3\frac{1}{4}$ (diam.) (6.2 x 8.2 cm). Gift of Mr. Edward Perry Warren h '26. 1923.30

In the manner of ONESIMOS, Greek, Attica (ca. 490-480 B.C.): *Fragment of a Red-Figure Cup.* Terra cotta, $2\frac{3}{8}$ x $1\frac{5}{8}$ x $\frac{3}{8}$ (6.1 x 4.2 x 0.4 cm). Gift of Mr. Edward Perry Warren h '26. 1923.18

Greek, Attica (ca. 480 B.C.): *Fragment of a Red-Figure Cup.* Terra cotta, $6\frac{9}{16}$ x $6\frac{5}{16}$ x $\frac{3}{16}$ (16.7 x 16.0 x 0.4 cm). Gift of Mr. Edward Perry Warren h '26. 1913.26

Syriskos Painter, Greek, Attica (ca. 480 B.C.): *Red-Figure Squat Lekythos.* Terra cotta, $5\frac{9}{16}$ x $4\frac{3}{8}$ (diam.) (14.1 x 11.1 cm). Gift of Mr. Edward Perry Warren h '26. 1920.4

In the manner of the Aigisthos Painter, Greek, Attica (ca. 480-470 B.C.): *Red-Figure Hydria.* Terra cotta, $11\frac{5}{8}$ x $10\frac{1}{16}$ (diam.) (29.5 x 25.5 cm). Gift of Mr. Edward Perry Warren h '26. 1913.32

Bowdoin Painter, Greek, Attica (ca. 480-470 B.C.): *Red-Figure Lekythos.* Terra cotta, $7\frac{1}{16}$ x $2\frac{3}{8}$ (diam.) (18.0 x 6.0 cm). Gift of Mr. Edward Perry Warren h '26. 1913.5

Heraion Painter, Greek, Attica (ca. 480-470 B.C.): *Red-Figure Pyxis with Cover.* Terra cotta, $1\frac{9}{16}$ x $2\frac{9}{16}$ (diam.) (4.0 x 6.5 cm). Gift of Mr. Edward Perry Warren h '26. 1915.14

Greek, Attica (ca. 475-450 B.C.): *Cup in the Form of a Female Head.* Terra cotta, 5 x $3\frac{9}{16}$ x $3\frac{1}{2}$ (12.7 x 9.1 x 8.9 cm). Gift of Mr. Edward Perry Warren h '26. 1923.19

Greek, Attica (ca. 475-450 B.C.): *Cup in the Form of a Head.* Terra cotta, $4\frac{7}{16}$ x $3\frac{5}{16}$ (diam.) (11.3 x 8.4 cm). Gift of Mr. Edward Perry Warren h '26. 1913.27

DOURIS, Greek, Attica (ca. 470 B.C.): *Fragment of a Red-Figure Cup.* Terra cotta, 1 x $2\frac{3}{16}$ x $\frac{3}{8}$ (2.6 x 5.6 x 0.4 cm). Gift of Mr. Edward Perry Warren h '26. 1913.18

⊞Pan Painter, Greek (ca. 460 B.C.): *Amphora.* Terra cotta, $12\frac{3}{16}$ x $7\frac{11}{16}$ (diam.) (31.0 x 19.6 cm). Gift of Mr. Edward Perry Warren h '26. 1913.30

⊞Niobid Painter, Greek (ca. 460-450 B.C.): *Hydria.* Terra cotta, $15\frac{15}{16}$ x $12\frac{1}{4}$ (diam.) (40.4 x 31.1 cm). Gift of Mr. Edward Perry Warren h '26. 1908.3

Greek, Attica (ca. 460-450 B.C.): *Red-Figure Mug.* Terra cotta, $2\frac{3}{4}$ x $3\frac{1}{8}$ (diam.) (7.0 x 7.9 cm). Gift of Mr. Edward Perry Warren h '26. 1930.2

School of the Achilles Painter, Greek, Attica (ca. 450 B.C.): *White-ground Lekythos.* Terra cotta, $12\frac{3}{8}$ x $3\frac{13}{16}$ (diam.) (31.5 x 9.7 cm). Gift of Mr. Edward Perry Warren h '26. 1923.26

Greek, Attica (ca. 450-400 B.C.): *Black-painted, Unfigured Lekanis.* Terra cotta, 5½ x 10 13/16 (diam.) (14.0 x 27.5 cm). Gift of Mr. Edward Perry Warren h '26. 1930.9

Greek, Attica (ca. 450-400 B.C.): *Circular Flask.* Terra cotta, 5½ x 4⅝ x 2 3/16 (13.9 x 11.7 x 5.5 cm). Gift of Mr. Edward Perry Warren h '26. 1915.29

Trophy Painter, Greek, Attica (ca. 440 B.C.): *Red-Figure Lekythos.* Terra cotta, 10 1/16 x 4 1/16 (diam.) (25.5 x 10.3 cm). Gift of Mr. Edward Perry Warren h '26. 1915.46

Greek, Attica (ca. 430 B.C.): *Red-Figure Column Krater.* Terra cotta, 16 7/16 x 15¾ (diam.) (41.8 x 40.0 cm). Gift of Mr. Edward Perry Warren h '26. 1913.8

Greek, Attica (ca. 430 B.C.): *Red-Figure Pyxis with Lid.* Terra cotta, 4⅞ x 4⅜ (diam.) (12.3 x 11.1 cm). Gift of Mr. Edward Perry Warren h '26. 1930.3

✠Phiale Painter, Greek (ca. 430 B.C.): *Lekythos.* Terra cotta, 14⅞ x 4 3/16 (diam.) (37.7 x 10.7 cm). Gift of Mr. Edward Perry Warren h '26. 1913.11

Greek, Attica (430-420 B.C.): *Fragment of a Red-Figure Bell Krater.* Terra cotta, 2 11/16 x 3⅝ x ¼ (6.9 x 9.2 x 0.6 cm). Gift of Mr. Edward Perry Warren h '26. 1927.3

Greek (ca. 425 B.C.): *Red-Figure Toy Oenochoë.* Terra cotta, 2 13/16 x 2 9/16 (diam.) (7.2 x 6.5 cm). Gift of Mr. Edward Perry Warren h '26. 1915.38

Quadrate Painter, Greek, Attica (ca. 425 B.C.): *White-ground Lekythos.* Terra cotta, 11½ x 3¼ (diam.) (29.2 x 8.3 cm). Gift of Mr. Edward Perry Warren h '26. 1923.25

Dinos Painter, Greek, Attica (ca. 425-420 B.C.): *Red-Figure Pelike.* Terra cotta, 14 13/16 x 11 7/16 (diam.) (37.7 x 29.1 cm). Gift of Mr. Edward Perry Warren h '26. 1895.2

Etruscan (ca. 420-400 B.C.): *Red-Figure Cup.* Terra cotta, 4 7/16 x 13 9/16 (diam.) (11.2 x 34.4 cm). Gift of Mr. Edward Perry Warren h '26. 1923.4

South Italian (ca. 420-400 B.C.): *Red-Figure Bell Krater.* Terra cotta, 12½ x 13 11/16 (diam.) (31.8 x 34.7 cm). Gift of Mr. Edward Perry Warren h '26. 1915.47

Greek, Attica (late 5th century B.C.): *Red-Figure Pyxis with Cover.* Terra cotta, 4⅞ x 2⅜ x 2 (12.4 x 6.0 x 5.1 cm). Gift of Mr. Edward Perry Warren h '26. 1923.31

Greek, Attica (late 5th century B.C.): *White-ground Lekythos.* Terra cotta, 10 15/16 x 3¼ (diam.) (27.8 x 8.2 cm). Gift of Mr. Edward Perry Warren h '26. 1913.31

Greek, Boeotia (late 5th century B.C.): *Red-Figure Bell Krater with Cover.* Terra cotta, $9\frac{7}{16}$ x $7\frac{3}{8}$ (diam.) (23.9 x 18.8 cm). Gift of Mr. Edward Perry Warren h '26. 1923.32

Greek, Attica (ca. 400 B.C.): *Red-Figure Squat Lekythos.* Terra cotta, $5\frac{3}{8}$ x $3\frac{7}{16}$ (diam.) (13.7 x 8.7 cm). Gift of Mr. Edward Perry Warren h '26. 1920.3

Italian, Apulia (4th century B.C.): *Red-Figure Cup and Lid.* Terra cotta, $3\frac{7}{8}$ x $5\frac{9}{16}$ (diam.) (9.8 x 14.2 cm). Gift of Dr. Chauncey W. Goodrich h '15. 1944.12.2

Italian, Campania (4th century B.C.): *Black-painted Bowl.* Terra cotta, $2\frac{15}{16}$ x $8\frac{15}{16}$ (diam.) (7.4 x 22.7 cm). Gift of Mrs. Lincoln MacVeagh in memory of her mother, Mrs. James McKeen. 1928.14

Italian, Campania (4th century B.C.): *Black-painted Bowl.* Terra cotta, $2\frac{5}{8}$ x $4\frac{7}{8}$ (diam.) (6.6 x 12.3 cm). Gift of Mrs. Lincoln Mac-Veagh in memory of her mother, Mrs. James McKeen. 1928.17

Italian, Campania (4th century B.C.): *Black-painted Plate with Stamped Designs.* Terra cotta, $1\frac{1}{2}$ x $10\frac{5}{8}$ (diam.) (3.8 x 26.9 cm). Gift of Mrs. Lincoln MacVeagh in memory of her mother, Mrs. James McKeen. 1928.5

Italian, Campania (4th century B.C.): *Black-painted Squat Lekythos.* Terra cotta, $5\frac{3}{8}$ x 5 (diam.) (13.6 x 12.7 cm). Gift of Mrs. Lincoln MacVeagh in memory of her mother, Mrs. James McKeen. 1928.11

Italian, Campania (4th century B.C.): *Black-painted Trefoil Oenochoë.* Terra cotta, $9\frac{11}{16}$ x $5\frac{15}{16}$ (diam.) (24.6 x 15.0 cm). Gift of Mrs. Lincoln MacVeagh in memory of her mother, Mrs. James McKeen. 1928.15

South Italian, Campania (4th century B.C.): *Black-glazed Unfigured Hydria.* Terra cotta, $12\frac{3}{8}$ x $9\frac{3}{16}$ (diam.) (31.4 x 23.2 cm). Gift of Mrs. Lincoln MacVeagh in memory of her mother, Mrs. James McKeen. 1928.16

Italian, Apulia (early 4th century B.C.): *Fragment of a Large Red-Figure Vase.* Terra cotta, $5\frac{9}{16}$ x $7\frac{5}{16}$ x $\frac{3}{8}$ (14.2 x 18.5 x 1.0 cm). Gift of Mr. Edward Perry Warren h '26. 1927.4

Italian, Apulia (early 4th century B.C.): *Red-Figure Lekanis with Cover.* Terra cotta, 6 x $8\frac{5}{16}$ (diam.) (15.2 x 21.1 cm). Gift of Mr. Edward Perry Warren h '26. 1928.4

Greek, Attica (ca. 375-350 B.C.): *Lekythos with Relief of Standing Nike.* Terra cotta, $6\frac{7}{16}$ x $3\frac{9}{16}$ x 2 (16.3 x 9.0 x 5.1 cm). Gift of Mr. Edward Perry Warren h '26. 1915.39

Italian, Campania (ca. 350 B.C.): *Figured Bowl with Cover.* Terra cotta, $5\frac{5}{8}$ x $5\frac{1}{16}$ (diam.) (14.3 x 12.9 cm). Gift of Mr. Edward Perry Warren h '26. 1928.7

Greek, Attica (ca. 350-325 B.C.): *Lekythos with Applied Relief.* Terra cotta, 7 x 2$\frac{13}{16}$ (diam.) (17.8 x 7.2 cm). Gift of Mr. Edward Perry Warren h '26. 1915.40

Italian, Apulia (ca. 350-325 B.C.): *Fragment of a Red-Figure Vase.* Terra cotta, 3$\frac{1}{8}$ x 4$\frac{3}{16}$ x $\frac{1}{2}$ (8.0 x 10.6 x 1.2 cm). Gift of Mr. Edward Perry Warren h '26. 1927.5

Italian, Apulia (ca. 350-300 B.C.): *Red-Figure Bell Krater.* Terra cotta, 10$\frac{11}{16}$ x 11$\frac{9}{16}$ (diam.) (27.1 x 29.3 cm). Gift of Mr. John Duveen. 1895.3

Etruscan (later 4th century B.C.): *Red-Figure Stamnos.* Terra cotta, 12$\frac{3}{4}$ x 13$\frac{1}{8}$ (diam.) (32.4 x 33.3 cm). Gift of Mr. Edward Perry Warren h '26. 1913.9

Sculpture and Reliefs

Assyrian (885-860 B.C.): *King Ashurnazirpal II with Attendants.* Gypsum, 35$\frac{7}{8}$ x 30$\frac{1}{16}$ x 6$\frac{1}{2}$ (91.2 x 76.3 x 16.5 cm). Gift of Dr. Henri B. Haskell M 1855. 1860.5

Assyrian (885-860 B.C.): *Two Griffin-Demons Fertilizing the Sacred Tree with Palm Spathe.* Gypsum, 56$\frac{3}{16}$ x 84$\frac{1}{4}$ x 6$\frac{1}{4}$ (142.7 x 214.0 x 15.8 cm). Gift of Dr. Henri B. Haskell M 1855. 1860.1

✠Assyrian (ca. 885-860 B.C.): *Winged Genius.* Gypsum, 90$\frac{9}{16}$ x 58$\frac{13}{16}$ x 6$\frac{7}{16}$ (230.0 x 149.3 x 16.3 cm). Gift of Dr. Henri B. Haskell M 1855. 1860.2

Assyrian (885-860 B.C.): *Winged Genius Anointing the Keeper of the King's Bow.* Gypsum, 65$\frac{5}{8}$ x 78$\frac{1}{8}$ x 6$\frac{3}{8}$ (166.8 x 198.5 x 16.2 cm). Gift of Dr. Henri B. Haskell M 1855. 1860.3

Assyrian (885-860 B.C.): *Winged Genius Fertilizing the Sacred Tree with Palm Spathe.* Gypsum, 91$\frac{7}{16}$ x 73$\frac{3}{16}$ x 5$\frac{7}{16}$ (232.2 x 185.9 x 13.8 cm). Gift of Dr. Henri B. Haskell M 1855. 1860.4

Cypriote (ca. 550-500 B.C.): *Bearded Man.* Limestone, 12$\frac{11}{16}$ x 8$\frac{3}{16}$ x 8$\frac{11}{16}$ (32.3 x 20.8 x 22.1 cm). Gift of Mr. Edward Perry Warren h '26. 1923.116

Cypriote (550-500 B.C.): *Head of a Flute Player.* Limestone, 4$\frac{1}{16}$ x 3$\frac{1}{4}$ x 2$\frac{7}{8}$ (10.2 x 8.3 x 7.3 cm). Gift of Mr. Dana Estes h 1898. 1902.15

Greek (ca. 425-300 B.C.): *Statuette of Cybele Enthroned.* Marble, 6$\frac{13}{16}$ x 3$\frac{3}{4}$ x 3$\frac{9}{16}$ (17.3 x 9.5 x 9.0 cm). Gift of Mr. Edward Perry Warren h '26. 1927.2

Greek (4th century B.C.): *Right Hand of a Woman.* Marble, 7$\frac{5}{16}$ x 3$\frac{1}{2}$ x 2$\frac{3}{16}$ (18.5 x 8.9 x 5.5 cm). Gift of Mr. Edward Perry Warren h '26. 1927.12

Greek (4th century B.C. or later): *Fragment of a Relief Depicting a*

Sleeping Heracles. Marble, $90\frac{9}{16}$ x $58\frac{13}{16}$ x $6\frac{7}{16}$ (230.0 x 149.3 x 16.3 cm). Gift of Mr. Edward Perry Warren h '26. 1906.2

Greek (4th century B.C. or later): *Fragmentary Statuette of Aphrodite.* Marble, 18 x $7\frac{3}{16}$ x $5\frac{11}{16}$ (45.7 x 18.2 x 14.5 cm). Gift of Mr. Dana Estes h 1898. 1904.1

Greek (4th century B.C. or later): *Fragmentary Statuette of a Youth.* Marble, $16\frac{9}{16}$ x $7\frac{3}{4}$ x $4\frac{7}{16}$ (42.0 x 19.7 x 11.3 cm). Gift of Mr. Edward Perry Warren h '26. 1913.60

Greek (4th century B.C. or later): *Head of Heracles.* Marble, $4\frac{5}{16}$ x $2\frac{9}{16}$ x $3\frac{1}{8}$ (11.0 x 6.5 x 8.0 cm). Gift of Mr. Edward Perry Warren h '26. 1927.17.1

Greek (4th century B.C. or later): *Head of Zeus or Heracles.* Marble, $4\frac{5}{16}$ x $2\frac{5}{8}$ x $3\frac{1}{8}$ (11.0 x 6.6 x 8.0 cm). Gift of Mr. Edward Perry Warren h '26. 1908.8

Greek (ca. 300 B.C.): *Two Horses' Heads.* Marble, $7\frac{1}{4}$ x $2\frac{1}{2}$ x $2\frac{11}{16}$ (18.4 x 6.4 x 6.8 cm) and $6\frac{5}{16}$ x $2\frac{9}{16}$ x $1\frac{7}{8}$ (16.0 x 6.5 x 4.7 cm). Gift of Mr. Edward Perry Warren h '26. 1915.36.1-.2

Roman (1st century B.C. or later): *Fragment of a Winged Nike.* Marble, $12\frac{7}{16}$ x $11\frac{1}{16}$ x $2\frac{1}{8}$ (31.6 x 28.1 x 5.4 cm). Gift of Mr. Edward Perry Warren h '26. 1913.35.1

Roman (1st century B.C. to 1st century A.D.): *Portrait Head of a Middle-aged Man.* Marble, $8\frac{11}{16}$ x $6\frac{1}{8}$ x $5\frac{9}{16}$ (22.0 x 15.5 x 14.2 cm). Gift of Mr. Edward Perry Warren h '26. 1927.19

Roman (1st century A.D.): *Fragment with Flowers in Relief.* Marble, $9\frac{1}{8}$ x $6\frac{3}{16}$ x $2\frac{1}{2}$ (23.2 x 15.7 x 6.3 cm). Gift of Mr. Edward Perry Warren h '26. 1923.42

Greco-Roman (1st or 2nd century A.D.): *Fragment of a Woman's Face.* Marble, $5\frac{3}{8}$ x 4 x $1\frac{3}{4}$ (13.7 x 10.2 x 4.5 cm). Gift of Mr. Edward Perry Warren h '26. 1927.13

Greco-Roman (1st or 2nd century A.D.): *Fragmentary Statuette of Aphrodite Anadyomene.* Marble, 9 x $3\frac{11}{16}$ x $2\frac{1}{2}$ (22.9 x 9.4 x 6.3 cm). Gift of Mr. Edward Perry Warren h '26. 1930.214

Greco-Roman (1st or 2nd century A.D.): *Fragmentary Statuette of Nike.* Marble, $17\frac{7}{8}$ x $7\frac{3}{16}$ x $8\frac{7}{16}$ (45.4 x 18.2 x 21.4 cm). Gift of Mr. Edward Perry Warren h '26. 1923.40

Greco-Roman (1st or 2nd century A.D.): *Fragmentary Statuette of a Satyr.* Marble, $7\frac{5}{8}$ x $5\frac{13}{16}$ x $2\frac{15}{16}$ (19.4 x 14.7 x 7.4 cm). Gift of Mr. Edward Perry Warren h '26. 1913.56

Greco-Roman (1st or 2nd century A.D.): *Male Torso.* Marble, $19\frac{1}{8}$ x $12\frac{1}{16}$ x $6\frac{1}{4}$ (48.5 x 30.6 x 15.9 cm). Gift of Mrs. Mortimer Warren in memory of Dr. Mortimer Warren 1896. 1950.3

Greco-Roman (1st or 2nd century A.D.): *Statuette of Hermes.* Marble, $8\frac{3}{16}$ x $5\frac{1}{4}$ x $2\frac{15}{16}$ (20.8 x 13.4 x 7.5 cm). Gift of Mr. Edward Perry Warren h '26. 1927.17.2

Greco-Roman (1st or 2nd century A.D.): *Torso of a Satyr.* Marble, $31\frac{1}{4}$ x $24\frac{15}{16}$ x 14 (79.3 x 63.4 x 35.5 cm). Gift of Mr. Edward Perry Warren h '26. 1923.110

Greco-Roman (1st or 2nd century A.D.): *Torso of an Unfinished Statuette of Heracles.* Marble, $8\frac{1}{4}$ x $5\frac{5}{8}$ x 4 (21.0 x 14.3 x 10.1 cm). Gift of Mr. Edward Perry Warren h '26. 1915.53

Cypriote (2nd century A.D.): *Fragmentary Statuette of Athena Parthenos.* Marble, $10\frac{7}{16}$ x $5\frac{1}{8}$ x $3\frac{3}{8}$ (26.5 x 13.1 x 8.5 cm). Gift of Mrs. John Mead Howells. 1960.48

✠Italian, Rome (ca. A.D. 140-150): *Head of Antoninus Pius.* Marble, $15\frac{1}{4}$ x $8\frac{3}{16}$ x $8\frac{11}{16}$ (38.7 x 20.8 x 22.1 cm). Gift of Mr. Edward Perry Warren h '26. 1906.1

Greco-Roman (2nd or 3rd century A.D.): *Head of a Bearded Man.* Marble, $5\frac{11}{16}$ x $3\frac{11}{16}$ x $4\frac{7}{8}$ (14.4 x 9.4 x 12.4 cm). Gift of Mr. Edward Perry Warren h '26. 1923.118

Terra Cottas

Greek, Boeotia (ca. 650-600 B.C.): *Standing Idol with Birdlike Head.* Terra cotta, $5\frac{13}{16}$ x $2\frac{9}{16}$ x $1\frac{1}{8}$ (14.8 x 6.5 x 2.8 cm). Gift of Mr. Edward Perry Warren h '26. 1923.27

Greek, Boeotia (ca. 550 B.C.): *Mounted Warrior with Shield.* Terra cotta, $7\frac{1}{16}$ x $5\frac{13}{16}$ x $1\frac{15}{16}$ (17.9 x 14.8 x 5.0 cm). Gift of Mr. Edward Perry Warren h '26. 1913.3

Greek, Boeotia (550-500 B.C.): *Standing Woman.* Terra cotta, $7\frac{7}{16}$ x $3\frac{3}{16}$ x $2\frac{15}{16}$ (18.9 x 8.0 x 7.4 cm). Gift of Mr. Edward Perry Warren h '26. 1923.3

Greek (5th century B.C.): *Whistle in the Form of a Boy's Head.* Terra cotta, $2\frac{1}{16}$ x $1\frac{1}{2}$ x $1\frac{3}{4}$ (5.3 x 3.8 x 4.5 cm). Gift of Mr. Edward Perry Warren h '26. 1930.91

South Italian (early 5th century B.C.): *Head of a Bearded Warrior.* Terra cotta, $4\frac{1}{2}$ x $2\frac{7}{8}$ x $3\frac{5}{16}$ (11.4 x 7.3 x 8.4 cm). Gift of Mr. Edward Perry Warren h '26. 1913.37

Greek, Melos (ca. 470 B.C.): *Crouching Sphinx.* Terra cotta, $2\frac{15}{16}$ x $3\frac{9}{16}$ x $\frac{3}{8}$ (7.5 x 9.0 x 1.0 cm). Gift of Mr. Edward Perry Warren h '26. 1923.7

Greek, Melos (ca. 470-460 B.C.): *Winged Woman.* Terra cotta, $2\frac{11}{16}$ x $3\frac{5}{16}$ x $\frac{1}{4}$ (6.8 x 8.4 x 0.6 cm). Gift of Mr. Edward Perry Warren h '26. 1923.6

Greek (mid-5th century B.C.): *Flute-playing Silenus.* Terra cotta, 4 x 2½ x 1¼ (10.2 x 6.4 x 3.2 cm). Gift of Mr. Edward Perry Warren h '26. 1930.84

South Italian (mid-5th century B.C.): *Head of a Youth.* Terra cotta, 4½ x 2¹³⁄₁₆ x 3¼ (11.5 x 7.1 x 8.2 cm). Gift of Mr. Edward Perry Warren h '26. 1913.39

Greek (late 5th century B.C.): *Jointed Female Doll.* Terra cotta, 6⅛ x 2¹⁄₁₆ x 1⁷⁄₁₆ (15.5 x 5.3 x 3.6 cm). Gift of Mr. Edward Perry Warren h '26. 1923.22

South Italian (ca. 425-350 B.C.): *Head of a Warrior.* Terra cotta, 3¾ x 2⅛ x 2½ (9.5 x 5.4 x 6.3 cm). Gift of Mr. Dana Estes h 1898. 1913.36

Greek (ca. 400 B.C.): *Standing Girl Holding a Dove.* Terra cotta, 6⅛ x 1¹⁵⁄₁₆ x 1⅝ (15.5 x 4.9 x 4.1 cm). Gift of Mr. Edward Perry Warren h '26. 1915.13

Cypriote (4th century B.C. or later): *Miniature Mask of a Satyr.* Terra cotta, 2¹³⁄₁₆ x 1¾ x 1¾ (7.2 x 4.5 x 4.5 cm). Gift of Mr. Dana Estes h 1898. 1902.42

Greek (4th century B.C. or later): *Head of an Old Woman.* Terra cotta, 3¾ x 2½ x 2¹⁵⁄₁₆ (9.5 x 6.4 x 7.4 cm). Gift of Mr. Edward Perry Warren h '26. 1913.35

Greek (4th century B.C. or later): *Satyr Holding the Infant Dionysus.* Terra cotta, 6¹³⁄₁₆ x 2¹⁵⁄₁₆ x 2¼ (17.3 x 5.9 x 5.7 cm). Gift of Mr. Edward Perry Warren h '26. 1923.12

Greek (4th century B.C. or later): *Standing Macedonian Youth.* Terra cotta, 6 x 2¹⁄₁₆ x 1⅝ (15.2 x 5.2 x 4.1 cm). Gift of Mr. Edward Perry Warren h '26. 1908.14

Greek (mid-4th century B.C.): *Jointed Female Doll Holding Rattles.* Terra cotta, 7½ x 3¹⁄₁₆ x 1³⁄₁₆ (19.0 x 7.7 x 3.0 cm). Gift of Mr. Edward Perry Warren h '26. 1913.28

Greek (late 4th century B.C. or earlier): *Standing Woman.* Terra cotta, 7⅝ x 2¹⁵⁄₁₆ x 2¼ (19.3 x 7.5 x 5.7 cm). Gift of Mr. Edward Perry Warren h '26. 1915.12.1

East Greek (late 4th century B.C. or later): *Comic Actor with Long Beard.* Terra cotta, 4³⁄₁₆ x 1⅞ x 1 (10.7 x 4.7 x 2.5 cm). Gift of Mr. Edward Perry Warren h '26. 1915.24

Greek (late 4th century B.C. or earlier): *Standing Woman.* Terra cotta, 3⁹⁄₁₆ x 2⁹⁄₁₆ x 2¹⁵⁄₁₆ (9.0 x 6.5 x 7.4 cm). Gift of Mr. Edward Perry Warren h '26. 1913.40

Greek, Tanagra (late 4th or early 3rd century B.C.): *Standing Woman Holding a Chapelet.* Terra cotta, 8¹⁄₁₆ x 3 x 2⅝ (20.4 x 7.6 x 6.7 cm). Gift of Mr. Edward Perry Warren h '26. 1908.10

Greek, Tanagra (late 4th or early 3rd century B.C.): *Standing Woman Leaning on a Pillar.* Terra cotta, 7$\frac{11}{16}$ x 3$\frac{3}{8}$ x 2$\frac{1}{16}$ (19.5 x 8.5 x 5.2 cm). Gift of Mr. Edward Perry Warren h '26. 1908.12

Greek, Tanagra (3rd century B.C.): *Standing Woman.* Terra cotta, 6$\frac{7}{8}$ x 2$\frac{11}{16}$ x 2$\frac{5}{16}$ (17.5 x 6.9 x 5.9 cm). Gift of Mr. Edward Perry Warren h '26. 1923.2

Greek (3rd or 2nd century B.C.): *Boy Wearing a Coat.* Terra cotta, 2$\frac{15}{16}$ x 1$\frac{3}{4}$ x $\frac{9}{16}$ (7.5 x 4.5 x 1.5 cm). Gift of Mr. Edward Perry Warren h '26. 1923.11

Greek (3rd or 2nd century B.C.): *Head of a Grotesque Man.* Terra cotta, 2$\frac{9}{16}$ x 2$\frac{3}{8}$ x 2$\frac{5}{16}$ (6.5 x 6.0 x 5.8 cm). Gift of Mr. Edward Perry Warren h '26. 1913.53

Greek (3rd or 2nd century B.C.): *Mask of a Young Faun.* Terra cotta, 6$\frac{11}{16}$ x 8$\frac{1}{4}$ x 3$\frac{9}{16}$ (17.0 x 20.9 x 9.0 cm). Gift of Mr. Edward Perry Warren h '26. 1913.42

Greek (3rd or 2nd century B.C.): *Winged Eros with Cymbals.* Terra cotta, 3$\frac{3}{8}$ x 2$\frac{3}{4}$ x 1$\frac{7}{8}$ (8.6 x 7.0 x 4.7 cm). Gift of Mr. Edward Perry Warren h '26. 1908.17

East Greek (2nd or 1st century B.C.): *Dwarf Carrying a Kid on His Shoulders.* Terra cotta, 3$\frac{1}{16}$ x 1$\frac{7}{8}$ x 1$\frac{1}{4}$ (7.8 x 4.7 x 3.2 cm). Gift of Mr. Edward Perry Warren h '26. 1915.51

East Greek (2nd or 1st century B.C.): *Mask of Eros.* Terra cotta, 5 x 5$\frac{1}{16}$ x 2$\frac{1}{16}$ (12.7 x 12.9 x 5.3 cm). Gift of Mr. Edward Perry Warren h '26. 1915.54

Greek (2nd or 1st century B.C.): *Flying Eros.* Terra cotta, 9 x 6$\frac{1}{8}$ x 3$\frac{1}{2}$ (22.9 x 15.5 x 8.8 cm). Gift of Mr. Edward Perry Warren h '26. 1908.13

Greek (2nd or 1st century B.C.): *Flying Eros in Phrygian Garb.* Terra cotta, 10$\frac{3}{4}$ x 7$\frac{5}{8}$ x 4$\frac{11}{16}$ (27.3 x 19.4 x 11.9 cm). Gift of Mr. Edward Perry Warren h '26. 1908.9

Greek (2nd or 1st century B.C.): *Male Bacchic Flute Player.* Terra cotta, 12$\frac{7}{8}$ x 4 x 5$\frac{11}{16}$ (32.8 x 10.2 x 14.4 cm). Gift of Mr. Edward Perry Warren h '26. 1908.18

Greek (2nd or 1st century B.C.): *Standing Slave.* Terra cotta, 5$\frac{7}{8}$ x 1$\frac{7}{8}$ x 1$\frac{1}{2}$ (14.9 x 4.7 x 3.8 cm). Gift of Mr. Edward Perry Warren h '26. 1915.22

East Greek (late 2nd century B.C.): *Standing Woman Holding a Winged Eros in Her Arms.* Terra cotta, 8$\frac{7}{8}$ x 2$\frac{15}{16}$ x 2$\frac{11}{16}$ (22.5 x 7.4 x 6.8 cm). Gift of Mr. Edward Perry Warren h '26. 1908.15

Greek (1st century B.C.): *Head of a Chubby Eros.* Terra cotta, 3$\frac{3}{8}$ x 2$\frac{1}{2}$ x 2$\frac{1}{8}$ (8.5 x 6.4 x 5.4 cm). Gift of Mr. Edward Perry Warren h '26. 1923.13

Roman (1st century B.C. or later): *Fragment of Sima with Eros Carrying a Cluster of Fruit.* Terra cotta, $7\frac{3}{16}$ x $5\frac{1}{8}$ x $1\frac{7}{8}$ (18.3 x 13.0 x 4.8 cm). Gift of Mr. Edward Perry Warren h '26. 1913.44

Cypriote (1st century A.D.): *Brown-glazed Lamp.* Terra cotta, 1 x 4 x $2\frac{15}{16}$ (2.5 x 10.2 x 7.4 cm). Gift of Mr. Dana Estes h 1898. 1902.5

Roman (1st century A.D.): *Fragment of Cresting with Satyrs Treading Grapes.* Terra cotta, $9\frac{11}{16}$ x $10\frac{5}{8}$ x $1\frac{1}{4}$ (24.6 x 26.9 x 3.2 cm). Gift of Mr. Edward Perry Warren h '26. 1913.29

Roman (1st century A.D.): *Fragment of Revetment Plaque with the Head of Ammon.* Terra cotta, $8\frac{1}{4}$ x $4\frac{3}{16}$ x $1\frac{1}{4}$ (21.0 x 10.7 x 3.2 cm). Gift of Mr. Edward Perry Warren h '26. 1913.48

Roman (1st century A.D.): *Fragment of Revetment Plaque with the Head of Dionysus.* Terra cotta, 7 x $7\frac{5}{16}$ x $2\frac{3}{8}$ (17.8 x 18.5 x 6.0 cm). Gift of Mr. Edward Perry Warren h '26. 1913.47

Roman (2nd century A.D.): *Fragments of Cresting with a Statue in the Colonnade of a Palaestra.* Terra cotta, $14\frac{3}{8}$ x $8\frac{1}{16}$ x $1\frac{3}{8}$ (36.5 x 20.5 x 3.5 cm). Gift of Mr. Edward Perry Warren h '26. 1927.24.1-.2

Miscellaneous Objects

Greek (ca. 650-600 B.C.): *Large Die.* Terra cotta, $1\frac{9}{16}$ x $1\frac{9}{16}$ x $1\frac{9}{16}$ (4.0 x 4.0 x 4.0 cm). Gift of Mr. Edward Perry Warren h '26. 1930.33

Greek (5th century B.C.): *Flask with Cap.* Alabaster, $7\frac{13}{16}$ x $1\frac{13}{16}$ (19.8 x 4.6 cm). Gift of Mr. Edward Perry Warren h '26. 1927.16

Roman (1st century A.D.): *Ladle with Shallow Bowl.* Silver, $6\frac{5}{8}$ x 2 (16.8 x 5.1 cm). Gift of Mr. Edward Perry Warren h '26. 1927.11

Roman (1st or 2nd century A.D.): *Hairpin with Carved Finial.* Bronze, $3\frac{1}{16}$ x $\frac{1}{2}$ (7.7 x 1.2 cm). Gift of Mr. Edward Perry Warren h '26. 1930.44

Roman (1st or 2nd century A.D.): *Music Pipe.* Ivory, $12\frac{7}{8}$ x $1\frac{1}{8}$ (32.7 x 2.9 cm). Gift of Mr. Edward Perry Warren h '26. 1928.2

Roman (1st or 2nd century A.D.): *Needle.* Ivory, $6\frac{1}{8}$ x $\frac{1}{4}$ (15.6 x 0.7 cm). Gift of Mr. Edward Perry Warren h '26. 1930.45

Roman (1st or 2nd century A.D.): *Spoon with Round Bowl.* Ivory, $4\frac{1}{2}$ x 1 (11.5 x 2.5 cm). Gift of Mr. Edward Perry Warren h '26. 1930.42

EUROPEAN PAINTING, SCULPTURE, AND DECORATIVE ARTS

Painting

The European paintings in the Bowdoin College Museum of Art were primarily acquired through bequest and donation. The major gifts are those of the Honorable James Bowdoin III of 1811, the Kress Foundation of 1961, and Mr. John H. Halford '07 and Mrs. Halford, whose generosity has ranged over a period of many years. Additional donors such as Colonel George Boyd 1810, the Misses Walker, and Miss Susan Dwight Bliss, to name only a few, also gave works of quality to the museum. Only in recent years have modest endowments and, in 1967, the Florence C. Quinby Fund in honor of Henry Cole Quinby h '16, permitted the active purchase of European paintings.

The collection began with the bequest of James Bowdoin III of approximately seventy European works. Many of these are copies, now confined to storage, rather than the originals James Bowdoin may have thought he was buying. The 1811 bequest remains nearly intact with the exception of a few paintings, including a copy of Titian's *Danae and the Golden Shower,* which were deaccessioned in the nineteenth century on the grounds that they were "unsuitable for public exhibition, and still more for the private inspection by the youth of either sex." James Bowdoin's tastes were very broad; he acquired mythological, religious, and genre subjects, sea- and landscapes, and portraits. By far the greatest number of paintings in the Bowdoin bequest were by seventeenth- and eighteenth-century Flemish artists. Several works in the original gift are thought to be copies after Renaissance and Baroque masters by the Scottish-born John Smibert, executed in his years of travel prior to departure for America. His version of Poussin's *The Continence of Scipio* (now in the Pushkin Museum, Moscow) must be considered one of the more intriguing "European" paintings from James Bowdoin III's bequest.

The next major holding of European paintings is the Kress Study Collection of twelve works given to the College by the Samuel H. Kress Foundation in 1961. The foundation, organized to disperse the art amassed by Samuel H. Kress, reserved for the study collections 150 works intended as gifts for universities and colleges "known to emphasize the teaching of Art History and to have a definite need for a collection of Renaissance paintings to enable them to enrich their presentation of the history of art." All but one of the paintings, *King David* by Pedro Berruguete, are attributed to Italian artists and range in date from circa 1350 for Allegretto Nuzi's *Christ Blessing* to circa 1750 for the unidentified allegorical scene by Giuseppe Bazzani.

The third of the major gifts of European paintings made to the Bowdoin Museum is comprised of primarily nineteenth-century works given by Mr. John H. Halford '07 and Mrs. Halford. Among this varied group of nearly thirty paintings are *The Lost Sheep Found,* attributed to the Spanish painter Pedro Orrente, and an oil sketch by Corot entitled *The Pond.* In 1976 Mr. John H. Halford, Jr. '38 and Mrs. Halford donated to the museum in honor of Mr. John H. Halford '07 *The Capture of a Spanish Convoy by Two English Frigates* by Dominique Serres.

Numerous other patrons have contributed over the years to the collection of European paintings. Of Colonel George Boyd's 1852 gift, which earned him the distinction of having the Boyd Gallery bear his name, only Bonaventura Peeters I's *Naval Engagement, Bay of Messina, Sicily* is shown today. The Walker sisters, responsible for donating the art museum itself, left a number of nineteenth-century paintings; among these are *Lion Cubs* by Rosa Bonheur and Hermanus Koekkoek's *Council of War.* Other important miscellaneous gifts of European paintings to the College include Miss Susan Dwight Bliss's over-door panels of *The Triumph of Love* and *Love Vanquished* attributed to Charles Joseph Natoire.

With the Quinby bequest of 1967, designated specifically for the purchase of art, important European paintings were added to the Bowdoin collections. Outstanding among these are *Lot and His Daughters,* a landscape attributed to a close follower of the sixteenth-century Flemish artist Herri met de Bles; *The Meeting of Jacob and Joseph in Egypt* of 1636 by Claes Cornelisz Moeyaert; and Hendrick van Vliet's *The Tomb of Admiral Jacob van Wassenaer in the Choir of the Jacobskerk at The Hague* of circa 1668-1670.

Sculpture

A plaster bust of *Benjamin Franklin,* given by Benjamin Vaughan in 1835 as the work of Jean-Antoine Houdon, was the first European sculpture to enter the collections other than nineteenth-century plaster and marble copies of ancient works. The Misses Walker's gift in 1894 of a wax model of *Young Man Mastering a Horse* by Antoine-Louis Barye was the first European sculpture to be acquired for the recently completed museum building. From those dates, the collection has grown slowly, with rare exception through donation and bequest.

Mr. Edward Perry Warren h '26, the brilliant connoisseur whose gifts form the major part of Bowdoin's ancient collection, presented two European sculptures to the College in 1906 and 1915. The first, an alabaster head of *John the Baptist,* is dated circa 1500 and attributed to a northern Italian workshop; the second, a limestone *Head of a King,* currently is dated to the second quarter of the thirteenth century and traced to Chartres Cathedral.

Despite the auspicious beginning indicated by these gifts, important acquisitions of European sculpture were not made again until the 1960s. Through the estate of Miss Susan Dwight Bliss, a number of pieces entered the collections in 1963, including a Flemish *Madonna and Child* and a French *Bust of a Pope,* both of the sixteenth century, a *Charity* by the French eighteenth-century sculptor Antoine Mouton, and twelve small bronzes of animals by Barye. An important Renaissance German wood sculpture, identified as the *Prophet Habakkuk,* was given in the same year by the friends of Mr. John W. Frost '04 in his memory. Major purchases of this period include a *Saint John Nepomuk* attributed to Ferdinand Maxmilian Brokov, Jean-Baptiste Carpeaux's bust of *Charles Garnier,* and François Rude's *Head of a Gaul,* possibly cast from an early model for the relief of *The Departure of the Volunteers* on the Arc de Triomphe. In 1969, three works by Jacob Epstein were acquired through the generosity of Lady Epstein.

The Bowdoin collection of European sculpture contains few masterworks but nonetheless is significant at the College for the teaching of art history, particularly in the area of French sculpture. The existing collection is complemented by the museum's holdings of medals and plaquettes—the Molinari collection, discussed in a separate section of the *Handbook,* and the recent gifts of Mr. and Mrs. Mark M. Salton and Mrs. Gerd Utescher.

Decorative Arts

The strongest collection of European decorative arts in the Bowdoin College Museum of Art is furniture, ranging in date from the fifteenth to the nineteenth centuries and including English, French, Italian, Flemish, and Portuguese examples. Eighteenth- and nineteenth-century English pieces are of interest both for their quality and because they serve as foils to the American collection of the same period. The museum's more limited collection of European silver includes several major gifts and bequests. The Daniel Cony Memorial Collection, the gift of Mrs. Mary Prentiss Ingraham Davies, contains a representative selection of silver spoons from the British Isles, while the bequest of Mrs. Sylvia E. Ross includes a variety of forms made by the eighteenth-century London firm of Hester Bateman. Among the works received by the museum from the bequest of Mr. Charles Potter Kling is an extensive collection of English silver and plated wares dating from the eighteenth and nineteenth centuries. The museum holdings also include a small collection of English and Continental pewter from the estate of Mr. Marshall P. Cram '04 and an extensive selection of Staffordshire figurines from the bequest of Mrs. Sylvia E. Ross. [K.J.W. & M.R.B.]

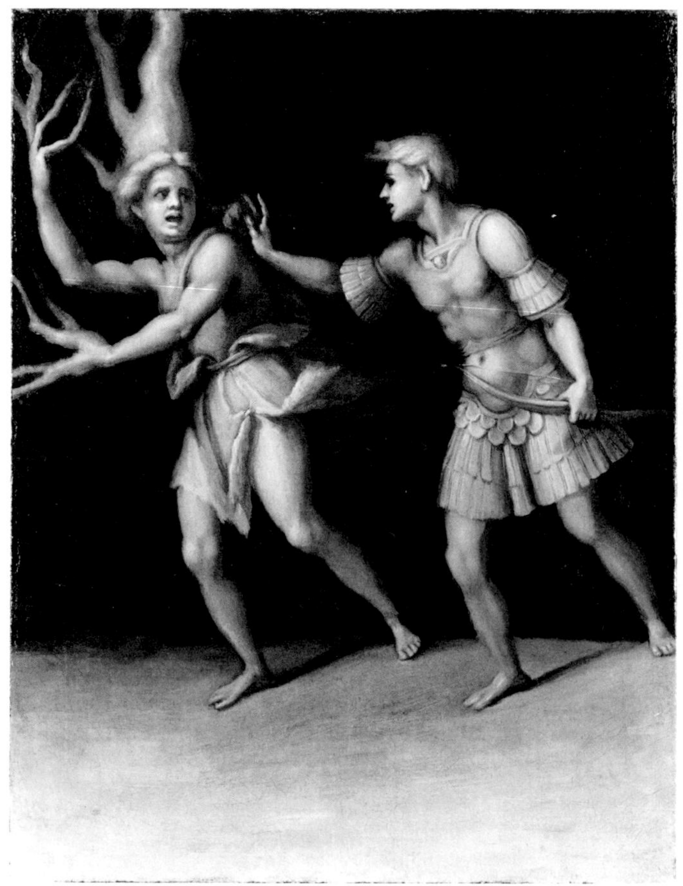

JACOPO DA CARRUCCI, CALLED PONTORMO (1494-1557), ITALIAN

Apollo and Daphne, 1513

Oil on canvas, 24⅜ x 19¼ (61.9 x 49.0 cm)

Gift of the Samuel H. Kress Foundation. 1961.100.9

The opening decades of the sixteenth century in Italy are distinguished by the culmination of artistic ideals originally developed during the Renaissance of the fifteenth century. This new phase, the High Renaissance, centering in Rome, Florence, and Venice, includes the work of Raphael, Andrea del Sarto, Leonardo da Vinci, Giorgione, and Titian. Yet even as a heroic classical style developed from the experiments and innovations of the previous century, younger artists were exploring new approaches to composition and color, resulting in a style referred to today as Mannerism, often defined as a reaction to the High Renaissance. One of the leading figures in the formation of the anti-classical Mannerist style was Jacopo da Carrucci, called Pontormo, the artist to whom Bowdoin's *Apollo and Daphne* is attributed.

Pontormo was the student of Piero di Cosimo and Mariotto Albertinelli. He became Andrea del Sarto's assistant in 1512. Giorgio Vasari reports in his *Lives of the Painters* (Volume III) that Pontormo admired Sarto's style and endeavored to imitate his work. Pontormo's first independent paintings date from about 1513, when he was still in the elder artist's studio. So strong was the influence of the master on his protégé that until recently *Apollo and Daphne* was attributed to the school of Andrea del Sarto.

Apollo and Daphne is done in grisaille, the technique of monochrome painting in shades of grey. The scene illustrated is from Ovid's *Metamorphoses,* a favorite source of subject matter for artists of the period. Research by John Shearman, reported in November 1962 in his *Burlington Magazine* article "Pontormo and Andrea del Sarto, 1513," indicates that the painting is most likely a very early work by Pontormo, dating from his association with Sarto's studio. According to documentary evidence compiled by Shearman, this painting and another, *Apollo and Cupid* (at Bucknell University, Lewisburg, Pennsylvania), were part of a series executed by Pontormo for a festival organized by the reinstated Medici for the rebellious Florentines in 1513. Two companies of lords and nobles commissioned decorated chariots which formed a ceremonial procession through the city; the Bowdoin and Bucknell canvases may have adorned one of those chariots.

In this painting, a passionate Apollo touches the chaste Daphne, who has called to her father, the river-god Peneus, imploring protection from her insistent suitor. In answer to her plea, Daphne is transformed into a laurel tree. It is this moment of metamorphosis that Pontormo has chosen to depict. Though the painting lacks the fullness and strength typical of the style of Sarto, it does, as Shearman points out, illustrate beautifully the sadness and gentle humor of Ovid's text.   [R.V.W.]

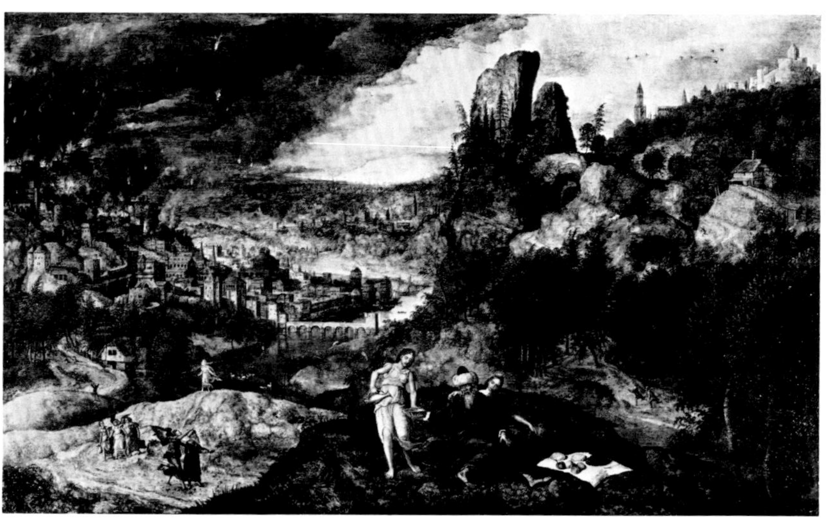

UNKNOWN ARTIST, FLEMISH

Lot and His Daughters, ca. 1550-1575

Oil on panel, 17½ x 28⅛ (44.3 x 71.3 cm)

Florence C. Quinby Fund in memory of Henry Cole Quinby h '16. 1970.78

Already in the first half of the fifteenth century, landscape was an important element in the work of such Flemish painters as Jan van Eyck, Rogier van der Weyden, and their followers. Later Hugo van der Goes and Hieronymus Bosch explored the use of landscape for compositional and emotional purposes, but in their work and that of other Flemish artists, as contrasted to Italian practice of the period, the two-dimensional rendition of space was for the most part instinctively realized through observation and not based on a scientific knowledge of perspective.

Throughout the sixteenth century, Flemish landscape remained empirical and became, with some exceptions, conventionalized spatially and coloristically. Following Bosch, painters such as Joachim Patinir and Herri met de Bles, who may have been Patinir's nephew, tended to use a high horizon with elevated foreground, the two united harmoniously by a sweeping panorama often including towns and mountains, forests and rivers, as in *Lot and His Daughters*. The same color scheme to indicate depth, a formula present in the Bowdoin painting, was frequently repeated: reddish brown in the foreground, green for the middle, and blue for the furthest distance. But, unlike their predecessors who treated landscape as a subsidiary part of usually religious narrative, Patinir and those painters closest to him, such as de Bles, allowed landscape a more dominant role and thus formed a bridge between the earlier masters and the great Pieter Brueghel in the development of Flemish landscape painting.

The narrative of *Lot and His Daughters* is drawn directly from the account in Genesis 19, and the separate episodes in the story are simultaneously related. With graceful gestures, the daughters of Lot woo their father on a low hill before a panoramic landscape. In the distance, fire destroys a city, probably their home, Sodom, and will soon spread to the neighboring Gomorrah. To the left, they can be seen again with Lot led from the cities by angels. They leave their mother, a figure who has turned to salt because she looked back at the destruction despite the Lord's warning. The next event in the biblical story, the refugees' stay in the city of Zoar, is perhaps alluded to by the town depicted near the distant horizon or the one nestled in the forest to the upper right. The conclusion of the narrative is clear from the foreground group: Lot's daughters will succeed in seducing him; their sons born of this union will father the Moabites and the children of Ammon.

Although *Lot and His Daughters* has traditionally been considered to be by Herri met de Bles, art historical scholars currently question this attribution. Despite the landscape's close similarity in style and composition to that artist's work, Professors Robert A. Koch of Princeton University and Craig Harbison of the University of Massachusetts have concluded in correspondence that the painting is somewhat later. According to Professor Koch, "it lies in the still shadowy period in Antwerp painting at the time of Pieter Brueghel in the middle decades of the sixteenth century." Additionally, Professor Walter S. Gibson of Case Western University suggests that the work is by a follower of Herri met de Bles, even a member of his workshop, and could have been executed circa 1550 by the Master of the Lille Sermon; with this tentative attribution, he acknowledges the work of Professor Giorgio Faggin on that master.   [K.J.W.]

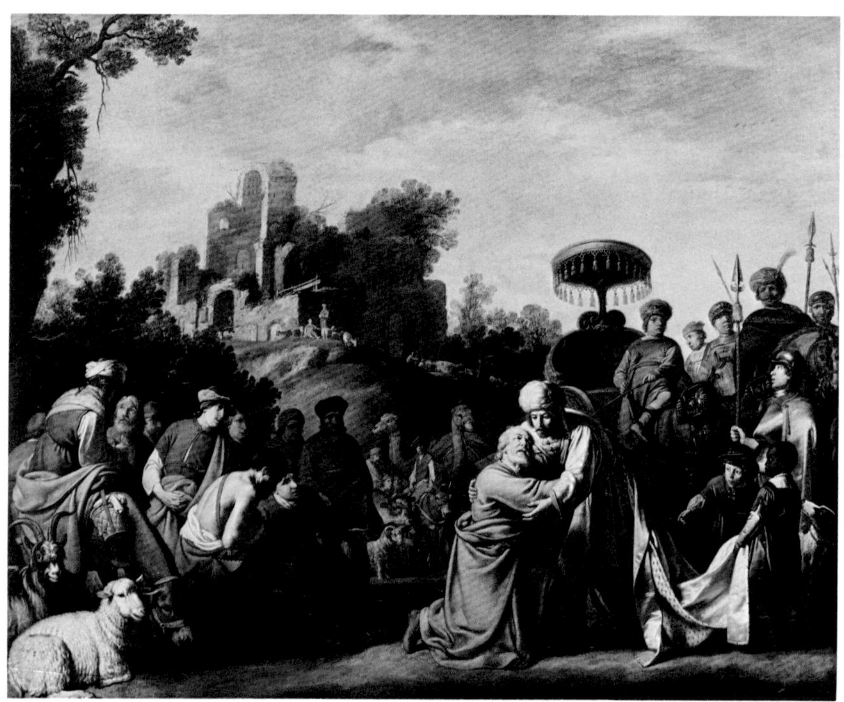

CLAES CORNELISZ MOEYAERT (1590/91-1655), DUTCH

The Meeting of Jacob and Joseph in Egypt, 1636

Oil on canvas, 54 x 64¾ (137.2 x 164.5 cm)

Florence C. Quinby Fund in memory of Henry Cole Quinby h '16. 1970.41

Due to the intense artistic and intellectual activity of the time, the seventeenth century has been called Holland's "Golden Age." Political and economic conditions allowed the arts to flourish, and an innovative and uniquely Dutch style was developed. This style was based primarily upon realism and the recognition of the beauty of everyday life and was expressed in landscape and still life as well as in genre painting and portraiture. Consideration of the achievements of this period cannot be confined to such masters as Rembrandt van Rijn, Frans Hals, and Jan Vermeer, but also must include other very talented though lesser known artists such as Claes Cornelisz Moeyaert.

Moeyaert's birthplace is uncertain, but it is known that he was in Amsterdam by 1604/5, where he worked for the remainder of his life. Little is known about his early training, which may have included a trip to Italy. The artist's first works were completed in 1624, and, beginning in 1631, he received numerous commissions from fellow Roman Catholics in Amsterdam. Though best known for history and religious paintings, Moeyaert executed throughout his career a large number of theatrical decorations and portraits of church clerics and officials. Documents regarding his many commissions and the description in his will of his considerable fortune indicate that he was one of the most highly respected and popular painters working in Amsterdam before the appearance of Rembrandt.

Moeyaert was part of a circle of artists, including Pieter Lastman and Jan and Jacob Pynas, who immediately preceded Rembrandt. These pre-Rembrandtists created realistic and straightforward paintings of historical subjects, often from the Old Testament. Though the pre-Rembrandtists worked within the traditions of seventeenth-century Dutch painting, the influence of Italian art on their oeuvre is significant.

Due to its similarity to Moeyaert's other dated works, *The Meeting of Jacob and Joseph in Egypt* is believed to have been executed in 1636. The artist illustrates the reunion of Jacob of Canaan with his long lost son Joseph, who had been serving as viceroy to the pharaoh in Egypt. The placement of Joseph's brothers around the father and the son, as

well as the classical format of the landscape and the Roman
ruins, are evidence of Moeyaert's adoption of Italian composition, style, and subject matter. The ruins, along with the
oriental garb of the Egyptians, illustrate an attempt at historical accuracy in the manner of Lastman. Moeyaert's concern with naturalism is apparent in the detail of the landscape and the individual features of the brothers of Joseph.

[R.V.W.]

HENDRIK CORNELISZ VAN VLIET (1611/12-1675), DUTCH

*The Tomb of Admiral Jacob van Wassanaer in the Choir
of the Jacobskerk at The Hague*

Oil on canvas, 37 x 28 (94.0 x 71.1 cm)

Florence C. Quinby Fund in memory of Henry Cole Quinby h '16.
1971.6

In the middle decades of the seventeenth century, Delft was
one of the great artistic centers of Holland. Carel Fabritius,
Jan Vermeer, Pieter de Hoogh, Evert and Willem van Aelst,
Gerard Houckgeest, and Emanuel de Witte reflected in their
paintings of religious themes, domestic and ecclesiastical interiors, street scenes, and still lifes the material well-being
and cultural refinement of the city's prosperous merchant
society. One of the least known today of this brilliant artistic
group, although a well-respected painter in his home town,
was Hendrik Cornelisz van Vliet.

Born in Delft, Vliet was taught by his uncle, Willem van
Vliet, and by Michiel van Miereveld. He joined the city's
painters' guild in 1632 and was noted early in his career as
a portraitist. Beginning in the 1650s and throughout his later
years, Vliet painted church interiors almost exclusively, particularly views of Delft's Old Church and New Church.

The Bowdoin College Museum of Art painting by Vliet
has been identified by Walter Liedtke as *The Tomb of Admiral Jacob van Wassanaer in the Choir of the Jacobskerk
at The Hague*. According to Liedtke, the work dates soon
after the completion in 1667 of the tomb, executed by Bartholomeus Eggers from a design by the painter C. Monincx.

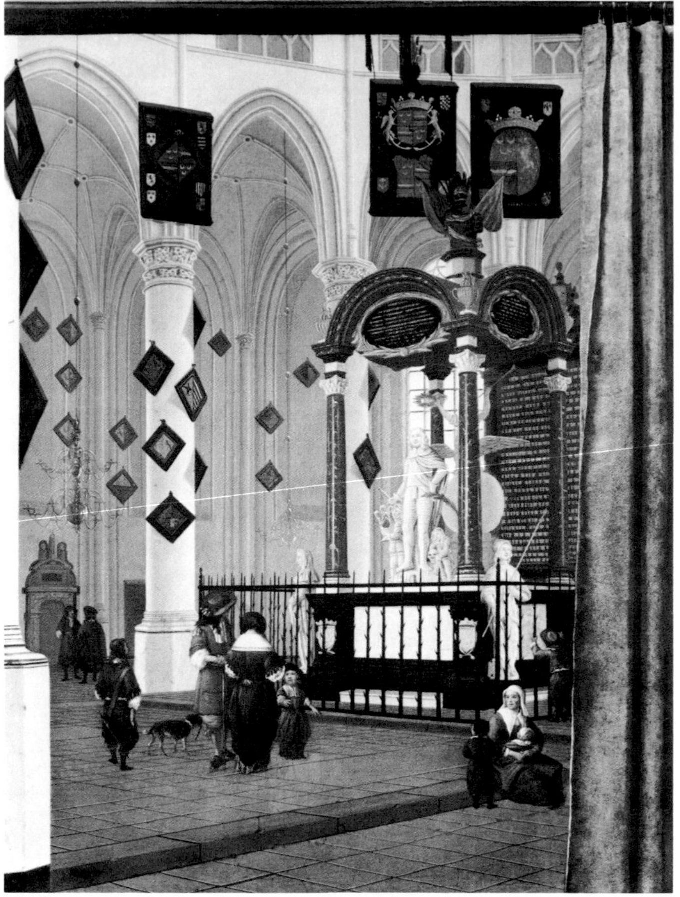

As with other paintings from this later period of Vliet's career, it indicates a shift from his relatively experimental compositions of the 1650s toward more rigidly ordered, coldly executed works. In this view of the Jacobskerk, Vliet, who placed his signature on the step at the lower left of the canvas, framed the composition on the right with a *trompe l'oeil* curtain. The bright yellow-green fabric on the painting surface, so close to the viewer, acts as a foil to the sunlit volumes and predominantly cream and white walls of the church and, with the pillar to the left, forms a frame within a frame, a transition between the reality of the viewer's space and the painted interior. The figures are placed as carefully as chess pieces on the grid pavement of the church to complement and check the compositional verticals of the tomb sculpture and massive pillars, the diagonals of floor stones, and the curves of vaulting and tomb structure. Vliet's painting meticulously records the sculptural and architectural details as well as the effects of light, which floods the choir window, illuminating the tomb and its statues and highlighting the starched white collars and cuffs of the costumes against the shadowed ambulatory. The work further serves as a *memento mori,* a reminder of the brevity of life and human glory, by its purposeful contrast between the human spectators and the lifeless tomb sculptures they quietly contemplate.   [K.J.W.]

FERDINAND MAXMILIAN BROKOV (1688-1731), BOHEMIAN

St. John Nepomuk, 1708-1710

Oak, 51¾ x 23⅜ x 17⅛ (131.4 x 59.3 x 43.4 cm)

Museum purchase. 1968.72

Following the failure of the Protestant Reformation in seventeenth-century Bohemia, the Roman Catholic clergy subjected the country to religious persecution and economic exploitation. The Baroque art of the Counter Reformation, imported by foreign artists from all over Europe, played a key role in the forced re-conversion of the country to Catholicism. By the early eighteenth century, however, Baroque art had become domesticated, and a few outstanding native artists, such as Ferdinand Maxmilian Brokov, brought to an end the artistic paralysis that had gripped Bohemia at the time.

Brokov, one of the outstanding figures in Bohemian as well as central European art, was born to a family of sculptors and worked with his brother Michal in the shop of their father, Jan. Unlike artists in other workshops of the time, the Brokovs created sculptures independently of one another. Though signed pieces from the atelier bear the name of Jan Brokov, an examination of style, technique, and iconography frequently make it possible to attribute the

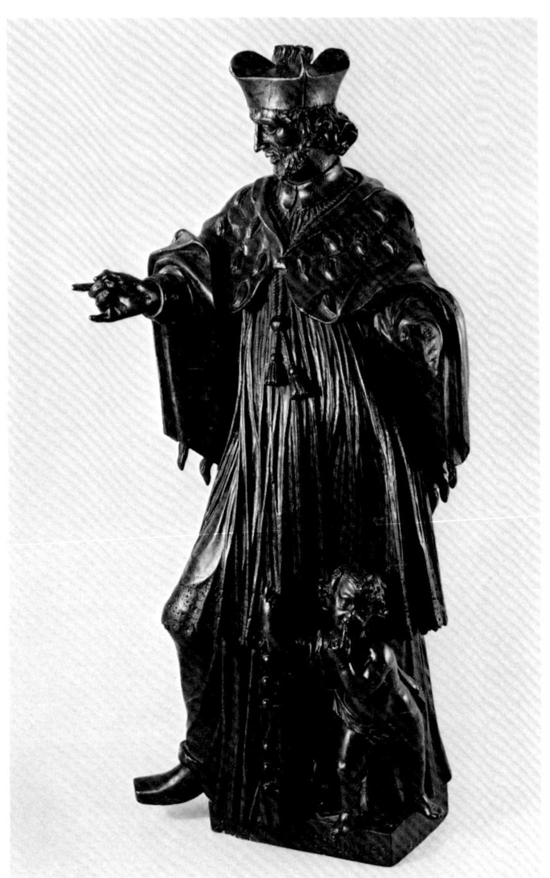

sculptures individually. Bowdoin's *St. John Nepomuk* relates to the Brokov workshop in concept and rendition; the
saint was a favorite subject of both father and sons. In this
case, however, the treatment of the form and volume and
the monumental aspiration and pose of the figure suggest
an attribution of the statue to Ferdinand. The body of the
saint is animated by a dramatic yet balanced distribution of
mass in a series of sweeping curves. The dynamic movement
so often associated with Baroque style is present, but St.
John is not wildly ecstatic. Rather, the activity of the body
and garment works more subtly to give life to the saint.

The cult of St. John Nepomuk was organized by the
Jesuits and supported by the general Catholic clergy and the

court of the Holy Roman Empire; it was of great political and ideological significance to the Counter Reformation in Bohemia. According to medieval tradition, St. John Nepomuk, confessor to the wife of Wenceslas IV, was tortured and thrown into the Vltava River in Prague after refusing to reveal the queen's confessional secrets to the king. Brokov depicts the saint with the symbols of a crucifix and a martyr's palm; the putto with finger raised to his lips represents the saint's determination to remain silent.

A more complete discussion of this sculpture and its attribution can be found in "The Bowdoin Sculpture of St. John Nepomuk," *Occasional Papers II* by Zdenka Volavka, published by the museum in 1975.   [z.v. & k.a.o.]

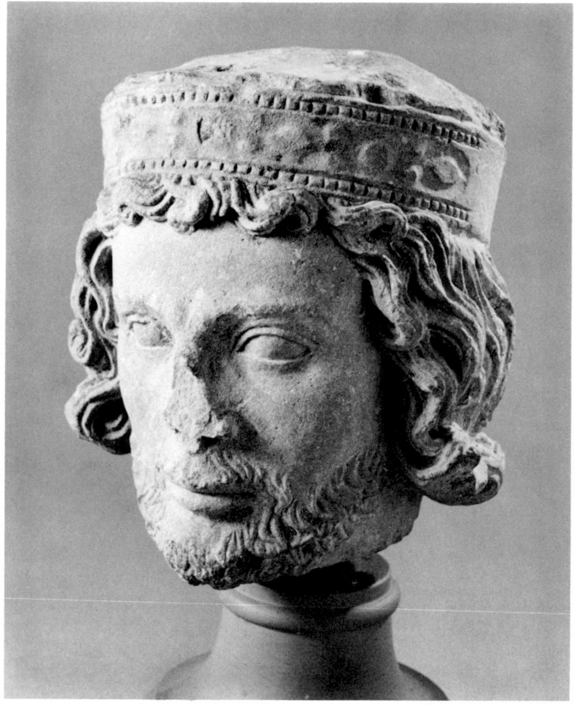

FRENCH

Head of a King, ca. 1220-1230

Limestone, $6\frac{1}{8}$ x $5\frac{13}{16}$ x $5\frac{1}{8}$ (15.6 x 14.7 x 13.0 cm)
Gift of Mr. Edward Perry Warren h '26. 1915.100

A synthesis of many artistic media, creating a total mystical vision of the church as "heaven on earth," is present in the Gothic cathedral, which achieved its highest form in the thirteenth century in Paris, Chartres, and Rheims. Sculpture was an integral part of ecclesiastical architecture, and hundreds of figures and decorative panels adorned the exterior of a cathedral and parts of its interior. The sculpture, along with stained glass and tapestries, formed rich iconographic programs which unfolded before the believer. Thus, the building became a visual catechism for those who could not read the scriptures.

Several different workshops of anonymous masons executed the sculpture of each cathedral. The pieces were not created at the building site but were virtually completed in the mason's yard. Only final fitting adjustments were made as the sculptures were put into place. The itinerant nature of the mason's trade and the fact that most of the sculpture is not signed make identification of geographic origin and dating of such works possible solely on the basis of style.

The sculpture of the thirteenth century marked a transition between the Romanesque style, characterized by rigid planar forms, stylized patterns of drapery, and exaggerated facial features, and the Gothic style, in which pattern was replaced by naturalism and linearity by plasticity. Drapery and facial modeling became softer and more varied; relaxed bodies moved more freely within the architectural setting. The style of the 1220s and 1230s, known as High Gothic, became extremely refined and delicate, and it is from this period that the Bowdoin *Head of a King* probably dates. Carving on the neck indicates that the piece was intended to be part of a complete figure; the unfinished state of the back of the head suggests that it may have been attached to an architectural structure. The face is naturalistic; the cheekbones are subtly modeled, creating an organic transition between the frontal and side planes not typical of earlier Gothic sculpture. The studied handling of the eyes and lips renders them expressive and lifelike. The beard and hair are finely carved, in a natural rather than a stylized manner; drillwork is used to create the full deep curls.

The *Head of a King* has been attributed to several workshops in the Île-de-France, the area surrounding Paris. Recent research by Dr. Brooks W. Stoddard has associated the
Bowdoin *Head* with sculptures from the choir screen, dating
from the 1230s and dismantled in the eighteenth century, of
the cathedral at Chartres. A plaster cast of the head was
fitted exactly to a torso fragment from the screen, which is
now in the Chapel of St. Martin in the crypt at Chartres. A
surviving head of a young king from the screen's depiction
of the *Dream of the Magi,* also in the crypt, bears a strong
stylistic resemblance to the Bowdoin sculpture.   [K.A.O.]

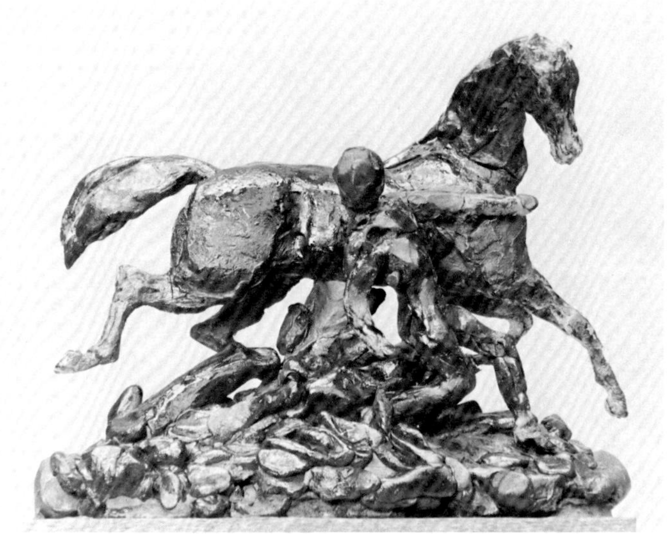

ANTOINE-LOUIS BARYE (1796-1875), FRENCH
Young Man Mastering a Horse, ca. 1855-1870
  Wax and plastiline, $8\frac{3}{8}$ x $3\frac{7}{8}$ x $9\frac{1}{8}$ (21.3 x 9.8 x 23.2 cm)
  Gift of the Misses Harriet and Sophia Walker. 1894.147

The son of a jeweler, Antoine-Louis Barye was born in
Paris in 1796. As a child he worked with his father and became skillful at modeling clay and wax from which bronze
ornaments were made. Following apprenticeships to a copper engraver and another jeweler, he studied sculpture briefly

with François-Joseph Bosio in 1816 and painting and drawing with Baron Antoine-Jean Gros during the next year. Barye's reputation as an artisan and the detail and literalism of his sculptures made success in academic circles difficult; as a result he returned to the jewelry trade in 1823 and worked with Jacques-Henri Fauconnier, with whom he remained for eight years. During this time, Barye concentrated on making small bronze animals, subjects he would later depict in his larger works.

Barye's art is at once scientific and romantic. He was deeply committed to the accurate portrayal of animals, making meticulous studies of anatomy and developing a scientist's understanding of bone and muscle structure. Yet Barye charged this anatomical precision with romantic expressionism, often depicting scenes of struggle, of natural enemies locked in combat, and of the strong devouring their prey. His animal subjects were described with the formal exactness and imbued with the emotional characteristics previously reserved for the presentation of the human figure.

In *Young Man Mastering a Horse,* Barye has captured in lumps of clay and wax the muscularity, weight, and speed of the horse, and the strength required of the young man to maintain control over it. Though the sculpture is a powerful work of art in its own right, it also was probably used as a model for bronze casts; from the model a plaster mold may have been made into which molten bronze was poured and a cast formed. Records of the provenance, which can be traced to Barye's studio, indicate that two bronze casts may have been made after the artist's death. A photograph of one of the casts, in the possession of the Tempelaere family in 1950, reveals that the head of the man was originally in a higher position and that the left hand touched the horse's mouth, implying that the fragile wax model once was broken and incorrectly mended.   [K.A.O.]

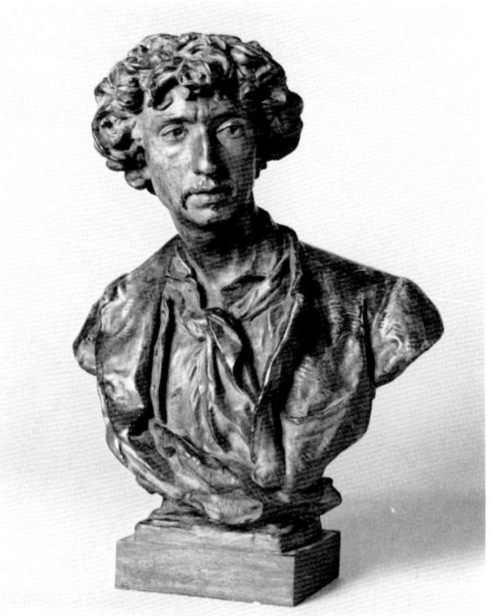

JEAN-BAPTISTE CARPEAUX (1827-1876), FRENCH
Bust of Charles Garnier, ca. 1869-1876

Plaster, $17\frac{9}{16}$ x $13\frac{3}{8}$ x $7\frac{1}{8}$ (44.6 x 34.0 x 18.1 cm)

Museum purchase. 1967.3

The son of a lacemaker and a stonemason, Jean-Baptiste Carpeaux was born in Valenciennes, France. After moving to Paris at the age of eleven, Carpeaux, with the assistance of his cousin Victor Liet, enrolled at the Petit École. There he learned the rudiments of sculpture and became friends with another student, Charles Garnier, later to become a prominent French architect. After two years at the Petit École, Carpeaux entered the École des Beaux Arts, where he studied first with François Rude and then with Francisque-Joseph Duret. In 1854, the young sculptor secured the *Prix de Rome,* his country's most coveted academic accolade.

Reaching Rome in 1856, Carpeaux began work on what was to become his masterpiece, *Ugolino and His Children,* and developed his talent as a portraitist. His return to Paris in 1862 was marked by increasing public acclaim; on August 17, 1865, his former classmate Garnier commissioned

Carpeaux to execute *The Dance,* one of the four sculptural groups on the main facade of the Paris Opéra, the crowning example of elegant architecture in Second Empire France, which Garnier had recently designed.

When the architect first sat for his portrait is not known, but Carpeaux exhibited Garnier's bust in the Paris Salon of 1869. This work in bronze is now in the Louvre. Another version, signed by the sculptor and dated 1869, was executed in marble. Additional copies in plaster are to be found in the École's collection and in the Musée de l'Opéra. In 1903 yet another version of this bust was incorporated into a memorial to the architect which was designed by M. Pascal and placed on the east side of the Opéra.

In 1868 Carpeaux purchased property at Auteuil, on the outskirts of Paris, where he built a large studio and established an atelier that produced large editions of his sculptures in bronze, marble, terra cotta, and plaster to satisfy popular taste. Identification markings—*Atelier Carpeaux* or *Propriété Carpeaux*—were apparently stamped on these multiple productions. Since the versions of the bust exhibited at the 1869 Salon and in the collection of the Louvre are listed as being sixty-five centimeters in height, Bowdoin's *Garnier* must be considered a reduction, most probably executed under Carpeaux's control in this atelier. It was probably colored to simulate bronze during its actual manufacture. The ease of duplicating sculpture and the lack of a substantive provenance for the bust render it impossible to determine the date of production or the number of replicas of this work on this scale.

An accomplished modeler and innovative designer, Carpeaux must be ranked as one of the giants of nineteenth-century sculpture. His style of portraiture combines a studied informality of pose with penetrating character analysis. The sharply focused eyes, jaunty turn of the head, and flowing locks of hair give the *Charles Garnier* a stunning physical immediacy. The lively modeling of surfaces that captures the textural differences of skin, hair, and clothing further demonstrates Carpeaux's mastery of portrait sculpture.

[M.R.]

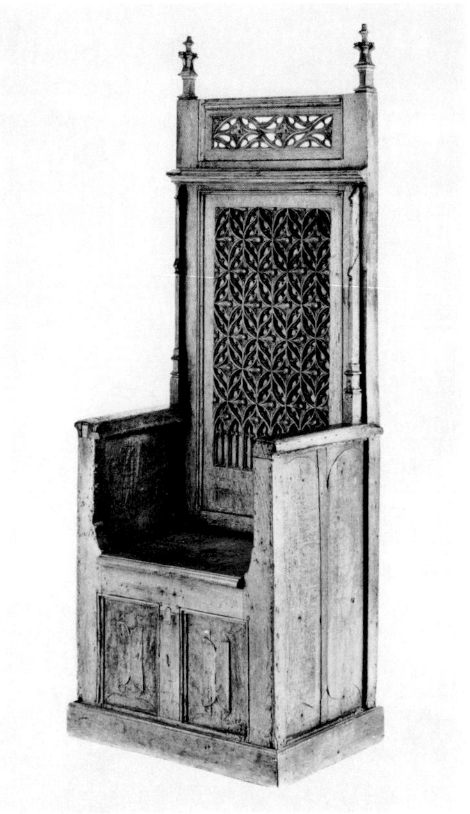

FRENCH

Chair, ca. 1500

Oak, $60\frac{7}{8}$ x $27\frac{1}{8}$ x $17\frac{3}{4}$ (154.6 x 68.9 x 45.0 cm)

Gift of Mr. Herbert H. Richardson from the estate of Mr. Curtis Appleton Perry 1877. 1931.14

In the Middle Ages, even elaborate homes were sparsely furnished. Pieces such as beds, chairs, and tables were few in number and often crudely constructed; medieval society treasured tapestries, imported fabrics, silver plate, and other decorative arts objects more highly than furniture. Although seating furniture of the time primarily included portable stools and benches, elaborate ceremonial chairs such as the example illustrated here were occasionally owned by the wealthy. Ecclesiastical in origin, such chairs were regarded as seats of honor and were generally reserved for the head of a family.

The style and decoration of furniture in the Middle Ages were chiefly derived from architecture. Motifs such as the carved linenfold decoration appearing on the sides and beneath the seat of the chair commonly accented interior wall paneling. The vertical thrust of the chair, as well as the pierced frieze and blind arcading adorning the back of the piece, generally reflect the decorative spirit of the Gothic cathedral; once brightly painted and probably gilded, the delicate carved tracery dividing the back panel suggests the intricacy and visual richness of a stained-glass window. The form of such chairs was also architectural, for the pieces were fastened together with mortise and tenon joints like interior paneling.

The chair may originally have been conceived as an integral part of the interior woodwork of an elaborate medieval room. It was once furnished with a deep cushion, and its arms were probably upholstered.   [M.R.B.]

ENGLISH

Pair of Side Chairs, 1700-1725

> Walnut and oak, $43\frac{5}{8}$ x $21\frac{3}{4}$ x $19\frac{1}{2}$ (110.8 x 55.2 x 49.5 cm)
>
> Gift of Mr. H. Ray Dennis, Jr. 1978.9.1-.2

English furniture of the late seventeenth and early eighteenth centuries was heavily influenced by Dutch and French design and by the influx of Dutch cabinetmakers following the reign of William III; such foreign motifs were absorbed and anglicized, resulting in a sober, restrained furniture style generally described as "Queen Anne," for its development and popularity can most conveniently be dated to the years of her reign (1702-1714). The Queen Anne style, in contrast to the elaborately turned and carved William and Mary style preceding it, was characterized by its subtle decorative outline and by its elegant curvilinear design. Much furniture, particularly case pieces such as chests of drawers, was veneered with thin sheets of figured woods and decorated with elaborate marquetry, specialized tech-

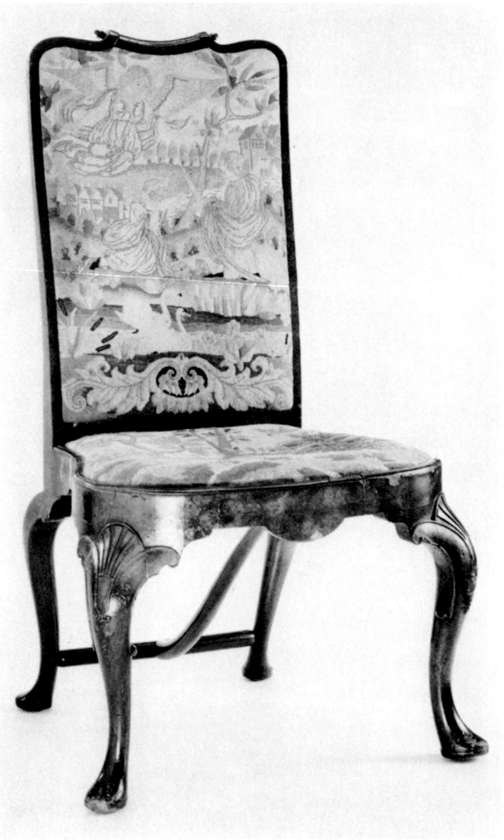

niques revealing the influence of Continental craftsmen. Though other woods such as oak, beech, yew, and elm do appear, walnut was most commonly utilized for furniture construction.

Chairmaking became a specialized craft during this period, and the high quality of its production is revealed by this pair of Queen Anne side chairs. As is typical of the style, the overall shape of each chair, including the seat, stretcher, and back, is composed of a series of curves which delicately interact, producing a restrained yet sophisticated composition. The cabriole, or S-shaped, leg was introduced during this period, often accented at the knee with crisp carving and terminating, as in the case of the Bowdoin chairs, in a simple pad foot. The chair rail is veneered with walnut. An unusual feature of the Bowdoin chairs is the turned rail connecting the stretcher to the underside of the seat frame, an element probably added for additional support.

The needlework seats and backs are original to the chairs and attest to the increased interest in upholstery in the early eighteenth century. Although imported velvets, brocades, or damask were utilized as upholstery materials on the very finest furniture, most pieces were covered in needlework, usually of canvas stitched with colored wool. Such furniture coverings were generally worked by the women of a household after published designs and patterns. Though the subjects illustrated were occasionally religious or historical, most needlework coverings depicted more general pastoral and decorative themes. [M.R.B.]

HESTER BATEMAN (1709-1794), ENGLISH

Teapot, 1782

Silver and wood, $5\frac{3}{8}$ x $9\frac{1}{2}$ x $3\frac{11}{16}$ (13.6 x 24.1 x 9.3 cm)

Gift of Mrs. Sylvia E. Ross. 1963.32.1

Probably part of a larger service, this handsome teapot is indicative of the rapid changes in silver styles in the final decades of the eighteenth century. A radical revolution in the form and design of the decorative arts was caused by a reaction against the fanciful freedom of the Rococo period and a renewed interest in classical sources. As seen in the teapot, the new style emphasized flat, unmodulated surfaces, simple linear decoration, and a complex interrelationship of geometric shapes. Such stylistic advances were further influenced by technological inventions such as rolling mills, which mass-produced thin silver sheets to be cut and seamed into the bodies of vessels, considerably reducing costly handwork.

The teapot exhibits a wide variety of decorative devices. Delicate floral swags, a common motif in the latter half of the eighteenth century, are chased, or tapped, into the surface of the teapot; strips of beaded decoration applied to the foot and lid of the piece and engraved initials further

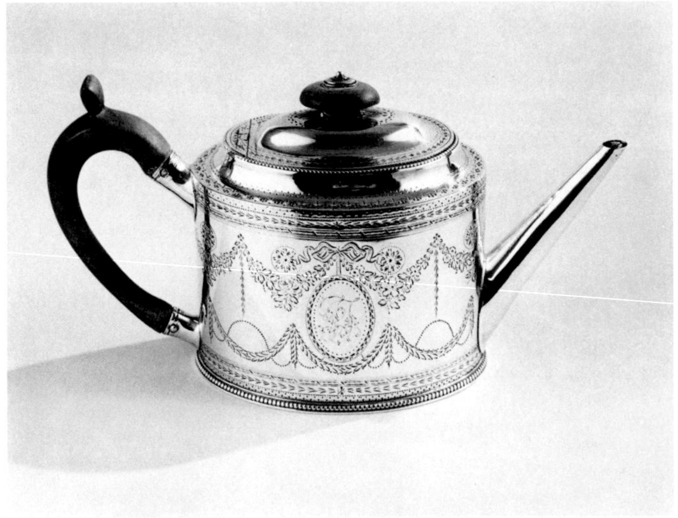

emphasize its delicate form. The teapot handle and finial are of wood, a poor conductor of heat.

The hallmarks on the teapot indicate that it was made by the London firm of Hester Bateman in 1782. Upon the death of her silversmith husband in 1760, Bateman inherited his modest business and registered her mark at Goldsmith's Hall the following year. Probably not personally involved in silver production, Bateman employed many assistants and developed the family business to compete successfully with the flourishing silverplate manufacturers of the late eighteenth century. Primarily aiming its wares at the middle-class market, the firm specialized in such useful pieces as salts, cream jugs, and teapots, which were noted for their high quality. The firm flourished in the 1780s and was continued under different hallmarks by her family following Hester Bateman's retirement in 1790 at the age of eighty-one.

[M.R.B.]

SELECTED WORKS FROM THE COLLECTION

Painting

[K.J.W. & K.A.O.]

School of Barnaba da Modena (14th century), Italian: *The Crucifixion.* Tempera on panel, 19¾ x 12¼ (52.0 x 31.1 cm). Gift of the Samuel H. Kress Foundation. 1961.100.2

Allegretto Nuzi (active 1346-1373/4), Italian: *Christ Blessing.* Tempera on panel, 7⅜ x 7¼ (18.7 x 18.1 cm). Gift of the Samuel H. Kress Foundation. 1961.100.4

Circle of the Master of the Griggs Crucifixion (15th century), Italian: *Scenes from the Ninfale Fiesolano.* Tempera on panel, 11⅜ x 49¾ (28.9 x 126.5 cm). Gift of the Samuel H. Kress Foundation. 1961. 100.1

School of Gherardo del Fora (active 1445-1497), Italian: *St. Mary of Egypt between St. Peter Martyr and St. Catharine of Siena.* Tempera on panel, 16¾ x 11¼ (42.5 x 28.5 cm). Gift of the Samuel H. Kress Foundation. 1961.100.11

Pedro Berruguete (ca. 1450-1504), Spanish: *King David.* Oil on panel, 32 x 38 (81.2 x 96.5 cm). Gift of the Samuel H. Kress Foundation. 1961.100.10

Giovanni Battista Bertucci (active 1475-1516), Italian: *St. Mary Magdalene.* Tempera on panel, 19½ x 16⅛ (49.5 x 41.0 cm). Gift of the Samuel H. Kress Foundation. 1961.100.6

Biagio d'Antonio da Firenze (1475-1515), Italian: *St. Jerome in the Wilderness.* Tempera on panel, 55¼ x 20 (140.1 x 50.8 cm). Gift of the Samuel H. Kress Foundation. 1961.100.3

School of Il Garofalo (Benevenuto da Tisio) (1481-1559), Italian: *The Presentation of the Virgin.* Oil on panel, 26¼ x 18⅜ (66.7 x 46.6 cm). Gift of the Samuel H. Kress Foundation. 1961.100.5

✠Jacopo da Carrucci (Pontormo) (1494-1557), Italian: *Apollo and Daphne.* Oil on canvas, 24⅜ x 19¼ (61.9 x 49.0 cm). Gift of the Samuel H. Kress Foundation. 1961.100.9

✠Unknown artist, Flemish (ca. 1550-1575): *Lot and His Daughters.* Oil on panel, 17½ x 28⅛ (44.3 x 71.3 cm). Florence C. Quinby Fund in memory of Henry Cole Quinby h '16. 1970.78

Pedro Orrente (1570-1644), Spanish: *The Lost Sheep Found.* Oil on canvas, 33 x 39 (83.8 x 99.1 cm). Gift of Mr. John H. Halford '07 and Mrs. Halford. 1957.2

Circle of Carlo Saraceni (1585-1620), Italian: *The Assumption of the*

Virgin. Oil on canvas, 37 x 30 (94.0 x 76.2 cm). Gift of Mr. John H. Halford '07 and Mrs. Halford. 1957.1

✠Claes Cornelisz MOEYAERT (1590/91-1655), Dutch: *The Meeting of Jacob and Joseph in Egypt*. Oil on canvas, 54 x 64¾ (137.2 x 164.5 cm). Florence C. Quinby Fund in memory of Henry Cole Quinby h '16. 1970.41

Cornelis SCHUT (1597-1655), Flemish: *Venus and Ceres*. Oil on canvas, 44 x 59 (111.7 x 149.8 cm). Bequest of the Honorable James Bowdoin III. 1813.12

Unknown artist (17th century), Spanish: *Portrait of an Unknown Youth*. Oil on canvas, 20⅜ x 15½ (51.8 x 39.4 cm). Gift of Mr. R. P. Manson. 1870.3

Frans FRANCKEN III (attributed) (1607-1667), Flemish: *Achilles at the Court of Lycomedes*. Oil on panel, 20½ x 31½ (52.1 x 80.0 cm). Bequest of the Honorable James Bowdoin III. 1813.2

Jan FYT (attributed) (1609-1661), Flemish: *Still Life, Birds*. Oil on canvas, 19½ x 26 (49.5 x 66.0 cm). Bequest of the Honorable James Bowdoin III. 1813.33

Jan FYT (attributed) (1609-1661), Flemish: *Still Life, Birds and Hare*. Oil on canvas, 19½ x 26 (49.5 x 66.0 cm). Bequest of the Honorable James Bowdoin III. 1813.34

✠Hendrik Cornelisz VAN VLIET (1611/12-1675), Dutch: *The Tomb of Admiral Jacob van Wassanaer in the Choir of the Jacobskerk at The Hague*. Oil on canvas, 37 x 28 (94.0 x 71.1 cm). Florence C. Quinby Fund in memory of Henry Cole Quinby h '16. 1971.6

Bonaventura PEETERS I (1614-1652), Flemish: *Naval Engagement, Bay of Messina, Sicily*. Oil on canvas, 42 x 60 (106.7 x 152.4 cm). Gift of Colonel George Boyd 1810. 1852.9

Giovanni Benedetto CASTIGLIONE (1616-1670), Italian: *Christ Cleansing the Temple*. Oil on canvas, 16¼ x 28 (41.3 x 71.2 cm). Gift of the Samuel H. Kress Foundation. 1961.100.12

Bernaert DE BRIDT (active 1688-1722), Flemish: *Still Life, Hare, Fruit, Bird*. Oil on canvas, 34½ x 27½ (87.6 x 69.8 cm). Bequest of the Honorable James Bowdoin III. 1813.37

Antonio BALESTRA (1666-1740), Italian: *Peter Delivered from Prison by an Angel*. Oil on canvas, 58 x 44 (147.3 x 111.8 cm). Bequest of the Honorable James Bowdoin III. 1813.22

Pieter ANGELLIS (1685-1734), Flemish: *Harvest Time*. Oil on canvas, 18 x 14 (45.7 x 35.6 cm). Bequest of Dr. Bernard Samuels. 1960.26

Giuseppe BAZZANI (1690-1769), Italian: *Erminia* (?). Oil on canvas, 46 x 44½ (116.8 x 113.0 cm). Gift of the Samuel H. Kress Foundation. 1961.100.8

School of Martinus II MYTENS (1695-1770), Swedish: *The Children of Maria Theresa.* Oil on canvas, 60 x 48 (152.4 x 121.9 cm). Bequest of Dr. Bernard Samuels. 1960.21

Charles Joseph NATOIRE (attributed) (1700-1777), French: *The Triumph of Love.* Oil on canvas, 32 x 60¾ (81.2 x 154.3 cm). Gift of Miss Susan Dwight Bliss. 1948.19

Charles Joseph NATOIRE (attributed) (1700-1777), French: *Love Vanquished.* Oil on canvas, 31 x 59 (78.7 x 149.9 cm). Gift of Miss Susan Dwight Bliss. 1948.20

Charles François DE LA CROIX (ca. 1700-1782), French: *Landscape Seaport with Fortress.* Oil on canvas, 14 x 17 (35.6 x 43.2 cm). Bequest of the Honorable James Bowdoin III. 1813.31

Dominique SERRES the Elder (1722-1793), English: *The Capture of a Spanish Convoy by Two English Frigates.* Oil on canvas, 41½ x 71¼ (105.4 x 181.0 cm). Gift of Mr. John H. Halford, Jr. '38 and Mrs. Halford and family in memory of Mr. John H. Halford '07. 1976.24

Thomas BEACH (1738-1806), English: *Portrait of Major Earl Hawker.* Oil on canvas, 30 x 25 (76.2 x 63.5 cm). Gift of Mrs. John H. Halford in memory of Mr. John H. Halford '07. 1970.60

Jean-Simon BERTHÉLEMY (attributed) (1743-1811), French: *Eponone and Sabinus Condemned before Vespasian.* Oil on canvas, 52½ x 41 (133.4 x 104.1 cm). Museum purchase with the aid of the Marvin S. Sadik h '79 and Gordon F. Linke '50 Funds. 1975.32

Jean Baptiste Camille COROT (1796-1875), French: *The Pond.* Oil on canvas, 16¼ x 19⅜ (41.3 x 49.2 cm). Gift of Mr. John H. Halford '07 and Mrs. Halford. 1962.1

School of Richard Bonington (1801-1828), English: *Martyr's Monument, Oxford.* Oil on panel, 14½ x 11 (36.8 x 27.9 cm). Bequest of Dr. Bernard Samuels. 1960.28

Eugène ISABEY (1803-1886), French: *Massacre of St. Bartholomew's Day.* Oil on panel, 21½ x 35¼ (54.5 x 89.5 cm). Florence C. Quinby Fund in memory of Henry Cole Quinby h '16. 1969.62

Henry GRITTEN (active 1835-1849), English: *Rue du Bec, Rouen.* Oil on panel, 18¾ x 14 (47.6 x 35.6 cm). Gift of Mrs. John H. Halford in memory of Mr. John H. Halford '07. 1970.66

Hermanus KOEKKOEK (1815-1882), Belgian: *Council of War.* Oil on canvas, 34¼ x 49⅝ (87.0 x 126.1 cm). Gift of the Misses Harriet and Sophia Walker. 1904.8

Charles François DAUBIGNY (1817-1878), French: *Woodland Scene.* Oil on canvas, 19¾ x 18¼ (50.1 x 46.3 cm). Gift of Mr. Alexander Standish '21 in memory of his father and mother, Mr. Myles Standish 1875 and Mrs. Louise M. Standish. 1941.5

Rosa Bonheur (1822-1899), French: *Lion Cubs.* Oil on canvas, 25 x 31$\frac{1}{4}$ (63.5 x 79.4 cm). Gift of the Misses Harriet and Sophia Walker. 1901.6

Eduardo Cano de la Peña (1823-1897), Spanish: *Street Scene in Seville.* Oil on canvas, 23$\frac{1}{2}$ x 31 (49.7 x 78.7 cm). Gift of Miss Mary T. Mason and Miss Jane Mason. 1955.11

Julien Dupré (1851-1910), French: *Women in the Fields.* Oil on canvas, 15 x 18 (38.1 x 45.7 cm). Bequest of Mrs. Ella Pratt. 1969.44

Amédée Ozenfant (1886-1967), French: *Fireworks, Bastille Day.* Oil on canvas, 57$\frac{1}{2}$ x 40 (146.1 x 101.6 cm). Gift of Miss Gertrude Kuebler. 1960.47

Sculpture

[K.J.W. & K.A.O.]

✠Unknown artist, French (ca. 1220-1230): *Head of a King.* Limestone, 6$\frac{1}{8}$ x 5$\frac{13}{16}$ x 5$\frac{1}{8}$ (15.6 x 14.7 x 13.0 cm). Gift of Mr. Edward Perry Warren h '26. 1915.100

Unknown artist (late 15th century), Milanese: *Head of St. John the Baptist.* Alabaster, 9$\frac{5}{8}$ x 8$\frac{5}{8}$ x 7$\frac{15}{16}$ (24.4 x 21.9 x 20.2 cm). Gift of Mr. Edward Perry Warren h '26. 1906.3

Heinrich Yselin (attributed) (late 15th-early 16th century), German: *The Prophet Habakkuk.* Wood, 11$\frac{1}{4}$ x 22$\frac{11}{16}$ x 7$\frac{13}{16}$ (28.5 x 57.7 x 19.8 cm). Gift of the friends of Mr. John W. Frost '04, in his memory. 1963.8

Unknown artist (16th century), Flemish: *Madonna and Child.* Limewood, 23$\frac{7}{8}$ x 8$\frac{7}{16}$ x 4$\frac{3}{16}$ (60.7 x 21.5 x 10.7 cm). Gift of Miss Susan Dwight Bliss. 1963.281

Unknown artist (16th century), French: *Bust of a Pope.* Oak, 22$\frac{3}{4}$ x 17$\frac{7}{8}$ x 8$\frac{9}{16}$ (57.8 x 45.4 x 21.7 cm). Gift of Miss Susan Dwight Bliss. 1963.255

Unknown artist (16th century), German: *St. John the Evangelist.* Wood, 34$\frac{7}{8}$ x 13$\frac{9}{16}$ x 1$\frac{1}{8}$ (88.7 x 34.5 x 2.9 cm). James Phinney Baxter Fund in memory of Professor Henry Johnson h '14, and Helen Johnson Chase Fund. 1962.14

Workshop of Martin and Michael Zürn (active 1636-1664), Austrian: *Moses.* Wood, 10$\frac{9}{16}$ x 11 x 6$\frac{3}{16}$ (26.8 x 27.9 x 15.7 cm). Museum purchase. 1965.23

✠Ferdinand Maxmilian Brokov (1688-1731), Bohemian: *St. John Nepomuk.* Oak, 51$\frac{3}{4}$ x 23$\frac{3}{8}$ x 17$\frac{1}{8}$ (131.4 x 59.3 x 43.4 cm). Museum purchase. 1968.72

Antoine Mouton (b. 1765-?), French: *Charity.* Terra cotta, 20$\frac{5}{8}$ x

$9\frac{1}{2}$ x $7\frac{1}{4}$ (52.5 x 24.2 x 18.4 cm). Gift of Miss Susan Dwight Bliss. 1963.245

François RUDE (1784-1855), French: *Head of a Gaul.* Bronze, $11\frac{1}{2}$ x $7\frac{3}{16}$ x $6\frac{15}{16}$ (29.2 x 18.3 x 17.6 cm). Museum purchase, Sylvia E. Ross Fund. 1970.80

Antoine-Louis BARYE (1796-1875), French: *A Group of 12 Animals.* Bronze, max. dim. $8\frac{1}{16}$ x $9\frac{1}{2}$ x $5\frac{1}{4}$ (20.5 x 24.2 x 13.3 cm). Gift of Miss Susan Dwight Bliss. 1963.249-.250, 1967.37.1-.10

✠Antoine-Louis BARYE (1796-1875), French: *Young Man Mastering a Horse.* Wax and plastiline, $8\frac{3}{8}$ x $3\frac{7}{8}$ x $9\frac{1}{8}$ (21.3 x 9.8 x 23.2 cm). Gift of the Misses Harriet and Sophia Walker. 1894.147

✠Jean-Baptiste CARPEAUX (1827-1876), French: *Bust of Charles Garnier.* Plaster, $17\frac{9}{16}$ x $13\frac{3}{8}$ x $7\frac{1}{8}$ (44.6 x 34.0 x 18.1 cm). Museum purchase. 1967.3

Nicolai Ivanovitch LIEBERICH (1828-1883), Russian: *Russian Wolf-Hunt.* Bronze, $9\frac{15}{16}$ x $21\frac{7}{16}$ x 10 (25.3 x 54.5 x 25.4 cm). Gift of the Misses Harriet and Sophia Walker. 1904.176

Jacob EPSTEIN (1880-1959), English: *Anthony.* Plaster, $16\frac{5}{8}$ x $14\frac{7}{8}$ x $8\frac{3}{8}$ (42.3 x 37.8 x 21.3 cm). Gift of Lady Epstein. 1969.96

Jacob EPSTEIN (1880-1959), English: *Kathleen.* Plaster, $21\frac{3}{4}$ x $17\frac{1}{16}$ x $12\frac{1}{16}$ (55.2 x 43.3 x 30.7 cm). Gift of Lady Epstein. 1969.95

Jacob EPSTEIN (1880-1959), English: *Seraph Head.* Plaster, $10\frac{7}{8}$ x $9\frac{9}{16}$ x $10\frac{7}{16}$ (27.6 x 24.3 x 26.5 cm). Gift of Lady Epstein. 1969.97

Furniture

[M.R.B. & K.A.O.]

Only primary woods are listed.

✠French (ca. 1500): *Chair.* Oak, $60\frac{7}{8}$ x $27\frac{1}{8}$ x $17\frac{3}{4}$ (154.6 x 68.9 x 45.0 cm). Gift of Mr. Herbert H. Richardson from the estate of Mr. Curtis Appleton Perry 1877. 1931.14

French (16th century): *Chest and Stand.* Oak; chest $14\frac{5}{8}$ x 22 x 16 (37.2 x 55.9 x 40.6 cm); stand $13\frac{1}{4}$ x $23\frac{5}{8}$ x $19\frac{1}{2}$ (33.7 x 60.0 x 49.5 cm). Gift of Miss Susan Dwight Bliss. 1948.22-.23

German (16th century): *Chest.* Oak, $36\frac{3}{16}$ x $73\frac{1}{2}$ x $24\frac{1}{2}$ (92.0 x 186.7 x 62.3 cm). Gift of Dr. Richard C. Webster. 1962.52

Italian (16th century): *Cassone.* Walnut, $22\frac{1}{2}$ x 72 x $22\frac{1}{2}$ (57.2 x 182.9 x 57.2 cm). Gift of the Honorable Percival P. Baxter 1898. 1962.33

English (17th century): *Clock.* Walnut, 85 x $18\frac{3}{4}$ x $9\frac{1}{4}$ (215.9 x 47.6 x 23.5 cm). Gift of Mr. John H. Halford, Jr. '38. 1966.85

Flemish or Italian (17th century): *Chest of Drawers.* Oak and walnut, $37\frac{1}{2}$ x 49 x $22\frac{1}{8}$ (94.7 x 124.5 x 56.2 cm). Gift of Miss Susan Dwight Bliss. 1948.24

Italian (18th century): *Looking Glass.* Gilded wood, 55 x $26\frac{1}{2}$ x $1\frac{3}{8}$ (139.7 x 67.0 x 3.5 cm). Bequest of Dr. Bernard Samuels. 1960.20

✠English (1700-1725): *Pair of Side Chairs.* Walnut and oak, $43\frac{5}{8}$ x $21\frac{3}{4}$ x $19\frac{1}{2}$ (110.8 x 55.2 x 49.5 cm). Gift of Mr. H. Ray Dennis, Jr. 1978.9.1-.2

French (ca. 1740-1770): *Commode.* Fruitwood, oak, ormolu, $33\frac{1}{2}$ x $56\frac{3}{4}$ x 25 (85.1 x 144.2 x 63.5 cm). Gift of Miss Susan Dwight Bliss. 1948.25

Portuguese (ca. 1770): *Settee.* Mahogany, $53\frac{1}{2}$ x $37\frac{1}{2}$ x 72 (35.9 x 95.3 x 182.9 cm). Gift of Mr. John H. Halford, Jr. '38. 1966.84

English (ca. 1780-1800): *Armchair.* Mahogany, $36\frac{3}{4}$ x $23\frac{3}{4}$ x 17 (93.4 x 60.4 x 43.2 cm). Bequest of Mrs. Sylvia E. Ross. 1963.23

English (ca. 1790-1810): *Sideboard.* Mahogany, $38\frac{1}{2}$ x $57\frac{7}{8}$ x 22 (97.8 x 147.0 x 55.9 cm). Bequest of Mrs. Sylvia E. Ross. 1963.13

English (ca. 1795-1810): *Armchair.* Mahogany, 35 x $23\frac{3}{8}$ x $17\frac{1}{2}$ (88.9 x 59.3 x 44.5 cm). Bequest of Mrs. Sylvia E. Ross. 1963.24

English (ca. 1800): *Dulcimer.* Zebrawood, $32\frac{1}{2}$ x $40\frac{1}{8}$ x $16\frac{1}{4}$ (82.5 x 102.9 x 41.3 cm). Anonymous gift. 1975.31

English (ca. 1805-1815): *Side Chair.* Mahogany, $36\frac{1}{2}$ x $20\frac{7}{8}$ x 18 (92.7 x 53.0 x 45.7 cm). Bequest of Mrs. Sylvia E. Ross. 1963.18

Silver

[M.R.B. & K.A.O.]

William SPRING (active 1701 and after), London: *Caster.* Silver, $8\frac{5}{16}$ x $3\frac{3}{4}$ (diam.) (21.1 x 9.5 cm). Gift of Mrs. Naomi Forsythe Phelps. 1979.79

Hester BATEMAN (1709-1794), London: *Ladle.* Silver, $17\frac{1}{8}$ x $2\frac{5}{16}$ (diam.) (18.1 x 5.9 cm). Bequest of Mrs. Sylvia E. Ross. 1963.45

Hester BATEMAN (1709-1794), London: *Sugar Tongs.* Silver, $5\frac{5}{16}$ x $1\frac{3}{4}$ (13.5 x 4.4 cm). Bequest of Mrs. Sylvia E. Ross. 1963.44

Hester BATEMAN (1709-1794), London: *Sugar Tongs.* Silver, $5\frac{9}{16}$ x $1\frac{7}{8}$ (14.1 x 4.8 cm). Bequest of Mrs. Sylvia E. Ross. 1963.93

✠Hester BATEMAN (1709-1794), English: *Teapot.* Silver and wood, $5\frac{3}{8}$ x $9\frac{1}{2}$ x $3\frac{11}{16}$ (13.6 x 24.1 x 9.3 cm). Gift of Mrs. Sylvia E. Ross. 1963.32.1

William GRUNDY (active 1748-1749 and after), London: *Mugs.* Silver,

$4\frac{15}{16}$ x $5\frac{3}{16}$ (12.5 x 13.2 cm). Gift of Miss Clara Bowdoin Winthrop. 1943.3.1-.2

Unknown maker (active 1767-1768 and after), London: *Candlesticks*. Silver, $11\frac{7}{8}$ x $4\frac{7}{16}$ (30.2 x 11.3 cm). Bequest of Mr. Charles Potter Kling. 1935.500-.503

Charles-Louis Auguste SPRIMAN (active 1775 and after), Paris: *Tureen*. Silver, $11\frac{1}{2}$ x 12 x $8\frac{1}{2}$ (29.2 x 30.5 x 21.6 cm). Gift of Miss Clara Bowdoin Winthrop in the name of the children of Mr. and Mrs. Robert C. Winthrop, Jr. 1924.3.1

Thomas SHEPHERD (active 1785 and after), London: *Creamer*. Silver, $5\frac{13}{16}$ x $4\frac{1}{16}$ (14.8 x 10.3 cm). Bequest of Mr. Charles Potter Kling. 1935.567

Peter and Ann BATEMAN (active 1791 and after), London: *Creamer*. Silver, $6\frac{1}{4}$ x $4\frac{1}{16}$ (15.9 x 10.3 cm). Bequest of Mrs. Sylvia E. Ross. 1963.38

Peter and Ann BATEMAN (active 1791 and after), London: *Sugar Basket*. Silver, $4\frac{11}{16}$ x $3\frac{13}{16}$ (11.9 x 9.7 cm). Bequest of Mrs. Sylvia E. Ross. 1963.37

Medals and Plaquettes
[K.J.W.]

Francesco DA SANGALLO (1494-1576), Italian: *Francesco da Sangallo and Helena Marsupina*. Bronze, $3\frac{11}{16}$ (9.4 cm). Gift of the Misses Harriet and Sophia Walker. 1895.35

European (16th-18th century): *A Group of Eighteen Plaquettes*. Bronze. Gift of Mrs. Gerd Utescher. 1978.40.1-.18

European (16th-18th century): *A Group of Fifty-Nine Medals and Plaquettes*. Brass, bronze, copper, lead, pewter, and silver. Gift of Mr. and Mrs. Mark M. Salton. 1978.32.1-.59

THE MOLINARI COLLECTION
OF MEDALS & PLAQUETTES

The Molinari collection of medals and plaquettes was given in 1966 by Amanda Marchesa Molinari in memory of her husband, Cesare Molinari d'Incisa. Consisting of more than 1,500 examples, it established at Bowdoin one of the major collections of medals and plaquettes in the United States. Notable for both its size and breadth, the collection contains some of the better known Italian Renaissance medals and plaquettes, European medals made through the nineteenth century, and northern European plaquettes.

A medal is a piece of metal, generally bronze or lead, which has been struck or cast in the form of a coin. Unlike coins, medals are commemorative in function and are not a medium of exchange. The value of a medal is determined by the quality of its design and its rarity rather than by the intrinsic worth of its material.

Generally the obverse of an early medal depicts a portrait of the person commemorated, and the reverse represents a device, called an *impresa,* with a motto related to the person or event. *Imprese* were intended to be difficult to decipher, and several continue to mystify modern scholars. Beginning in the sixteenth century, *imprese* were frequently replaced by inscriptions or narrative depictions of the events for which the medal was cast.

In the fifteenth century, medals were cast; later they were also struck, like coins, from dies. Although striking resulted in a loss of warmth on the surface of the medal as well as a reduction in size (the pressure of striking often cracks a large die), it enabled the artist to depict greater detail and, more importantly, to produce medals more quickly and less expensively.

Probably first conceived as an imitation of Roman commemorative medallions and coins, the modern medal is a creation of the Italian Renaissance. The Renaissance medal was a vehicle for local diplomacy and personal friendship. In the seventeenth century, with governments evolving from city-states and duchies to nations and empires, medals were utilized for national propaganda. This change in function occurred at the court of Louis XIV, whose monumental *Histoire métallique* became the model for other medallic series, several of which are represented in the Molinari collection. Series of the popes, the dukes and duchesses of Lorraine, Queen Christina of Sweden, the rulers of England, the Medici, and events from German history attest to the popularity of the form. At the same time, at the court of the later Medici grand dukes in Florence, a revival of the cast medal technique, now in Baroque guise, was taking place. The French continued to determine the style of the European medal through the nineteenth century.

A plaquette is a small, flat piece of metal cast with the relief on one face. While medals are personal commemorative documents, plaquettes are narrative or devotional images, generally used as decoration for functional or religious objects. Like the medal, the plaquette reflected period or geographic styles, but its production methods and function changed very little.

A complete study of the collection can be found in the museum's 1975 publication *Medals and Plaquettes from the Molinari Collection at Bowdoin College* by Andrea S. Norris and Ingrid Weber.   [A.S.N.]

PISANELLO (1395-1455), ITALIAN

John VIII Palaeologus, Emperor of Constantinople, 1425-1448

> *Obv.: Bust to right, wearing hat with tall crown and upturned brim. Around:* ΙΩΑΝΝΗC · ΒΑCΙΛΕVC · ΚΑΙ · ΑVΤΟ · ΚΡΑ[ΤΩΡ] ΡΩΜΑΙΩΝ · Ο · ΠΑΛΑΙΟΛΟΓΟC✚ *(John, King and Emperor of the Romans, Palaeologus)*
>
> *Without reverse*
>
> Lead, $4\frac{1}{8}$ (10.5 cm) (diam.). 1966.103

Antonio di Puccio Pisano, called Pisanello, is considered the founder of the modern medal. His fame as a painter had

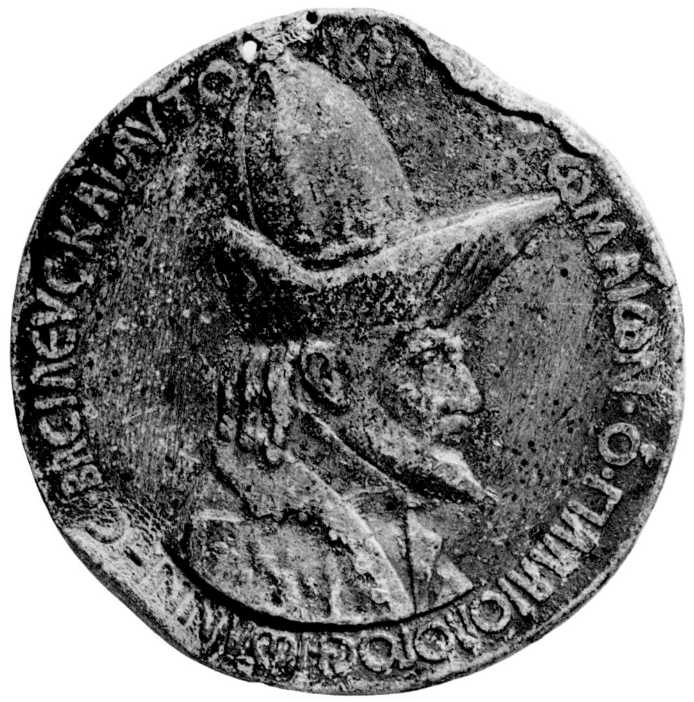

already been established when he cast his first medal, a depiction of John VIII Palaeologus, emperor of Constantinople, in 1438. At that date, Palaeologus was in Italy attending the Council of the Two Churches. The council, which had begun in Basel in 1431 and closed in Rome in 1443, mainly concerned itself with the union of the Greek and Latin churches and the protection of Constantinople from the Turks.

The obverse of the medal depicts the emperor in profile. While the Molinari example is uniface, some castings of the medal exhibit on the reverse a scene of the ruler with his retinue stopping at a crossroad. The style of the portrait and the Greek lettering and equestrian figures of the reverse suggest that Pisanello imitated imperial medallions and coins, appropriate models for the medal of this most recent emperor. The visit of the emperor of the Eastern Roman Empire was a major event in Italy, and for years his costume (particularly his peaked hat) and those of his retinue were copied in art whenever images of exotic personages were required.

The Molinari specimen is made of lead, a soft metal with a low melting point. Since lead readily takes up the image from the mold in all its detail, it is an excellent material for medal casting. However, lead medals are fragile and were probably rarely distributed. Instead, they were used in the workshop as test pieces and models from which new molds could be made. Contact with air causes lead to form a dark skin with a soft lustre which adds warmth to the impression.

[A.S.N.]

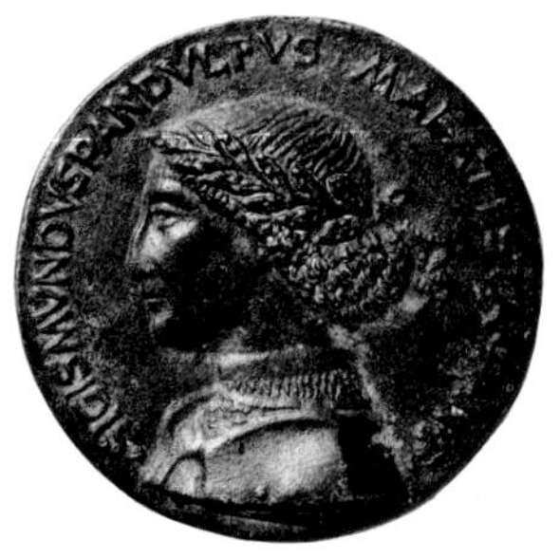 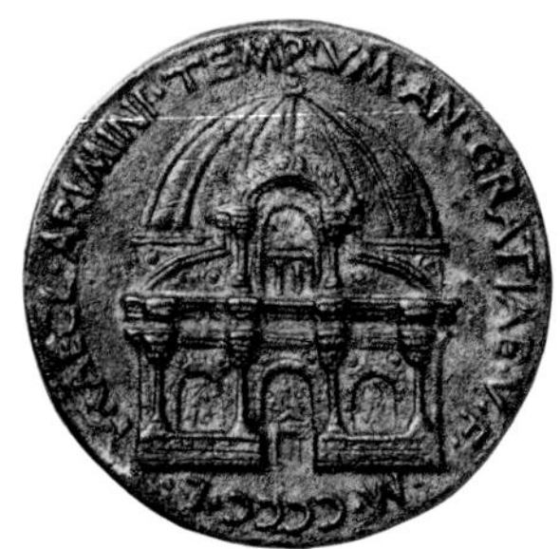

MATTEO DE' PASTI (active 1441-1467/8), ITALIAN
Sigismondo Pandolfo Malatesta, 1450

Obv.: Bust to left, laureate. Around: • SIGISMVNDVS PAN-DVLFVS MALATESTA • PAN • F •

Rev.: View of façade of San Francesco, Rimini, based on Alberti's proposed reconstruction. Around: PRAECL • ARIMINI • TEM-PLVM • AN • GRATIAE • V • F • M • CCCC • L •

Bronze, $1\frac{7}{16}$ (4.0 cm) (diam.). 1966.104.1

Matteo de' Pasti was Pisanello's most able follower. Born in Verona, he spent most of his life working at the court of Sigismondo Malatesta, lord of Rimini. Pasti was a versatile artist: an accomplished painter, book illuminator, architect, and sculptor as well as medalist.

In about 1450 Sigismondo commissioned Leon Battista Alberti, the artist and writer on art, letters, philosophy, and science, to remodel the church of San Francesco at Rimini as a mausoleum for himself, his mistress Isotta degli Atti, and the illustrious men at his court. Alberti left the execution of his classicizing remodeling to Matteo de' Pasti, directing the work by letter from Rome. The rebuilding was left incomplete when Sigismondo died.

Several specimens of this medal were placed in the foundations of the church, called the Tempio Malatestiana in recognition of the classicism intended in the reconstruction. The medal is the best evidence of Alberti's original design for the building. Although the church facade was never completed above the entablature, it is apparent that Alberti intended to place a high arch above the central door and curved walls above the side bays; the medal also shows the monumental dome intended for the church crossing.

The original function of this medal was to celebrate the transformation of the church into a personal monument for a Renaissance tyrant. Today it serves as the sole documentation of Alberti's intention for the completed design.

[A.S.N.]

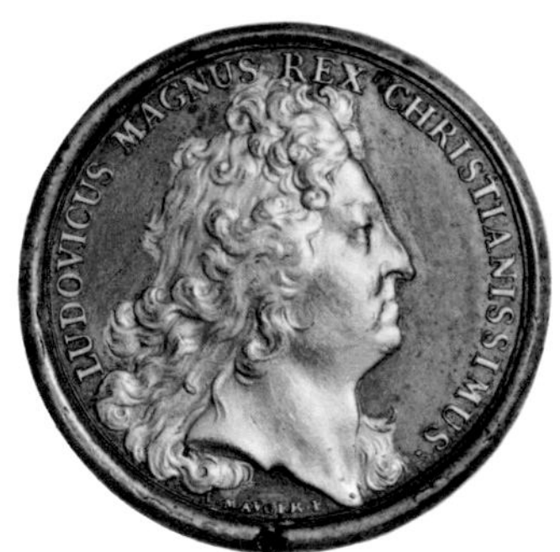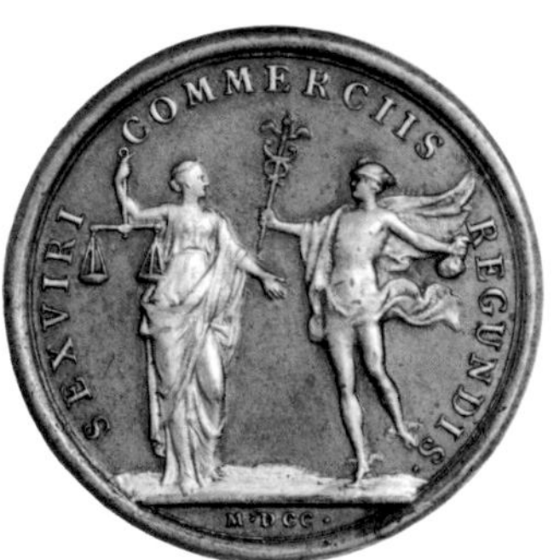

JEAN MAUGER (1648-1722), FRENCH

Louis XIV, Chamber of Commerce, 1700

> *Obv.: Head to right. Around:* LUDOVICUS MAGNUS REX CHRISTIANISSIMUS · *Below:* I · MAVGER · F ·
>
> *Rev.: Justice and Mercury. Around:* SEXVIRI COMMERCIIS REGUNDIS · *In exergue:* M·DCC ·
>
> Bronze, partly gilt and silvered, 1⅝ (4.1 cm) (diam.). 1966.131.1

During the reign of Louis XIV, the arts were directed toward the glorification of the king and his government. Like other artists, medalists had to suppress individual styles of creative expression; an official style based on an imitation of classical antiquity was considered the only art worthy of the Sun King.

The academies were responsible for the unification and direction of the arts. In 1663 Louis's advisor, J. B. Colbert, directed the members of the powerful Petite Académie to design and execute a series of medals illustrating the reign of Louis XIV in terms that would make them an effective instrument of propaganda in and around France. Literary figures such as Jean Racine were assigned to devise reverses depicting contemporary events transposed into allegory. Submitted to the academy, the images were revised and given appropriate legends; a drawing was made of the reverse for the die engraver to copy exactly. Because of the length and vicissitudes of Louis's reign, the devices of the medal reverses had to be changed frequently. As a result, a medal commemorating one event could employ as many as four different reverses.

The medals were struck in gold, silver, and bronze and initially were of various sizes and designs. In the 1690s, the academy decided to standardize the size and design of the existing medals and to strike new specimens to illustrate unrepresented events. The first *Histoire métallique* was completed in 1702 and was accompanied by a book of engravings and descriptions of the medals, *Médailles sur les principaux événements du Règne de Louis le Grand avec des explications historiques.* Louis presented the series to ambassadors and others whose favors he sought. A revision of the series, demanded by the king, was not completed until 1725, long after his death.

This medal from the first Uniform Series of the *Histoire métallique* is by Jean Mauger, one of the artists occupied on the *Histoire* for many years. It indicates the method of translating a contemporary event into classical allegory. To illustrate the establishment of the Chamber of Commerce in 1700, the designer depicted a meeting between Mercury (a symbol of commerce) and Justice. This specimen is bronze enriched with gold and silver. Like other artists, Mauger was given minimal opportunity for individual expression and concentrated his efforts on virtuoso execution.   [A.S.N.]

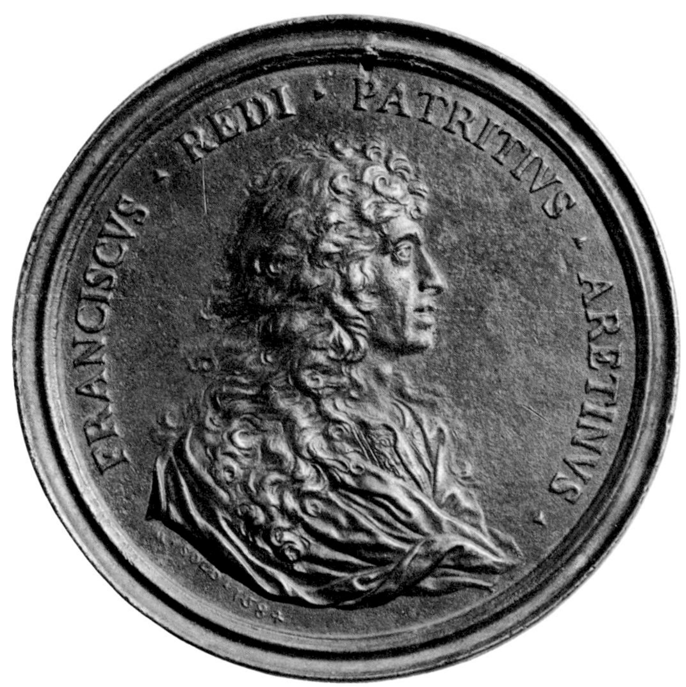

MASSIMILIANO SOLDANI-BENZI (1656-1740), ITALIAN

Francesco Redi (1628-1698), 1684

> *Obv.: Bust to right. Around:* FRANCISCVS · REDI · PATRI-
> TIVS · ARETINVS · *Below:* M · SOLD · 1684
> *Rev.: Bacchus and Silenus with maenads and satyrs. In exergue:*
> CANEBAM *flanked by small* M *and* S
> Bronze, $3\frac{7}{16}$ (8.7 cm) (diam.). 1966.126.2

Massimiliano Soldani was a bronze sculptor at the Medici
court in Florence. He was sent by Cosimo III de' Medici to
study in Rome at the Grand-Ducal Academy and later to
Paris. Master of the Florentine mint for forty years, Soldani
revived the tradition of the cast medal in Italy. This medal
portraying Francesco Redi is perhaps his finest example.

Francesco Redi, the chief physician to Ferdinand II and
Cosimo III de' Medici, was also a famous scientist, poet, and
philosopher. Soldani was commissioned by Cosimo to make
three medals of Redi, each with a reverse illustrating a different facet of his activity. On the reverse of this medal

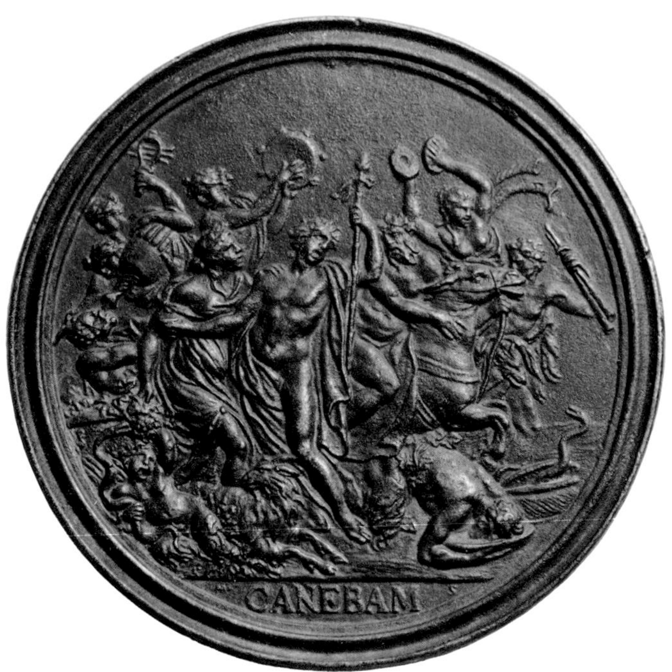

referring to Redi's poetry, Bacchus (with the staff), Silenus (riding the donkey), and Ariadne stand surrounded by maenads and satyrs. Soldani easily unites the classical subject with a late Baroque emphasis on movement, atmosphere, and florid detail. The curve of Bacchus's nude body and the gestures of the bacchantes, which pull them back toward the center of the medal, reinforce its circular shape. In the exergue below, the inscription CANEBAM means "I sang." The bacchanal scene is a reference to the highly praised dithyramb by Redi, *Bacco in Toscana,* published in 1685.   [A.S.N.]

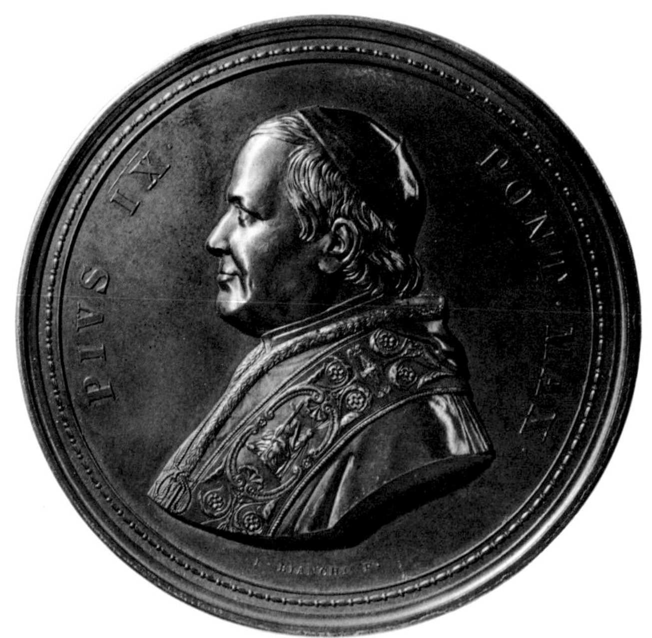

IGNAZIO BIANCHI (active 1848-1869), ITALIAN
Pius IX Mastai-Ferretti (pope 1846-1878), 1854

Obv.: Bust to left, wearing skullcap, mozzetta, and stole. Around:
PIVS IX · PONT · MAX · *Below:* I · BIANCHI F ·

Rev.: Interior of Basilica of Saint Paul. Around: PIVS · IX · P ·
M · BASILICAM · PAVLI · APOST · AB · INCENDIO · RE-
FECTAM · SOLEMNI · RITV · CONSECRAVIT · IV · ID ·
DEC · MDCCCLIV ✿ *Below:* I · BIANCHI · F · *In exergue:*
AL · POLETTI · ARCH · INV ·

Bronze, 3¼ (8.2 cm) (diam.). 1966.114.2

Beginning with the reign of Paul II in the fifteenth century,
the papacy was a major patron of medalists. Like temporal
rulers, the pope used medals to publicize his activities and
foster diplomacy.

This medal by Ignazio Bianchi commemorates the recon-
secration of the Basilica of Saint Paul in 1854. Burned in
1823, the church was rebuilt under Pius IX and his predecessors. The medal depicts Luigi Poletti as the architect of
the reconstruction of the church.

Active at the papal mint as a medalist and coin engraver
from 1848 to 1869, Ignazio Bianchi was a specialist in archi-

tectural designs. With its sophisticated treatment of perspective, this example of his work displays the detail made possible by the highly refined nineteenth-century methods of striking. Although the medal lacks the warmth and soft texture of a cast medal, it is a masterpiece of design and technological skill. [A.S.N.]

UNKNOWN ARTIST (first quarter of the 17th century), SOUTH GERMAN

Pan and Syrinx, from the series Twenty-four Scenes from Ovid's *Metamorphoses*

> *Syrinx, garments fluttering, flees into a stream filled with rushes, which are embraced by the pursuing Pan. On the left, a bridge and architecture; to the right, reeds and a tree*

Bronze, gilt, $2\frac{13}{16}$ x 5 (7.1 x 12.7 cm) (diam.). 1967.16.10

Like the medal, the plaquette is a creation of the Italian Renaissance, when it was used as decoration for other objects or collected for its own sake. Appearing north of the Alps in the sixteenth century, plaquettes became models for goldsmiths and other artisans as well as decorative elements

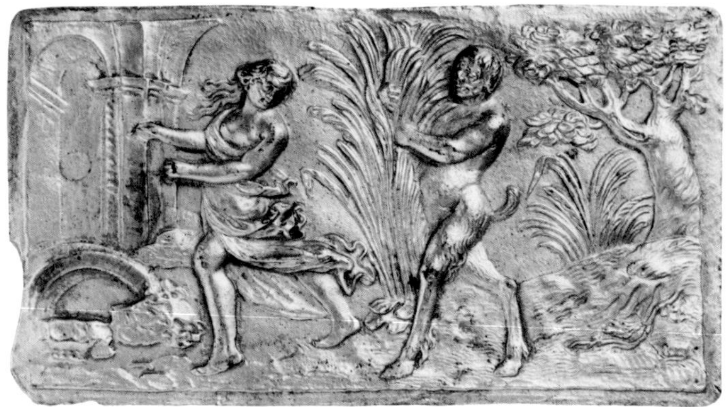

on furniture and other objects. Attributions to specific artists and geographic areas are frequently difficult since plaquettes are rarely signed; their designs were often derived from prints.

The Molinari collection is particularly strong in northern European plaquettes and contains two impressive series, the Life of Christ by the circle of Matthias Wallbaum, and Twenty-Four Scenes from Ovid's *Metamorphoses* by an unknown seventeenth-century South German artist. Several of the motifs from the latter series derive from woodcut illustrations by Virgil Solis (after woodcuts by Bernard Salomon) for Ovid's *Metamorphosen,* printed in 1563.

An example from the *Metamorphoses* series is reproduced here. Pursued and nearly captured by Pan, the nymph Syrinx is transformed by her sister nymphs into a clump of reeds; at the same moment, Pan grasps the reeds from which he later made his pipe.

Several plaquettes are sometimes used to depict one *Metamorphoses* episode. For example, one plaquette illustrates Phaeton struck down by Jupiter's thunderbolt after failing to drive the sun god's chariot; the next plaquette represents Phaeton's sisters mourning over his tomb and being transformed into poplar trees.

Dazzling gilding, vast and detailed landscape settings, vigorously gesturing figures, and graphic clarity of the compositions enhance these charming depictions of classical myths.   [A.S.N.]

SELECTED WORKS FROM THE COLLECTION

[A.S.N.]

Medals

Only diameter measurements are given in this section.

✠Pisanello (1395-1455), Italian: *John VIII Palaeologus, Emperor of Constantinople.* Lead, 4⅛ (10.5 cm). 1966.103

✠Matteo de' Pasti (active 1441-1467/8), Italian: *Sigismondo Pandolfo Malatesta.* Bronze, 1 7/16 (4.0 cm). 1966.104.1

Matteo de' Pasti (active 1441-1467/8), Italian: *Sigismondo Pandolfo Malatesta.* Bronze, 3 3/16 (8.1 cm). 1966.106.7

Francesco Laurana (1420/5-ca. 1502), Italian: *Jean d'Anjou, Duke of Calabria and Lorraine.* Bronze, 3⅜ (8.6 cm). 1966.106.23

Giovanni Candida (Giovanni di Salvatore Filangieri) (before 1450-after 1495), Italian: *Maximilian of Austria and Maria of Burgundy.* Bronze, 1 15/16 (4.9 cm). 1966.107.3

Sperandio of Mantua (1425/31-1504), Italian: *Ludovico Carbone.* Bronze, 3⅞ (8.5 cm). 1966.106.22

Niccolò Fiorentino (attributed) (1430-1514), Italian: *Stefano Taverna.* Bronze, 3⅛ (7.9 cm). 1966.104.9

Cristoforo di Geremia (active 1456-1476), Italian: *Alfonso V of Aragon.* Lead, 2 15/16 (7.5 cm). 1966.107.4

Andrea Guacialoti (Guazzalotti) (1435-1495), Italian: *Pius II Piccolomini.* Bronze, 2 1/16 (5.3 cm). 1966.107.6

Bartolommeo Melioli (1448-1514), Italian: *Francesco II Gonzaga.* Bronze, 2 13/16 (7.1 cm). 1966.104.5

Medalist of the Roman Emperors (active third quarter of the 15th century), Italian: *Faustina I and Antoninus Pius.* Bronze, 4 5/16 (11.0 cm). 1966.105.1

Caradosso (ca. 1452-1526/7), Italian: *Julius II della Rovere.* Bronze, 2 3/16 (5.6 cm). 1966.113.55

Jacopo Tatti (Sansovino) (1486-1570), Italian: *Tommaso Rangone of Ravenna.* Bronze, 1½ (3.8 cm). 1966.108.13

Unknown artist (16th century), possibly Netherlandish: *Charles V.* Lead, 3 15/16 (10.0 cm). 1966.111

Giovanni del Cavino (1500-1570), Italian: *Nero.* Bronze, 1⅞ (3.7 cm). 1966.108.9

Jacopo Nizolla da Trezzo (1515/19-1589), Italian: *Gianello della Torre.* Bronze, 3⅛ (8.0 cm). 1966.108.10

Marc Bechot (1520-1557), French: *Henry II.* Bronze, $2\frac{3}{8}$ (6.0 cm). 1966.117.3

Alfonso da Tomaso Ruspagiari (1521-1576), Italian: *Ercole II d'Este.* Lead, $2\frac{9}{16}$ (6.5 cm). 1966.108.3

Alfonso da Tomaso Ruspagiari (1521-1576), Italian: *Unknown Ladies.* Bronze, $2\frac{7}{16}$ (6.2 cm). 1966.104.16

Unknown artist (active mid-16th century), Italian: *Pierio Valeriano Bolzanio.* Bronze, $2\frac{3}{8}$ (6.0 cm). 1966.106.12

Jacob Jonghelinck (1530-1606), Netherlandish: *Anton Strale, Duke of Merxem and Dambrugge.* Bronze, $2\frac{3}{16}$ (5.5 cm). 1966.131.64

Nicolò de Bonis (active 1580-1592), Italian: *Sixtus V Peretti.* Bronze, $1\frac{11}{16}$ (4.3 cm). 1966.113.15

Paolo Sanquirico (1565-1630), Italian: *Paul V Borghese.* Bronze, $2\frac{5}{16}$ (5.9 cm). 1966.113.13

Guillaume Dupré (ca. 1576-1643), French: *Francesco de' Medici.* Bronze, $3\frac{11}{16}$ (9.3 cm). 1966.117.15

Guillaume Dupré (ca. 1576-1643), French: *Maria Magdalena of Austria.* Bronze, $3\frac{11}{16}$ (9.3 cm). 1966.117.36

Unknown artist (17th century), Netherlandish: *Johann and Cornelius de Witt.* Silver, $1\frac{7}{8}$ (4.8 cm). 1966.131.63

Jean Varin (ca. 1604-1672), French: *Armand-Jean Duplessis.* Bronze, $3\frac{1}{16}$ (7.7 cm). 1966.117.20

Johann Höhn (active ca. 1637-1693), German: *In Memory of the Peace of Oliva.* Bronze, $2\frac{3}{4}$ (7.0 cm). 1966.131.48

Gioacchino Francesco Travani (d. 1675), Italian: *Alexander VII Chigi.* Bronze, $3\frac{11}{16}$ (9.4 cm). 1966.113.39

Gioacchino Francesco Travani (d. 1675), Italian: *Alexander VII Chigi.* Bronze, $2\frac{9}{16}$ (6.5 cm). 1966.114.73

Johann Jakob Kornmann (Giovanni Jacopo Cormano) (mid-17th century), Italian: *Filippo Pirovani.* Bronze, $3\frac{9}{16}$ (9.0 cm). 1966.106.19

Antoine Benoist (1632-1717), French: *Louis XIV.* Bronze, $3\frac{7}{16}$ (8.8 cm). 1966.131.2

Charles Jean François Chéron (1635-1698), French: *Pietro da Cortona.* Bronze, $2\frac{13}{16}$ (7.2 cm). 1966.118.2

Giovanni Hamerani (1646-1705), Italian: *Queen Christina of Sweden.* Bronze, $3\frac{3}{8}$ (3.6 cm). 1966.127.8

✠Jean Mauger (1648-1722), French: *Louis XIV, Chamber of Commerce.* Bronze, partly gilt and silvered, $1\frac{5}{8}$ (4.1 cm). 1966.131.1

✠Massimiliano Soldani-Benzi (1656-1740), Italian: *Francesco Redi.* Bronze, $3\frac{7}{16}$ (8.7 cm). 1966.126.2

Massimiliano Soldani-Benzi (1656-1740), Italian: *Pietro Matteo Maggi.* Bronze, $3\frac{5}{16}$ (8.5 cm). 1966.126.5

Ferdinand de Saint-Urbain (1658-1738), Italian: *Leopold I.* Bronze, $2\frac{9}{16}$ (6.5 cm). 1966.131.89

Giovacchino Fortini (1671/2-1736), Italian: *Cosimo II de' Medici.* Bronze, $3\frac{1}{4}$ (8.3 cm). 1966.131.60

Antonio Selvi (1679-1753), Italian: *Ferdinand II de' Medici.* Bronze, $3\frac{7}{16}$ (8.8 cm). 1966.130.48

Antonio Lazari (active 1709-1734), Italian: *Laura Maria Caterina Bassi.* Gilt bronze, $2\frac{3}{4}$ (7.0 cm). 1966.107.8

Joseph Charles Roettiers (1692-1779), French: *Elizabeth, Duchess of Orleans, Princess Palatine.* Bronze, $2\frac{13}{16}$ (7.2 cm). 1966.130.45

Jacques Antoine Dassier (1715-1759), French: *Count Giovanni Maria Mazzucchelli.* Bronze, $2\frac{1}{8}$ (5.5 cm). 1966.131.77

Jacques Antoine Dassier (1715-1759), French: *Maurice, Comte de Saxe.* Bronze, $2\frac{1}{8}$ (5.5 cm). 1966.130.37

Benjamin Duvivier (1730-1819), French: *Louis XVI.* Bronze, $2\frac{1}{16}$ (5.3 cm). 1966.131.26

Leonhard Posch (1750-1831), German: *Unknown Female Sitter.* Iron, $3\frac{1}{8}$ (8.0 cm). 1966.137.163

Giuseppe Girometti (1780-1851), Italian: *Pius IX Mastai-Ferretti.* Bronze, 2 (5.1 cm). 1966.114.23

Pierre Jean David d'Angers (1788-1856), French: *Dieudonné, Comte de Las-Cases.* Bronze, 5 (12.7 cm). 1966.135.6

Pierre Jean David d'Angers (1788-1856), French: *Jean Paul Marat.* Bronze, $4\frac{13}{16}$ (12.3 cm). 1966.135.5

Jean Jacques Barre (1793-1855), French: *Alexander I.* Bronze, $1\frac{9}{16}$ (4.0 cm). 1966.137.48

Jean François Antoine Bovy (1795-1877), French: *Louis Philippe I.* Copper, $4\frac{7}{16}$ (11.3 cm). 1966.137.173

✠Ignazio Bianchi (active 1848-1869), Italian: *Pius IX Mastai-Ferretti.* Bronze, $3\frac{1}{4}$ (8.2 cm). 1966.114.2

Gaspare Galeazzi (active mid-19th century), Italian: *George, Lord Byron.* Bronze, $2\frac{1}{4}$ (5.7 cm). 1966.137.106

Stefano Johnson (firm active mid-19th century), Italian: *Rebuilding of Campanile, Venice.* Bronze, $1\frac{11}{16}$ (4.3 cm). 1966.138.1

Jules Clément CHAPLAIN (1839-1903), French: *Albert Dumont.* Bronze, 3⅞ (9.8 cm). 1966.137.174

Louis Oscar ROTY (1846-1911), French: *Prize Medal of the Ministry of the Interior.* Silvered bronze, 1⅜ (3.6 cm). 1966.137.180

Plaquettes

Unknown artist (late 15th or early 16th century), Italian: *Hercules and the Nemean Lion.* Bronze, 2¹⁵⁄₁₆ x 2³⁄₁₆ (7.5 x 5.6 cm). 1967.20.19

Peter FLÖTNER (ca. 1485-1546), German: *Christ and the Samaritan Woman.* Lead, 2³⁄₁₆ x 4⅜ (5.5 x 11.1 cm). 1967.11.2

Peter FLÖTNER (ca. 1485-1546), German: *Temptation of Faith.* Bronze, 3¾ x 4³⁄₁₆ (9.6 x 10.7 cm). 1967.11.28

Unknown artist (16th century), Italian: *Madonna and Child with Saint John.* Bronze, 5¼ x 3½ (13.4 x 8.9 cm). 1967.20.36

Antonio ABONDIO (ca. 1538-1591), South German: *Toilet of Venus.* Lead, 3¹¹⁄₁₆ x 2¹³⁄₁₆ (9.3 x 7.2 cm). 1967.20.42

Unknown artist (active last quarter of the 16th century), Netherlandish: *Triumph of Humility,* from the series Triumphal Processions of Human Fortunes. Bronze, 2½ x 4⅝ (6.3 x 11.8 cm). 1967.11.23

Unknown artist (active late 16th century), Venetian: *Madonna of Loreto.* Bronze, 3¹⁵⁄₁₆ x 2⁹⁄₁₆ (9.8 x 6.5 cm). 1967.20.79

Monogrammist AVB (Arent VAN BOLTEN) (1573-ca. 1625), Netherlandish: *Christ on Gethsemane,* from the series The Passion of Christ. Bronze, 3½ x 2½ (8.9 x 6.4 cm). 1967.11.15

Hans Jakob BAYR (attributed) (1574-1628), Netherlandish: *Rape of the Sabine Women.* Bronze, 5⅝ (diam.) (14.3 cm). 1967.11.17

Unknown artist (active ca. 1600), possibly French: *The Conversion of St. Paul.* Bronze, 6 x 7⅞ (15.2 x 19.9 cm). 1967.20.61

Circle of the Wallbaum Workshop (ca. 1600), South German: *Eight Plaquettes,* from the series Events from the Life of Christ. Bronze, max. dim. 3⅞ x 2¹⁵⁄₁₆ (9.8 x 7.5 cm). 1967.15.1-.6, 1967.15.8, 1967.11.5

Circle of the Wallbaum Workshop (ca. 1600), South German: *Two Plaquettes,* from the series The Passion of Christ. Lead, max. dim. 2¼ x 1¹¹⁄₁₆ (5.7 x 4.3 cm). 1967.11.21, 1967.11.9

Unknown artist (active first quarter of the 17th century), South German: *Noli Me Tangere.* Bronze, 3¼ x 2½ (8.3 x 6.4 cm). 1967. 11.12

✠Unknown artist (first quarter of the 17th century), South German: *Pan and Syrinx,* from the series Twenty-four Scenes from Ovid's Metamorphoses. Bronze, gilt, 2¹³⁄₁₆ x 5 (7.1 x 12.7 cm). 1967.16.10

Unknown artist (active first half of the 17th century), possibly Flemish: *The Repentant Magdalene.* Bronze, $6\frac{13}{16}$ x $5\frac{3}{16}$ (17.3 x 13.2 cm). 1967.17.3

Unknown artist (ca. 1700), possibly German: *The Repentant Magdalene.* Bronze, $4\frac{7}{8}$ x $3\frac{3}{4}$ (11.8 x 9.6 cm). 1967.20.83

Unknown artist (second half of the 18th century), possibly French: *Madonna and Child with the Infant Saint John.* Bronze, $4\frac{3}{16}$ x $3\frac{1}{8}$ (10.7 x 7.9 cm). 1967.20.56

AMERICAN PAINTING, SCULPTURE, AND DECORATIVE ARTS

Painting

American paintings have been a major part of the collections of the Bowdoin College Museum of Art since the bequest of the Honorable James Bowdoin III in 1813. Including the famous likenesses of Thomas Jefferson and James Madison by Gilbert Stuart, and the *Portrait of Samson Occom* by Nathaniel Smibert, Bowdoin's contribution forms a significant nucleus around which the museum's extraordinary collection of Colonial and early Federal portraits has grown.

Generous gifts from such Bowdoin family descendants as Mrs. Sarah Bowdoin Dearborn and Mrs. Lucy Flucker Knox Thatcher, which included outstanding works by Joseph Badger, Joseph Blackburn, John Singleton Copley, Robert Feke, John Smibert, and Gilbert Stuart, expanded the original collection during the nineteenth century. The paintings are valuable both aesthetically and historically, as nearly all of the sitters were connected by blood, marriage, or close personal ties with the Bowdoin family, and most of the paintings were in the family's possession from the time they were executed until they were given to the College. The collection, including more recent additions, is fully explored in the catalogue *Colonial and Federal Portraits at Bowdoin College* by Marvin S. Sadik, published by the museum in 1966.

The museum's nineteenth- and twentieth-century American paintings strongly augment the works of the earlier period and were generally more recently acquired. Among the important acquisitions are works by J. Foxcroft Cole and William Trost Richards, donated to the collection by the Misses Harriet and Sophia Walker. In 1961 a fund was established by Mr. and Mrs. George Otis Hamlin for the purchase and exhibition of American art. Such support has led to the acquisition of numerous works, including the *Portrait of A. Bryan Wall* by Thomas Eakins, *Montclair, New Jersey* by George Inness, *The Fall Hunter* by Thomas Doughty, and *Washington Allston in His Studio* by David Claypoole Johnston. In the 1960s and 1970s, a fund established by Mrs. Florence C. Quinby in memory of her husband, Mr. Henry Cole Quinby h '16, allowed the acquisition of works by Worthington Whittredge, Thomas Hill, and Albert Bierstadt, among others. More than a dozen fine paintings, including works by Alexander Wyant, John Neagle, and Rembrandt Peale, have become part of the museum's collection as a result of gifts from Mr. John H. Halford '07 and Mrs. Halford.

The first major gifts of twentieth-century works came in the 1950s when paintings by William Glackens and Raphael Soyer were donated by Mr. Stephen Etnier h '69. In 1961 nineteen oils by John Sloan, including *Sunday Afternoon in Union Square* and *The Cot,* were received as part of the bequest of Mr. George Otis Hamlin, who purchased them from the artist in 1923. A series of gifts to the museum in 1964, 1965, and 1966 from Mr. Walter K. Gutman '24 included paintings by Guy Pène du Bois, Alex Katz, and Jack Tworkov. Six oils by Rockwell Kent, a complement to the large holdings of Kent watercolors and drawings, were purchased in 1971 with the aid of an anonymous gift.

Sculpture

An important bronze portrait relief of Theophilus Wheeler Walker by Daniel Chester French, the gift to the College in 1894 of the Misses Harriet and Sophia Walker, marked the beginning of the American sculpture collection. Early in the twentieth century the Walker sisters also donated a bronze relief of Robert Louis Stevenson by Augustus Saint-Gaudens. Sculptural examples of particular historic value to the College include a bronze bust of Rear Admiral Robert E. Peary 1877 by William Ordway Partridge and a nineteenth-century plaster bust of Brown University Professor George W. Greene by Thomas Crawford, a gift from Greene's friend Henry Wadsworth Longfellow 1825. Other works of particular note are nineteenth-century marble portrait busts by Longworth Powers, Franklin Simmons, and Erastus Dow Palmer. The museum is fortunate to have a few excellent examples by prominent contemporary sculptors, including several bronzes by Leonard Baskin, a bronze cast of a sketch for a figure in the foyer of Radio City Music Hall by William Zorach h '58, and a mobile by Alexander Calder.

Decorative Arts

The furniture is considered to be the strongest of the American decorative arts in the museum's collection; a general introduction to the furniture collection can be found in the exhibition catalogue *The Art of American Furniture* by R. Peter Mooz, published by the museum in 1974.

The earliest gift to the American furniture collection came to the College in 1872, when a fully documented seventeenth-century joined armchair from Ipswich, Massachusetts, was given to the College by Mr. E. Wilder Farley 1836. While the collection of furniture is not large, it does include fine representative examples of eighteenth- and nineteenth-century pieces from the extended New England area. Examples of particular note are a nineteenth-century Philadelphia armchair which belonged to Theophilus Wheeler Walker; an eighteenth-century Massachusetts oxbow-front desk, said to have been owned by Nathaniel Hawthorne 1825; and a nineteenth-century stenciled New England side chair which, according to tradition, was owned by Henry Wadsworth Longfellow 1825 while he was a student at Bowdoin. The generosity of various donors has brought the museum such fine examples as an eighteenth-century Rhode Island Chippendale chest of drawers, an early nineteenth-century New England tambour desk, and a pair of eighteenth-century Philadelphia Chippendale side chairs. Many of the finest pieces of furniture are on display in the James Bowdoin and Sophia Walker Galleries, offering, through their juxtaposition with paintings, pewter, and silver, a historical picture of the periods represented.

The collection of American silver and pewter is characterized by fine eighteenth-century pieces and a representative selection of nineteenth-century examples. Several pieces of silver bearing the Bowdoin crest or coat of arms of particular importance to the collection are permanently installed in the James Bowdoin Gallery. In addition to gifts of silver from Mr. Edward H. Tevriz '26 and from the bequest of Mr. Charles Potter Kling, the College received from Mrs. Mary Prentiss Ingraham Davies a large collection of English and American silver donated in memory of her great-grandfather, the Honorable Daniel Cony, an overseer of the College from 1794 to 1797; the Cony collection is particularly strong in the area of silver spoons. A representative collection of pewter and glass completes the museum's holdings in American decorative arts.   [L.H.]

JOHN SMIBERT (1688-1751)
Portrait of James Bowdoin II, 1736
   Oil on canvas, 34⅞ x 26⅞ (88.6 x 68.3 cm)
   Bequest of Mrs. Sarah Bowdoin Dearborn. 1826.5

According to the artist's notebook, John Smibert painted this portrait of "James Bodween Jnr" early in 1736, near the height of his American career. This straightforward work portrays the young gentleman, with his string bow and arrow, as a hunter in a rural landscape. As was frequently the case with contemporary portraiture, the composition of the painting was undoubtedly not drawn from life; rather, the pose and clothing of the boy were probably derived from an English print of the period, and it is likely that the artificial landscape, resembling a stage set, was drawn from the artist's imagination. Smibert's full modeling and lively brushwork indicate his modest proficiency in the court portraiture style of Sir Godfrey Kneller, which dominated English painting in the early eighteenth century. The boy's lack of facial expression, heavily lidded eyes, slightly upturned mouth, and fatty jaw and chin, details repeated con-

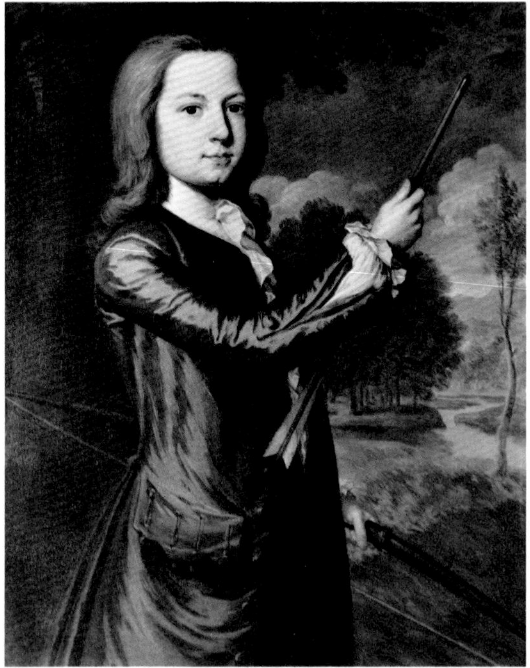

sistently in Smibert's oeuvre, reveal the artist's aesthetic limitations.

Smibert's influence in America in the eighteenth century far surpassed his painterly talents, for he was among the first significant artists to immigrate to the New World, settling in Boston in 1730. The city's ample patronage, a lack of local artistic competition, and the social prestige resulting from his marriage that year to the prominent Mary Williams led to his establishment as the leading New England portrait painter during the first half of the eighteenth century. His foreign training, informally received in London, Florence, and Rome prior to his coming to America, further enhanced his artistic reputation.

Smibert's American influence extended beyond the stylistic impact of his work upon that of local painters. Soon after his arrival in Boston, he organized an art exhibition, including recently completed portraits and copies of Italian paintings which he had executed abroad and transported to

America; further, in 1734, the artist opened in his home a store for the sale "of Colours, dry or ground, with Oils and Brushes" and "the best Metzotinto, Italian, French, Dutch and English Prints...." Smibert's studio, which also contained copies of old master paintings and a sculpture collection, aided in the introduction of European art to native painters and, later inhabited by such figures as John Greenwood and John Trumbull, remained a Boston artistic center long after his death.   [M.R.B.]

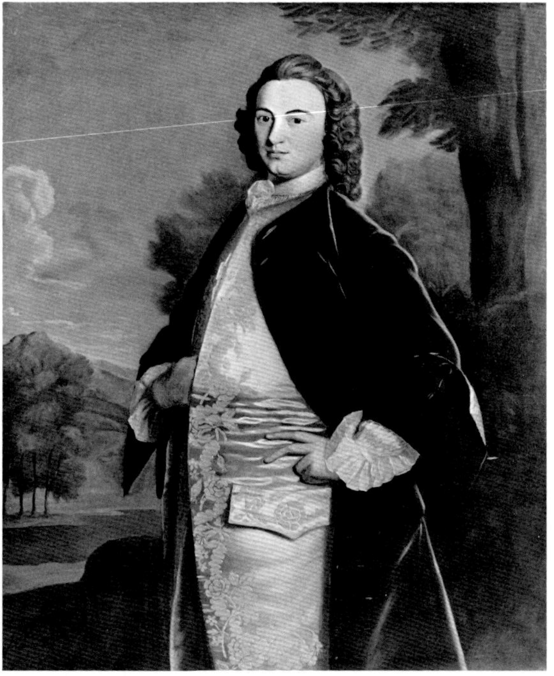

ROBERT FEKE (1707-1752)
Portrait of James Bowdoin II, 1748
> Oil on canvas, 50 x 40 (127.0 x 101.6 cm)
> Bequest of Mrs. Sarah Bowdoin Dearborn. 1826.8

Despite exhaustive investigation, many details regarding the life of Robert Feke remain obscure; recent research has, however, provided a foundation on which to base further study of the career of this native American painter. Probably born in Oyster Bay, Long Island, Feke may have traveled abroad as a mariner throughout his life. He began to paint in 1741. He settled briefly in Newport in 1742 and was exposed either there or in New York to the work of John Smibert, whose influence upon him was significant. A comparison of Smibert's well-known painting *The Bermuda Group* (1728-1729) with Feke's *Isaac Royall and His Family* (1741) reveals that the younger artist's composition is derived from Smibert's earlier work; however, Feke's lack of formal training is evident in the linear, planar, more decorative patterning of *Isaac Royall*. During his brief artistic career, Feke painted in Philadelphia, Boston, and Newport, and his technical expertise consistently developed.

Feke's *Portrait of James Bowdoin II,* probably a wedding portrait, represents the painter's style at the peak of his career in Boston, where he filled an artistic gap created by Smibert's retirement. Within a graceful, unified composition, the artist has sculpturally defined the broad idealized portrait of Bowdoin, though the background remains a flat backdrop. Feke's mastery of texture and use of pastel color suggest an awareness of the elegant, delicate work of such English Rococo artists as Thomas Hudson and Joseph Highmore, which he may have seen abroad during his voyages.

Feke painted several portraits of members of the prominent Bowdoin family in the 1740s. An astute politician and an ardent supporter of the American Revolution, James Bowdoin II was elected governor of Massachusetts in 1785; he was a founder of the American Academy of Arts and Sciences in 1780 and became the first president of the Massachusetts Bank.   [M.R.B.]

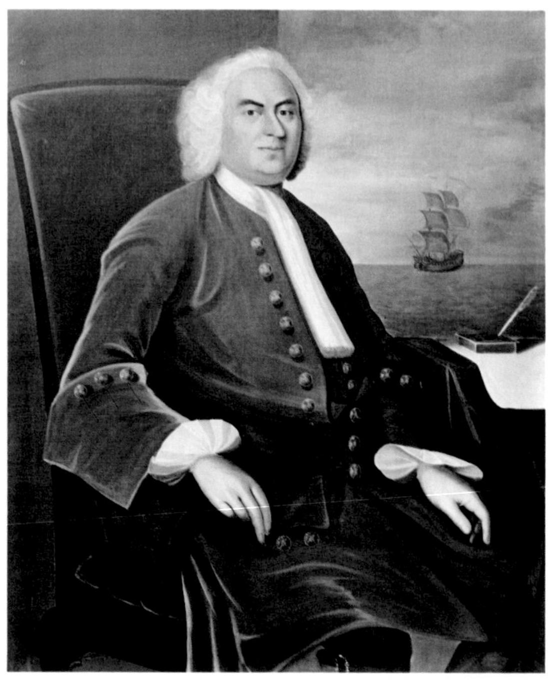

JOSEPH BADGER (1708-1765)

Portrait of James Bowdoin I, ca. 1747

Oil on canvas, 50¼ x 40¼ (127.6 x 102.3 cm)

Bequest of Mrs. Sarah Bowdoin Dearborn. 1826.6

The son of a Charlestown, Massachusetts, tailor, Joseph Badger worked as a house and sign painter and glazer before turning his attention to portrait painting, a pursuit he continued part time from about 1740 until his death. Badger is thought to have received no formal artistic training and, unlike other local artists such as John Smibert and Peter Pelham, he did not advertise his skills as a portrait painter. That his artistic talent was well respected, however, is indicated by the number and prominence of his sitters; like such painters as Robert Feke and John Greenwood, he completed numerous important local commissions between about 1747, when failing eyesight forced the retirement of John Smibert, and 1755, when Joseph Blackburn arrived in Boston.

Although he was undoubtedly aware of the work of the prominent local portrait painter John Smibert, Badger's artistic style suggests little direct influence from him. Rather, Badger more generally worked in the tradition of late seventeenth—early eighteenth-century English portraiture and, like other artists, relied on mezzotints after such artists as Sir Peter Lely and Sir Godfrey Kneller as sources for his compositions. Badger's considerable difficulties with proportion and draughtsmanship, use of lurid and unharmonious colors, and problems with capturing a lively likeness suggest his lack of formal training.

Badger's three-quarter length *Portrait of James Bowdoin I* was probably executed in Boston about 1747. Badger completed a second, nearly identical, version of the portrait, which also descended in the Bowdoin family and is owned by the Detroit Institute of Arts; the precise reason for the dual commission is not known. Badger apparently derived the costume and composition of this work from a 1726 mezzotint of *Sir Isaac Newton* by Johan Faber the Younger after a painting by Johan van der Banck, a print which he and other artists used as a source for numerous portraits. As was his custom, Badger slightly altered the mezzotint to include, instead of a column in the background of the Bowdoin portrait, a ship, signifying the sitter's mercantile interests and ownership of Long Wharf in Boston.   [M.R.B.]

JOSEPH BLACKBURN (active in America 1754-1763)
Portrait of James Bowdoin III and His Sister Elizabeth,
ca. 1760

Oil on canvas, 36⅞ x 58 (93.7 x 147.4 cm)
Gift of Mrs. Sarah Bowdoin Dearborn. 1826.11

One of the most elusive figures in American art, Joseph Blackburn was probably born in England and trained in London. Active in America between 1754 and 1763, he painted in Bermuda and Newport before arriving in Boston in 1755. Schooled in the latest fashionable taste and facing little local competition, Blackburn received numerous portrait commissions from prominent Boston residents. John

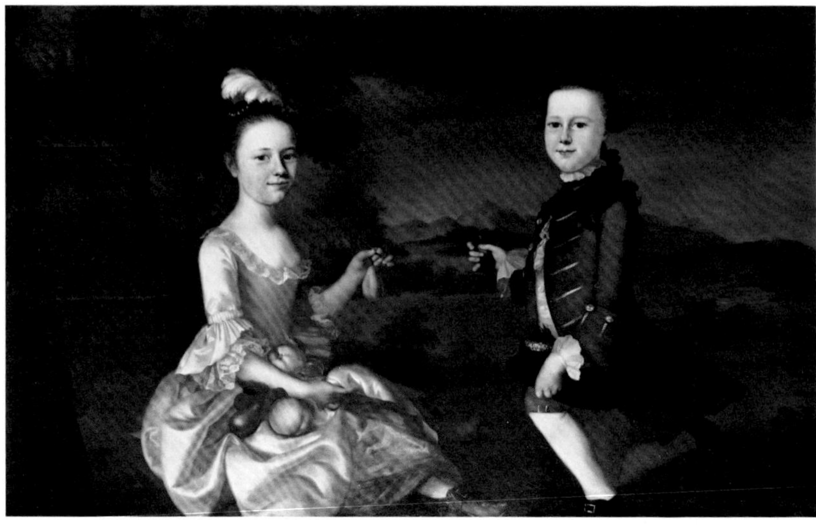

Singleton Copley's early paintings suggest a considerable awareness of Blackburn's style, although by 1758 the linear clarity and strong tonal contrasts of the younger artist's work had influenced Blackburn's more delicate manner. In addition to his Boston work, Blackburn completed several portraits in Portsmouth, New Hampshire, before returning to England in 1763, where he continued his promising career.

In this delightful double portrait, Blackburn has depicted Elizabeth and James Bowdoin III, the children of James Bowdoin II and his wife Elizabeth Erving. The portrait reveals the dependence of American Colonial painting on English style and fashion. The delicate handling, pastel palette, and elegant textures indicate Blackburn's interest in the Rococo style, which he introduced to the New England colonies. The architectural details, elaborate clothing, and contrived poses of the sitters suggest that Blackburn may have followed his usual practice of consulting an English print source for the composition and details of the painting. The children appear to occupy a space distinctly apart from the idealized landscape, which, with its awkward composition, color variations, and lack of perspective devices, resembles a stage set; the background was undoubtedly drawn

from a secondary source or from the imagination of the
artist, a practice which contrasts greatly with the nineteenth-century artistic interest in portraying the wonder of
the American landscape.　　　　　　　　　　[M.R.B.]

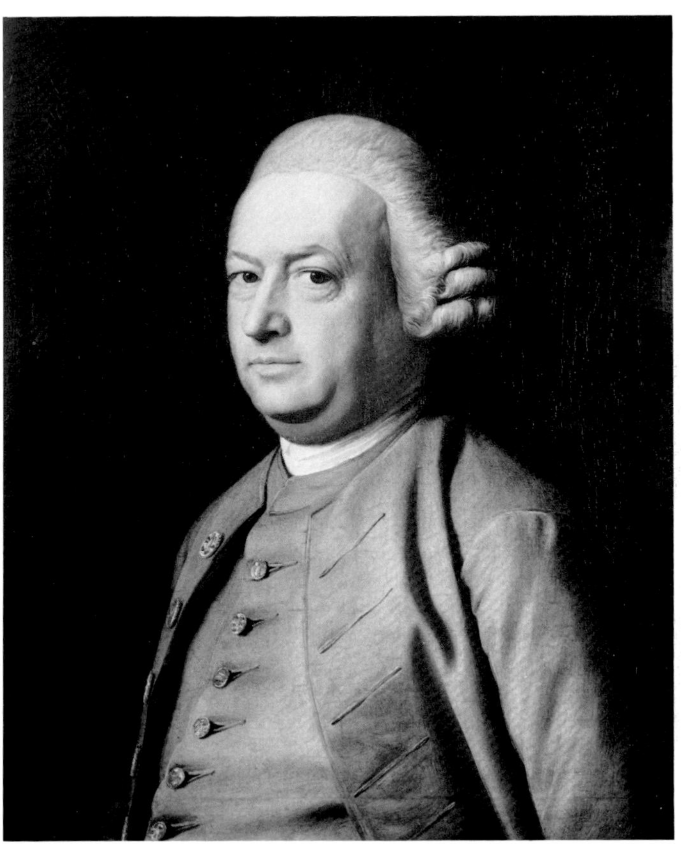

JOHN SINGLETON COPLEY (1738-1815)

Portrait of Thomas Flucker, ca. 1770-1772

 Oil on canvas, 28⅞ x 24 (73.3 x 60.9 cm)

 Bequest of Mrs. Lucy Flucker Knox Thatcher. 1855.1

Though he was primarily self-taught, John Singleton Copley
probably acquired his early interest in art from his step-
father, Peter Pelham, a Boston mezzotint engraver and
portrait painter.

 Copley's formative works reveal an ambitious interest in

classical studies and history painting, subjects he pursued later in England, but he was aware of the limited American art market and so directed his talents to the painting of portraits. Copley's early works reflect the richness and variety of the artistic tradition in eighteenth-century Boston and were particularly influenced by the painterly technique of Robert Feke and John Greenwood and the sophisticated, elegant portraits by Joseph Blackburn. By the late 1750s, his mature style, based on masterly technical proficiency and penetrating observation, attracted numerous commissions and established Copley as a leading portrait painter in America. In 1774, as a result of artistic aspirations and political complications, Copley permanently moved to England, where his subject matter and style altered dramatically, reflecting contemporary taste.

This sober quarter length *Portrait of Thomas Flucker* illustrates Copley's stylistic evolution in the latter part of his American career. Unlike his early portraits, which often include lavish settings, costumes, and decorative accessories to suggest the individual's social position, Copley's works of this period focus more directly on the actual sitter. As seen in the *Portrait of Thomas Flucker,* architectural and decorative details are eliminated, the palette is limited to muted tones, and the figure and face of the sitter are sharply illuminated. This simplified, nearly abstract presentation vitalizes and intensifies the image, producing a heightened sense of realism. Like most of his portraits, Copley's objective depiction of Flucker, a wealthy Tory, betrays none of the artist's political attitudes. The portrait was given to the College by the sitter's granddaughter.   [M.R.B.]

GILBERT STUART (1755-1828)

Portrait of Thomas Jefferson, 1805-1807

  Oil on canvas, 48⅜ x 39¾ (122.9 x 101.0 cm)
  Bequest of the Honorable James Bowdoin III. 1813.55

Born in Newport, Rhode Island, Gilbert Stuart expressed an early interest in portrait painting. He probably received his first formal training from Cosmo Alexander, a Scottish artist

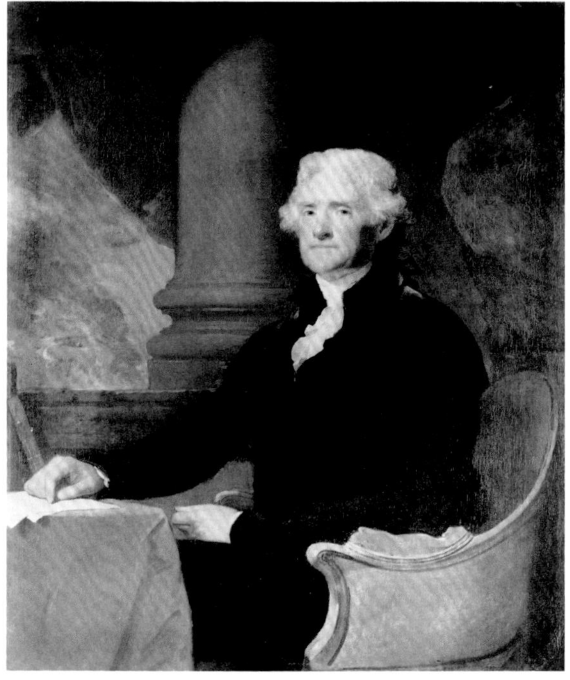

whom Stuart accompanied to Edinburgh in 1771 as an apprentice. Alexander's death the following year and lack of patronage forced Stuart to return home in 1773, and he worked as a portrait painter in Newport, Boston, and Philadelphia before traveling to London in 1775. There, as a close friend and pupil of the influential American artist Benjamin West, Stuart's style and important social contacts developed quickly. Upon the exhibition of his painting *The Skater* at the Royal Academy in 1782, Stuart received immediate recognition and was widely patronized in London and in Dublin, where he relocated in 1787. Stuart continued his successful career in America, to which he returned in 1793, and worked in New York, Philadelphia, and Washington, D. C., before finally settling in Boston in 1805.

Aesthetically and historically significant, Stuart's *Portrait of Thomas Jefferson* was commissioned in 1805 by James Bowdoin III, an avid Jeffersonian. In a letter to his Washington friend, General Henry Dearborn, secretary of war,

Bowdoin stated: "I shall be much obliged to you to procure me the portraits of Mr. Jefferson and Mr. Madison if a good painter can be found at Washington, and they should be willing to take the trouble of sitting therefor. I should like to have them done by Stuart, could he be induced to execute them." Research suggests that the Bowdoin painting, one of several portraits Stuart executed of the president, was based on another 1805 likeness of Jefferson which Stuart had painted from life; Stuart enlarged and elaborated upon the earlier work, finishing the portrait in Boston in 1807. Stuart also derived the *Portrait of James Madison* requested in Bowdoin's letter from a life portrait executed in 1804; this work is also in the Bowdoin collection. As James Bowdoin III had requested, the portraits were executed as pendants; nearly identical in size, their compositions are similar though reversed. Generally considered to be Stuart's most masterful portrait of Jefferson, this painting clearly demonstrates the vitality and freshness of the artist's style. Schooled in the tradition of such British artists as George Romney and Sir Henry Raeburn, Stuart employed a lively palette and an elaborate system of transparent glazes in his portraits to produce a radiant luminosity. The artist's lavish use of pigment and fluid brushstrokes contrast markedly with the crisp, linear style of many contemporary American artists. A charming and sophisticated figure, Stuart attracted many students to his Boston studio and strongly influenced the style and development of American portraiture in the first half of the nineteenth century.   [M.R.B.]

MARTIN JOHNSON HEADE (1819-1904)
Newburyport Marshes: Passing Storm, 1865-1870
   Oil on canvas, 15 x 30 (38.1 x 76.2 cm)
   Museum purchase with the aid of the Sylvia E. Ross Fund.   1964.45

Born in rural Lumberville, Pennsylvania, Martin Johnson Heade studied painting with Edward Hicks before traveling abroad to complete his artistic education. Heade began his career as an itinerant painter, producing numerous portraits and genre scenes and exhibiting widely. While working in

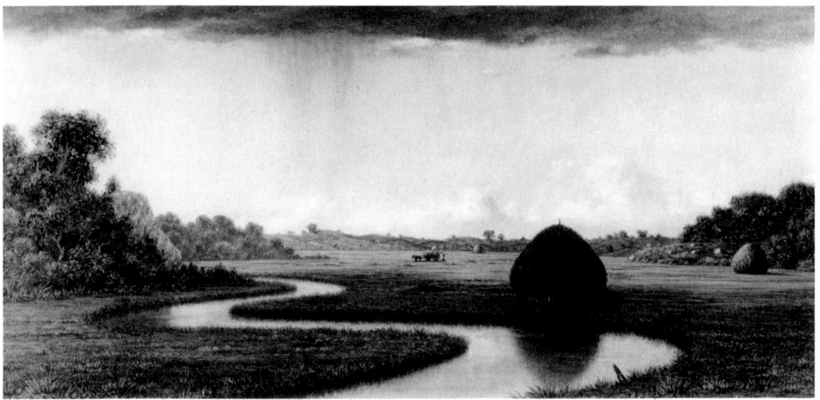

1859 at the 10th Street Studio Building in New York City, he met leading members of the popular Hudson River School and developed a close friendship with Frederick Church; as a result, Heade's interest in portraying the beauty of the natural landscape developed rapidly, and, following several trips to South America, he began to specialize in the depiction of exotic flora and fauna.

Though he executed similar scenes in New Jersey, Rhode Island, and Florida, Heade is most admired for his portrayals of the salt marshes in the area of Newburyport, Massachusetts, in the 1860s. Heade differed from numerous Hudson River School painters whose aim in portraying the natural landscape was to reproduce popular topographical wonders; rather, Heade repeatedly depicted the serene salt marsh, subtly varying the basic elements of the composition, the river, haystacks, and clouds, in an effort to achieve a perfectly balanced painting. Heade's pleasing if somewhat simple variation on the marsh theme uses a standard panoramic format which focuses on a single haystack and a river receding gently into the background. Heade was also interested in capturing nature's moments of transition. In this painting, he sensitively illustrates the changes in sunlight, mood, and atmosphere caused by the oncoming storm. Unlike other nineteenth-century artists who utilized a series format, Heade's interest in the method was aesthetic rather than narrative. Though his style differs radically from that of the Impressionist Claude Monet, like the French artist he frequently composed work in series to carefully record temporal changes in nature. As is so frequently the case in Heade's work, man plays a small but central role in this carefully controlled composition, where he exists in total harmony with his natural environment.   [M.R.B.]

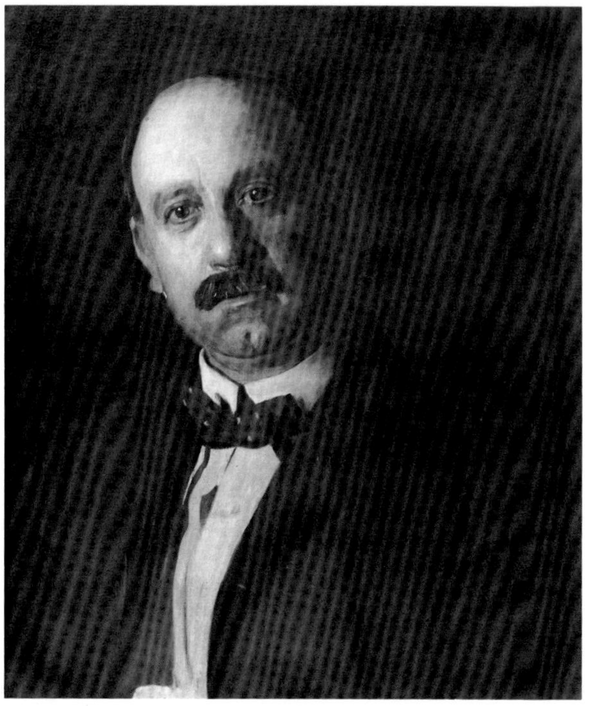

THOMAS EAKINS (1849-1916)
Portrait of A. Bryan Wall, 1904
   Oil on canvas, 23 x 19½ (58.4 x 49.5 cm)
   Hamlin Fund. 1962.16

One of America's outstanding Realist painters, Thomas Eakins was born in Philadelphia, the city which throughout his life was to be the focus of his artistic efforts. Having studied drawing at the Pennsylvania Academy of the Fine Arts and anatomy at Jefferson Medical School, Eakins went to Paris in 1866 and entered the École des Beaux Arts. There he worked with the painters Jean Léon Gérôme and Léon Bonnat and, briefly, with the sculptor Augustin Dumont. Untouched by avant-garde European trends, Eakins greatly admired such artists as Rembrandt, Ribera, and Velasquez, who strongly influenced his later style. Eakins returned to Philadelphia in 1870 and for several years primarily painted genre scenes and portraits of his friends; in 1876 he began teaching evening classes at the Pennsylvania Academy, becoming director of the school in 1882.

Eakins's teaching methods strongly reflected his preference of realistic expression to academic refinement. Eakins encouraged his students to draw not from plaster casts but directly from the nude model; he emphasized thorough anatomical knowledge and initiated dissecting classes at the academy. Eakins required his students to paint a subject directly, without relying upon a series of preliminary drawings to organize the composition. His radical educational approach led to political complications and forced his resignation from the academy in 1886. Reclusive by nature, he received few commissions, and his works were rarely exhibited and little appreciated prior to his death in 1916.

Eakins is usually viewed as a leading figure in the tradition of American Realism. Like John Singleton Copley in the eighteenth century, Eakins recorded the appearance of his sitters with remarkable accuracy and vitality. Eakins's portraits, however, rarely were commissioned and seldom functioned as records of the sitter's social position. Rather, such acutely personal portraits objectively capture the dignity and humanity of his family and closest friends. Further, Eakins's approach to nature was coolly scientific. In addition to his anatomical research, Eakins utilized his photographic studies and experiments with sculpture and perspective as tools in his search for realistic acccuracy.

In his *Portrait of A. Bryan Wall,* Eakins clearly demonstrates his mastery of the Realist mode. With its somber palette and vigorous brushwork, this non-idealized portrait captures the sitter's introspective personality. Like Eakins, Wall was a reclusive, relatively unknown painter. Born near

Pittsburgh, the son of the artist Alfred S. Wall, he was self-taught and specialized in landscape painting. Eakins signed the reverse of the canvas, "TO MY FRIEND/ A. BRYAN WALL/ THOMAS EAKINS/ 1904."   [M.R.B.]

JOHN SLOAN (1871-1951)
Sunday Afternoon in Union Square, 1912
   Oil on canvas, 26¼ x 32¼ (66.7 x 81.9 cm)
   Bequest of Mr. George Otis Hamlin. 1961.63

John Sloan has achieved recognition not just as an accomplished graphic artist and painter but also as an influential teacher and champion of liberalized exhibition opportunities. His early career in the 1890s was spent as a newspaper illustrator in Philadelphia. Sloan was a working associate of William Glackens, George Luks, and Everett Shinn and often attended classes with them at the Pennsylvania Academy of the Fine Arts, where he became a close friend of Robert Henri. In 1904 he sought work as a free-lance illustrator in New York, and the following year he won critical acclaim for his New York City Life etchings, which depicted the vitality and humanity of the everyday urban environment. Despite such artistic recognition, Sloan found few patrons for his prints and oil paintings, a medium he began to seriously explore in the early twentieth century. Though admired for their freshness and vitality of expression, Sloan's works were more frequently criticized for their vulgar, everyday subject matter and lack of academic refinement and conventional beauty.

Under the leadership of Henri, Sloan and a number of his friends, including Glackens, Luks, and Shinn, held an important exhibition in the MacBeth Gallery in February 1908; the group, dubbed "The Eight," and somewhat misleadingly the "Ash Can School," as a result of the realistic urban subject matter depicted in the work of several participants, sought increased opportunities for American artists to exhibit. Though Sloan sold nothing, the show aroused broad interest and the works were sent on a national tour. In 1910 he again joined Henri in staging the non-juried Exhibition

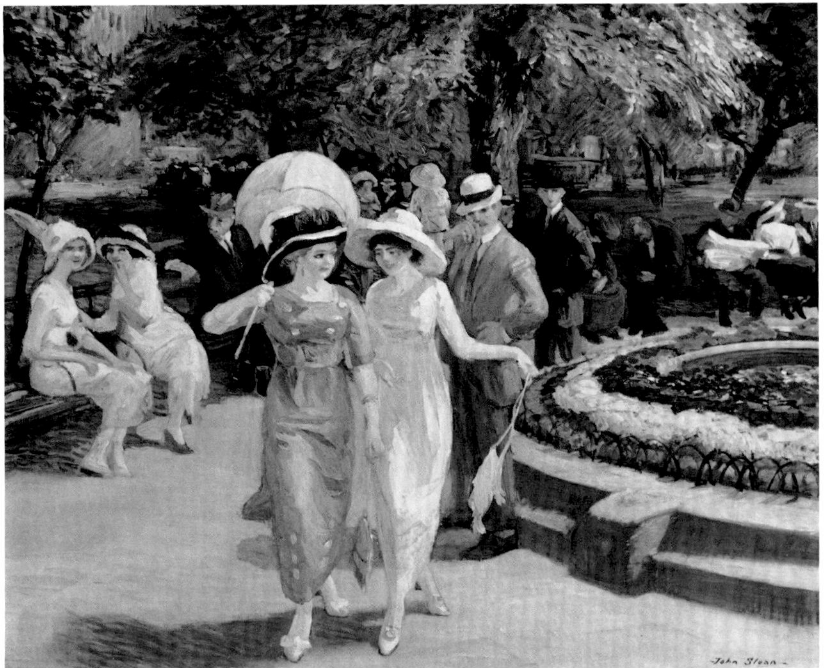

of Independent Artists, aimed at offering unknown artists a place to show their works.

In *Sunday Afternoon in Union Square,* Sloan broadly illustrates the activity and energy displayed in a New York park on a sunny afternoon, a favorite subject at this period of his career. His ability to capture the momentary nuances and subtleties of the scene perhaps resulted from his training as a newspaper illustrator. The work also demonstrates Sloan's ability to separate his painting and his politics. Like many contemporary artists, Sloan's liberal philosophies and hatred of social injustice led to his temporary involvement in the Socialist Party; although his diary notes, "Union Square was the scene of a large Socialist meeting on May 1, 1912," there is no hint of urban unrest in the painting.

Following the modernist impact of the 1913 Armory Show, Sloan's works were no longer considered to be part of the aesthetic avant-garde, but he continued to experiment throughout his career. His most direct influence on younger artists was as a highly respected teacher at the Art Students

League from 1916 to 1938. His first major patron was Mr. George Otis Hamlin, who purchased twenty oils from him in 1923, an important collection he later bequeathed to Bowdoin College. [M.R.B.]

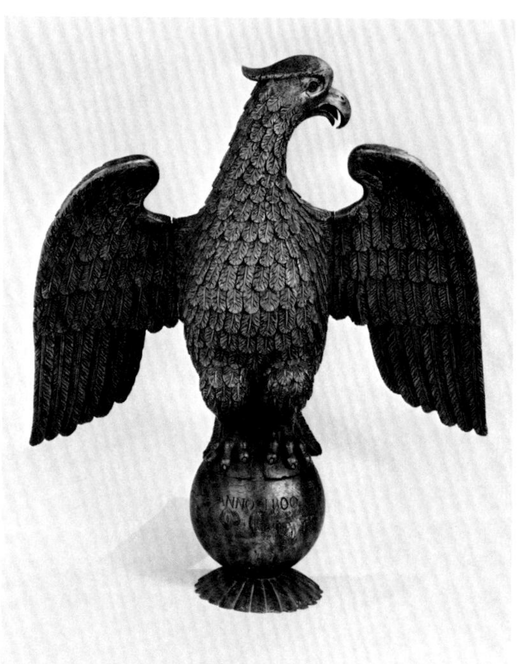

UNKNOWN ARTIST

Eagle, ca. 1800

Wood, $31\frac{1}{8}$ x $27\frac{13}{16}$ x 15 (79.1 x 70.7 x 38.1 cm)

Museum purchase with the aid of the Helen Johnson Chase Fund. 1965.24

In the early years of the American republic, most of this country's sculpture was created for specific purposes or practical situations and was executed by amateur carvers. When the embellishment of public buildings called for sculptural decoration, it was nearly always performed by foreign-born professionals. While the identity of the early native artisans is difficult to determine, examples of their indigenous craftsmanship have fortunately survived.

Not only is the artisan who made Bowdoin's eagle unknown, but the reasons for the creation of this sculpture are not readily understandable. Certainly the inscription on the globe, "Anno 1800," has some commemorative significance, but the only thread it provides for clarifying the historical fabric of this piece is a *terminus post quem* for the eagle's execution. Because of the horizontal frontality of the pose, it is possible that this piece served as an architectural embellishment, perhaps attached to an elaborate podium or lectern. The absence of deterioration of the wood's surface further indicates that this avian national emblem was an interior, rather than exterior, decorative element.

Because the eagle in the eighteenth century was popularly considered to be lacking in moral character, Benjamin Franklin, in 1782, strenuously objected to its selection as the country's symbol by the Continental Congress. Nevertheless, American folk artists produced numerous representations of this bird of prey throughout the nineteenth century. The breadth of conception and technical diversity of the artisans who made them render the eagle one of the appealing images in American folk sculpture. The craftsman who created the eagle at the Bowdoin College Museum of Art was particularly interested in translating the bird's essential characteristics—alertness, strength, and power—into three-dimensional form. The expressive curve of the beak is sensitively repeated in the eagle's twisting neck and sinuous wings. While the carving strokes employed by the artisan in rendering the eagle's feathers have an almost hypnotic uniformity, the physical prowess of this majestic bird is tangibly conveyed. The eagle's posture, perhaps ruffling its feathers or flapping its wings as it prepares to fly, suggests the carver's desire to portray a specific moment in time. This compositional device was probably based not on detailed observation but rather on the desire of the artisan to capture a rhythmic pattern of surface design and texture.

This American folk artist's enthusiasm for his subject is genuine; the proud eagle becomes not only an animated sculptural work but also a spirited emblem of America's newly emerging national identity.   [M.R.]

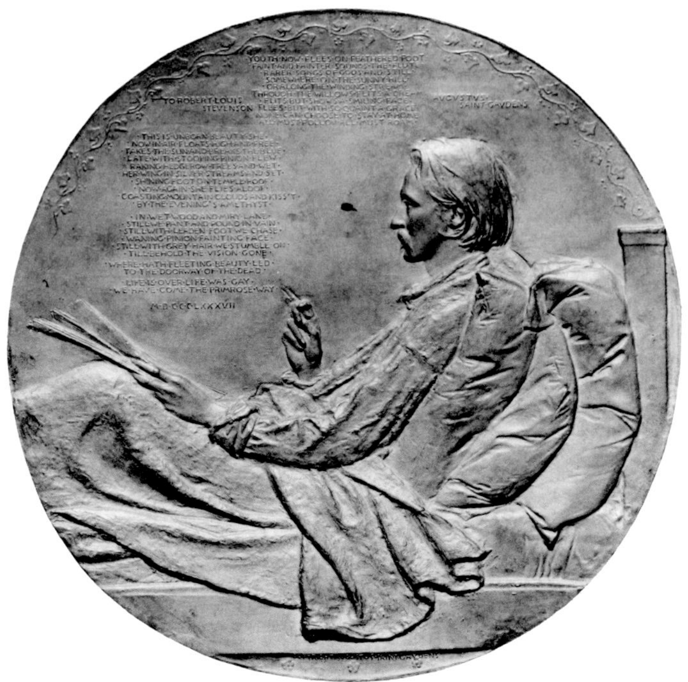

AUGUSTUS SAINT-GAUDENS (1848-1907)

Robert Louis Stevenson, ca. 1887-1901

Bronze, $\frac{3}{16}$ x $17\frac{3}{4}$ (diam.) (.5 x 45.0 cm)

Gift of the Misses Harriet and Sophia Walker. 1904.29

Although Augustus Saint-Gaudens did not meet Robert Louis Stevenson until the poet's visit to America in the fall of 1887, the sculptor had remarked prophetically ten years earlier: "If Stevenson ever crossed to this side of the water, I should consider it an honor if he would allow me to make his portrait." Their first meeting took place in Stevenson's rooms at the Hotel Albert in New York City. The portrait was finished the following spring in Manasquan, New Jersey. Of these sessions Saint-Gaudens remarked to their mutual friend Will H. Low: "My episode with Stevenson has been one of the events of my life. I am in a beatific state. It makes me very happy."

As originally planned, the relief was to have been rectangular. Why Saint-Gaudens substituted a circular format is not known, but he often labored on his sculptures both in clay and in plaster to perfect his artistic conception. Ostensibly this change only eliminated a portion of the bed on which Stevenson lay, but within the tondo the sculptor was now able to juxtapose in an imaginative composition the profile portrait with three stanzas of the poet's *Underwoods*. Not only was Saint-Gaudens able to capture the casual atmosphere of the poet's hotel room, as observed in the wrinkled nightshirt, rumpled hair, and loosely held cigarette, but the sculptor was also able to create a moving eulogy of a universally acclaimed poet. Stevenson, ill with tuberculosis, was bedridden, but this dramatic bronze could never be considered a maudlin portrayal of a sick man. Propped up by three pillows, the alert, thirty-seven-year-old poet, his knees slightly bent to support a manuscript, pauses in his reading, musing approvingly on what he has written.

On receiving his bronze in Samoa in July 1894, Stevenson wrote to its creator: "We have it in a very good light which brings out the artistic merits of the god-like sculptor to great advantage. As for my own opinion, I believe it to be a speaking likeness." This bronze, 36 inches in diameter, has not been located, but it and at least three other replicas of the same size that were cast before 1900 provide important insights into the production of sculpture. Without any modification to the portrait, Saint-Gaudens insured the uniqueness of each bronze by varying the length or placement of the various inscriptions, by altering the treatment of the bed linens, or by changing the design of the bed post. Not only were these calculations deliberately made in the large relief, but the same type of alterations were also introduced either by the sculptor himself or by his assistants into the smaller replicas, reliefs of 12-inch and $17\frac{3}{4}$-inch diameters produced in quantity during the artist's life and after his death. One series, cast before 1897, contains no reference to the word "copyright." A second series produced after this date is inscribed: "Copyright Augustus Saint-Gaudens." After 1901, all replicas of the *Stevenson* relief bore a small copyright stamp that was either applied on the surface of the finished bronze or imprinted during the casting.

It is not known how the Walkers acquired their relief, which was given to Bowdoin in 1903, but external evidence indicates that the bronze was made between 1897 and 1901. The number of replicas in this series is not recorded.

Born in Dublin, Ireland, Saint-Gaudens came to America at the age of six months. Studying first at the National Academy of Design in New York and later at the École des Beaux Arts in Paris, he produced some of this country's greatest public monuments, including the *Farragut Memorial* (1876-1881) and the *Sherman Memorial* (1892-1903) in New York, the *Shaw Memorial* (1884-1897) in Boston, and the *Adams Memorial* (1886-1892) in Washington, D. C. Equally renowned as a relief sculptor, Saint-Gaudens's consummate mastery of this medium is most strikingly demonstrated in the *Stevenson*. Not only is the likeness of the poet brilliantly rendered, but the relief itself is a paradigm of design. Saint-Gaudens's intimacy of portrayal is circumspect rather than intrusive. No greater tribute to a fellow artist exists in American art than this portrait of Robert Louis Stevenson by Augustus Saint-Gaudens.   [M.R.]

DANIEL CHESTER FRENCH (1850-1931)

Portrait of Theophilus Wheeler Walker, 1893-1894

Bronze, 53 x 29½ x 3¼ (134.6 x 74.9 x 8.2 cm)

Gift of the Misses Harriet and Sophia Walker. 1894.148

Daniel Chester French was widely acclaimed during his lifetime as a prolific sculptor of public monuments, an art form that reflected America's growing self-confidence and economic optimism in the years following the Civil War. To supplement such major commissions as the *Minute Man* (1871-1875) in Concord, Massachusetts, and the seated *Abraham Lincoln* (1911-1922) at the Lincoln Memorial in Washington, D. C., which occupied much of his time, French was also able to execute bas-relief portraits, which further attest to his stylistic diversity and creative sensitivity. In December 1892, the sculptor agreed to execute the relief of Mr. Theophilus Wheeler Walker, a major Bowdoin College

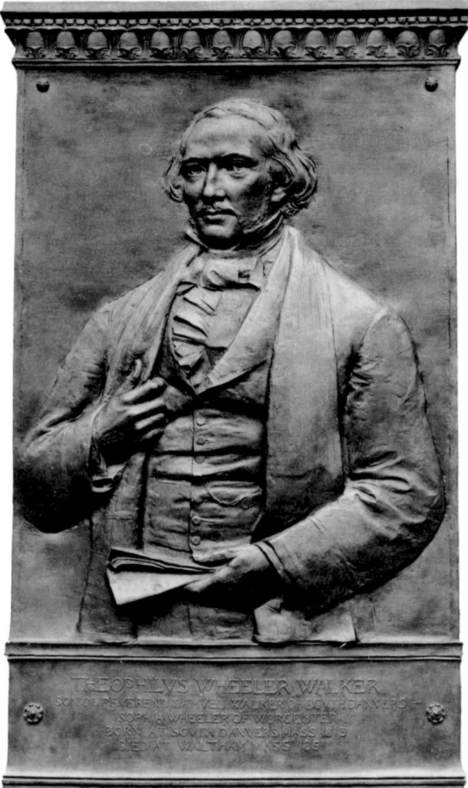

patron, who had envisioned a permanent location for the College's expanding art collection. In fulfillment of their uncle's wishes, the Misses Harriet and Sophia Walker provided the funds for the Walker Art Building, a Beaux Arts structure designed by Charles Follen McKim.

In response to a letter from Harriet Walker regarding the relief, French wrote on December 5, 1892: "It is very gratifying for me to learn that Mr. McKim has suggested me to you as the possible sculptor of the relief of Mr. Walker for the new Art Building." In a letter of May 5, 1893 to Miss Walker, French stressed the need of working closely with the architect: "I have seen Mr. McKim ... recently and he has promised to go to Brunswick with me to determine as to the position, size and character of the work and the kind of setting required. It does not seem possible for me to decide these questions without going to the place, though I am very sorry to retard the work."

The Bowdoin College Museum of Art collection includes a portrait of Walker by Joseph Alexander Ames, depicting him in three-quarter view seated in a chair. This painting was undoubtedly the primary source for the relief. French modified the composition by having the figure stand, by changing the position of his hands, and by providing a necessary horizontal emphasis to the vertical relief by including sheets of paper which Walker grasps in his left hand. The breadth of execution and liveliness of modeling exhibited in the work demonstrate French's assimilation of the international art trends he had encountered in Florence between 1874 and 1876 and later in Paris from the fall of 1876 to the summer of 1877.

French executed the *Walker* in clay before it was cast in plaster in the summer of 1893. Following the approval of the plaster by the patrons, the largest and most ambitious of French's portrait reliefs was sent to a New York City foundry, the Henry-Bonnard Bronze Company. The finished tablet was shipped to Bowdoin and installed in the Walker Art Building, which was dedicated on June 7, 1894.

[M.R.]

WILLIAM ZORACH h '58 (1887-1966)
Spirit of the Dance, ca. 1950
   Bronze, 26 x 16⅛ x 10¼ (66.0 x 41.0 x 26.0 cm)
   Museum purchase. 1953.4

From the outset of his sculptural career in 1917, William Zorach created volumeric compositional studies, carved directly in wood or stone, of animals and members of his family. In these sculptures he was preoccupied with exploiting the physical properties of the materials with which he worked and with the mechanical labor of carving. Often the shape of a block of wood or a piece of stone influenced the final appearance of a sculpture. Although he occasionally made small three-dimensional studies in clay during the 1920s, Zorach was a carver and not a modeler. For him,

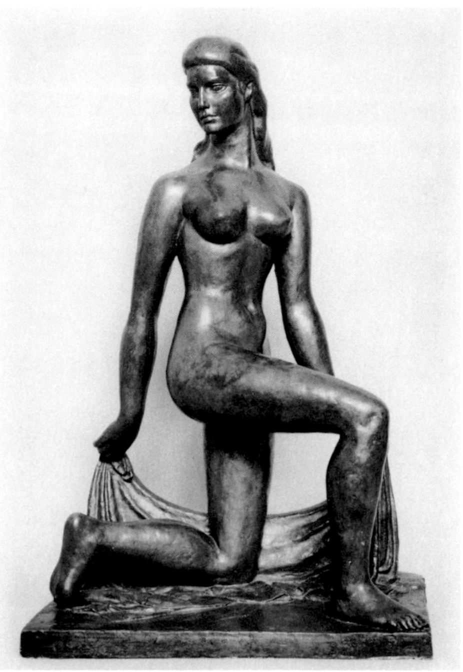

creation was a thoughtful, one-step, manual confrontation between the sculptor and his material.

The opportunity for Zorach to model his first large figure came in 1932 with a commission from Nelson A. Rockefeller for a statue to be placed in the foyer of New York's Radio City Music Hall. Edward Durell Stone, the architect, and other collaborators on the Rockefeller Center project contacted the sculptor. On examining a portfolio of his drawings, they selected as an appropriate composition a figure of "a dancer kneeling just at the finale of the dance." On finishing his preparatory model, the artist and the music hall's interior designer, Donald Deskey, agreed that the statue, originally to have been three feet high, would have to be larger, in proportion to the size of the foyer. During the spring and summer of 1932, Zorach worked on the full-scale model of his seventy-eight-inch kneeling nude.

Cast in aluminum, the statue was set in place in early December but was soon removed by the manager of the music hall, S. L. "Roxy" Rothafel. It was reinstalled in January

1933, after considerable public outcry. Hoping for a sale, Zorach had a second cast of *Spirit of the Dance* made in bronze. When no buyer was found, this replica was installed at the sculptor's summer studio at Robinhood Cove, Maine.

When Zorach decided to have the "third-scale" or working model of *Spirit of the Dance* cast in bronze is not known, but by 1950 at least one statuette was in existence, for it was loaned to Bowdoin College for a summer art exhibition. Three years later it was purchased from the sculptor; Bowdoin's bronze is one of seven castings of this figure that were either made during the sculptor's lifetime or authorized by his estate.

Although his proficiency as a carver is unmatched in the history of American sculpture, Zorach's talents as a modeler, as *Spirit of the Dance* so evocatively reveals, were considerable. This beautifully proportioned, structurally compact nude is a vibrating study of shapely volumes and sensuous surfaces. Aware of where the statue would be placed, the sculptor permitted the essential frontality of the figure to be subtly interrupted by the downturned head, the drawn-back arms, and the jutting right knee. Concerned also with public response, Zorach introduced a piece of drapery into the composition. Unquestionably this detail was included to provide the dancer a degree of respectability. In both conception and execution, *Spirit of the Dance* remains one of William Zorach's most appealing and impressive sculptures.   [M.R.]

ALEXANDER CALDER (1898-1976)

Red Fossils, 1970

Steel and wire, 48 x 70 (121.9 x 177.8 cm)

Gift of the family and friends of Charles Baird Price III '74. 1973.6

A significant innovator in twentieth-century sculpture, Alexander Calder was born into an environment of more traditional artistic endeavor, for his grandfather, Alexander Milne Calder, and his father, Alexander Stirling Calder, were noted academic sculptors in Philadelphia in the late nineteenth and early twentieth centuries. Despite his artistic upbringing, Calder was initially drawn to engineering and

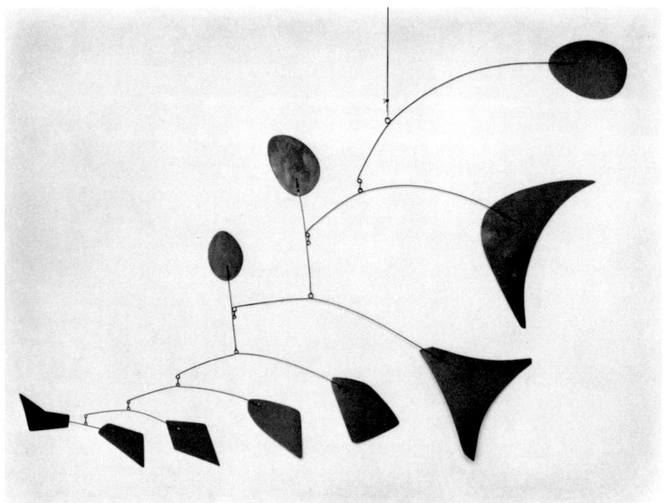

graduated from the Stevens Institute of Technology in 1919. Following a variety of engineering jobs and travel, Calder enrolled at the Art Students League in 1923. Arriving in Paris in 1926, he experimented with the creation of open wire figurines and animals. Calder's humorous figural sculpture attracted the attention of the leading artists in Paris and led to a period of fertile experimentation in the artist's career. The influence of Piet Mondrian introduced bold primary colors into Calder's work and encouraged his interest in abstract and geometrical composition. Through the influence of the Russian Constructivists, Calder began to examine methods of incorporating motion into his work. His earliest constructions were activated by hand or electric motor and were dubbed "mobiles" by Marcel Duchamp. By 1933 he had created his first wind-operated, free-floating sculpture to explore the constantly shifting relationship of colors and form in space through spontaneous movement. Calder's friendship with Jean Miró in 1933 led to the final stage of his artistic development, for the Spaniard's fascination with dream imagery and fantasy stimulated his interest in organic form and rhythm.

The mobile *Red Fossils* in the Bowdoin College collection

represents a mature example from the sculptor's work. The flat steel discs in a variety of shapes are connected by wires at different intervals and are suspended in asymmetrical equilibrium. The slightest breeze disrupts the delicate balance and alters the relationship of the colors and forms to each other in space. Suspended from the ceiling and not fixed by a traditional base, the piece interacts freely with its environment; the variety and unpredictability of the resulting formal relationships are the essence of Calder's sculpture.

Calder's fertile imagination continued to flourish, and he experimented with painting, lithography, jewelry design, and book illustration throughout his career. His immobile metal constructions, first developed in the 1930s and referred to as "stabiles" by Jean Arp, assumed monumental proportions in the 1960s. Before his death in 1976, Calder was one of the most highly recognized artists in America, and his work is widely admired today for its vitality, humor, and organic expression. [M.R.B.]

School of WILLIAM SEARLE (1634-1667) / THOMAS DENNIS (active 1667-1706)
Armchair, ca. 1665-1670
  Oak, 48½ x 25½ x 15¼ (123.2 x 64.8 x 38.8 cm)
  Gift of Mr. E. Wilder Farley 1836. 1872.1

This armchair traditionally has been attributed to Thomas Dennis, a joiner of Ipswich, Massachusetts. Together with a second chair, a tape loom, a box with drawer, and a chest, all exhibiting similar decorative motifs and style, this example descended directly in the family of Thomas Dennis; it was given to the museum in 1872.

Little is known of Dennis's origins or training. In 1667 he moved from Portsmouth, New Hampshire, to Ipswich, where he married the widow of another joiner, William Searle, the following year. Dennis was active in public affairs in Ipswich and served in King Philip's War. He trained his son and several apprentices in the joinery trade before his death in 1706.

Despite its traditional attribution, recent research suggests

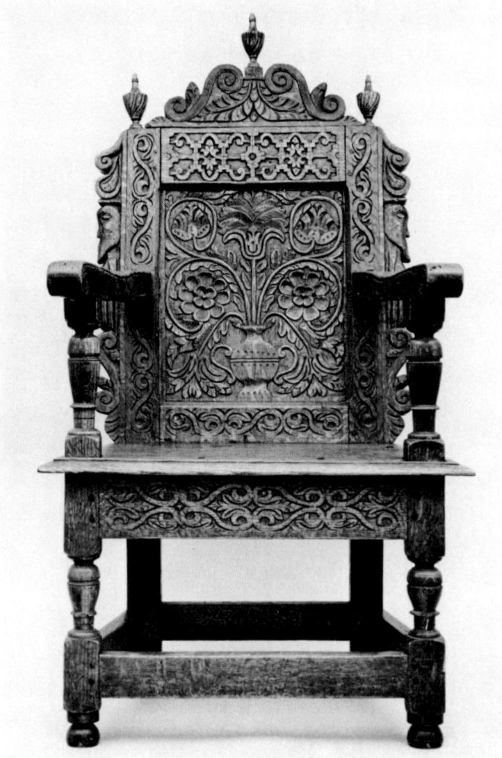

that the armchair could have been made by Searle rather than by Dennis. The decorative motifs and quality of the carving relate directly to a body of fixed church woodwork and ornamental plasterwork in coastal Somerset and Devonshire; Searle was born in Ottery Saint Mary, Devonshire, where he was trained by his father. Searle transmitted the Devonshire style to Ipswich, and several land transfers between Searle and Dennis may indicate that Dennis was also from Devonshire and knew Searle in England. Because it is difficult to distinguish between the hands of two craftsmen trained in the same English provincial joinery tradition, some scholars refuse to divide the family heirlooms and related objects into Searle and Dennis groups, but the marked difference in quality between this example and the second family armchair, now owned by the Essex Institute, Salem,

Massachusetts, has prompted others to attribute the Bowdoin chair to Searle, whose inventory of 1667 included "one Chaire," assigned the surprisingly high value of one pound.

The two Searle/Dennis armchairs are among the most elaborately decorated of seventeenth-century American joined furniture examples, and they were originally further decorated with red and black paint, now largely faded. The three urn finials are restorations but take the place of similar originals. [R.F.T. & M.R.B.]

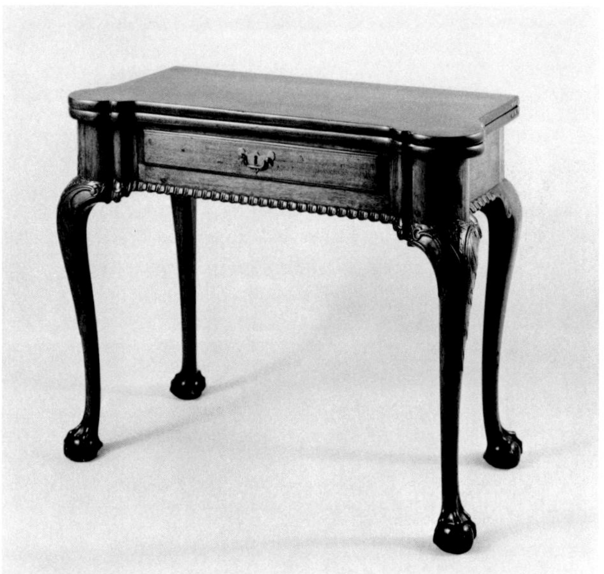

PENNSYLVANIAN, PHILADELPHIA

Gaming table, ca. 1765-1780

Mahogany and oak, 20 x 34¾ x 16½ (50.8 x 88.3 x 41.9 cm)

Gift of Mr. John H. Halford '07 and Mrs. Halford. 1964.38

In the second quarter of the eighteenth century, the city of Philadelphia emerged as a leading cultural and commercial center in the American colonies. Upper-class residents desired an architectural and decorative arts style corresponding to their growing wealth and increasingly sophisticated taste. As a result, Philadelphia furniture of the period 1765 to

1780 is highly regarded for its fine craftsmanship and so-phisticated design.

The quality of Philadelphia furniture is revealed in this mahogany gaming table of the Chippendale style. The complex formal interrelationship of cabriole legs to case, delicate naturalistic foliate carving, and finely executed ball-and-claw feet suggest a Philadelphia origin. The particularly strong English influence upon Philadelphia design and con-struction partially accounts for the sophistication of furni-ture produced in the city. Numerous craftsmen immigrated to Philadelphia from the British Isles, and furniture design books such as Thomas Chippendale's *The Gentleman and Cabinet-Maker's Director* (1754) and Robert Manwaring's *Cabinet and Chair-Maker's Real Friend and Companion* (1765) were available locally.

A higher standard of living in the American colonies by the mid-eighteenth century led to the popularity of such specialized furniture forms as card, gaming, tea, and break-fast tables. Like other gaming tables, this one has recessed oval pockets, made to contain coins or gaming chips, which appear on the table surface when it is open; candlesticks were placed on the projections at the table corners. Probably the indented table top was originally covered with baize, a napped woolen or cotton fabric which provided an ideal sur-face for card playing.   [M.R.B.]

PAUL REVERE (1735-1818)
Punch Ladle, ca. 1760

  Silver and wood, 13⅝ x 4 x 1⅛ (34.6 x 10.2 x 2.9 cm)
  Gift of Mrs. Clara Bowdoin Winthrop. 1943.3.3

Included in the 1774 inventory of James Bowdoin II is the intriguing reference to a punch ladle marked with the Bow-doin crest and the maker's name, "Riviere." Stamped with the mark of Paul Revere and engraved with the family crest, this punch ladle appears to be the item noted in Bowdoin's inventory. The ladle, which descended directly in the family of James Bowdoin II before being given to the College in 1943, underscores the cultural relationship between Bowdoin

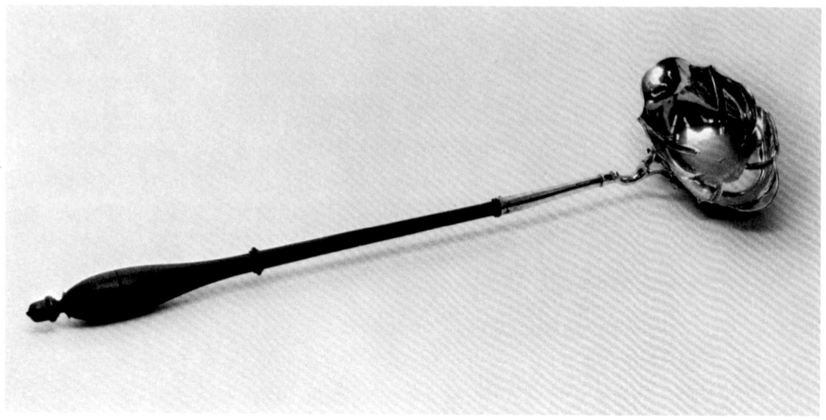

and Revere, who were both descended from Huguenot stock. The son of a silversmith, Revere carried on the family trade after his father's death in 1754. In addition to his skill as a silversmith, the craftsman was noted for his talent as a copperplate engraver. Endowed with a creative mind and an acute business sense, he conducted a flourishing hardware business and owned rolling mills and a bell and cannon foundry later in his career.

The high quality of Revere's silver production is evident in this elegant ladle. Of particular note is the punchmark, a "PR" encased in a rectangle, which is stamped in the center of the ladle bowl; appearing in the work of the elder Revere, this mark was inherited and utilized by his son in the early years of his career. Throughout the seventeenth and eighteenth centuries, American silver design was profoundly influenced by English prototypes, a reflection of the colonies' social and cultural dependence upon the mother country. The sinuous curves of the ladle's form and the lively scalloped flutes of the hammered bowl and delicately turned handle attest to the sophistication and restraint of English Rococo taste in Boston. In keeping with period fashion, Revere later adopted the more geometric Neoclassical style and rejected completely the robust, energetic designs of the more fanciful Rococo period. [M.R.B.]

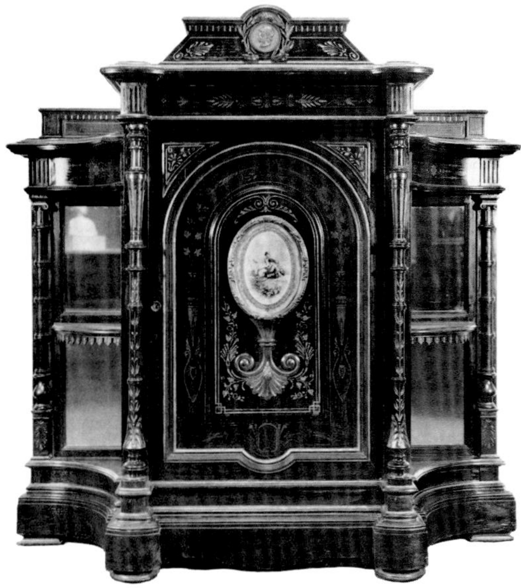

ALEXANDER ROUX (ca. 1813-1886)

Cabinet, ca. 1867-1877

Rosewood, maple, metal, porcelain, and mirrors, $52\frac{1}{2}$ x $51\frac{1}{2}$ x $19\frac{1}{2}$
(133.4 x 130.8 x 49.5 cm)

Hamlin Fund. 1974.42

This sophisticated cabinet bears the label of the fashionable
New York cabinetmaker Alexander Roux. Born in France
and probably trained in Paris, Roux immigrated to New
York City, where his name first appears in the 1837 *City
Directory*. His furniture business expanded rapidly, and by
1855 he employed over 120 craftsmen. The firm continued
in operation for sixty-one years, achieving its pinnacle of
success in the 1870s. Following Roux's retirement in 1881,
his son continued the highly prosperous business until 1898.

Roux's success can partially be attributed to his fashionable
training, for in the mid-nineteenth century sophisticated designs by other French cabinetmakers, such as Charles Bau-
douine, Emmanuel Ringuet Le Prince, and Leon Marcotte,
were equally in demand. In addition, Roux was able to
supply the variety of furniture styles necessary to satisfy
nineteenth-century taste. Period fashion dictated the use of

particular historic styles for specific rooms, and Roux's establishment could supply tasteful furniture in the Gothic, Renaissance, Louis XIV, and Rococo styles. In his influential *Architecture of Country Houses* (1850), Andrew Jackson Downing recommended Roux for both the quality and quantity of his designs.

By the 1860s, historic styles in the decorative arts were often eclectically combined to produce complex works of magnificent color and texture. The heavy form and architectural qualities of the cabinet are features typical of the Renaissance Revival style; characteristics of the Louis XVI period, such as the painted porcelain plaque and metal moldings, are juxtaposed with such decorative motifs as incised carving and stylized marquetry to increase the lavish visual effect. Due to the high quality of its craftsmanship and the opulence of its ornamentation, the cabinet can be regarded as an aesthetic climax in Victorian decorative arts.

[M.R.B.]

LOUIS COMFORT TIFFANY (1848-1933)

Vase, ca. 1900

Glass, $3\frac{3}{4}$ x $2\frac{5}{16}$ (diam.) (9.5 x 5.9 cm)
Gift of Mrs. Sylvia E. Ross. 1963.53

The eldest son of the founder of the silver and jewelry firm of Tiffany & Company, Louis Comfort Tiffany studied with George Inness and began his career as a painter. Becoming increasingly interested in the decorative and applied arts, he and Candace Wheeler, Samuel Colman, and Lockwood de Forest formed the Associated Artists group in 1879. The group created luxurious, refined interiors for the fashionable New York market. His interest in the decorative arts and medieval craftsmanship encouraged Tiffany to experiment with ornamental glass techniques, and his early production included colorful glass tiles and stained-glass windows. Such ventures led to the establishment of the Tiffany Glass Company in 1885.

Tiffany's aim was to educate popular taste by mass-producing functional as well as beautiful art objects and by

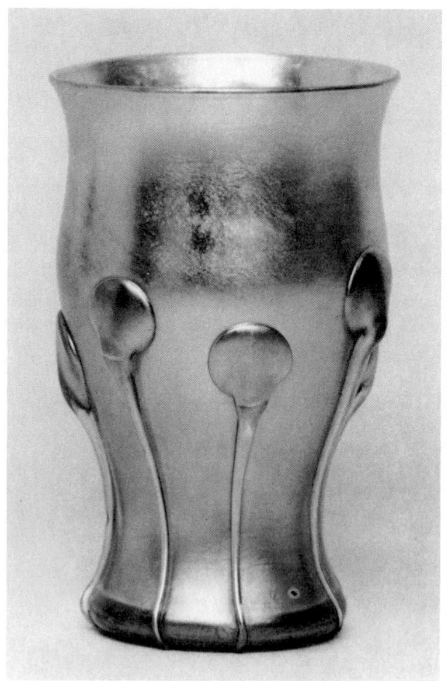

maintaining high standards of craftsmanship; in contrast to the decorative excesses of the Victorian era, he theorized that the form of an object, rather than its applied decoration, is essential and should be derived naturally from its material. The firm was most noted for its blown "Favrile" glass, described as "a composition of various colored glasses, worked together while hot"; registered in 1894, the Favrile trademark is derived from an Old English term signifying "handmade." The process utilized in the production of Favrile pieces involved the incorporation of tiny bits of glass of different colors and textures into a ball of hot iridescent glass; after repeatedly adding color and bits of glass, the piece was blown into its final form. The fine color and design of Favrile glass, often derived from exotic or organic forms, helped establish Tiffany as a leader in the American Art Nouveau movement.

The form of this miniature gold Favrile vase is decorated with applied drops of molten glass producing the "lily pad" pattern common in the Tiffany oeuvre. The initials "LCT" and a production number are scratched into the base of the vase. [M.R.B.]

SELECTED WORKS FROM THE COLLECTION

[M.R.B.]

Painting

John SMIBERT (1688-1751), after Nicholas Poussin (1594-1665), French: *The Continence of Scipio.* Oil on canvas, 46 x 62 (116.8 x 157.5 cm). Bequest of the Honorable James Bowdoin III. 1813.10

✠John SMIBERT (1688-1751): *Portrait of James Bowdoin II.* Oil on canvas, 34⅞ x 26⅞ (88.6 x 68.3 cm). Bequest of Mrs. Sarah Bowdoin Dearborn. 1826.5

John SMIBERT (1688-1751): *Portrait of Reverend James McSparran.* Oil on canvas, 30 x 25 (76.2 x 63.5 cm). Bequest of Mr. Charles Edward Allen 1835. 1897.1

Unknown artist (18th century): *Portrait of James Bowdoin I.* Oil on canvas, 36¼ x 29¾ (92.1 x 75.6 cm). Bequest of Mrs. Sarah Bowdoin Dearborn. 1826.4

Unknown artist (18th century): *Portrait of William Bowdoin.* Oil on canvas, 30¼ x 25 (76.9 x 63.5 cm). Bequest of Mrs. Sarah Bowdoin Dearborn. 1826.3

Robert FEKE (1707-1752): *Portrait of Brigadier General Samuel Waldo.* Oil on canvas, 96¾ x 60¼ (245.7 x 153.0 cm). Bequest of Mrs. Lucy Flucker Knox Thatcher. 1855.3

✠Robert FEKE (1707-1752): *Portrait of James Bowdoin II.* Oil on canvas, 50 x 40 (127.0 x 101.6 cm). Bequest of Mrs. Sarah Bowdoin Dearborn. 1826.8

Robert FEKE (1707-1752): *Portrait of Mrs. James Bowdoin II.* Oil on canvas, 50⅛ x 40⅛ (127.2 x 101.7 cm). Bequest of Mrs. Sarah Bowdoin Dearborn. 1826.7

Robert FEKE (1707-1752): *Portrait of Mrs. William Bowdoin.* Oil on canvas, 50¼ x 40⅜ (127.6 x 102.5 cm). Bequest of Mrs. Sarah Bowdoin Dearborn. 1826.9

Robert FEKE (1707-1752): *Portrait of William Bowdoin.* Oil on canvas, 50¼ x 40¼ (127.6 x 102.2 cm). Bequest of Mrs. Sarah Bowdoin Dearborn. 1826.10

✠Joseph BADGER (1708-1765): *Portrait of James Bowdoin I.* Oil on canvas, 50¼ x 40¼ (127.6 x 102.3 cm). Bequest of Mrs. Sarah Bowdoin Dearborn. 1826.6

✠Joseph BLACKBURN (active in America 1754-1763): *Portrait of James Bowdoin III and His Sister Elizabeth.* Oil on canvas, 36⅞ x 58 (93.7 x 147.4 cm). Gift of Mrs. Sarah Bowdoin Dearborn. 1826.11

Joseph BLACKBURN (active in America 1754-1763): *Portrait of Mrs. Thomas Flucker.* Oil on canvas, 50¼ x 40 (127.6 x 101.6 cm). Bequest of Mrs. Lucy Flucker Knox Thatcher. 1855.2

Nathaniel SMIBERT (1735-1756): *Portrait of Samson Occom.* Oil on canvas, 30¼ x 24¾ (76.8 x 62.8 cm). Bequest of the Honorable James Bowdoin III. 1813.4

✠John Singleton COPLEY (1738-1815): *Portrait of Thomas Flucker.* Oil on canvas, 28⅞ x 24 (73.3 x 60.9 cm). Bequest of Mrs. Lucy Flucker Knox Thatcher. 1855.1

Benjamin WEST (1738-1820): *Portrait of Sir Robert Stuart, Lord of the Admiralty.* Oil on canvas, 30 x 25 (76.2 x 63.5 cm). Gift of Mr. John H. Halford '07 and Mrs. Halford. 1955.6

Samuel KING (1749-1819): *Portrait of Elizabeth Bowdoin, Lady Temple.* Oil on canvas, 30⅞ x 26⅜ (78.5 x 67.0 cm). Bequest of Mrs. Sarah Bowdoin Dearborn. 1826.2

John JOHNSTON (ca. 1753-1818): *Portrait of Judge David Sewall.* Oil on canvas, 35⅜ x 28⅞ (89.8 x 73.4 cm). Museum collections. 1870.8

Gilbert STUART (1755-1828): *Portrait of Elizabeth Bowdoin, Lady Temple.* Oil on panel, 28 x 23 (71.1 x 58.4 cm). Gift of Mr. Robert Winthrop. 1966.89

Gilbert STUART (1755-1828): *Portrait of General Henry Alexander Scammell Dearborn.* Oil on panel, 27¼ x 22½ (69.2 x 57.2 cm). Bequest of Miss Mary J. E. Clapp. 1921.3

Gilbert STUART (1755-1828): *Portrait of James Bowdoin III.* Oil on canvas, 28½ x 24 (72.4 x 60.9 cm). Bequest of Mrs. Sarah Bowdoin Dearborn. 1870.6

Gilbert STUART (1755-1828): *Portrait of Mrs. Henry Alexander Scammell Dearborn.* Oil on panel, 27½ x 22½ (69.8 x 57.2 cm). Bequest of Miss Mary J. E. Clapp. 1921.4

Gilbert STUART (1755-1828): *Portrait of Mrs. James Bowdoin III.* Oil on canvas, 30 x 25⅛ (76.2 x 63.7 cm). Bequest of Mrs. Sarah Bowdoin Dearborn. 1870.7

Gilbert STUART (1755-1828): *Portrait of Mrs. Sarah Winthrop Sullivan.* Oil on panel, 28 x 23 (71.1 x 78.4 cm). Gift of Mr. Robert Winthrop. 1966.90

Gilbert STUART (1755-1828): *Portrait of Mrs. Thomas C. Upham.* Oil on canvas, 29½ x 24½ (74.9 x 62.2 cm). Gift of Mr. Edward D. Jameson. 1919.1

Gilbert STUART (1755-1828): *Portrait of President James Madison.* Oil on canvas, 48¼ x 39¾ (102.6 x 101.0 cm). Bequest of the Honorable James Bowdoin III. 1813.54

✠Gilbert STUART (1755-1828): *Portrait of Thomas Jefferson.* Oil on canvas, 48⅜ x 39¾ (122.9 x 101.0 cm). Bequest of the Honorable James Bowdoin III. 1813.55

John TRUMBULL (1756-1843): *Portrait of Professor Chauncey Allen Goodrich.* Oil on panel, 25⅛ x 20½ (63.8 x 52.2 cm). Gift of the Reverend Chauncey W. Goodrich h '15. 1954.29

Christian GULLAGER (1759-1826): *Portrait of James Bowdoin II.* Oil on panel, 11 x 8¾ (27.9 x 22.2 cm). Bequest of Mrs. Sarah Bowdoin Dearborn. 1894.2

Christian GULLAGER (1759-1826): *Portrait of James Bowdoin II.* Oil on panel, 10¾ x 8½ (27.3 x 21.6 cm). Gift of Miss Clara Bowdoin Winthrop. 1924.1

James EARL (1761-1796): *Portrait of a Man.* Oil on canvas, 30 x 25 (76.2 x 63.5 cm). Gift of Mr. John H. Halford '07 and Mrs. Halford. 1952.4

Joshua JOHNSTON (active 1796-1824): *Portrait of a Cleric.* Oil on canvas, 28 x 22 (71.1 x 55.8 cm). Hamlin Fund. 1963.490

Rembrandt PEALE (1778-1860): *Portrait of Mr. Morton.* Oil on canvas, 30¼ x 25 (76.8 x 63.5 cm). Gift of Mrs. John H. Halford in memory of John H. Halford '07. 1970.59

Rembrandt PEALE (1778-1860): *Portrait of Mrs. William Allen.* Oil on canvas, 26½ x 22 (67.3 x 55.8 cm). Gift of Mrs. Malleville McC. Howard. 1950.14

Rembrandt PEALE (1778-1860): *Portrait of William Allen.* Oil on canvas, 26 x 22 (66.0 x 55.8 cm). Gift of Mrs. Malleville McC. Howard. 1950.13

Thomas SULLY (1783-1872): *Portrait of Miss Elizabeth Anne Bates.* Oil on canvas, 30 x 25 (76.2 x 63.5 cm). Gift of Mr. John H. Halford '07 and Mrs. Halford. 1962.2

Thomas SULLY (1783-1872): *Portrait of John Vaughan.* Oil on canvas, 30 x 25 (76.2 x 63.5 cm). Gift of the Reverend Edward Abbott. 1908.27

Charles Bird KING (1785-1862): *Portrait of an Artist.* Oil on panel, 17½ x 13¾ (44.4 x 34.9 cm). Gift of Mr. Ross Levett. 1974.47

Thomas DOUGHTY (1793-1856): *The Fall Hunter.* Oil on canvas, 16¼ x 24⅛ (41.3 x 61.2 cm). Hamlin Fund. 1967.6

David Claypoole JOHNSTON (1799-1865): *Washington Allston in His Studio.* Oil on board, 10½ x 9 (26.6 x 22.9 cm). Hamlin Fund. 1965.14

John NEAGLE (1799-1865): *Portrait of Huizinger Messehert.* Oil on canvas, 16 x 12¾ (40.6 x 32.4 cm). Gift of Mr. John H. Halford '07 and Mrs. Halford. 1966.87

John Neagle (1799-1865): *Portrait of Mrs. Huizinger Messehert.* Oil on canvas, 16 x 12¾ (40.6 x 32.4 cm). Gift of Mr. John H. Halford '07 and Mrs. Halford. 1966.88

Unknown artist (19th century): *View of Bowdoin Campus.* Oil on canvas, 12 x 16⅛ (30.5 x 40.8 cm). Museum collections. T1977.22

Charles Codman (1800-1842): *Down East.* Oil on canvas, 24 x 35 (60.9 x 88.9 cm). Gift of Mrs. Marshall P. Slade. 1939.164

Fitz Hugh Lane (1804-1865): *Gloucester Harbor.* Oil on canvas, 24 x 36 (60.9 x 91.5 cm). Gift of Mrs. Hope P. Gillmor. 1971.42

John Greenleaf Cole (1806-1858): *Portrait of Mrs. Henry C. Buswell.* Oil on canvas, 29¼ x 24½ (74.3 x 62.2 cm). Gift of Mr. John H. Halford '07 and Mrs. Halford. 1965.32

William Matthew Prior (attributed) (1806-1873): *Portrait of Charles S. Nash.* Oil on canvas, 29 x 25½ (73.7 x 64.8 cm). Gift of Mr. Charles F. Adams '12. 1956.15

John H. Carmiencke (1810-1867): *Valley of the Catskills.* Oil on canvas, 16 x 24 (40.6 x 60.9 cm). Gift of Mr. Charles F. Adams '12. 1963.11

Thomas Badger (active 1836-1857): *Portrait of Joseph McKeen.* Oil on canvas, 26 x 21 (66.1 x 53.3 cm). Gift of the Misses E. F. and A. F. McKeen. 1895.7

Thomas Badger (active 1836-1857): *Portrait of William Allen.* Oil on canvas, 30 x 25 (76.2 x 63.5 cm). Gift of the children of William Allen. 1871.1

Joseph Ropes (1812-1885): *Mount Washington from North Conway.* Oil on canvas, 7 x 11 (17.8 x 27.9 cm). Gift of Mrs. John H. Halford in memory of John H. Halford '07. 1970.56

George P. A. Healy (1813-1864): *Portrait of Henry Wadsworth Longfellow.* Oil on canvas, 50 x 40 (127.0 x 101.6 cm). Bequest of Mrs. Annie Louise Cary Raymond. 1921.5

Daniel Huntington (1816-1906): *Coast Scene, Storm Passing Off.* Oil on canvas, 21¾ x 27 (55.3 x 68.6 cm). Florence C. Quinby Fund in memory of Henry Cole Quinby h '16. 1970.1

Benjamin Champney (1817-1907): *Carnations.* Oil on canvas, 14 x 10 (35.5 x 25.4 cm). Hamlin Fund. 1974.35

James Hope (1818-1892): *Waterfall in the Mountains.* Oil on canvas, 27 x 38 (68.6 x 96.5 cm). Gift of Miss Susan Dwight Bliss. 1948.16

James Hamilton (1819-1878): *Sunset at the Seacoast.* Oil on canvas, 20 x 30 (50.8 x 76.2 cm). Florence C. Quinby Fund in memory of Henry Cole Quinby h '16. 1970.16

✠Martin Johnson Heade (1819-1904): *Newburyport Marshes: Passing*

Storm. Oil on canvas, 15 x 30 (38.1 x 76.2 cm). Museum purchase with the aid of the Sylvia E. Ross Fund. 1964.45

Worthington Whittredge (1820-1910): *Second Beach, Newport*. Oil on canvas, 14¾ x 21¾ (37.5 x 55.2 cm). Florence C. Quinby Fund in memory of Henry Cole Quinby h '16. 1969.81

John G. Brown (active 1821-1858): *Bowdoin Campus*. Oil on canvas, 29 x 37 (73.6 x 94.0 cm). Gift of Mr. Harold L. Berry '01. 1961.82

William M. Hart (1823-1894): *Steer Study*. Oil on canvas, 9¼ x 12¼ (23.5 x 31.2 cm). Hamlin Fund. 1970.44

Eastman Johnson (1824-1906): *Babes in the Woods*. Oil on canvas, 36 x 30¼ (91.4 x 76.8 cm). Gift of the Honorable Percival P. Baxter 1898. 1962.31

Eastman Johnson (1824-1906): *Portrait of Daniel B. Fayerweather*. Oil on canvas, 42 x 33 (106.6 x 83.8 cm). Museum collections. 1898.22

Eastman Johnson (1824-1906): *Portrait of John Stuart Kennedy*. Oil on canvas, 24 x 20 (60.9 x 50.8 cm). Museum purchase. 1910.02

George Inness (1825-1894): *Montclair, New Jersey*. Oil on canvas, 16 x 24 (40.6 x 60.9 cm). Hamlin Fund. 1968.15

John Bunyan Bristol (1826-1909): *An Autumn Afternoon near Bolton, Lake George*. Oil on canvas, 14 x 23 (35.5 x 58.4 cm). Florence C. Quinby Fund in memory of Henry Cole Quinby h '16. 1970.23

John Rollen Tilton (1828-1888): *Temple, Aegina*. Oil on canvas, 30¾ x 48 (78.0 x 121.9 cm). Gift of the Misses Harriet and Sophia Walker. 1904.15

Jervis McEntee (1828-1891): *Evening Landscape, Late Autumn*. Oil on canvas, 18⅛ x 14⅛ (46.3 x 35.8 cm). Florence C. Quinby Fund in memory of Henry Cole Quinby h '16. 1970.53

Thomas Hill (1829-1908): *New Hampshire Mountain Scene*. Oil on canvas, 20 x 30 (50.8 x 76.2 cm). Florence C. Quinby Fund in memory of Henry Cole Quinby h '16. 1970.2

Albert Bierstadt (1830-1902): *Cloud Study (Moonlight)*. Oil on paper, 12⅝ x 9¼ (32.0 x 23.5 cm). Florence C. Quinby Fund in memory of Henry Cole Quinby h '16. 1969.68

Albert Bierstadt (1830-1902): *The Mountain Pool*. Oil on paper, 13 x 12⅝ (33.0 x 32.1 cm). Gift of Mr. Michael H. Strater. 1979.82

Harrison Brown (1831-1915): *Country Road*. Oil on canvas, 13¼ x 16¼ (33.7 x 41.3 cm). Hamlin Fund. 1964.35

Harrison Brown (1831-1915): *Portland Harbor*. Oil on canvas, 24¾ x 40 (62.8 x 101.6 cm). Bequest of Mr. William S. Linnell '07. 1968.20

Harrison Brown (1831-1915): *Woodland Pool.* Oil on cardboard, $11\frac{1}{4}$ x $9\frac{1}{2}$ (28.7 x 24.2 cm). Hamlin Fund. 1965.1

Hermann Herzog (1832-1932): *View of Lake Luzerne opposite Brunnen.* Oil on board, 11 x 15 (27.9 x 38.1 cm). Florence C. Quinby Fund in memory of Henry Cole Quinby h '16. 1970.21

William Trost Richards (1833-1905): *In the Woods.* Oil on canvas, $15\frac{5}{8}$ x 20 (39.7 x 50.8 cm). Gift of the Misses Mary T. and Jane Mason. 1955.10

William Stanley Haseltine (1835-1900): *Coast of New England.* Oil on canvas, 15 x 23 (38.1 x 58.4 cm). Gift of Mrs. Helen Haseltine Plowden. 1952.1

William Stanley Haseltine (1835-1900): *Coastal Cliffs.* Oil on canvas, $32\frac{1}{4}$ x $26\frac{1}{4}$ (81.9 x 66.7 cm). Gift of Mrs. Estelle K. Butler in memory of her husband, Henry F. Butler. 1964.37

John La Farge (1835-1910): *Athens.* Oil on canvas, 108 x 240 (276.9 x 615.4 cm). Gift of the Misses Harriet and Sophia Walker. 1893.35

Alexander Helwig Wyant (1836-1892): *A Clearing in the Woods.* Oil on canvas, 20 x 16 (50.8 x 40.6 cm). Gift of Colonel Francis M. Weld. 1946.53

Alexander Helwig Wyant (1836-1892): *Landscape.* Oil on canvas, 14 x 20 (35.6 x 50.8 cm). Gift of Mrs. John H. Halford in memory of Mr. John H. Halford '07. 1970.55

Elihu Vedder (1836-1923): *Rome.* Oil on canvas, 144 x 288 (369.0 x 731.5 cm). Gift of the Misses Harriet and Sophia Walker. 1893.37

Joseph Foxcroft Cole (1837-1892): *The Annisquam River, near Gloucester, Massachusetts.* Oil on canvas, 34 x 47 (86.4 x 119.4 cm). Gift of the Misses Harriet and Sophia Walker. 1894.8

Joseph Foxcroft Cole (1837-1892): *Landscape.* Oil on panel, $13\frac{1}{2}$ x $24\frac{1}{2}$ (34.3 x 62.2 cm). Gift of Mrs. Martha B. Angell. 1917.1

Edmund Darch Lewis (1837-1910): *Lake George.* Oil on canvas, 30 x 50 (76.2 x 127.0 cm). Florence C. Quinby Fund in memory of Henry Cole Quinby h '16. 1970.32

William Keith (1839-1911): *Landscape.* Oil on canvas, 30 x 50 (76.2 x 127.0 cm). Gift of Mr. S. A. DeSantis. 1973.59

Edwin Deakin (1840-1925): *California Landscape.* Oil on canvas, 30 x 25 (76.2 x 63.5 cm). Gift of Mr. and Mrs. Philmon G. Hatch. 1964.1

William Merritt Chase (1849-1916): *Portrait of the Art Dealer, Otto Fleischmann.* Oil on canvas, 26 x 21 (66.1 x 53.3 cm). Gift of Dr. Max Hirshler. 1953.41

William Merritt Chase (1849-1916): *Portrait of William John Curtis.* Oil on canvas, 59½ x 39½ (151.1 x 100.4 cm). Gift of Mrs. William J. Curtis. 1927.28

✠Thomas Eakins (1849-1916): *Portrait of A. Bryan Wall.* Oil on canvas, 23 x 19½ (58.4 x 49.5 cm). Hamlin Fund. 1962.16

Abbott Thayer (1849-1921): *Florence.* Oil on canvas, 144 x 288 (369.0 x 731.5 cm). Gift of the Misses Harriet and Sophia Walker. 1893.36

John Francis Murphy (1853-1921): *Stormy Twilight.* Oil on canvas, 12 x 19 (30.5 x 48.2 cm). Gift of Mrs. Arthur Poillon. 1949.18

John Frederick Peto (1854-1907): *Mug, Pipe, and Biscuits.* Oil on board, 6 x 9 (15.2 x 22.8 cm). Hamlin Fund. 1975.3

Henry Pember Smith (1854-1907): *A Country Landscape.* Oil on canvas, 12 x 13 (30.4 x 33.0 cm). Florence C. Quinby Fund in memory of Henry Cole Quinby h '16. 1970.22

Kenyon Cox (1856-1919): *Venice.* Oil on canvas, 144 x 288 (369.0 x 731.5 cm). Gift of the Misses Harriet and Sophia Walker. 1893.38

Kenyon Cox (1856-1919): *Venice.* Oil on canvas, 29¾ x 61 (75.6 x 154.9 cm). Gift of Colonel Leonard Cox, Mrs. Caroline Cox Lansing, and Mr. Allyn Cox. 1959.3.1

Howard Russell Butler (1856-1937): *The Coast Patrol.* Oil on canvas, 31 x 39 (78.8 x 99.1 cm). Gift of Mr. Howard Russell Butler, Jr. 1968.116

Walter Griffin (1861-1935): *Fishing Boats, Brittany, France.* Oil on canvas, 11½ x 29½ (29.2 x 75.0 cm). Gift of Mrs. George J. Johnston. 1975.29

Frederick J. Waugh (1861-1940): *The Cove.* Oil on board, 12 x 14 (30.4 x 35.5 cm). Gift of Mr. and Mrs. Stuart P. Feld. 1974.51

Frederick J. Waugh (1861-1940): *Rocky Shore.* Oil on masonite, 30¼ x 36¼ (76.9 x 92.1 cm). Bequest of Mr. Frederick E. Hasler h '43. 1974.3

Anson Kent Cross (1862-1944): *Across Boothbay Harbor.* Oil on canvas, 17 x 24½ (43.2 x 62.0 cm). Gift of Mrs. Anson Kent Cross. 1961.79

Anson Kent Cross (1862-1944): *Portrait of Mrs. Robert Vonnoh.* Oil on canvas, 17 x 21 (43.2 x 53.3 cm). Gift of Mrs. Anson Kent Cross. 1948.35

Louis Michel Eilshemius (1864-1941): *The Bather.* Oil on composition board, 22 x 16¾ (55.8 x 42.5 cm). Gift of Mr. James N. Rosenberg. 1946.56

Louis Michel Eilshemius (1864-1941): *The Gulls.* Oil on board, 19⅞ x 10⅝ (50.5 x 27.0 cm). Gift of Mr. James N. Rosenberg. 1948.3

Robert Henri (1865-1929): *Coal Breaker.* Oil on canvas, 26 x 32 (66.1 x 81.2 cm). Hamlin Fund. 1970.48

William Glackens (1870-1938): *Captain's Pier.* Oil on canvas, 25 x 30 (63.5 x 76.2 cm). Gift of Mr. Stephen M. Etnier h '69. 1957.127

John Sloan (1871-1951): *Alert Nude.* Oil on canvas, 24 x 19⅞ (61.0 x 50.5 cm). Bequest of Mr. George Otis Hamlin. 1961.61

John Sloan (1871-1951): *Blonde Nude.* Oil on canvas, 20 x 24 (50.8 x 61.0 cm). Bequest of Mr. George Otis Hamlin. 1961.53

John Sloan (1871-1951): *Buttes, New Mexico (Coyote Mesa).* Oil on canvas, 26⅛ x 32 (66.2 x 81.2 cm). Bequest of Mr. George Otis Hamlin. 1961.67

John Sloan (1871-1951): *Clouds and Sunlight.* Oil on canvas, 24 x 30 (61.0 x 76.2 cm). Bequest of Mr. George Otis Hamlin. 1961.66

John Sloan (1871-1951): *Clouds over Great South Mountain.* Oil on canvas, 20 x 24 (50.8 x 61.0 cm). Bequest of Mr. George Otis Hamlin. 1961.59

John Sloan (1871-1951): *The Cot.* Oil on canvas, 36¼ x 30 (92.1 x 76.2 cm). Bequest of Mr. George Otis Hamlin. 1961.62

John Sloan (1871-1951): *Cottage on a Stormy Night.* Oil on canvas, 18 x 22 (45.7 x 55.8 cm). Bequest of Mr. George Otis Hamlin. 1961.58

John Sloan (1871-1951): *Deep Blue Sea.* Oil on canvas, 19¾ x 23⅞ (50.2 x 60.6 cm). Bequest of Mr. George Otis Hamlin. 1961.57

John Sloan (1871-1951): *Flats at Low Tide.* Oil on canvas, 24 x 19⅞ (61.0 x 50.5 cm). Bequest of Mr. George Otis Hamlin. 1961.64

John Sloan (1871-1951): *Island and Wistaria.* Oil on canvas, 19⅞ x 23⅞ (50.5 x 60.6 cm). Bequest of Mr. George Otis Hamlin. 1961.55

John Sloan (1871-1951): *Near Sunset, Gloucester.* Oil on canvas, 20 x 24 (50.8 x 61.0 cm). Bequest of Mr. George Otis Hamlin. 1961.52

John Sloan (1871-1951): *Pig-Pen-Sylvania.* Oil on canvas, 20 x 23¾ (50.8 x 60.3 cm). Bequest of Mr. George Otis Hamlin. 1961.51

John Sloan (1871-1951): *Purple Rocks and Green Sea.* Oil on canvas, 20 x 24 (50.8 x 61.0 cm). Bequest of Mr. George Otis Hamlin. 1961.68

John Sloan (1871-1951): *The Road to Cienaga.* Oil on canvas, 18 x 22 (45.7 x 55.8 cm). Bequest of Mr. George Otis Hamlin. 1961.60

John Sloan (1871-1951): *Rosette.* Oil on canvas, 26 x 32 (66.0 x 81.2 cm). Bequest of Mr. George Otis Hamlin. 1961.65

John Sloan (1871-1951): *Signals.* Oil on canvas, 19⅞ x 24 (50.5 x 61.0 cm). Bequest of Mr. George Otis Hamlin. 1961.56

⊞John Sloan (1871-1951): *Sunday Afternoon in Union Square.* Oil on canvas, 26¼ x 32¼ (66.7 x 81.9 cm). Bequest of Mr. George Otis Hamlin. 1961.63

John Sloan (1871-1951): *White Lace Cap.* Oil on canvas, 23⅞ x 20 (60.6 x 50.8 cm). Bequest of Mr. George Otis Hamlin. 1961.54

John Sloan (1871-1951): *A Window on the Street.* Oil on canvas, 26 x 32 (66.0 x 81.2 cm). Bequest of Mr. George Otis Hamlin. 1961.50

Eugene Higgins (1874-1958): *Homeward Bound.* Oil on panel, 16 x 12 (40.7 x 30.5 cm). Florence C. Quinby Fund in memory of Henry Cole Quinby h '16. 1970.24

Ernest Haskell (1876-1925): *Fruit Shop, Paris.* Oil on panel, 6¹¹⁄₁₆ x 4³⁄₁₆ (17.0 x 10.7 cm). Gift of Mrs. Josephine Aldridge in memory of Mrs. Ernest Haskell, Sr. 1976.14.4

Ernest Haskell (1876-1925): *Lady with a Hat.* Oil on canvas, 10¼ x 9 (26.0 x 22.8 cm). Gift of Mrs. Josephine Aldridge in memory of Mrs. Ernest Haskell, Sr. 1976.8

Marsden Hartley (1877-1943): *Maine Coast at Vinalhaven.* Oil on academy board, 28¼ x 22¼ (71.7 x 56.5 cm). Gift of Mrs. Charles Philip Kuntz. 1950.8

Rockwell Kent (1882-1971): *Asgaard—Cloud Shadows.* Oil on canvas, 28 x 38 (71.1 x 96.5 cm). Museum purchase with funds donated anonymously. 1971.78

Rockwell Kent (1882-1971): *Greenland People, Dogs, and Mountains.* Oil on canvas, 28 x 48¼ (71.2 x 122.6 cm). Museum purchase with funds donated anonymously. 1971.77

Rockwell Kent (1882-1971): *Into the Sun.* Oil on canvas, 28 x 44½ (71.2 x 113.1 cm). Gift of Mrs. Charles F. Chillingworth. 1957.126

Rockwell Kent (1882-1971): *Landscape, Ireland.* Oil on panel, 15⅞ x 19¾ (40.3 x 50.2 cm). Museum purchase with funds donated anonymously. 1971.76

Rockwell Kent (1882-1971): *Sun, Manana, Monhegan.* Oil on canvas, 20 x 24 (50.8 x 61.0 cm). Museum purchase with funds donated anonymously. 1971.73

Guy Pène Du Bois (1884-1958): *Wooden Soldier.* Oil on board, 25 x 20 (63.5 x 50.8 cm). Gift of Mr. Walter K. Gutman '24. 1966.37

Waldo Peirce (1884-1970): *Johnny and Mike.* Oil on canvas, 43 x 31 (109.2 x 78.7 cm). Gift of the artist. 1959.57

Leon Kroll (1884-1974): *Monhegan Landscape.* Oil on panel, 8¾ x 10¾ (22.2 x 27.3 cm). Hamlin Fund. 1970.79

Marguerite Zorach (1887-1968): *The Family Evening.* Oil on canvas, 34 x 44 (86.3 x 111.1 cm). Gift of Mrs. Dahlov Ipcar and Mr. Tessim Zorach. 1979.77

Henry Strater (b. 1896): *The Ranch on Beaver Creek.* Oil on canvas, 30 x 40 (76.2 x 101.6 cm). Gift of the artist. 1953.7

Reginald Marsh (1898-1954): *Untitled* (r). Egg tempera on board. *Untitled* (v). Egg tempera and oil wash on board, 12 x 9 (30.4 x 22.8 cm). Bequest of Mrs. Felicia Meyer Marsh. 1979.32a & b

Raphael Soyer (b. 1899): *Girl on Sofa.* Oil on canvas, 26 x 32 (66.0 x 81.2 cm). Gift of Mr. Stephen M. Etnier h '69. 1956.1

Jack Tworkov (b. 1900): *Untitled.* Oil on canvas, 36 x 42 (91.5 x 106.7 cm). Gift of Mr. Walter K. Gutman '24. 1964.59

Jack Tworkov (b. 1900): *Untitled.* Oil on canvas, 19 x 22 (48.2 x 55.8 cm). Gift of Mr. Walter K. Gutman '24. 1964.60

Jack Tworkov (b. 1900): *Untitled.* Oil on masonite, 28 x 26 (71.1 x 66.0 cm). Gift of Mr. Walter K. Gutman '24. 1964.62

Stephen Etnier h '69 (b. 1903): *Old Brunswick Airport.* Oil on canvas, 24 x 35 (61.0 x 88.9 cm). Gift of Mr. John D. MacDonald. 1960.61

Walter K. Gutman '24 (b. 1903): *Strong Woman.* Oil on canvas, 18 x 14 (45.7 x 40.6 cm). Gift of the artist. 1965.45

Calvert Coggeshall (b. 1907): *Horizontal.* Oil on canvas, 45⅛ x 65⅛ (114.6 x 165.3 cm). Anonymous gift. 1977.16

John Muench (b. 1914): *Dark Harbor.* Oil on masonite, 22 x 42 (55.9 x 106.7 cm). Gift of the artist. 1961.1

John Grillo (b. 1917): *Untitled.* Oil on canvas, 26½ x 30¾ (67.3 x 78.1 cm). Gift of Mr. Walter K. Gutman '24. 1965.35

Seymour Remenick (b. 1923): *East River Drive, Philadelphia.* Oil on canvas, 16 x 18 (40.6 x 45.7 cm). Gift of Mr. Samuel Pesin. 1960.87

Alex Katz (b. 1927): *Edwin Denby.* Oil on masonite, 24 x 24 (61.0 x 61.0 cm). Gift of Mr. Walter K. Gutman '24. 1966.30

Alex Katz (b. 1927): *Landscape.* Oil on board, 13½ x 14½ (34.2 x 36.8 cm). Gift of Mr. Walter K. Gutman '24. 1965.43

Donald Hugo Stoltenberg (b. 1927): *Interior with Glass Dome.* Oil on canvas, 30 x 20 (76.2 x 50.8 cm). Gift of Mr. and Mrs. John D. MacDonald. 1977.9

Lennart Anderson (b. 1928): *Still Life with Earthenware Vessel.* Oil on canvas, 60 x 50 (152.4 x 127.0 cm). Gift of the American

Academy of Arts and Letters, through the Childe Hassam Fund. 1974.6

Laurence SISSON (b. 1928): *Monhegan, A.M.* Oil on canvas, 24 x 36 (61.0 x 91.5 cm). Gift of the Boston Society of Independent Artists. 1952.5

Alan GUSSOW (b. 1931): *Delphinium.* Oil on canvas, $24\frac{1}{8}$ x 26 (61.3 x 66.0 cm). Hamlin Fund. 1975.17

Sculpture

✠Unknown artist (ca. 1800): *Eagle.* Wood, $31\frac{1}{8}$ x $27\frac{13}{16}$ x 15 (79.1 x 70.7 x 38.1 cm). Museum purchase with the aid of the Helen Johnson Chase Fund. 1965.24

Thomas CRAWFORD (1814-1857): *Portrait of Professor George W. Greene.* Plaster, $27\frac{5}{8}$ x $21\frac{1}{16}$ x $8\frac{15}{16}$ (70.2 x 53.5 x 22.8 cm). Gift of Mr. Henry Wadsworth Longfellow 1825. 1879.1

Erastus Dow PALMER (1817-1904): *Portrait of a Woman.* Marble, 21 x $16\frac{3}{8}$ x $11\frac{5}{16}$ (53.4 x 41.6 x 28.7 cm). Hamlin Fund. 1971.19

John A. JACKSON (1825-1879): *Portrait of General Joshua Chamberlain.* Plaster, $28\frac{3}{4}$ x 23 x $11\frac{1}{2}$ (73.0 x 58.4 x 29.2 cm). Gift of Miss Rosamond Allen. 1973.13

✠Augustus SAINT-GAUDENS (1848-1907): *Robert Louis Stevenson.* Bronze, $\frac{3}{16}$ x $17\frac{3}{4}$ (diam.) (0.5 x 45.0 cm). Gift of the Misses Harriet and Sophia Walker. 1904.29

Franklin SIMMONS (1842-1913): *Portrait of a Man.* Marble, $29\frac{1}{4}$ x $19\frac{3}{16}$ x $11\frac{5}{8}$ (74.3 x 48.8 x 29.5 cm). Sylvia E. Ross Fund. 1966.29

Longworth POWERS (d. 1904): *Priscilla.* Marble, $18\frac{13}{16}$ x $12\frac{11}{16}$ x $6\frac{5}{8}$ (47.8 x 32.3 x 16.9 cm). Bequest of the Honorable DeAlva S. Alexander 1870 and Mrs. Alexander. 1926.4

✠Daniel Chester FRENCH (1850-1931): *Portrait of Theophilus Wheeler Walker.* Bronze, 53 x $29\frac{1}{2}$ x $3\frac{1}{4}$ (134.6 x 74.9 x 8.2 cm). Gift of the Misses Harriet and Sophia Walker. 1894.148

William Ordway PARTRIDGE (1861-1930): *Portrait of Alfred, Lord Tennyson.* Bronze, $20\frac{5}{8}$ x 13 x $8\frac{9}{16}$ (52.4 x 33.0 x 21.7 cm). Museum purchase. 1973.19

William Ordway PARTRIDGE (1861-1930): *Portrait of Rear Admiral Robert E. Peary.* Bronze, $27\frac{3}{4}$ x 25 x $16\frac{1}{2}$ (70.5 x 63.5 x 41.9 cm). Museum collections. 1925.17

Frederick MacMONNIES (1863-1937): *Portrait of Max Gibson Newman.* Plaster, $13\frac{5}{8}$ x $8\frac{3}{4}$ x $11\frac{1}{8}$ (34.6 x 22.2 x 28.3 cm). Gift of Mr. Paul J. Newman '09. 1968.74

Paul Wayland BARTLETT (1865-1925): *Head of a Kid.* Bronze, $6\frac{3}{4}$ x

$8\frac{1}{16}$ x $6\frac{5}{8}$ (17.2 x 20.4 x 16.9 cm). Gift of Mr. Arthur T. Parker 1876 in memory of Mr. Arlo Bates 1876. 1937.7

Paul Wayland BARTLETT (1865-1925): *Nude.* Bronze, $19\frac{3}{8}$ x $6\frac{13}{16}$ x $4\frac{7}{8}$ (49.2 x 17.3 x 12.3 cm). Gift of Mr. Walter Griffin. 1932.9.

Mabel CONKLING (1871-1966): *Portrait of Frederick MacMonnies.* Bronze, $14\frac{9}{16}$ x $12\frac{1}{4}$ x $1\frac{5}{16}$ (37.1 x 31.2 x 3.3 cm). Hamlin Fund. 1964.46

Anna Hyatt HUNTINGTON (1876-1973): *White Horses of the Sea.* Bronze, $18\frac{5}{8}$ x $24\frac{3}{8}$ x $20\frac{3}{8}$ (47.4 x 61.9 x 51.7 cm). Gift of the artist. 1938.10

Malvina HOFFMAN (1887-1966): *Portrait of Mme. Marguerite Your-cenar.* Plaster, 15 x $8\frac{3}{8}$ x $9\frac{7}{8}$ (38.1 x 21.3 x 25.1 cm). Gift of Mme. Marguerite Yourcenar h '68. 1980.7

William ZORACH h '58 (1887-1966): *The Lineman.* Granite, $50\frac{1}{2}$ x $23\frac{1}{2}$ x $24\frac{1}{2}$ (128.3 x 59.7 x 62.2 cm). Gift of the artist. 1960.50

⌘William ZORACH h '58 (1887-1966): *Spirit of the Dance.* Bronze, 26 x $16\frac{1}{8}$ x $10\frac{1}{4}$ (66.0 x 41.0 x 26.0 cm). Museum purchase. 1953.4

⌘Alexander CALDER (1898-1976): *Red Fossils.* Steel and wire, 48 x 70 (121.9 x 177.8 cm). Gift of the family and friends of Charles Baird Price III '74. 1973.6

William MUIR (1902-1964): *Growth.* Redwood, $29\frac{5}{8}$ x $4\frac{3}{16}$ x $4\frac{1}{4}$ (75.2 x 10.6 x 10.8 cm). Museum purchase. 1955.12

Arnold BURCHESS (b. 1912): *Chimera #7.* Silicon bronze, $6\frac{1}{2}$ x $10\frac{5}{16}$ x $2\frac{5}{8}$ (16.5 x 26.2 x 6.7 cm). Gift of the artist. 1974.56

Leonard BASKIN (b. 1922): *Bouquet.* Bronze, $14\frac{1}{8}$ x $4\frac{9}{16}$ x $\frac{5}{16}$ (36.0 x 11.6 x 0.8 cm). Gift of the artist. 1966.99

Leonard BASKIN (b. 1922): *Dead Man.* Bronze, $16\frac{7}{16}$ x $23\frac{11}{16}$ x $\frac{5}{8}$ (41.8 x 60.1 x 1.6 cm). Gift of Mr. Marvin S. Sadik h '78. 1974.53

Leonard BASKIN (b. 1922): *Imaginary Flowers.* Bronze, $8\frac{3}{8}$ (diam.) x $\frac{1}{4}$ (21.3 x 0.6 cm). Gift of the artist. 1966.97

Leonard BASKIN (b. 1922): *Small Thistle.* Bronze, $13\frac{9}{16}$ x 5 x $\frac{11}{16}$ (34.4 x 12.7 x 1.7 cm). Gift of the artist. 1966.98.

Leonard BASKIN (b. 1922): *Thistle.* Bronze, $21\frac{15}{16}$ x $15\frac{1}{8}$ x $\frac{7}{8}$ (55.7 x 38.4 x 2.3 cm). Gift of the artist. 1963.240

Marianna PINEDA (b. 1925): *The Visitation.* Bronze, $7\frac{13}{16}$ x $10\frac{5}{8}$ x $2\frac{7}{8}$ (19.8 x 27.0 x 7.3 cm). Museum purchase. 1960.6

Charles WELLS (b. 1935): *Head.* Marble, $10\frac{3}{4}$ x $7\frac{1}{8}$ x $8\frac{1}{16}$ (27.3 x 18.3 x 20.6 cm). Florence C. Quinby Fund in memory of Henry Cole Quinby h '16. 1969.94

Furniture

Only primary woods are listed.

✠School of William Searle (1634-1667)/Thomas Dennis (active 1667-1706): *Armchair.* Oak, 48½ x 25½ x 15¼ (123.2 x 64.8 x 38.8 cm). Gift of Mr. E. Wilder Farley 1836. 1872.1

Connecticut (1710-1780): *Side Chair.* Maple, 44½ x 19½ x 14½ (113.0 x 49.5 x 36.3 cm). Museum purchase. 1973.8

Massachusetts (1730-1760): *Side Chair.* Walnut, 39 x 21¼ x 17¼ (99.1 x 54.0 x 43.8 cm). Gift of Mr. Henry Gilman 1897. 1968.115

Massachusetts or Rhode Island (1740-1765): *Chest of Drawers.* Walnut, 30 x 37 x 21⅜ (76.2 x 94.0 x 54.3 cm). Gift of Mr. John H. Halford '07 and Mrs. Halford. 1964.39

Massachusetts (ca. 1750): *High Chest of Drawers.* Mahogany, 87 x 40¼ x 22½ (121.0 x 102.3 x 57.1 cm). Museum collections. 1964.28

New England (1760-1780): *Desk.* Mahogany, 44½ x 42¹¹⁄₁₆ x 12¼ (113.0 x 108.5 x 59.3 cm). Bequest of Mrs. Edith L. K. Sills h '52, given through the generosity of her sister, Mrs. Eleanor R. Campbell. 1979.61

American (1760-1790): *Looking Glass.* Mahogany, 34 x 19⅝ x ⅞ (86.4 x 49.9 x 2.2 cm). Bequest of Mrs. Sylvia E. Ross. 1963.27

✠Pennsylvania (ca. 1765-1780): *Gaming Table.* Mahogany and oak, 20 x 34¾ x 16½ (50.8 x 88.3 x 41.9 cm). Gift of Mr. John H. Halford '07 and Mrs. Halford. 1964.38

Pennsylvania (1765-1790): *Desk and Bookcase.* Walnut, 101½ x 42½ x 22⅛ (157.8 x 108.0 x 56.2 cm). Gift of Mrs. Charles F. Parker, Jr. 1966.17

Massachusetts (ca. 1770): *Desk.* Mahogany, 42⅞ x 45¼ x 22 (109.9 x 114.9 x 55.9 cm). Gift of the Misses Harriet and Sophia Walker. 1897.2

Pennsylvania (ca. 1770): *Side Chairs.* Mahogany, 40½ x 22⅜ x 17¾ (102.9 x 56.8 x 45.1 cm). Gift of Mr. John H. Halford, Jr. '38. 1966.57a & b

American (ca. 1790): *Card Table.* Mahogany, 29 x 36 x 16¾ (73.7 x 91.4 x 42.6 cm). Bequest of Mrs. Sylvia E. Ross. 1963.15

American (1790-1815): *Card Table.* Mahogany, 29¼ x 36⅛ x 17½ (74.3 x 91.8 x 44.5 cm). Bequest of Dr. Bernard Samuels. 1960.40

American (1790-1820): *Chest of Drawers.* Mahogany, 33½ x 38⅞ x 21⅛ (85.1 x 98.8 x 53.7 cm). Gift of the Honorable Percival P. Baxter 1898. 1962.32

Massachusetts (1795-1815): *Card Table.* Mahogany, 29¼ x 35¾ x

17½ (74.3 x 90.8 x 44.5 cm). Bequest of Mrs. Sylvia E. Ross. 1963.16

Massachusetts (1800-1825): *Tambour Desk.* Mahogany, 48⅛ x 40½ x 20⅛ (122.3 x 102.9 x 51.1 cm). Bequest of Mrs. Sylvia E. Ross. 1963.14

American (1800-1830): *Armchair.* Mahogany, 42¼ x 25⅝ x 21 (107.4 x 65.1 x 53.5 cm). Gift of Miss Edith J. Boardman. 1935.19

American (1815-1830): *Looking Glass.* Pine, 45¾ x 28¼ x 5¼ (116.3 x 71.7 x 13.3 cm). Museum collections. 1974.5

American (1820-1835): *Card Table.* Mahogany, 29 x 35½ x 18 (73.6 x 90.2 x 45.7 cm). Bequest of Miss Edith J. Boardman. 1936.11

American (1820-1840): *Sofa.* Mahogany, 35 x 61¾ x 22⅛ (88.9 x 156.8 x 56.2 cm). Gift of Miss Edith J. Boardman. 1935.41

American (1825-1840): *Pier Table.* Pine, 36¾ x 42 x 18 (93.4 x 106.7 x 45.7 cm). Bequest of Mr. Frederick C. Lee 1900. 1964.12

American (ca. 1830): *Side Chair.* Maple, 31½ x 19⅛ x 15¼ (80.0 x 48.6 x 38.7 cm). Bequest of Miss Mabel S. Davies. 1947.22

John JELLIFF (1813-1893), New Jersey: *Arm Chair.* Rosewood, 36½ x 26¼ x 25 (92.7 x 66.7 x 63.5 cm). Hamlin Fund. 1975.19

✠Alexander ROUX (ca. 1813-1886): *Cabinet.* Rosewood, maple, metal, porcelain, and mirrors, 52½ x 51½ x 19½ (133.4 x 130.8 x 49.5 cm). Hamlin Fund. 1974.42

American (ca. 1840): *Armchair.* Mahogany, 34½ x 23¾ x 22 (87.6 x 60.3 x 56.0 cm). Gift of the Misses Harriet and Sophia Walker. 1896.6

American (ca. 1870): *Table.* Mahogany, 29 x 29 x 38 (73.6 x 73.6 x 96.5 cm). Hamlin Fund. 1974.50

Christian HERTER (1840-1883), New York: *Side Chair.* Rosewood, 34 x 16⅞ x 18¾ (86.9 x 42.9 x 47.6 cm). Hamlin Fund. 1975.8

Gustave STICKLEY (1857-1942), New York: *Side Chair.* Oak, 35¾ x 17 x 18¾ (90.8 x 43.2 x 47.6 cm). Hamlin Fund. 1974.43

Silver

John POTWINE (1698-1792), Massachusetts: *Tankard.* Silver, 7³⁄₁₆ x 6¹¹⁄₁₆ (18.3 x 17.0 cm). Gift of Mrs. Nina Lennox in memory of Mr. Edmund Bridge Bowman 1823. 1945.60

Thomas TOWNSEND (1701-1777), Massachusetts: *Tankard.* Silver, 7¹⁵⁄₁₆ x 7¼ (20.1 x 18.4 cm). Gift of Mr. Henry Brewer Quinby 1869 in memory of Mr. Henry Cole Quinby h '16. 1923.108

✠Paul REVERE (1735-1818): *Punch Ladle.* Silver and wood, 13⅝ x 4 x

1⅛ (34.6 x 10.2 x 2.9 cm). Gift of Mrs. Clara Bowdoin Winthrop. 1943.3.3

David MOSELEY (1753-1812), Massachusetts: *Punch Ladle*. Silver, 14⅜ x 4½ (diam.) (36.5 x 11.4 cm). Bequest of Mrs. Frances Erving Weston. 1912.4.2

Ebenezer MOULTON (1768-1824), Massachusetts: *Ladles*. Silver, 6$\frac{3}{16}$ x 2⅛ (diam.) (17.3 x 5.4 cm). Gift of Miss Clara Bowdoin Winthrop. 1956.10.1-.2

Eleazer WYER (1768-1848), Maine: *Teaspoons*. Silver, 5$\frac{5}{16}$ x 1½ (diam.) (13.5 x 3.8 cm). Gift of Mrs. Mary Prentiss Ingraham Davies, Daniel Cony Memorial Collection. 1928.19.4-.5

Enoch MOULTON (1780-1815), Maine: *Salt Spoons*. Silver, 4$\frac{5}{16}$ x 1 (diam.) (11.0 x 2.5 cm). Gift of Mrs. Mary Prentiss Ingraham Davies, Daniel Cony Memorial Collection. 1928.19.2-.3

Charles ALDIS (active 1814 and after), Massachusetts: *Tea Service*. Silver; teapot 8$\frac{13}{16}$ x 11⅞ (22.4 x 30.2 cm); sugar bowl 7$\frac{13}{16}$ x 8$\frac{15}{16}$ (19.8 x 22.7 cm); cream pitcher 7⅛ x 6$\frac{1}{16}$ (18.1 x 15.4 cm); waste bowl 5$\frac{13}{16}$ x 5$\frac{9}{16}$ (14.8 x 14.1 cm). Bequest of Mr. Harry Peter Faulkner '15. 1961.9.1-.4

William LADD (active 1830 and after). New York: *Salver*. Silver, ⅞ x 9⅜ (diam.) (2.3 x 23.9 cm). Gift of Mr. Edward H. Tevriz '26. 1962.37

THE WINSLOW HOMER COLLECTION

The Winslow Homer Collection is comprised of three main groups acquired from a variety of sources: a selection of Homer's paintings, a collection of memorabilia pertaining to his career, and a comprehensive set of examples of his work in the graphic arts.

Appropriately, the first painting was contributed from the private collection of the Walker sisters. Entitled *The End of the Hunt,* it was given in 1894, the opening date of the Walker Art Building. The next important addition came in 1933 in the form of the watercolor *Marine,* donated by the Honorable Augustus F. Moulton 1873, author of *Old Prout's Neck* and friend of the artist. *Marine* is a pendant to *Taking an Observation,* still owned by a member of the Homer family. Mrs. Charles Savage Homer, Jr. continued these benefactions in 1938 by giving the noted and unusual oil painting *The Fountains at Night.*

In 1964 members of Homer's family donated the notable body of memorabilia closely associated with the personal life of the artist. These objects are located in a memorial gallery in the renovated museum, the only room in the building devoted to the work of a single artist. A special place must be accorded the memorabilia collection because of the unique insights it provides into the life and character of the artist, Maine's principal old master and devoted son by adoption. The items were formerly in Homer's studio at Prout's Neck and thus are of paramount biographical interest and importance. Prominent are two pictures, probably the earliest extant works from Homer's hand: a pencil drawing of a boy dreaming in a meadow, done when Homer was ten years of age, and a landscape rendered in watercolor when he was eleven. Related to these youthful efforts is a group of watercolors of flowers and birds by his mother, who encouraged his early leanings toward art.

Also important are a large collection of letters written to

members of his family over three decades and an album of newspaper clippings preserved by his mother; his sister-in-law, Mrs. Charles S. Homer, Jr. (the "Dear Mattie" of many of the letters); and his nephew, Mr. Charles L. Homer. Related in a personal way are several examples of Homer's etchings which were his own or were given by him to members of his family. Also included are a number of photographs taken by the artist during his travels which parallel the configuration of forms, use of light and dark, and subject matter of his pictures. There are also photographs of members of his family and friends and their Prout's Neck environment in the 1880s and 1890s.

Contributing to the importance of the memorabilia are numerous items connected with the artist's career: a pass issued to him as an artist-correspondent for *Harper's Weekly* at the Civil War front; a diploma admitting him to full membership in the National Academy of Design in 1866; a guidebook used during his first trip to Nassau in 1884; an 1868 edition of a French dictionary inscribed with the address of his studio in the New York University building; two wooden mannequins dressed like the fisherwomen of Tynemouth, England, acquired during his visit of 1881-1882; a booklet listing him as a member of the Tourilli Club, a favorite backwoods haunt in Canada; and a certificate awarded to him by the French government denoting the purchase of his oil *A Summer Night* at the time of the Exposition Universelle of 1900 at Paris. Relating directly to his art are his watercolor box, a set of brushes, two of his palettes, and a mahlstick for oil painting.

The third important part of the Homer Collection, primarily acquired in 1974, consists of over two hundred fine quality wood engravings designed by Homer between 1857 and 1880, the span of his activity in this medium. The nearly complete set includes his first engraving and the next to his last effort produced in this medium. Closely related to the wood engravings is an important selection of etchings. This rarer species, joined with the wood engravings and other printed examples, provides an excellent cross-section of Homer's work in the graphic arts.   [P.C.B.]

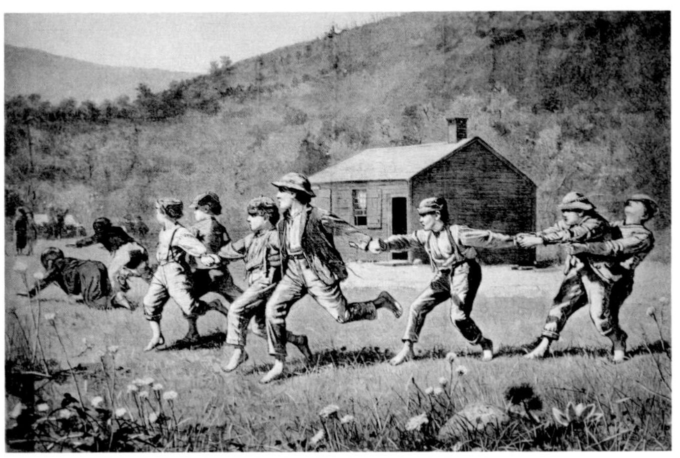

WINSLOW HOMER (1836-1910)

Snap the Whip

Wood engraving, 13½ x 20½ (34.3 x 52.1 cm)
Museum purchase. 1974.1.176

During the early and middle years of his career, from 1857 to 1875, Winslow Homer was known to the public primarily as a highly productive illustrator of daily life for the popular magazines of the day, most notably for *Harper's Weekly,* the *Life* magazine of that era, for which *Snap the Whip* was designed. It is an excellent example of his work in the graphic arts for several reasons. Although Homer had established himself as a serious painter in oil and would soon emerge as a leading practitioner of watercolor, he frequently based designs for engravings on oil or watercolor paintings which had proved to be successful, indicating a kind of priority among his output by his choices. *Snap the Whip* was his engraved version of the oil he had done in 1872 which received an award at the Centennial Exhibition of 1876 at Philadelphia. It thus got off to a good start and has remained an esteemed picture to this day. The original painting is now in the Butler Art Institute in Youngstown, Ohio. By the use of the two media, Homer addressed two constituencies: the general public with its contemporary interests and the serious collectors with long-range aims. Homer's long experience as a designer of woodcuts had a lasting effect upon his art, drilling him in descriptive draughtsmanship, in the use of clear-cut outlines, and in the handling of broadly patterned areas of light and dark. These features, inherent in wood engraving, remained characteristic of his art to the end.

The theme and spirit of *Snap the Whip* also are expressive of his attitude during those years. Compared to the powerful but somber marines of his later Prout's Neck years, the boys depicted at play are lighthearted Tom Sawyers at recess time, not students diligently reading indoors. In effect, they speak for Homer; no scholar himself, he depicted boys relaxing by preference in the out-of-doors. This subscription to the pleasant view of life advanced by such artists as William Sidney Mount and called by John Wilmerding in his 1972 *Winslow Homer* "Homer's Walt Whitman phase," speaks for the gentility of the post-Civil War days. It pervaded Homer's output of the 1870s, which was often inspired by carefree youths and handsome young belles on vacation at the seashore or mountain resorts.

There is a critical consensus that Homer reached the height of his skill as a designer of wood engravings in the mid-1870s. *Snap the Whip* is a fine example of his work of that period. It also is widely applauded as the counterpart to the universally popular *Breezing Up* of the same years. *Harper's Weekly* anticipated this acceptance by according it a large format and a two-page spread. *Snap the Whip* thus is a high point of the large collection of Homer's wood engravings owned by the museum.　　　　　[P.C.B.]

WINSLOW HOMER (1836-1910)
Surf and Rocks near Cannon Rock, Prout's Neck, 1884
    Charcoal and chalk, 17⅛ x 23⅜ (43.5 x 59.3 cm)
    Museum purchase. 1967.40

After his return from Tynemouth, England, in 1882, Homer began a new chapter in his life by moving from New York City to Prout's Neck, Maine, where he painted the marines which are the principal foundation of his fame. In the en-

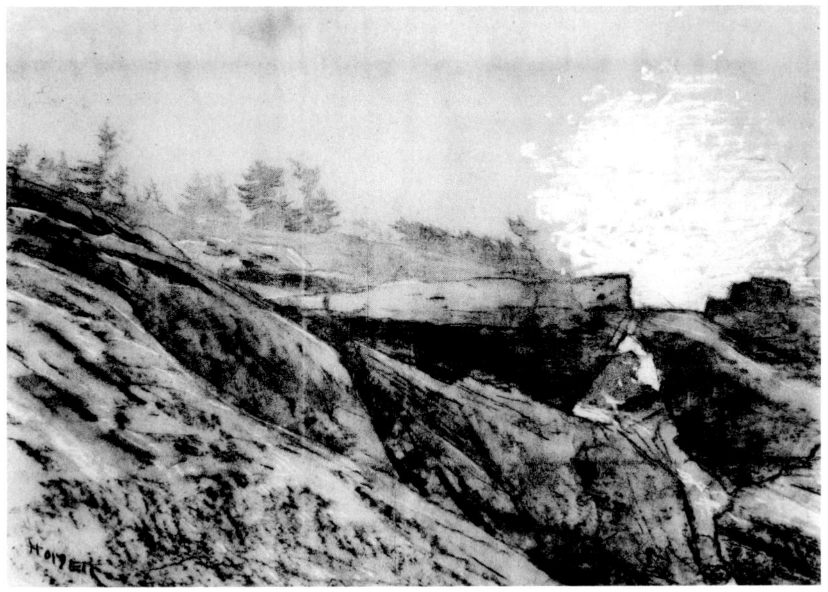

suing years, he used the formations along the rocky, ocean-
front promontory as a specific point of departure for his
comments on the universal conflict between the dynamic
world of the ocean and the stable, resisting coastline. This
commentary was saved from formula and stereotype by
Homer's daily and incisive study of the many formations
which extended from the doorstep of his studio to the far
end of the neck. Like artists before him, Homer used drawings for his closest studies of the physical characteristics of
nature and oils for his interpretations of nature's larger
meanings. Since Homer's final vision on canvas is the one
most frequently exhibited in galleries and museums, it is
instructive for those who are concerned with the creative
process to have an opportunity to consider the artist's procedure at its beginning.

This drawing furnishes a significant opportunity for study
in two ways: it is a drawing from the earliest period of
Homer's Prout's Neck residence, and it delineates an arch-
like waterfront formation with literal, almost photographic,
accuracy. It thus speaks for Homer during an exploratory
stage when, in 1883 or 1884, he was familiarizing himself

with the myriad of formations available near his new studio-home, and before he was prepared to use them as the broad elements in his marines.

It is worth noting that Homer assimilated his lessons and distilled the meanings of nature's forms profoundly but slowly. Although the motif for his celebrated painting *Cannon Rock* was located only a few yards away, he did not utilize it until nearly a decade of study had transpired. The charcoal drawing of the arch near Cannon Rock is therefore the typical beginning of a process which led to a superb conclusion.

Although Homer exhibited the drawing at the Doll and Richards Gallery in Boston in 1884, he recognized it for what it is—a study—and preserved it in his studio collection, from which it was acquired by the museum in 1967 from the Homer family. [P.C.B.]

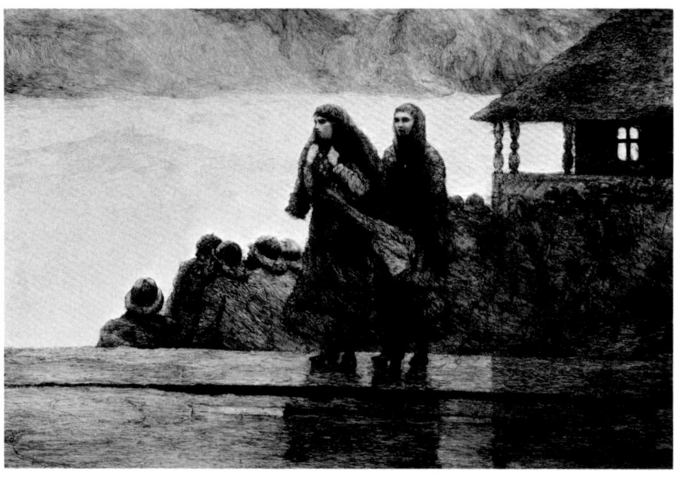

WINSLOW HOMER (1836-1910)

Perils of the Sea, 1888

Etching, 16 x 21¼

Gift of Mr. Fred A. Neuren. 1969.1

When, in the late 1880s, Winslow Homer turned his hand brilliantly but briefly to etching, the enterprise was an artistic success but a financial failure. The products of his etching needle thus are rare in comparison to his voluminous body of work in wood engraving in a ratio of about eight to nearly two hundred. The etchings also represent a profound change in Homer's outlook on life, most notably in a shift from the bland attitude of his middle years, expressed through *Snap the Whip,* to the great marines of his later years and a new conception of the relationship of human beings to the sea.

This dramatic change has been described by John Wilmerding as a shift from Walt Whitman's view of life to the somber vision of Melville. It can be subsumed as a new recognition of the *Perils of the Sea,* Homer's own title for this etching. The inspiration for this revelation came to Homer during a brief but crucial visit to Europe in 1881 and 1882, when he eschewed Paris in favor of Tynemouth, on the stormy North Sea coast of England. Inasmuch as seven of his small group of etchings done in the late 1880s derive either directly or indirectly from his experience of 1881-1882, he seems never to have forgotten those years or the people of Tynemouth. They truly caused a turning point in his life, as manifested by the differences between *Snap the Whip* and *Perils of the Sea.* In the one, carefree boys play in a benign rural landscape; in the other, two women wait anxiously but helplessly for news of the fate of their men, who are caught in a storm at sea. A turbulent ocean fills the background, silhouetting the Coast Guard watch tower and the rows of men in foul weather gear who wait and watch, prepared to spring to rescue work if necessary.

The deeper shadows and infinite atmospheric effects possible with the etching process, in contrast to the sharper, more mechanical attributes of wood engraving, have been exploited with a sure eye for the expressive potentialities of the needle and plate. The feeling of foreboding and anxiety, the poignant appeal of helpless waiting, came home strongly to Homer during his two years' stay in Tynemouth. He identified especially with the position of the hard-working fisherwomen obliged to wait stoically at home. They comprise a new gallery of female subjects, far different from the bathing resort belles of former years, and were remembered and treated with respect by Homer throughout the rest of his life.

One similarity between the etching and the wood engraving is that both had prototypes in outstanding paintings. *Perils of the Sea* follows the watercolor of the same title which Homer did in 1881 while he was actually at Tynemouth. The original is in the Sterling and Francine Clark Art Institute at Williamstown, Massachusetts, and the etching is a later confirmation of Homer's regard for it.

[P.C.B.]

WINSLOW HOMER (1836-1910)
The End of the Hunt, 1892

 Watercolor, 15⅛ x 21⅜ (38.4 x 54.3 cm)

 Gift of the Misses Harriet and Sophia Walker. 1894.11

The End of the Hunt, while far removed from the marines inspired by Prout's Neck, derived from two prominent aspects of Homer's career: his personal restlessness and his genius for the medium of watercolor. His dynamic temperament caused him to travel ceaselessly throughout his life, with Prout's Neck serving only as a base of operations during times propitious for marine painting. At other times, Homer took his brushes and watercolors the ideal traveler's painting kit—to far-flung points on the Atlantic seaboard, from Cuba, the Caribbean, the Bahamas, Bermuda, and Florida to Canada and the Adirondacks. In the meantime, he increased his facility with watercolor, a medium congenial to a restless temperament, until he transformed it from a process associated with genteel young ladies to one expressive of the most robust feelings. He elevated it, in short, to a major modern medium.

Homer had discovered the Adirondacks in the 1870s, responding to their wildness rather than interpreting them in the idyllic manner of the Hudson River School of painters. He was especially active there with his watercolor paints in the period from 1889 to 1894 and created *The End of the Hunt* in 1892 with an unmatched feeling for the freshness

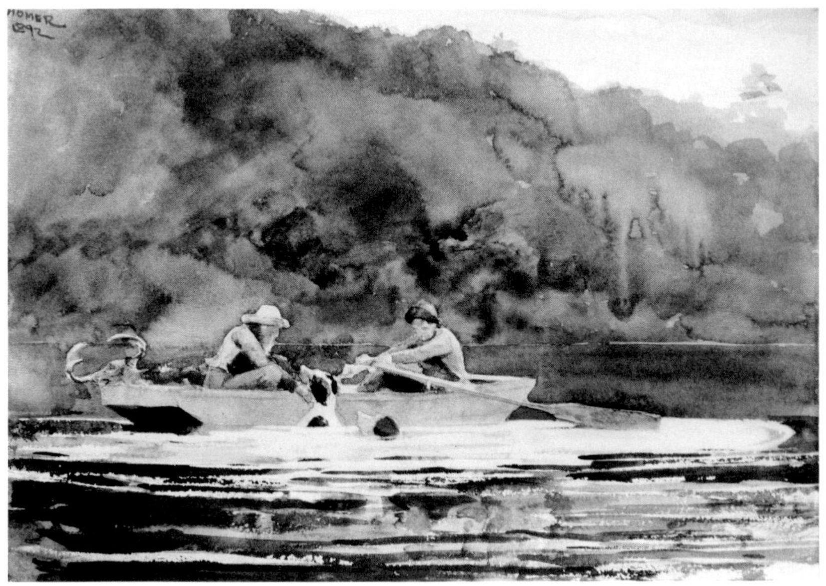

of the medium. This record of the unspoiled wilderness and
the rugged men who lived—or survived—there was exhibited
at the Doll and Richards Gallery in Boston, where it was
bought by the Walker sisters of Waltham, Massachusetts,
who gave it to Bowdoin College with their personal collection at the time of the opening of the Walker Art Building.
Their purchase of the picture was a mark of their progressive
attitude, for Homer's career was at a low ebb in terms of
sales, partly because his realistic and uncompromising portrayal of hunting scenes, in which deer seemed to be
slaughtered wantonly by drowning, repelled Victorian sen-
sibilities. For this and similar pictures he was harshly criticized on the grounds of content and, by some, for his so-
called crude (or non-academic) handling of pigments.
Homer, an excellent fisherman though not a hunter, refused
to editorialize on the harsh facts of life in the Adirondacks.
In all probability, the Walker sisters, ahead of their day in a
number of respects, purchased the picture because they per-
ceived it to be a superb example of watercolor painting. Time
and the nationwide exhibition of the picture have proved
the soundness of their judgment.   [P.C.B.]

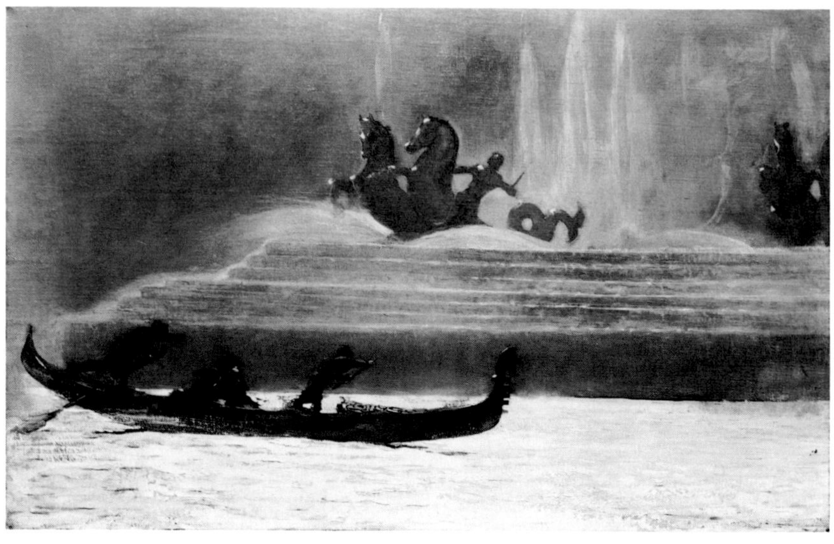

WINSLOW HOMER (1836-1910)

The Fountains at Night, World's Columbian Exposition,
1893

Oil on canvas, 16 x 25 (40.7 x 63.5 cm)

Bequest of Mrs. Charles S. Homer, Jr. 1938.2

When, in 1938, Bowdoin College was given a choice of one
of the paintings which Winslow Homer had given to his
older brother and sister-in-law, *The Fountains at Night* was
selected from those available for a variety of special reasons.

Despite the fact that it was, in many ways, atypical of the
work of the great marine painter, it was deemed to be a
brilliant example of his later facility with the oil medium,
especially in his superb representation of light sparkling on
water. The picture also exemplified Homer's lifelong affinity
for the effective manipulation of the neutral scale from
black to white and the intermediate greys—a command
which he gained during his years of work in the graphic
arts. The picture also was appealing because of the significance of the setting depicted, for both Homer and the na-
tion. The World's Columbian Exposition was Chicago's
triumphant "coming of age" in the domain of culture, as
well as America's dedication to faith in unlimited material

progress. A great art exhibition was held which attracted entries from the entire Western world, and Homer was highly pleased to have his oil *The Gale* selected for an award. Perhaps as a consequence of this recognition, he made one of his few trips west of the Hudson and his only known visit to Chicago to see the fair at first hand. *The Fountains at Night* is the most recognizable product of that visit to come from his brush. It is a singular memento in that it shows Homer's ability to avoid the bizarre aspects of the spectacle—the sculpture atop the fountain designed by Frederick MacMonnies—while concentrating on the most popular features of the fair, the fountain's illumination by electric lights at night and the network of lagoons over which visitors were whisked Venetian-style in swiftly moving gondolas. These elements provided a visual excitement which captured the magic of the fair as reported by its throngs of visitors.

The notion was once current that Homer painted the picture by electric light, an unlikely procedure. More probably he painted it with verve upon his return to Prout's, while still under the stimulus of his trip. He gave the painting to Charles and Mattie—a sign in itself of his own approval—and Mrs. Homer was said to have prized it especially.   [P.C.B.]

SELECTED WORKS FROM THE COLLECTION
[K.A.O.]

Snap the Whip. Wood engraving, $13\frac{1}{2}$ x $20\frac{1}{2}$ (34.3 x 52.1 cm). Museum purchase. 1974.1.176

Marine. Watercolor, $9\frac{3}{4}$ x $13\frac{1}{2}$ (24.8 x 34.3 cm). Bequest of the Honorable Augustus F. Moulton 1873. 1933.1

Saved (The Lifeline). Etching, $16\frac{7}{8}$ x $27\frac{3}{4}$ (42.9 x 70.5 cm). Gift of the Homer family. 1964.69.202

✠*Surf and Rocks near Cannon Rock, Prout's Neck.* Charcoal and chalk, $17\frac{1}{8}$ x $23\frac{3}{8}$ (43.5 x 59.3 cm). Museum purchase. 1967.40

Royal Palms, Santiago de Cuba. Graphite and white chalk, $12\frac{1}{16}$ x $18\frac{1}{4}$ (30.6 x 46.4 cm). Hamlin Fund. 1969.24

Eight Bells. Etching, $18\frac{7}{8}$ x $24\frac{1}{2}$ (48.0 x 62.3 cm). Gift of Mr. Charles S. Payson. 1967.67

Mending the Nets. Etching, $16\frac{3}{8}$ x 22 (41.6 x 55.8 cm). Gift of the Homer family. 1964.69.201

✠*Perils of the Sea.* Etching, 16 x $21\frac{1}{4}$ (40.6 x 54.0 cm). Gift of Mr. Fred A. Neuren. 1969.1

Fly Fishing, Saranac. Etching, $17\frac{5}{16}$ x $22\frac{5}{16}$ (39.9 x 56.6 cm). Gift of the Homer family. 1964.69.203

✠*The End of the Hunt.* Watercolor, $15\frac{1}{8}$ x $21\frac{3}{8}$ (38.4 x 54.3 cm). Gift of the Misses Harriet and Sophia Walker. 1894.11

✠*The Fountains at Night, World's Columbian Exposition.* Oil on canvas, 16 x 25 (40.7 x 63.5 cm). Bequest of Mrs. Charles S. Homer, Jr. 1938.2

Wolfe's Cove. Watercolor, $13\frac{3}{4}$ x $20\frac{1}{8}$ (35.0 x 51.2 cm). Museum purchase. 1955.2

MEMORABILIA

The Bowdoin College Museum of Art contains an extensive collection of Homer memorabilia, largely the gift of the Homer family, including a collection of over 120 letters from Homer to his family and friends; Homer's sketchbook and daybook; over 80 photographs of Homer, his family and friends, and Prout's Neck; over 60 books, exhibition catalogues, and articles about Homer or owned by him; artist's materials, including a watercolor box, brushes, palettes, and mannequins; and personal belongings, such as fishing and camping gear, certificates, citations, and scrapbooks.

DRAWINGS, PRINTS, WATERCOLORS, AND PHOTOGRAPHS

Drawings

The Bowdoin College Museum of Art contains the first American collegiate drawing collection, given to the school in 1811 by the Honorable James Bowdoin III. The circumstances under which Bowdoin assembled his collection are remarkable, and his importance as one of the first American art collectors abroad is undisputed.

A friend and political associate of Thomas Jefferson's, and possibly influenced by Jefferson's own art collecting, Bowdoin was commissioned minister plenipotentiary to Spain in 1804. He never arrived at the court of Madrid; however, from 1805 to 1808 he lived primarily in Paris, a city which presented an unusual opportunity for art collecting during those years. Napoleon's armies were returning with the contents of art galleries from across the continent, and Italy was particularly well represented in their booty. The drawings Bowdoin bequeathed to the College in 1811 were largely collected at that time; another group may have been purchased by Bowdoin en masse from Smibert's studio.

The 1811 drawings collection consists of 142 sheets, several of which have verso drawings, bringing the total number of works to 152. Sixteenth- and seventeenth-century drawings form the majority of the bequest, but fifteenth- and eighteenth-century works are included as well. Approximately ninety Italian drawings form the nucleus of the collection; there are nearly forty more Dutch and Flemish drawings, fifteen French and one or two each of German and English drawings. Beccafumi, Boscoli, Cambiaso, Poccetti, Giulio Romano, Vanni, and Zuccaro are represented in the sixteenth-century Italian drawing collection; seventeenth-century artists include Corenzio, Gimignani, Giovanni da San Giovanni, Ricci, Maratta, and Petri. Works by Dutch, Flemish, and French artists such as Moeyaert, Koninck, Breenbergh, Weenix, Diepenbeeck, Vellert, Quillard, and Bouchardon are also included in the collection. The supreme drawing from the bequest is *View of Waltersburg* by Pieter Brueghel the Elder.

The drawings collection was significantly enlarged in the 1890s. In the period between 1894 and 1904, the Misses Harriet and Sophia Walker gave approximately twenty drawings dating from the nineteenth century. English drawings comprise the majority of the group, which contains works by Burne-Jones and attributed to Gainsborough.

The next major gift of drawings came to the collection in 1930 when a small but very fine group of charcoal figure studies by John Singer Sargent was given to the College by Miss Emily Sargent and her sister, Mrs. Francis Ormond. The James Phinney Baxter Fund, established in memory of Professor Henry Johnson h '14, was first used in 1932 to purchase thirty-five European drawings from the late Professor Johnson's collection; the majority of the drawings are Italian, of the sixteenth and seventeenth centuries. The Charles Potter Kling bequest of 1935, primarily a teaching collection, includes European drawings of the sixteenth and seventeenth centuries, the majority of which are Italian.

The next period of major growth in the drawings collection occurred in the 1950s and 1960s. Eighteen drawings by Elihu Vedder, all of them preliminary studies for his mural *Rome* in the rotunda of the Walker Art Building, were a gift in 1955 from the American Academy of Arts and Letters. In 1956 and 1967, Miss Susan Dwight Bliss gave the College 102 European and American drawings, primarily Italian works from the seventeenth and eighteenth centuries, French drawings from the eighteenth and nineteenth centuries, and English and American drawings from the nineteenth century. Of particular merit are two sketchbooks and a portfolio by John La Farge and a group of drawings and watercolors by John Ruskin. The Helen Johnson Chase bequest in 1958 included *Thisbe Committing Suicide* by Peter Paul Rubens, one of the best-known works in the museum collection. Through the generosity of Colonel Leonard Cox,

Mrs. Caroline Cox Lansing, and Mr. Allyn Cox, the College received in 1959 a significant group of drawings and sketches by Kenyon Cox, including preparatory studies for his mural *Venice* in the rotunda of the Walker Art Building. Gifts from Mr. George Otis Hamlin in 1961 and from Mrs. Helen Farr Sloan in 1962 brought to Bowdoin several drawings by John Sloan, complementing the already major holdings of that artist's graphic works and paintings.

Twenty drawings were given to the College in 1964, 1965, and 1966 by Mr. Walter K. Gutman '24. Artists such as Gorky, Guston, Kline, Cruz, Nakian, and Segal are represented; the group is unique in that all of the artists were either friends or acquaintances of Mr. Gutman.

A group of eight drawings by Ernest Haskell, a contribution in 1976 by Mrs. Josephine Aldridge in memory of Mrs. Ernest Haskell, Sr., was a welcome addition to the collection of prints previously presented by other members of the Haskell family.

In 1957 and 1958 the museum began to expand its collection of twentieth-century drawings with the purchase of works by Klimt, Schiele, Marcks, and Archipenko. From 1958 to the present time, American and European drawings of importance to the Bowdoin collection have been acquired with the help of several purchase funds, including the Hamlin Fund and the Florence C. Quinby Fund given in memory of Henry Cole Quinby h '16. Fifty-three drawings by Rockwell Kent were purchased in 1971 with funds donated anonymously. In 1976 and 1977 representative drawings by such artists as Christo, Pearlstein, Lichtenstein, and LeWitt were added to the collection with the assistance of a matching grant from the National Endowment for the Arts, a federal agency. [L.H. & STAFF]

Prints

Although a few prints were part of the bequest of the Honorable James Bowdoin III, the collection did not grow significantly until 1923. In that year, Mr. Charles A. Coffin h '22, presented to the College his print collection, which included works by Corot, Daubigny, Haden, Hassam, Manet, Millet, Piranesi, and Pissarro. The Charles Potter Kling bequest of 1935 continued the expansion of the print collection with Boydell's *Shakespeare Gallery* and a Callot. Thirty lithographs and etchings by Childe Hassam were received as a gift in 1940 from Mrs. Maud Hassam, the artist's wife. The museum's extensive collection of Ernest Haskell's works was begun in 1947 with a nucleus of twenty-seven etchings given by Mrs. Ernest Haskell, Sr. In 1974 and 1975 Mrs. Ernest Haskell, Jr. presented the College with a collection of 118 items, including engravings, etchings, lithographs, and a scrapbook; Mrs. Josephine Aldridge generously extended the Haskell collection in 1976 with thirty-four etchings given in memory of Mrs. Ernest Haskell, Sr. The greatest growth in the print collection occurred in the 1950s and early 1960s, when the interest of Miss Susan Dwight Bliss in the Bowdoin College Museum of Art resulted in a series of substantial gifts. In 1956 she donated a large collection of prints extending from a Dürer woodcut series to works by Meryon and Whistler. Sixteenth-, seventeenth-, and eighteenth-century European graphics were represented in Miss Bliss's collection and included, among works by other artists, prints of Vorsterman, van Vliet, Vico, Bartolozzi, Marieschi, Reni, and Canaletto. Miss Bliss's concern with the teaching potential of prints is noteworthy; in 1963 she gave 199 prints for the purpose of creating a collection which could be circulated to schools in Maine. A nearly complete representation of the graphic work of John Sloan was established in 1961 by Mr. George Otis Hamlin, who donated to the museum 189 prints and drawings by the artist. The collection was further expanded in 1962 by Mrs. Helen Farr Sloan, the artist's wife.

In more general terms, the museum's print collection is strong in nineteenth- and twentieth-century French, English, and American works, with excellent examples by such artists as Millet, Pissarro, Daubigny, Legros, Blake, Bone, Haden, Cameron, Whistler, Hassam, Higgins, and Baskin. Late nineteenth- and early twentieth-century German prints also are well represented, particularly those of the German

Expressionists Beckmann, Heckel, Kollwitz, Nolde, Pechstein, and Schmidt-Rottluff. The collection is more thor-
oughly examined in *500 Years of Printmaking: Prints and
Illustrated Books at Bowdoin College* by David P. Becker
'70, published by the museum in 1978.   [STAFF]

Watercolors

In 1894 the Misses Harriet and Sophia Walker donated to
the collection its first small group of watercolors, including
Winslow Homer's *The End of the Hunt.* Ten years later the
Misses Walker gave the College three watercolors by John
La Farge, creating a small but significant nucleus of works
around which the remainder of the collection has grown.

Paintings by American watercolorists comprise the majority of the collection, which also contains two watercolors
by John Ruskin given by Miss Susan Dwight Bliss in 1956.
Additional watercolors by Winslow Homer came to the
collection in 1933 and in 1955; *Marine* through the bequest
of the Honorable Augustus F. Moulton 1873, and *Wolfe's
Cove* the gift of Mr. Neal W. Allen '07, Mr. John F. Dana
1898, Mr. John H. Halford '07, Mr. William W. Lawrence
1898, and Mr. Benjamin R. Shute '31.

Many important gifts came to the museum during the
1960s and 1970s. Mr. Stephen Etnier h '69 and Mrs. Etnier
gave Andrew Wyeth's *Bermuda* in memory of Mr. S. Foster
Yancey '30. In 1962 Mr. Eliot O'Hara, himself a watercolor-
ist, presented sixty-one watercolors, most of which are contemporary works. Thirteen watercolors by Augustus A.
Gibson were the gift in 1968 and 1969 of Mr. Paul J. Newman '09. In the mid-1970s thirty-two watercolors came to the
College as a gift from Mr. William F. Bonner, Jr.

Several watercolors by Rockwell Kent were donated to the
museum in 1971 as part of a larger collection of the artist's
work. Nine watercolors by Ernest Haskell were a gift to the
College in 1976 from Mrs. Josephine Aldridge in memory of
Mrs. Ernest Haskell, Sr.   [STAFF]

Photographs

Though presently limited in size, the photography collection at the Bowdoin College Museum is constantly expanding. Included are works by such major twentieth-century photographers as Berenice Abbott, Ansel Adams, Manuel Alvarez Bravo, Harry Callahan, and Edward Weston.   [STAFF]

PIETER BRUEGHEL THE ELDER (ca. 1525-1569), FLEMISH

View of Waltersburg, ca. 1553-1554

    Pen and ink, 12⅝ x 10⅝ (32.1 x 27.0 cm)

    Bequest of the Honorable James Bowdoin III. 1811.142

This view of Waltersburg in the Swiss Alps is one of the best-known and most important drawings in the Bowdoin College Museum of Art collection. The work was probably acquired by James Bowdoin III during a diplomatic mission abroad in the early nineteenth century and was donated to the College at the time of his death in 1811.

Following his acceptance as a master in the Antwerp painter's guild in 1551, Brueghel began a "Wanderjahr" through France to southern Italy. This sheet is one of a small number of drawings of spectacular Alpine scenery dating from the artist's return trip from Italy to Antwerp; related examples are included in the holdings of such institutions as Chatsworth, the Fogg Art Museum, and the Pierpont Morgan Library, and in the collection of the late Count Antoine Seilern.

Brueghel's travels through the Alps and the drawings he made there were critical to his later art, for the high mountains, rocky outcrops, low valleys, and spectacular views were depicted in his paintings; thus, in a well-known statement, the seventeenth-century writer Karel van Mander observed that Brueghel devoured the Alps in order to spit them out again in his homeland.

Brueghel's depiction of Waltersburg appears to be more than a precise, accurate portrayal of the pictorial landscape;

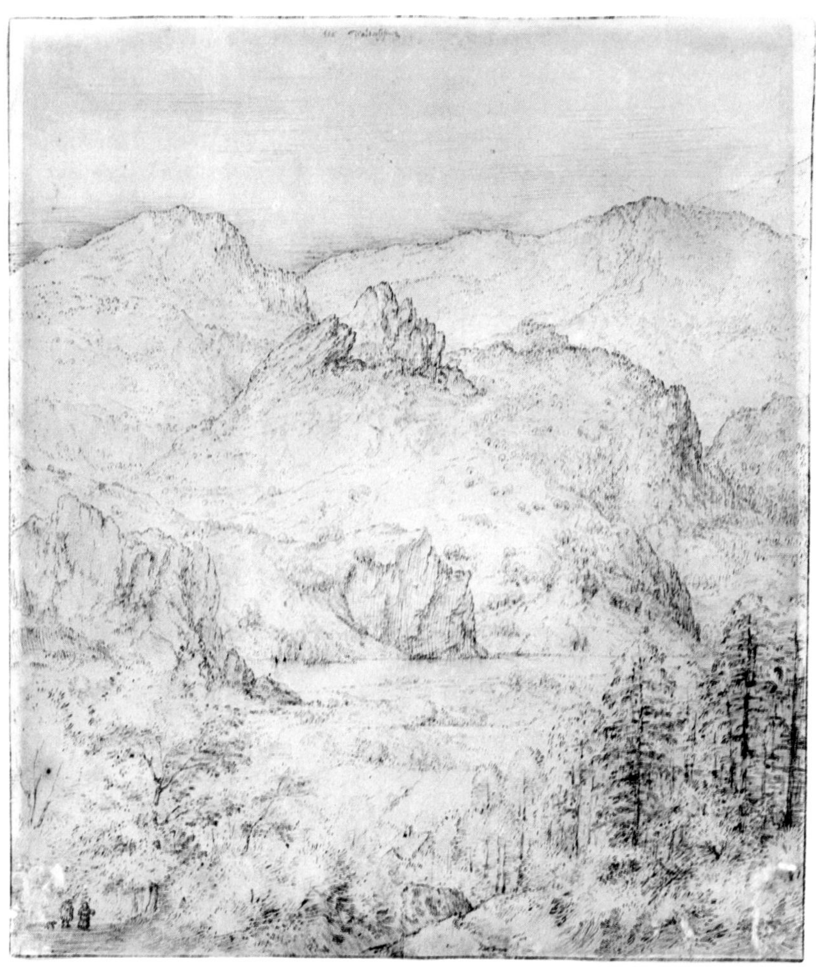

rather, the artist seems to have created an idealized composite of a variety of natural forms to produce an embracing vision of nature. The minimal use of continuous contours and contrast between the minutely depicted foreground details with the more generalized background treatment produces the impression of vast, enveloping space. Brueghel's energetic, expressive line activates the composition; through the size, variety, and direction of his strokes, he captures both the fleeting, atmospheric qualities and the ruggedly picturesque aspects of the Alpine landscape. [J.D.B.]

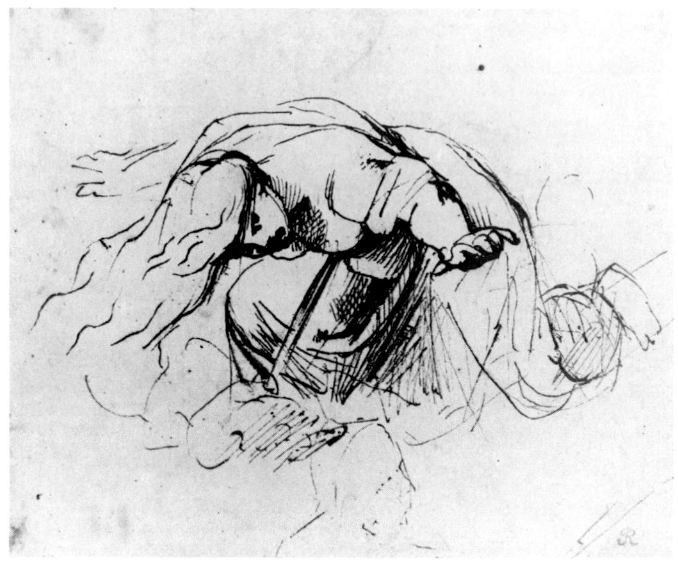

PETER PAUL RUBENS (1577-1640), FLEMISH
Thisbe Committing Suicide, ca. 1602-1605
  Pen and ink, 5⅝ x 6½ (14.3 x 16.5 cm)
  Bequest of Mrs. Helen Johnson Chase. 1958.67

Ovid's tale of the tragic lovers Pyramus and Thisbe was a popular subject for artists and decorative craftsmen in the Renaissance and Baroque periods. Although there is no known painting by the artist of this subject, Rubens completed five other studies of Thisbe committing suicide. These five works, to which the Bowdoin drawing relates, were done in Rome early in Rubens's career, and appear on a single sheet in the collections of the Louvre. In this drawing, Rubens depicts the moment when Thisbe, "Fell forward on the blade, still warm and reeking/ With her lover's blood" (Ovidius Naso, Publius, *Metamorphoses,* trans. Rolfe Humphries [Bloomington: Indiana University Press, 1955, pp. 164-5]). Originally given to Rubens, the drawing was later attributed to Anthony van Dyck; in fact, the work was considered by Frank Jewett Mather, Jr., in his article "Drawings by Old Masters at Bowdoin College Ascribed to Northern Schools: II" published in *Art in America* in February

1914, to be "far too good for [Rubens]." Recent scholarship, particularly by Julius S. Held, in his 1959 *Rubens Selected Drawings,* has reaffirmed the traditional attribution.

Mather misread the collector's monogram in the lower left corner as that of Sir Joshua Reynolds, rather than that of Jonathan Richardson, Sr. (Lugt 2184). A number of drawings in the Richardson collection did come to Sir Joshua through his teacher, Sir Thomas Hudson, so such a provenance is possible though difficult to determine. No documentary knowledge exists for the drawing's location from the time of the Richardson sale in 1747 until it appeared in a scrapbook of studies from the old masters from the library of Dr. Barnard Davis of London, which was purchased by Professor Henry Johnson h '14, the first director of the Bowdoin College Museum of Art, in 1892.   [R.V.W.]

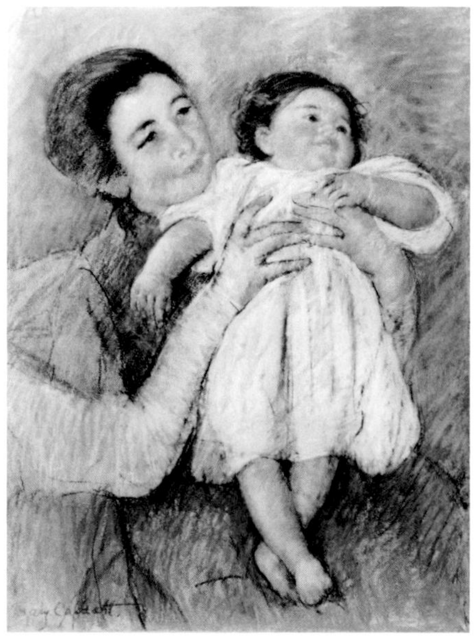

MARY CASSATT (1845-1926), AMERICAN
The Barefoot Child, 1897

Pastel, 28 x 21 (71.1 x 53.3 cm)

Gift of Mrs. Murray S. Danforth in memory of her husband, Dr. Murray S. Danforth '01. 1953.42

Though she is frequently categorized as a member of the French Impressionist group, Mary Cassatt was decidedly American, born in Pennsylvania to a prosperous and prominent family. Her early training included four years of rigorous academic study at the Pennsylvania Academy of the Fine Arts, which she entered in 1861. Seeking artistic freedom and inspiration, and independent by nature, she traveled to Paris in 1866, where she studied briefly with the fashionable academic painter Charles Chaplin. Her further training involved extensive travel to Italy and Spain; she was influenced not only by such old master painters as Corregio, Goya, and Velasquez but also by such revolutionary modern artists as Courbet and Manet. In 1877 Cassatt met Edgar Degas, who recognized her talent and determination and invited her to exhibit with the French Impressionists. Cassatt worked closely with Degas, in whom she found artistic and spiritual companionship, and her work was included in the fourth Impressionist exhibition of 1879, as well as in later Impressionist shows. Like Degas, she admired Japanese art for its pattern and flat asymmetrical design and also was influenced by the compositional effects appearing in early informal, instantaneous photographs. Both Cassatt and Degas shared a reverence for the form and discipline of drawing, and Degas encouraged her experimentation with printmaking, a medium in which she perhaps achieved her most successful results.

The Barefoot Child illustrates Cassatt's facility at the height of her career in the 1890s with the medium of pastel. The subject of mother and child, captured with such lively expression and luminous color, was a dominant theme for Cassatt, who concentrated upon the domestic world so familiar to her. The obvious freedom and spontaneity of this and other pastels prevented Cassatt's work in the medium from being seriously considered by contemporary critics, who demanded detailed academic execution in a work of art. Cassatt's pastel technique is similar to that of Degas, who used steam and a fixative solution to manipulate the chalk particles while building up the surface of the work.

This pastel was originally purchased by Alfred Atmore

Pope, one of the friends of the artist whose taste for Impressionist art Cassatt helped to form.   [M.R.B.]

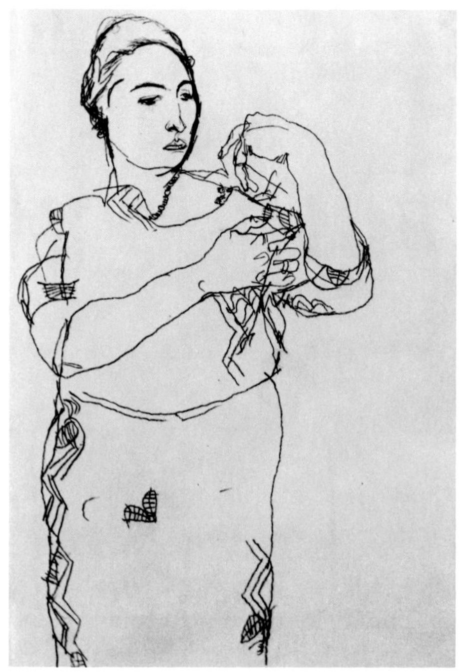

EGON SCHIELE (1890-1918), AUSTRIAN
Standing Woman, ca. 1917-1918
  Graphite, 19¼ x 12⅝ (48.6 x 32.1 cm)
  Museum purchase. 1957.87

The "enfant terrible" of the Vienna art world in the 1910s, the Austrian Expressionist painter Egon Schiele attended the Vienna Academy of Fine Arts from 1907 to 1909, where he studied with Gustav Klimt and knew Oskar Kokoschka. Schiele was heavily influenced by the linear arabesque and decorative patterning of the Art Nouveau movement, but incorporated into the style an intense nervous angularity. Unlike many European art capitals in the twentieth century, Vienna embraced portraiture, and Schiele executed numerous portraits of patrons and close friends which are remarkable for their psychological intensity and penetration. The artist is most noted today for his tormented series of nude self-portraits, which painfully examine his struggle for self-knowledge and -realization. Except for a brief period of success prior to his death, Schiele received limited recognition during his career. Befriended by the influential art critic Arthur Roessler, who encouraged several patrons to collect his work, and by the art historian Otto Benesch, Schiele was granted a one-man show at the Vienna Secession exhibition in 1918.

This pencil drawing, *Standing Woman,* indicates Schiele's overriding interest in portraying the human figure and suggests the artist's more reflective style in the later years of his career. While the drawing lacks the frenzied intensity and emotional impact of Schiele's Expressionist figural studies, it displays the linear precision and sensitivity so typical of his oeuvre.   [M.R.B.]

ARSHILE GORKY (1905-1948), AMERICAN
Untitled, 1943

   Pencil and crayon, 15½ x 22½ (39.4 x 57.2 cm)
   Gift of Mr. Walter K. Gutman '24. 1966.91

Arshile Gorky, born Vusdanig Manoog Adoian, immigrated to the United States in 1920 from Armenia. Though he studied briefly at the Rhode Island School of Design and at the New School of Design in Boston, the artist was largely self-taught. Gorky carefully studied art books and reproductions, and his early work is dominated by an awareness of the art of Cézanne and Picasso. His career in the 1920s was marked by desperate poverty. In 1925 he moved to New York and adopted the name of Arshile (the Georgian equivalent of the Armenian royal name Arshak) Gorky (meaning "bitterness" in Russian). Gorky's work of the 1930s reveals his struggle to assimilate the influences of Cubism and Surrealism to produce a truly independent artistic form. In Cubism he discovered structural and spatial solutions to his artistic problems, while in Surrealism he found the symbolic vocabulary of images and shapes to express spontaneously his inner consciousness.

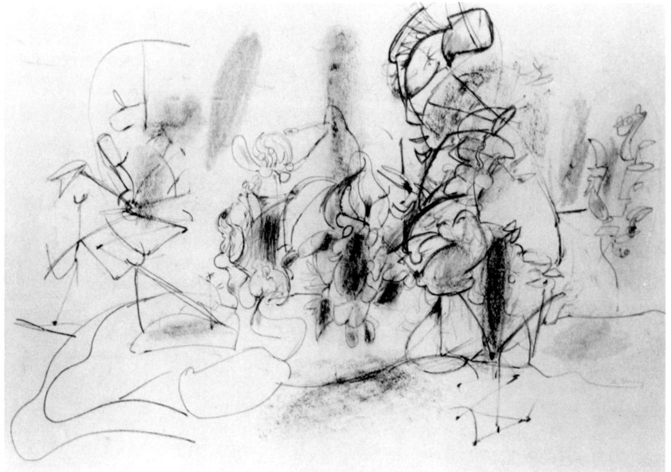

Gorky's mature and independent style emerged in the early 1940s, a critical period of self-discovery for the artist. During the summer of 1943, which he spent on his wife's farm in Virginia, the artist executed dozens of sketches based on an acute observation of nature. Drawings, both the studies for his monumental paintings and independent exercises in design, had always played a significant role in Gorky's art, for the artist appreciated the immediacy of their execution and consistently preferred line to color as a means of expression. Bowdoin's untitled drawing dates from this period of intense creativity and indicates the Expressionist freedom his art attained in its maturity. Gorky's heightened imagination transforms the landscape of his immediate perception to evoke passionately the fertility of nature. The artist's interest in surface and texture is revealed in his use of the wax crayon, a medium with which he constantly experimented at that time. Strokes of color punctuate, though never overwhelm, the excited linear network.

Gorky's key role as a transmitter of European Modernism and as a leader in the development of Abstract Expressionism is widely appreciated today. His art received limited recognition and acceptance in the 1940s, however, and in 1948, despondent and after personal difficulties, he committed suicide in Sherman, Connecticut.   [M.R.B.]

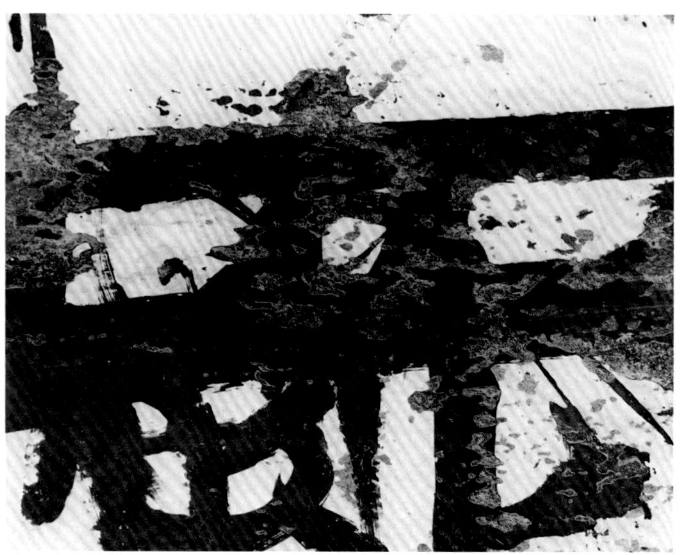

FRANZ KLINE (1910-1962), AMERICAN
Untitled, 1955

    Gouache, $19\frac{11}{16}$ x $14\frac{3}{4}$ (50.2 x 37.5 cm)

    Gift of Mr. Walter K. Gutman '24. 1964.65

Born in Wilkes-Barre, Pennsylvania, Franz Kline attended classes at Girard College in Philadelphia and at Boston University's School of Fine and Applied Arts. Following additional study in England, Kline moved to New York in 1938. He worked there in the 1940s, primarily exhibiting portraits, figural studies, and street scenes. Kline continuously simplified his style, and by the time of his first one-man exhibition at Egan Gallery in 1950, his paintings were totally abstract and frequently reduced to a monochromatic color scheme.

The artist is primarily noted for his use of a dominating black image on a white background, a configuration often compared in structure, though not in symbolic content, to oriental calligraphy. Kline is equally concerned with the energetic application of paint, and the gestural brushstroke so evident in his work establishes a dramatic tension between the overlay of paint and the surface of the canvas. The scale of Kline's paintings is monumental and tends to envelop the viewer; the pigment was frequently applied with a house painter's brush on canvases of enormous size. Kline's immediately recognizable images met with instant success, and, due to his interest in the physical act of painting, he quickly became identified as a master of Abstract Expressionism, a school of painting which emerged in America during the postwar era.

Though small, Kline's untitled drawing conveys the dramatic impact of his larger paintings. The power of his brush and the conflict between the inked surface and bare paper create a composition of great visual excitement. Like his larger canvases, the drawing suggests an interest in formal structure, the manipulation of materials, and a raw energy and violence of execution.   [M.R.B.]

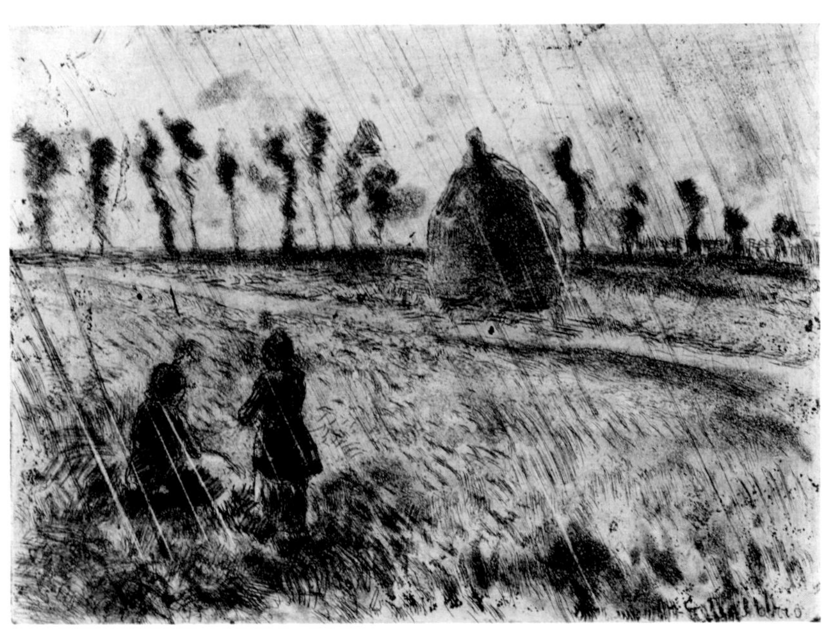

CAMILLE PISSARRO (1830-1903), FRENCH
Effect of Rain, 1879
   Etching, aquatint, and drypoint, 6¼ x 8⅜ (15.8 x 21.4 cm)
   Gift of Miss Susan Dwight Bliss. 1963.328

The oldest member of the Impressionist group, Camille Pissarro was noted for his wisdom, kindness, loyalty, and patience; he was among the first to recognize the talents of Degas, Cézanne, and Gauguin and strongly encouraged them in their artistic pursuits. Born in the Virgin Islands, Pissarro arrived in Paris in 1855, where he quickly became involved in avant-garde artistic circles. Never a radical innovator, he was interested in capturing the transient effects of light and atmospheric conditions in a landscape while maintaining the discipline of well-defined contours and formal structure. Pissarro was the only member of the Impressionist circle to exhibit in all eight of the group shows; although for most of his career his financial situation was difficult if not desperate, his reputation was modestly established in 1892 in a large retrospective exhibition organized by Durand-Ruel.

One of the few Impressionist artists to be involved in printmaking, Pissarro regarded his works in this medium as private expressions, like drawings; despite their enormous current appeal to connoisseurs of Impressionism, Pissarro's prints were never published during his lifetime. *Effect of Rain,* with its depiction of haystacks and outdoor subjects and its studied effects of light and changing climatic conditions, is close to the very core of Pissarro's art. The print illustrates his masterful application of intaglio techniques. The open, regular grain of aquatint suggests the effervescent quality of the atmosphere. The wispy cypress trees created with aquatint tones fill in the etched outlines of figures and details of the fields. The diagonal rainfall, a convention of Japanese prints, was added in this final state with a drypoint needle and by wiping the plate clean in straight, thin strokes. This print is one of only a few impressions, perhaps not more than ten, which were taken from the plate during Pissarro's lifetime.   [J.D.B.]

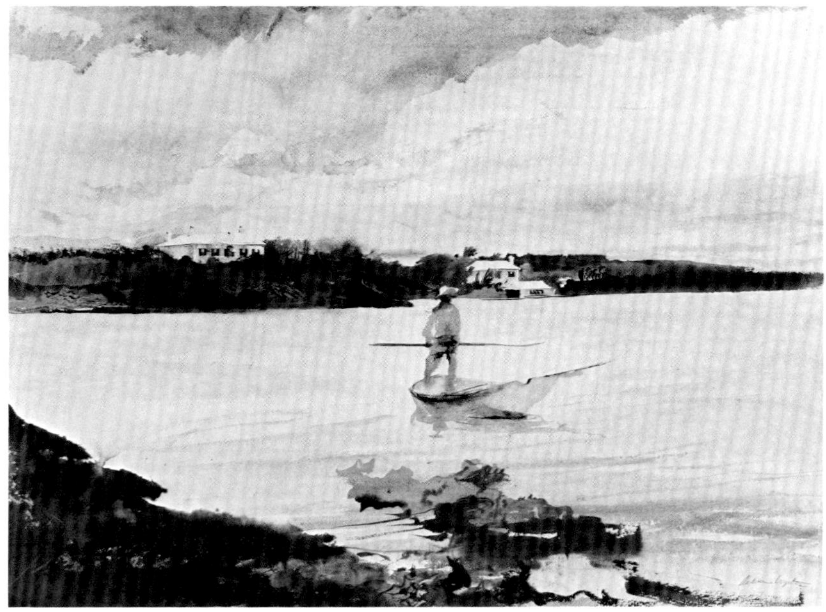

ANDREW WYETH (b. 1917), AMERICAN

Bermuda, ca. 1950

Watercolor, $21\frac{7}{16}$ x $29\frac{1}{2}$ (54.5 x 74.9 cm)

Gift of Mr. Stephen Etnier h '69 and Mrs. Etnier in memory of Mr. S. Foster Yancey '30. 1961.98

Undoubtedly the most popular living American artist, Andrew Wyeth is the son of the gifted and successful illustrator N. C. Wyeth. Rigorously and academically trained by his father, the young artist became a meticulous craftsman and developed an exceptional ability to duplicate the natural appearance of the visible world. Living and working almost exclusively in Chadds Ford, Pennsylvania, and Cushing, Maine, Wyeth has succeeded in capturing more than simply the physical reality of his environment; in his intense examination of a scene, Wyeth penetrates beyond the subject itself, invoking memory and imagination and altering elements of composition and light to suggest the essence and inner life of the objects which compose his world.

Though most highly respected for his tempera paintings and regarded as a painstaking draughtsman, Wyeth is also noted for his work in watercolor, which he regards as a major medium. Wyeth began working in watercolor early in his career, and his first one-man exhibition at Macbeth Gallery in 1937 was of works in this medium. His early watercolors were free and spontaneous in comparison to his later works, which exhibit a greater interest in precision and exact control of the medium. The watercolor *Bermuda* is somewhat unusual both for the extreme looseness and softness of its technique as well as for its subject matter; though he can hardly be described as provincial, Wyeth rarely travels or paints away from the Pennsylvania and Maine worlds so familiar to him. [M.R.B.]

SELECTED WORKS FROM THE COLLECTION

[D.P.B. & STAFF]

For drawings and watercolors, sheet size is included. For intaglio prints, the measurements are to the plate mark; for all other prints, they are to the edge of the image itself.

Drawings

Giovanni Francesco Caroto (attributed) (1470-1546), Italian: *Madonna and Child*. Red chalk, $5\frac{3}{16}$ x $4\frac{1}{4}$ (13.2 x 10.8 cm). Bequest of the Honorable James Bowdoin III. 1811.33

Domenico di Pace Beccafumi (1486-1551), Italian: *The Tribune Publius Mutius Condemning His Colleagues to Be Burnt*. Red chalk, $7\frac{1}{2}$ x $11\frac{1}{8}$ (18.9 x 28.5 cm). Bequest of the Honorable James Bowdoin III. 1811.85

Giulio Romano (1492-1546), Italian: *The Sacking of Troy*. Pen and ink, $10\frac{1}{16}$ x 8 (25.6 x 20.3 cm). Bequest of the Honorable James Bowdoin III. 1811.6

Dirk Jacobsz Vellert (active 1518-1540), Flemish: *Six Designs for Windows at King's College, Cambridge*. Pen and ink with wash, $6\frac{5}{8}$ x $6\frac{7}{8}$ (16.8 x 17.4 cm). Bequest of the Honorable James Bowdoin III. 1811.109

Unknown artist (16th century), Genoese: *Madonna and Child with Saints*. Pen and ink with sepia wash, 10⅞ x 8⅛ (27.6 x 20.6 cm). Bequest of the Honorable James Bowdoin III. 1811.4

Jan VAN DER STRAET (STRADANUS) (1523-1605), Flemish: *Jesus with the Doctors*. Pen and ink with wash, 16⅛ x 10½ (41.0 x 27.6 cm). Bequest of the Honorable James Bowdoin III. 1811.129

Jan VAN DER STRAET (STRADANUS) (1523-1605), Flemish: *Mode of Catching Snakes in Holland*. Pen and ink with wash, 7 x 10½ (17.8 x 26.6 cm). Gift of Miss Susan Dwight Bliss. 1956.24.266

Paolo FARINATO (attributed) (1524-1606), Italian: *Woman and Child*. Pen and sepia, 8¾ x 5⅜ (22.2 x 13.7 cm). Bequest of the Honorable James Bowdoin III. 1811.35

✠Pieter BRUEGHEL the Elder (ca. 1525-1569), Flemish: *View of Waltersburg*. Pen and ink, 12⅝ x 10⅝ (32.1 x 27.0 cm). Bequest of the Honorable James Bowdoin III. 1811.142

Giovanni BALDUCCI (attributed) (active 1550-1603), Italian: *John the Baptist Preaching*. Pen and ink with wash, 10½ x 12¾ (26.7 x 32.4 cm). James Phinney Baxter Fund in memory of Professor Henry Johnson h '14. 1932.42

Luca CAMBIASO (1527-1585), Italian: *Apotheosis*. Pen and ink, 14 x 10¾ (35.6 x 27.3 cm). James Phinney Baxter Fund in memory of Professor Henry Johnson h '14. 1932.8

Luca CAMBIASO (attributed) (1527-1585), Italian: *The Scourging in the Temple*. Sepia with wash, 7⅜ x 5⅜ (18.7 x 13.7 cm). Bequest of the Honorable James Bowdoin III. 1811.11

Bernardino INDIA (1528-1590), Italian: *Madonna and Child*. Pen and ink with sepia wash, 6¾ x 6⅛ (17.1 x 15.6 cm). Bequest of the Honorable James Bowdoin III. 1811.5

Frederik SUSTRIS (ca. 1540-1599), Dutch: *Fresco Study*. Pen and ink with wash, 7⅞ x 3¾ (20.0 x 9.5 cm). Bequest of the Honorable James Bowdoin III. 1811.15

Federico ZUCCARO (ca. 1540-1609), Italian: *The Choice of Hercules*. Sepia with wash, 9 x 7⅝ (22.9 x 19.2 cm). Bequest of the Honorable James Bowdoin III. 1811.62

Karel VAN MANDER (1548-1606), Dutch: *Shepherds Feasting*. Pen and ink with wash, 4³⁄₁₆ x 4³⁄₁₆ (10.6 x 10.6 cm). Bequest of the Honorable James Bowdoin III. 1811.89

Bernardino POCCETTI (1548-1612), Italian: *Woman and Child Standing*. Black and red crayon, 8¹¹⁄₁₆ x 6¾ (22.4 x 16.2 cm). Bequest of the Honorable James Bowdoin III. 1811.10

Andrea BOSCOLI (1550-1606), Italian: *The Visitation*. Graphite with wash, 5⁹⁄₁₆ x 9⅛ (14.1 x 23.2 cm). Bequest of the Honorable James Bowdoin III. 1811.7

Belisario Corenzio (1558/60-1640/3), Italian: *Five Figures Gathered around an Obelisk*. Blue wash, 9⅜ x 5⅞ (24.0 x 14.9 cm). Bequest of the Honorable James Bowdoin III. 1811.58

Francesco Vanni (1563/65-1609/10), Italian: *Madonna with Infant Jesus and St. John* (?). Red chalk, 6¹⁵⁄₁₆ x 5¼ (17.7 x 13.4 cm). Bequest of the Honorable James Bowdoin III. 1811.9

Georges Lallemand (ca. 1575-1635), French: *St. Sebastian Nursed by St. Irene and Attendant*. Graphite with wash, 10⅜ x 14⅜ (25.7 x 36.1 cm). Bequest of the Honorable James Bowdoin III. 1811.96

Unknown artist (late 16th century), Flemish: *Ecce Homo*. Pen and ink with wash, 10⅛ x 8¹⁄₁₆ (25.9 x 20.5 cm). Bequest of the Honorable James Bowdoin III. 1811.39

✠Peter Paul Rubens (1577-1640), Flemish: *Thisbe Committing Suicide*. Pen and ink, 5⅝ x 6½ (14.3 x 16.5 cm). Bequest of Mrs. Helen Johnson Chase. 1958.67

Marc Antonio Bassetti (1588-1630), Italian: *Joseph and the Wife of Potiphar*. Pen and ink with wash, 6⅛ x 8¾ (15.6 x 21.3 cm). Museum collections. 1930.184

Esaias van de Velde (1590-1630), Dutch: *Two Men and a Dog*. Graphite, 2¹³⁄₁₆ x 2⅞ (7.2 x 7.4 cm). Gift of Miss Susan Dwight Bliss. 1956.24.269

Giovanni Mannozzi da San Giovanni (1590/92-1636), Italian: *Entombment*. Sepia with wash, 7¼ x 7¹⁵⁄₁₆ (18.3 x 20.1 cm). Bequest of the Honorable James Bowdoin III. 1811.8

Claes Cornelisz Moeyaert (1592-1655), Dutch: *Christ and the Samaritan Woman*. Graphite, 7⅝ x 10⅛ (19.5 x 25.7 cm). Bequest of the Honorable James Bowdoin III. 1811.94

Claes Cornelisz Moeyaert (1592-1655), Dutch: *The Flight into Egypt*. Red chalk, 6⅞ x 10⅝ (17.5 x 27.0 cm). Bequest of the Honorable James Bowdoin III. 1811.52

Claes Cornelisz Moeyaert (1592-1655), Dutch: *Tobias Frightened by the Fish*. Sepia with wash, 8¾ x 6⅜ (21.3 x 16.2 cm). Bequest of the Honorable James Bowdoin III. 1811.63

Abraham van Diepenbeeck (1596-1675), Flemish: *Frontispiece for "Costumen van het Graefschap van Vlaenderen."* Pen and ink with wash, 13⁹⁄₁₆ x 8⅝ (34.4 x 22.0 cm). Bequest of the Honorable James Bowdoin III. 1811.135

Bartholomeus Breenbergh (1599-ca. 1663), Dutch: *Roman Ruins*. Pen and ink with wash, 10¹⁄₁₆ x 13⁹⁄₁₆ (25.5 x 34.4 cm). Bequest of the Honorable James Bowdoin III. 1811.132

Unknown artist (17th century), Florentine, after Sebastiano del Piombo (ca. 1485-1547), Italian: *Head of a Bishop* (r). Graphite.

Figure of a Bishop Seated (v). Graphite and red chalk, $13\frac{1}{16}$ x $8\frac{7}{8}$ (33.2 x 22.6 cm). Museum collections. 1930.133

Jacob A. BACKER (1608-1651), Dutch: *Archer.* Black chalk, $12\frac{13}{16}$ x $7\frac{5}{8}$ (35.1 x 19.3 cm). Museum collections. 1930.231

Giovanni Benedetto CASTIGLIONE (1610/16-1665/70), Italian: *Madonna and Child with Angels.* Pen and ink, $8\frac{5}{8}$ x $7\frac{5}{8}$ (21.8 x 19.4 cm). Gift of Miss Susan Dwight Bliss. 1956.24.196

Giovanni Benedetto CASTIGLIONE (1610/16-1665/70), Italian: *Madonna and Child with Angels.* Pen and ink with wash, $8\frac{3}{8}$ x $6\frac{5}{8}$ (21.3 x 16.8 cm). Gift of Miss Susan Dwight Bliss. 1956.24.197

Salvator ROSA (attributed) (1615-1673), Italian: *Mountainous Landscape.* Sepia with wash, 13 x $17\frac{1}{2}$ (33.0 x 44.5 cm). Bequest of the Honorable James Bowdoin III. 1811.70

Michel DORIGNY (1617-1665), after Simon Vouet (1590-1649), French: *Sample Designs for Panels.* Pen and ink with wash, $15\frac{1}{4}$ x 17 (38.8 x 43.3 cm). Gift of Miss Susan Dwight Bliss. 1956.24.273

Philips DE KONINCK (1619-1688), Dutch: *River Scene.* Sepia with wash, $7\frac{11}{16}$ x $12\frac{1}{2}$ (19.8 x 31.7 cm). Bequest of the Honorable James Bowdoin III. 1811.82

Philips DE KONINCK (1619-1688), Dutch: *Sheds on a Wharf.* Sepia with wash, $7\frac{7}{8}$ x $12\frac{1}{2}$ (19.9 x 31.7 cm). Bequest of the Honorable James Bowdoin III. 1811.79

Claes or Nicholaes BERCHEM (1620-1683), Dutch: *Laundresses and Cowherds.* Pen and ink with sepia wash, $9\frac{1}{2}$ x 14 (24.7 x 35.1 cm). Gift of Miss Susan Dwight Bliss. 1956.24.187

Jan-Baptist WEENIX (attributed) (1621-1663), Dutch: *Landscape.* Red chalk, $10\frac{11}{16}$ x $16\frac{1}{8}$ (27.5 x 41.0 cm). Bequest of the Honorable James Bowdoin III. 1811.140

Carlo MARATTA (1625-1713), Italian: *Allegory of the City of Rome.* Chalk, pen and ink with wash, $18\frac{3}{4}$ x $14\frac{3}{4}$ (47.6 x 37.5 cm). Gift of Miss Susan Dwight Bliss. 1956.24.230

Carlo MARATTA (1625-1713), Italian: *Fame Being Led toward Parnassus* (?). Black and red chalk, $10\frac{7}{8}$ x $23\frac{1}{2}$ (27.6 x 59.7 cm). Bequest of Mrs. Helen Johnson Chase. 1958.70

Niccolo BERRETTONI (1637-1682), Italian: *Study of Venus.* Red chalk, $15\frac{7}{8}$ x $10\frac{3}{8}$ (40.3 x 26.4 cm). James Phinney Baxter Fund in memory of Professor Henry Johnson h '14. 1932.16

Lodovico GIMIGNANI (1643-1697), Italian: *Israelites Gathering Manna* (?). Crayon, 11 x $8\frac{13}{16}$ (27.8 x 22.4 cm). Bequest of the Honorable James Bowdoin III. 1811.16

Sebastiano RICCI (1659-1734), Italian: *Bathsheba.* Sepia with wash,

5⁵⁄₁₆ x 5⅛ (13.5 x 13.1 cm). Bequest of the Honorable James Bowdoin III. 1811.41

Pietro DA PETRI (1663/71-1716), Italian: *Assumption of the Virgin.* Sepia with wash, 10⁷⁄₁₆ x 7⅝ (26.6 x 19.4 cm). Bequest of the Honorable James Bowdoin III. 1811.26

Pietro DA PETRI (1663/71-1716), Italian: *Christ at the Bedside of a Dying Man* (r). Crayon. *Christ at the Bedside of a Dying Man* (v). Pen and ink, 10³⁄₁₆ x 7⅞ (25.9 x 20.0 cm). Bequest of the Honorable James Bowdoin III. 1811.27

Pietro DA PETRI (1663/71-1716), Italian: *Entombment of Christ* (r). Sepia with wash. *Ascension* (v). Pen and ink, 12 x 8⁷⁄₁₆ (30.5 x 21.4 cm). Bequest of the Honorable James Bowdoin III. 1811.28

Pietro DA PETRI (1663/71-1716), Italian: *Europa and the Bull.* Red chalk, 7¾ x 10½ (19.7 x 26.7 cm). Bequest of the Honorable James Bowdoin III. 1811.23

Pietro DA PETRI (1663/71-1716), Italian: *The Flight into Egypt.* Sepia with wash, 10½ x 7¾ (26.6 x 19.7 cm). Bequest of the Honorable James Bowdoin III. 1811.25

Pietro DA PETRI (1663/71-1716), Italian: *Group before Michelangelo's Statue of Moses* (r). Red chalk. *Musicians* (v). Graphite, 10½ x 7¾ (26.7 x 19.7 cm). Bequest of the Honorable James Bowdoin III. 1811.22

Pietro DA PETRI (1663/71-1716), Italian: *Peter Delivered from Prison by the Angel.* Red chalk, 10⅝ x 7¹¹⁄₁₆ (27.0 x 19.5 cm). Bequest of the Honorable James Bowdoin III. 1811.20

Pietro DA PETRI (1663/71-1716), Italian: *Peter Denouncing the Sorcerer* (r). Chalk. *Christ Delivering the Keys to St. Peter* (v). Chalk, 10⁷⁄₁₆ x 7¾ (26.5 x 18.7 cm). Bequest of the Honorable James Bowdoin III. 1811.19

Pietro DA PETRI (1663/71-1716), Italian: *The Visitation.* Sepia with wash, 10½ x 7¹⁵⁄₁₆ (26.7 x 20.2 cm). Bequest of the Honorable James Bowdoin III. 1811.24

Pietro DA PETRI (attributed) (1663/71-1716), Italian: *Solomon's Decision between the Two Mothers.* Red chalk, 10⅝ x 7½ (27.0 x 19.0 cm). Bequest of the Honorable James Bowdoin III. 1811.21

Jean-Baptiste OUDRY (1686-1755), French: *Pomeranian Dog.* Black chalk, 12½ x 15½ (31.8 x 39.4 cm). Museum purchase. 1964.58

Edme BOUCHARDON (1698-1762), French: *Allegory of Justice.* Red chalk, 9½ x 5⅝ (24.0 x 14.3 cm). Bequest of the Honorable James Bowdoin III. 1811.59

Edme BOUCHARDON (1698-1762), French: *Allegory of Prudence.* Red chalk, 9 x 5³⁄₁₆ (22.8 x 13.2 cm). Bequest of the Honorable James Bowdoin III. 1811.74

Girolamo Brusaferro (1700-1760), Italian: *Allegory of America.* Pen and ink with wash, $6\frac{5}{16}$ x $5\frac{1}{16}$ (16.0 x 12.9 cm). Gift of Miss Susan Dwight Bliss. 1956.24.193

Pierre-Antoine Quillard (1701-1733), French: *Garden Scene with Three Figures.* Red chalk, $7\frac{7}{8}$ x $10\frac{3}{8}$ (20.1 x 26.4 cm). Bequest of the Honorable James Bowdoin III. 1811.38

Thomas Gainsborough (attributed) (1727-1788), English: *Horses Feeding.* Graphite, $8\frac{1}{4}$ x $9\frac{3}{4}$ (21.0 x 24.8 cm). Gift of the Misses Harriet and Sophia Walker. 1894.15

Giovanni Domenico Tiepolo (1727-1804), Italian: *Head Study.* Red chalk, $10\frac{1}{2}$ x $8\frac{1}{4}$ (26.7 x 21.0 cm). Florence C. Quinby Fund in memory of Henry Cole Quinby h '16. 1972.14

John Flaxman (1755-1826), English: *Hector Chiding Paris.* Pen and ink with graphite, $8\frac{3}{8}$ x $12\frac{1}{8}$ (21.3 x 30.8 cm). Museum purchase. 1918.1

John Flaxman (1755-1826), English: *Telemachus in Search of His Father.* Pen and ink with graphite, $8\frac{1}{4}$ x $10\frac{7}{8}$ (21.0 x 27.6 cm). Museum purchase. 1918.2

Thomas Rowlandson (1756-1827), English: *The Picnic Party.* Pen and ink with wash, $11\frac{5}{8}$ x 18 (29.6 x 45.7 cm). Gift of Miss Susan Dwight Bliss. 1956.24.256

Charles Balthazar Julien Févret de Saint-Mémin (1770-1852), French: *Portrait of the Honorable Silas Lee.* Crayon, $21\frac{3}{8}$ x 15 (56.9 x 38.1 cm). Gift of Mrs. P. S. J. Talbot. 1869.1

Charles Balthazar Julien Févret de Saint-Mémin (1770-1852), French: *Portrait of Mrs. Silas Lee.* Crayon, $20\frac{1}{2}$ x 15 (50.8 x 38.1 cm). Gift of Mrs. P. S. J. Talbot. 1869.2

Samuel Melcher III (1775-1862), American: *Congregational Church, Wiscasset.* Pen and ink, graphite, and wash, $29\frac{3}{4}$ x $15\frac{7}{8}$ (75.6 x 40.1 cm). Museum collections. T1976.27

Nicolas-Toussaint Charlet (1792-1845), French: *Profile Bust of a Grenadier, Small Comic Figure, and Face of a Negro.* Pen and ink, 7 x $4\frac{3}{8}$ (17.8 x 11.1 cm). Hamlin Fund. 1964.24

Théodore Rousseau (1812-1867), French: *Landscape.* Graphite, $7\frac{5}{8}$ x 11 (19.3 x 27.9 cm). Gift of Miss Susan Dwight Bliss. 1956.24.255

John Ruskin (1819-1900), English: *Entrance to Feldkirch, Tyrol.* Pen and ink with graphite, $8\frac{3}{4}$ x $10\frac{1}{2}$ (22.2 x 26.7 cm). Gift of Miss Susan Dwight Bliss. 1956.24.261

John Ruskin (1819-1900), English: *St. Mark's and the Ducal Palace, Venice.* Pen and ink with graphite, $10\frac{5}{8}$ x $7\frac{5}{16}$ (28.0 x 18.5 cm). Gift of Miss Susan Dwight Bliss. 1956.24.264a

Charles MERYON (1821-1868), French: *The Old Louvre.* Graphite, 4⅜ x 10 (11.2 x 25.4 cm). Gift of Miss Susan Dwight Bliss. 1956.24.227a

Alexandre CABANEL (1824-1889), French: *Allegorical Female Figure.* Chalk, 21 3/16 x 12 1/16 (53.8 x 30.6 cm). Gift of the Misses Harriet and Sophia Walker. 1904.23

David JOHNSON (1827-1908), American: *Maple.* Graphite and white chalk, 11⅝ x 17 11/16 (29.5 x 45.3 cm). Museum purchase. 1968.70

James M. HART (1828-1901), American: *Trees and Stream.* Graphite, 13½ x 17½ (34.3 x 44.5 cm). Florence C. Quinby Fund in memory of Henry Cole Quinby h '16. 1969.78

Samuel COLMAN (1832-1920), American: *Old Orchard at Newport.* Graphite and watercolor, 6 15/16 x 12 3/16 (17.6 x 31.0 cm). Florence C. Quinby Fund in memory of Henry Cole Quinby h '16. 1969.80

Edward BURNE-JONES (1833-1898), English: *Female Figure.* Chalk and gouache, 14 x 6 15/16 (35.5 x 17.5 cm). Gift of the Misses Harriet and Sophia Walker. 1897.6

John LA FARGE (1836-1910), American: *Portfolio of Sketches.* 22 sheets, graphite, max. dim. 9¼ x 7¾ (23.5 x 19.7 cm). Gift of Miss Susan Dwight Bliss. 1956.24.223.3

John LA FARGE (1836-1910), American: *Sketchbook.* 84 sheets, watercolor, pen and ink, graphite, 8 x 10 (20.3 x 25.4 cm). Gift of Miss Susan Dwight Bliss. 1956.24.223.1

John LA FARGE (1836-1910), American: *Sketchbook.* 62 sheets, graphite, 5½ x 7¾ (14.0 x 19.7 cm). Gift of Miss Susan Dwight Bliss. 1956.24.223.2

Elihu VEDDER (1836-1923), American: *Amore.* Black and white crayon, 8¾ x 9½ (22.2 x 24.1 cm). Gift of the American Academy of Arts and Letters. 1955.4.6

Elihu VEDDER (1836-1923), American: *Anima.* Black and white crayon, 15¼ x 11 (38.7 x 27.9 cm). Gift of the American Academy of Arts and Letters. 1955.4.9

Elihu VEDDER (1836-1923), American: *Natura.* Black and white crayon, 17⅛ x 12⅝ (43.5 x 32.1 cm). Gift of the American Academy of Arts and Letters. 1955.4.3

Thomas MORAN (1837-1926), American: *Distant City.* Graphite, 11⅛ x 14⅛ (28.3 x 36.0 cm). Florence C. Quinby Fund in memory of Henry Cole Quinby h '16. 1971.3

✠Mary CASSATT (1845-1926), American: *The Barefoot Child.* Pastel, 28 x 21 (71.1 x 53.3 cm). Gift of Mrs. Murray S. Danforth in memory of her husband, Dr. Murray S. Danforth '01. 1953.42

Eugène CARRIÈRE (1849-1906), French: *Apparition.* Charcoal, 12 1/16 x

$7\frac{3}{4}$ (30.6 x 19.7 cm). Florence C. Quinby Fund in memory of Henry Cole Quinby h '16.   1969.63

Kenyon Cox (1856-1919), American: *Study of the Campanile of San Giorgio Maggiore* for the mural *Venice* in the Bowdoin College Museum of Art. Graphite, $6\frac{1}{4}$ x $3\frac{7}{8}$ (15.9 x 9.8 cm). Gift of Colonel Leonard Cox, Mrs. Caroline Cox Lansing, and Mr. Allyn Cox. 1959.3.6

Kenyon Cox (1856-1919), American: *Study for Figure of Commerce* for the mural *Venice* in the Bowdoin College Museum of Art. Graphite, $15\frac{5}{8}$ x $18\frac{7}{8}$ (39.7 x 47.9 cm). Museum collections. 1959.9

Kenyon Cox (1856-1919), American: *Study for Figure of Venice* for the mural *Venice* in the Bowdoin College Museum of Art. Graphite, $3\frac{7}{8}$ x $6\frac{1}{4}$ (9.8 x 15.9 cm). Gift of Colonel Leonard Cox, Mrs. Caroline Cox Lansing, and Mr. Allyn Cox. 1959.3.7

John Singer SARGENT (1856-1925), American: *Figure Study.* Charcoal, $18\frac{1}{2}$ x $24\frac{1}{2}$ (47.0 x 62.2 cm). Gift of Miss Emily Sargent and Mrs. Francis Ormond. 1930.75

John Singer SARGENT (1856-1925), American: *Figure Study.* Charcoal, $18\frac{3}{4}$ x $24\frac{3}{4}$ (47.6 x 63.0 cm). Gift of Miss Emily Sargent and Mrs. Francis Ormond. 1930.76

John Singer SARGENT (1856-1925), American: *Study.* Charcoal, 19 x $24\frac{3}{8}$ (48.3 x 62.5 cm). Gift of Miss Emily Sargent and Mrs. Francis Ormond. 1930.77

James ENSOR (1860-1949), Belgian: *The Artist's Mother and Sister.* Graphite, $9\frac{1}{2}$ x $11\frac{3}{4}$ (24.1 x 29.8 cm). Museum purchase. 1963.485

Walter GRIFFIN (1861-1935), American: *Untitled Landscape.* Pastel, 12 x $7\frac{15}{16}$ (30.4 x 20.1 cm). Bequest of Mrs. Edith L. K. Sills h '52. 1979.64

Gustav KLIMT (1862-1918), Austrian: *Seated Woman.* Blue chalk, $17\frac{5}{8}$ x $12\frac{3}{8}$ (44.8 x 31.4 cm). Museum purchase. 1957.38

John SLOAN (1871-1951), American: *The Fisherman.* Pen and ink, $13\frac{3}{16}$ x $7\frac{1}{8}$ (33.5 x 18.1 cm). Bequest of Mr. George Otis Hamlin. 1961.69.15

John SLOAN (1871-1951), American: *Visitors to an Exhibition.* Graphite, $6\frac{1}{4}$ x $9\frac{5}{8}$ (15.9 x 24.5 cm). Gift of Mrs. John Sloan. 1962.6

Frantisek KUPKA (1871-1957), Czechoslovakian: *Initiation II.* Charcoal and chalk, 12 x $6\frac{15}{16}$ (30.5 x 17.6 cm). Florence C. Quinby Fund in memory of Henry Cole Quinby h '16. 1970.35

Joseph STELLA (1880-1946), American: *Seated Man with Cane.* Graphite, $10\frac{7}{16}$ x $6\frac{1}{2}$ (26.5 x 16.5 cm). Hamlin Fund. 1964.2

Joseph STELLA (1880-1946), American: *Study of a Bearded Man.* Graphite, $5\frac{1}{8}$ x $6\frac{3}{8}$ (13.0 x 16.2 cm). Hamlin Fund. 1964.3

Abraham WALKOWITZ (1880-1965), American: *Untitled*. Pastel, graphite, and watercolor, $12\frac{1}{16}$ x $8\frac{13}{16}$ (30.6 x 22.3 cm). Hamlin Fund. 1979.45

George BELLOWS (1882-1925), American: *Emma Bellows, Walking*. Graphite, 11 x $7\frac{3}{4}$ (27.9 x 19.7 cm). Gift of Mr. Walter K. Gutman '24. 1925.7

Rockwell KENT (1882-1971), American: *Nude in Dancing Pose*. Graphite, 19 x $12\frac{1}{2}$ (48.3 x 31.1 cm). Anonymous gift. 1971.79.21

Rockwell KENT (1882-1971), American: *Portrait of T. M. Cleland*. Graphite and chalk, $18\frac{1}{2}$ x $14\frac{3}{8}$ (47.0 x 36.5 cm). Anonymous gift. 1971.79.19

Rockwell KENT (1882-1971), American: *Study for Revisitation*. Graphite and wash, $5\frac{1}{2}$ x $7\frac{5}{8}$ (14.0 x 19.4 cm). Anonymous gift. 1971.79.7

Rudolf GROSSMANN (b. 1882), German: *Head of Max Lieberman*. Graphite, 12 x $9\frac{1}{2}$ (30.4 x 24.1 cm). Museum purchase. 1957.93

Elie NADELMAN (1885-1946), American: *Head Turned Right, Looking Down*. Pen and ink, $12\frac{1}{4}$ x 8 (31.2 x 20.3 cm). Hamlin Fund. 1979.44

Alexander ARCHIPENKO (1887-1964), American: *Nude Study*. Red and blue crayon, $16\frac{5}{8}$ x $10\frac{3}{16}$ (42.2 x 25.9 cm). Museum purchase. 1958.49

LE CORBUSIER (Charles Edouard Jeanneret) (1887-1965), French: *Plan for a Model City*. Chalk, $42\frac{1}{2}$ x $90\frac{1}{4}$ (108.0 x 229.2 cm). Gift of Mrs. Edith L. K. Sills h '52. 1976.47

Marguerite ZORACH (1887-1968), American: *Untitled*. Graphite, $11\frac{1}{2}$ x $10\frac{7}{16}$ (29.2 x 26.5 cm). Gift of Mrs. Dahlov Ipcar and Mr. Tessim Zorach. 1979.72

Oskar SCHLEMMER (1888-1943), German: *Head in Profile on a Black Sectioned Background*. Graphite and chalk, $11\frac{3}{16}$ x $8\frac{5}{8}$ (28.4 x 21.8 cm). Florence C. Quinby Fund in memory of Henry Cole Quinby h '16. 1970.34

Gerhard MARCKS (b. 1889), German: *Head of a Woman*. Graphite, $10\frac{7}{16}$ x $8\frac{1}{2}$ (26.5 x 21.6 cm). Museum purchase. 1958.1

⌖Egon SCHIELE (1890-1918), Austrian: *Standing Woman*. Graphite, $19\frac{1}{8}$ x $12\frac{5}{8}$ (48.6 x 32.1 cm). Museum purchase. 1957.87

Robert LAURENT (1890-1970), American: *Torso—Three Quarters*. Graphite and crayon, $20\frac{1}{4}$ x $13\frac{1}{2}$ (51.5 x 34.2 cm). Hamlin Fund. 1979.50

Reuben NAKIAN (b. 1897), American: *Untitled*. Pen and ink, $11\frac{3}{8}$ x $14\frac{1}{4}$ (28.9 x 36.2 cm). Gift of Mr. Walter K. Gutman '24. 1965.46

Louise KRUGER (20th century), American: *Running Figure, Left, Right, and Center Views.* Pen and ink with watercolor, 12¼ x 11⅛ (31.1 x 28.2 cm). Hamlin Fund with the aid of a matching grant from the National Endowment for the Arts in Washington, D. C., a federal agency. 1977.21

Rico LEBRUN (1900-1964), American: *Restless Figures.* Pen and ink, graphite with wash, 38¼ x 27¾ (97.2 x 70.5 cm). Gift of Mr. and Mrs. Herbert C. Lee. 1965.52

Arshile GORKY (1904-1948), American: *Untitled.* Crayon, 19⅞ x 26 (50.5 x 66.0 cm). Gift of Mr. Walter K. Gutman '24. 1964.63

✠Arshile GORKY (1904-1948), American: *Untitled.* Pencil and crayon, 15½ x 22½ (39.4 x 57.2 cm). Gift of Mr. Walter K. Gutman '24. 1966.91

✠Franz KLINE (1910-1962), American: *Untitled.* Gouache, 19 11/16 x 14¾ (50.0 x 37.5 cm). Gift of Mr. Walter K. Gutman '24. 1964.65

Hyman BLOOM (b. 1913), American: *Landscape #21: Moonlight.* Charcoal, 65 x 42½ (165.1 x 108.0 cm). Anonymous gift. 1970.17

Philip GUSTON (b. 1913), American: *Untitled.* Pen and ink, 23¼ x 18 (58.9 x 45.7 cm). Gift of Mr. Walter K. Gutman '24. 1964.64

Leonard BASKIN (b. 1922), American: *Head.* Pen and ink, 30½ x 22 (77.5 x 55.9 cm). Gift of the artist. 1965.53

Roy LICHTENSTEIN (b. 1923), American: *Two Studies for Guitars.* Graphite, 7 1/16 x 9⅛ (17.9 x 23.2 cm). Hamlin Fund with the aid of a matching grant from the National Endowment for the Arts in Washington, D. C., a federal agency. 1976.37

Philip PEARLSTEIN (b. 1924), American: *Seated Female Model on Couch.* Graphite, 17⅞ x 23¾ (45.5 x 60.3 cm). Hamlin Fund with the aid of a matching grant from the National Endowment for the Arts in Washington, D. C., a federal agency. 1976.30

George SEGAL (b. 1924), American: *Untitled.* Pastel, 17⅞ x 12 (45.4 x 30.5 cm). Gift of Mr. Walter K. Gutman '24. 1966.35

Sol LEWITT (b. 1928), American: *The Location of a Blue Square, a Red Trapezoid, a Yellow Circle, and a Black Triangle.* Graphite and colored ink, 18 x 18 (45.7 x 45.7 cm). Hamlin Fund with the aid of a matching grant from the National Endowment for the Arts in Washington, D. C., a federal agency. 1977.23

CHRISTO (Javacheff) (b. 1935), American: *Running Fence.* Graphite, pastel, charcoal, and fabric, 22¼ x 28¼ (56.5 x 72.0 cm). Hamlin Fund with the aid of a matching grant from the National Endowment for the Arts in Washington, D. C., a federal agency. 1976.38

Charles WELLS (b. 1935), American: *Two Seated Nudes.* Charcoal and wash, 39¾ x 28 (101.0 x 71.1 cm). Hamlin Fund. 1966.8

Emilio Cruz (b. 1938), American: *Untitled*. Pen and ink with wash, 17-9/16 x 26-9/16 (44.7 x 59.9 cm). Gift of Mr. Walter K. Gutman '24. 1965.40

DeWitt Hardy (b. 1940), American: *Portrait of Ethan*. Graphite and watercolor, 13⅝ x 10¾ (34.5 x 27.0 cm). Hamlin Fund with the aid of a matching grant from the National Endowment for the Arts in Washington, D. C., a federal agency. 1977.1

Patt Franklin (b. 1941), American: *Orchid*. Graphite, 7-1/16 x 7-1/16 (18.0 x 18.0 cm). Hamlin Fund. 1979.54

Mark Forrester Libby (b. 1948), American: *Dead Tree*. Pen and ink, 14 x 10 (35.6 x 25.4 cm). Hamlin Fund. 1968.71

Joseph Nicoletti (b. 1948), American: *Studio Nude, Seated*. Graphite and watercolor, 22½ x 15 (57.2 x 38.1 cm). Hamlin Fund with the aid of a matching grant from the National Endowment for the Arts in Washington, D. C., a federal agency. 1977.5

Prints

Unknown artist (15th century), German: *Moses Commissioning Joshua*. Woodcut, 4½ x 7⅜ (11.5 x 18.7 cm). Anonymous gift. 1978.8

Unknown artist (15th century), Italian: *The Triumphs of Petrarch*. Set of 6 woodcuts, max. dim. 9⅜ x 6¼ (23.9 x 16.0 cm). Anonymous gift. 1978.12.1-.6

Albrecht Dürer (1471-1528), German: *Life of the Virgin*. Set of 20 woodcuts, max. dim. 11-13/16 x 8¼ (30.5 x 21.0 cm). Gift of Miss Susan Dwight Bliss. 1956.24.44.1-.20

Albrecht Dürer (1471-1528), German: *Pilate Washing His Hands*. Woodcut, 5 x 3⅞ (12.8 x 9.9 cm). Anonymous gift. 1978.4

George Pencz (active 1500-1550), German: *Procris Slain by Cephalis*. Engraving, 4⅝ x 2-15/16 (11.7 x 7.4 cm). James Phinney Baxter Fund in memory of Professor Henry Johnson h '14. 1979.20

Jean De Gourmont I (active 1501-1556), French: *The Marriage of St. Catharine*. Engraving, 3-1/16 x 4¼ (7.8 x 10.8 cm). Gift of Miss Susan Dwight Bliss. 1963.452

Albrecht Altdorfer (1480-1538), German: *Pyramus and Thisbe*. Engraving, 2⅜ x 1-9/16 (6.0 x 3.9 cm). Sylvia E. Ross Fund. 1972.3

Hans Leonhard Schauffelin (1480-1539), German: *The Ascension*. Woodcut, 9⅜ x 6¾ (23.8 x 16.3 cm). Museum collections. 1930.165

Urs Graf (1485/90-1529), German: *Christ Mocked*. Woodcut, 8½ x 6¼ (21.6 x 15.9 cm). Museum collections. 1930.176

Hans HOLBEIN the Younger (1497-1543), German: *Death Leading the Blind*. Woodcut, $2\frac{9}{16}$ x $1\frac{13}{16}$ (6.4 x 4.6 cm). Gift of Mr. Philip Hofer. 1976.18

Barthel BEHAM (1502-1540), German: *Battle for the Banner*. Engraving, $2\frac{1}{2}$ x $11\frac{3}{8}$ (6.4 x 29.0 cm). Anonymous gift. 1978.5

Enea VICO (1523-1567), Italian: *A Decorated Urn*. Engraving, $8\frac{5}{8}$ x $6\frac{5}{8}$ (21.7 x 16.7 cm). Gift of Miss Susan Dwight Bliss. 1956.24.369

Unknown artist after Jan van der Straet (Stradanus) (1523-1605), Flemish: *Cranes Catching Snakes*. Engraving, $8\frac{1}{16}$ x $10\frac{11}{16}$ (20.4 x 27.2 cm). Anonymous gift. 1976.39

Hendrick GOLTZIUS (1558-1617), Dutch: *Christ before Pilate*. Etching, 8 x $5\frac{5}{16}$ (20.3 x 13.5 cm). Museum collections. 1930.164

Annibale CARRACCI (1560-1609), Italian: *Susanna and the Elders*. Etching and engraving, $13\frac{5}{8}$ x $12\frac{1}{4}$ (34.6 x 31.1 cm). Anonymous gift. 1978.17

Andrea ANDREANI (ca. 1560-1623), Italian: *The Triumph of Caesar*. Chiaroscuro woodcut, $14\frac{9}{16}$ x $14\frac{11}{16}$ (37.0 x 37.3 cm). Museum purchase. 1965.47

Crispin DE PASSE the Elder (1565-1637), Dutch: *Saul Orders the Priests to Be Slain*. Engraving, $7\frac{5}{8}$ x $5\frac{5}{8}$ (19.4 x 14.3 cm). Susan Dwight Bliss Fund. 1970.49

Guido RENI (1575-1642), Italian: *St. John and the Infant Jesus*. Etching, $4\frac{11}{16}$ x $6\frac{11}{16}$ (11.9 x 17.0 cm). Gift of Miss Susan Dwight Bliss. 1956.24.144

Christoffel VAN SICHEM II (1581-1658), Dutch, after Hendrick Goltzius (1558-1617), Dutch: *Judith with Head of Holofernes*. Chiaroscuro woodcut, $5\frac{1}{4}$ x 4 (13.5 x 10.2). Anonymous gift. 1978.6

Hendrik GOUDT (1585-1630), Dutch, after Adam Elsheimer (1578-1610), Dutch: *The Flight into Egypt*. Engraving, $11\frac{1}{2}$ x $15\frac{5}{8}$ (29.2 x 39.7 cm). Anonymous gift. 1977.6

Jacques CALLOT (1592-1635), French: *St. Armand*. Etching, $7\frac{11}{16}$ x $11\frac{1}{16}$ (19.6 x 28.1 cm). Sylvia E. Ross Fund. 1972.4

Claes Cornelisz MOEYAERT (1592-1655), Dutch: *Jacob's Dream*. Etching, $6\frac{1}{4}$ x $8\frac{7}{8}$ (15.9 x 22.5 cm). Helen Johnson Chase Fund. 1975.4

Lucas VORSTERMAN (1595-1675), Flemish: *Emperor Charles V*. Engraving, 17 x $12\frac{5}{8}$ (43.2 x 32.1 cm). Gift of Miss Susan Dwight Bliss. 1956.24.370

Anthony VAN DYCK (1599-1641), Flemish: *Portrait of Joannes de Wael*. Etching, $9\frac{5}{8}$ x $6\frac{7}{8}$ (24.5 x 17.4 cm). Gift of Mr. Charles A. Coffin h '22. 1923.97

Claude Lorrain (Claude Gellée) (1600-1682), French: *The Dance by the Waterside*. Etching, $5\frac{3}{16}$ x $7\frac{5}{8}$ (13.2 x 19.4 cm). Gift of Mr. Charles A. Coffin h '22. 1923.65

Jan Georg van Vliet (1610-1633), Dutch: *Beggar on Two Crutches; Beggar Seated on a Knoll*. Etchings; 1) $3\frac{5}{8}$ x $2\frac{1}{2}$ (9.2 x 6.5 cm); 2) $3\frac{3}{4}$ x $2\frac{5}{8}$ (9.4 x 6.6 cm). Gift of Miss Susan Dwight Bliss. 1956.24. 157

Stefano della Bella (1610-1664), Italian: *Interior of St. Laurant Church*. Etching, $10\frac{1}{4}$ x $8\frac{1}{4}$ (26.0 x 21.0 cm). Museum collections. 1930.160

Stefano della Bella (1610-1664), Italian: *Woman Seen from Behind*. Etching, $9\frac{7}{8}$ x $7\frac{3}{8}$ (25.0 x 18.7 cm). James Phinney Baxter Fund in memory of Professor Henry Johnson h '14. 1979.8

Adriaen van Ostade (1610-1684), Dutch: *The Cheerful Smoker*. Etching, $4\frac{1}{8}$ x $3\frac{5}{8}$ (10.5 x 9.2 cm). Gift of Mr. Charles A. Coffin h '22. 1923.99

Adriaen van Ostade (1610-1684), Dutch: *The Dance at the Inn*. Etching, $10\frac{1}{8}$ x $12\frac{3}{4}$ (25.8 x 32.5 cm). Gift of Mr. Charles A. Coffin h '22. 1923.82

Dirk Stoop (1610-1686), Dutch: *Horse Being Led*. Etching, $5\frac{7}{8}$ x $7\frac{5}{8}$ (14.9 x 19.4 cm). James Phinney Baxter Fund in memory of Professor Henry Johnson h '14, and David C. Warner '76. 1979.14

Jan-Dirksz Both (ca. 1618/22-1652), Dutch: *The Wooden Bridge at Sulmona near Tivoli*. Etching, $7\frac{5}{16}$ x $10\frac{5}{16}$ (18.6 x 26.2 cm). Helen Johnson Chase Fund. 1975.5

Robert Nanteuil (1623-1678), French: *Don Juan of Austria*. Engraving, $9\frac{1}{4}$ x $6\frac{1}{8}$ (23.5 x 15.6 cm). Gift of Miss Susan Dwight Bliss. 1956.24.342

Pietro da Petri (1663/71-1716), Italian: *Purgatory*. Etching and engraving, $15\frac{3}{8}$ x $10\frac{1}{4}$ (39.1 x 26.0 cm). Anonymous gift. 1979.17

Jean Antoine Watteau (1684-1721), French: *Recruits Going to Join the Regiment*. Etching, $9\frac{13}{16}$ x $13\frac{11}{16}$ (24.9 x 34.8 cm). Museum purchase with anonymous gifts. 1980.2

Michele Marieschi (1696-1743), Italian, after Giuseppe Zocchi (1711-1767), Italian: *View of the Arno River*. Engraving, $12\frac{1}{8}$ x $18\frac{3}{4}$ (30.8 x 47.7 cm). Gift of Miss Susan Dwight Bliss. 1956.24.335

Giovanni Antonio Canale (Canaletto) (1697-1768), Italian: *The Market at Dolo*. Etching, $5\frac{3}{4}$ x $8\frac{1}{4}$ (14.6 x 21.0 cm). Gift of Miss Susan Dwight Bliss. 1963.344

Giambattista Piranesi (1720-1778), Italian: *Pyramid of Caius Cestius, Rome*. Etching, $15\frac{9}{16}$ x $21\frac{1}{8}$ (39.5 x 53.7 cm). Bequest of Mrs. Morgan B. Cushing. 1960.54

Giambattista Piranesi (1720-1778), Italian: *Tomb of Cecilia Metella.* Etching, $17\frac{7}{8}$ x $25\frac{1}{4}$ (45.7 x 64.1 cm). Museum collections. 1954.1.14

Francesco Bartolozzi (1727-1815), Italian: *The Marlborough Family.* Engraving, $4\frac{1}{4}$ x $3\frac{1}{2}$ (10.6 x 9.0 cm). Gift of Miss Susan Dwight Bliss. 1956.24.278

Jean Honoré Fragonard (1732-1806), French: *Bacchanal.* Set of 4 etchings, max. dim. $7\frac{1}{4}$ x $9\frac{5}{8}$ (18.5 x 24.5 cm). Gift of Miss Susan Dwight Bliss. 1956.24.52.1-.4

François Janinet (1752-1813), French, after Jacques Charlier (ca. 1720-1790), French: *Venus.* Engraving, $6\frac{3}{4}$ x 8 (17.2 x 20.2 cm). Gift of Miss Susan Dwight Bliss. 1956.24.322

William Blake (1757-1827), English: *Thou Hast Fulfilled the Judgment of the Wicked,* from the series The Book of Job. Engraving, $7\frac{7}{8}$ x $6\frac{1}{2}$ (20.7 x 16.5 cm). Museum purchase. 1970.50

Carle Vernet (1758-1836), French: *Cavalry Battle.* Lithograph, $7\frac{1}{8}$ x $20\frac{3}{4}$ (18.1 x 52.7 cm). Anonymous gift. 1975.1

Baron Antoine-Jean Gros (1771-1835), French: *Chief of the Mamelukes.* Lithograph, $12\frac{5}{8}$ x $9\frac{1}{4}$ (32.1 x 23.5 cm). James Phinney Baxter Fund in memory of Professor Henry Johnson h '14. 1957.45

Joseph Mallord William Turner (1775-1851), English: *Aesacus and Hesperié.* Etching and engraving, $11\frac{9}{16}$ x $8\frac{1}{4}$ (29.3 x 20.9 cm). Museum purchase with the aid of the Hamlin Fund. 1979.56

John Martin (1789-1854), English: *Paradise Lost.* Mezzotint, 10 x 14 (25.4 x 35.6 cm). Museum purchase. 1973.4

Théodore Géricault (1791-1824), French: *Mecklemburg Horse.* Lithograph, $8\frac{3}{8}$ x $9\frac{1}{4}$ (20.7 x 23.4 cm). Florence C. Quinby Fund in memory of Henry Cole Quinby h '16. 1970.11

Thomas Doughty (1793-1856), American: *Cabinet of Natural History and American Rural Sports.* Set of 24 engravings and lithographs, max. dim. $6\frac{5}{8}$ x $8\frac{3}{4}$ (16.8 x 21.7 cm). James Phinney Baxter Fund in memory of Professor Henry Johnson h '14. 1970.18.1-.24

Jean Baptiste Camille Corot (1796-1875), French: *The Outskirts of Rome.* Etching and aquatint, $12\frac{1}{2}$ x $9\frac{3}{8}$ (31.8 x 23.9 cm). Gift of Miss Susan Dwight Bliss. 1963.448

Jean Baptiste Camille Corot (1796-1875), French: *Remembrance of Italy.* Etching, $12\frac{9}{16}$ x $9\frac{5}{16}$ (31.9 x 23.6 cm). Gift of Mr. Charles A. Coffin h '22. 1923.72

Eugène Delacroix (1798-1863), French: *Portrait of Goethe.* Lithograph, $5\frac{3}{4}$ x $6\frac{1}{8}$ (14.7 x 15.5 cm). James Phinney Baxter Fund in memory of Professor Henry Johnson h '14. 1979.7

Eugène Delacroix (1798-1863), French: *What then? A rat?,* illustration from *Hamlet* by William Shakespeare. Lithograph, $9\frac{9}{16}$ x $7\frac{5}{8}$ (24.2 x 19.3 cm). Museum collections. 1930.161

Eugène-Louis-Gabriel Isabey (1803-1886), French: *The Outskirts of Dieppe.* Lithograph, $8\frac{3}{8}$ x $11\frac{3}{16}$ (21.3 x 28.4 cm). Museum purchase. 1957.49

Samuel Palmer (1805-1881), English: *Opening the Fold.* Etching, $6\frac{3}{8}$ x $8\frac{7}{8}$ (16.2 x 22.7 cm). Gift of Miss Susan Dwight Bliss. 1963.327

Honoré Daumier (1808-1879), French: *At the Café d'Aguesseau ...,* from the series Men of Law. Lithograph, $10\frac{5}{8}$ x $8\frac{3}{16}$ (27.1 x 20.8 cm). Museum purchase. 1952.3.1

Honoré Daumier (1808-1879), French: *(Bearded Woman)—Impudent! ...,* from the series Actualités. Lithograph, $10\frac{3}{4}$ x $8\frac{3}{4}$ (27.3 x 22.2 cm). Museum purchase. 1952.8.3

Honoré Daumier (1808-1879), French: *Charivari ...,* from the series Actualités. Lithograph, $10\frac{5}{8}$ x $8\frac{1}{4}$ (26.8 x 21.0 cm). Museum purchase. 1952.8.2

Honoré Daumier (1808-1879), French: *A modest animal ...,* from the series Actualités. Lithograph, $8\frac{3}{8}$ x $10\frac{1}{4}$ (21.3 x 26.0 cm). Museum purchase. 1952.8.1

Honoré Daumier (1808-1879), French: *Revival of Turenne,* from the series Actualités. Lithograph, $9\frac{15}{16}$ x $8\frac{3}{8}$ (25.4 x 21.3 cm). Museum purchase. 1952.8.4

Honoré Daumier (1808-1879), French: *Successor of Charlemagne,* from the series Actualités. Lithograph, $10\frac{7}{8}$ x $9\frac{1}{4}$ (27.6 x 23.5 cm). Museum purchase. 1952.8.5

Théodore Rousseau (1812-1867), French: *Landscape with Rocks.* Etching, $4\frac{7}{8}$ x $6\frac{11}{16}$ (12.5 x 17.0 cm). Gift of Mr. Charles A. Coffin h '22. 1923.64

Charles Jacque (1813-1894), French: *Herd of Pigs.* Etching, $7\frac{1}{4}$ x $9\frac{7}{16}$ (18.5 x 24.0 cm). Museum collections. 1930.170

Jean François Millet (1814-1875), French: *The Man with the Wheelbarrow.* Etching, $6\frac{3}{8}$ x $5\frac{3}{16}$ (16.2 x 13.2 cm). Gift of Mr. Charles A. Coffin h '22. 1923.68

Jean François Millet (1814-1875), French: *Starting Out for Work.* Etching, $15\frac{3}{16}$ x $12\frac{1}{16}$ (38.6 x 30.7 cm). Gift of Mr. Charles A. Coffin h '22. 1923.89

Charles François Daubigny (1817-1878), French: *Crows in a Tree.* Etching, $8\frac{1}{2}$ x $11\frac{13}{16}$ (21.5 x 30.0 cm). Museum collections. 1930.172

Charles François Daubigny (1817-1878), French: *The Grape Harvest.* Etching, $7\frac{3}{4}$ x $13\frac{1}{8}$ (19.7 x 33.4 cm). Gift of Mr. Charles A. Coffin h '22. 1923.75

Charles François Daubigny (1817-1878), French: *The Shepherds.*

Etching, $11\frac{7}{16}$ x $8\frac{3}{4}$ (29.0 x 22.2 cm). Gift of Miss Susan Dwight Bliss. 1956.24.38

Francis Seymour Haden (1818-1910), English: *Challow Farm.* Etching, $5\frac{7}{8}$ x $8\frac{3}{4}$ (14.9 x 22.2 cm). Gift of Miss Susan Dwight Bliss. 1956.24.61

Francis Seymour Haden (1818-1910), English: *Evening.* Etching, $5\frac{7}{8}$ x $3\frac{3}{4}$ (14.9 x 9.5 cm). Gift of Miss Susan Dwight Bliss. 1956.24.57

Francis Seymour Haden (1818-1910), English: *Harlech.* Engraving, $8\frac{13}{16}$ x $12\frac{3}{8}$ (22.4 x 31.5 cm). Gift of Mr. Charles A. Coffin h '22. 1923.80

Francis Seymour Haden (1818-1910), English: *Self Portrait.* Etching, $7\frac{3}{4}$ x $10\frac{5}{8}$ (19.8 x 26.9 cm). Gift of Mr. Charles A. Coffin h '22. 1923.86

Johann Barthold Jongkind (1819-1891), Dutch: *Anvers.* Etching, $6\frac{1}{4}$ x $9\frac{5}{16}$ (15.9 x 23.7 cm). Museum collections. 1930.175

Charles Meryon (1821-1868), French: *The Bridge at the Exchange, Paris.* Etching, $6\frac{1}{8}$ x $13\frac{1}{4}$ (15.6 x 33.2 cm). Florence C. Quinby Fund in memory of Henry Cole Quinby h '16. 1969.76

Charles Meryon (1821-1868), French: *Collège Henri IV* or *Lycée Napoléon.* Etching, $11\frac{5}{8}$ x $18\frac{7}{8}$ (29.5 x 48.1 cm). Gift of Miss Susan Dwight Bliss. 1956.24.109

Charles Meryon (1821-1868), French: *The Gallery of Notre Dame.* Etching, $11\frac{1}{8}$ x $6\frac{15}{16}$ (28.3 x 17.6 cm). Gift of Miss Susan Dwight Bliss. 1956.24.123

Charles Meryon (1821-1868), French: *The Naval Ministry.* Etching, $6\frac{5}{8}$ x $5\frac{3}{4}$ (16.8 x 14.6 cm). Gift of Miss Susan Dwight Bliss. 1956.24.115

Charles Meryon (1821-1868), French: *Oceania—Fishing near Palm Trees.* Etching, $6\frac{3}{16}$ x $13\frac{5}{16}$ (15.7 x 33.8 cm). Susan Dwight Bliss Fund. 1974.36

Charles Meryon (1821-1868), French: *The Petit Pont.* Etching, $10\frac{1}{4}$ x $7\frac{1}{2}$ (26.0 x 19.0 cm). Florence C. Quinby Fund in memory of Henry Cole Quinby h '16. 1970.68

Charles Meryon (1821-1868), French, after Félix Bracquemond (1833-1917), French: *Portrait of Meryon.* Etching, $5\frac{7}{8}$ x $3\frac{15}{16}$ (14.9 x 10.0 cm). Gift of Miss Susan Dwight Bliss. 1956.24.17

Charles Meryon (1821-1868), French: *Rue de Chantres, Paris.* Etching, $11\frac{13}{16}$ x $5\frac{7}{8}$ (30.0 x 14.8 cm). Gift of Miss Susan Dwight Bliss. 1956.24.124

Charles Meryon (1821-1868), French: *Rue des Toiles, Bourges.* Etching, $8\frac{7}{16}$ x $4\frac{5}{8}$ (21.4 x 11.8 cm). Gift of Mr. Charles A. Coffin h '22. 1923.59

Charles MERYON (1821-1868), French: *Saint Etienne-du-Mont.* Etching, $9\frac{11}{16}$ x $5\frac{1}{8}$ (24.7 x 13.0 cm). Gift of Miss Susan Dwight Bliss. 1956.24.122

Charles MERYON (1821-1868), French: *The Vampire.* Etching, $6\frac{1}{2}$ x $5\frac{1}{8}$ (16.6 x 12.9 cm). Gift of Miss Susan Dwight Bliss. 1956.24.119

Rodolphe BRESDIN (1822-1885), French: *The Stream in the Gorge.* Transfer lithograph, $4\frac{3}{8}$ x $5\frac{7}{8}$ (11.2 x 14.8 cm). Anonymous gift. 1978.7

Maxime LaLANNE (1827-1886), French: *The Canal at the Bridge of St. Maxence.* Etching, $6\frac{9}{16}$ x $9\frac{1}{4}$ (16.7 x 23.2 cm). Gift of Mr. Charles A. Coffin h '22. 1923.94

⌖Camille PISSARRO (1830-1903), French: *Effect of Rain.* Etching, aquatint, and drypoint, $6\frac{1}{4}$ x $8\frac{3}{8}$ (15.8 x 21.4 cm). Gift of Miss Susan Dwight Bliss. 1963.328

Camille PISSARRO (1830-1903), French: *The Plow.* Lithograph, $9\frac{3}{16}$ x $5\frac{15}{16}$ (23.4 x 15.0 cm). Gift of Miss Susan Dwight Bliss. 1963.476

Camille PISSARRO (1830-1903), French: *Rue Damiette in Rouen.* Etching and aquatint, $7\frac{5}{8}$ x $5\frac{3}{4}$ (19.4 x 14.6 cm). Gift of Miss Susan Dwight Bliss. 1963.424

Camille PISSSARRO (1830-1903), French: *Under the Trees at the Hermitage.* Aquatint, $8\frac{9}{16}$ x $10\frac{1}{2}$ (21.8 x 26.7 cm). Gift of Mr. Charles A. Coffin h '22. 1923.70

Camille PISSARRO (1830-1903), French: *The Weeder.* Etching and drypoint, $6\frac{1}{4}$ x $4\frac{3}{8}$ (15.9 x 11.1 cm). Gift of Miss Susan Dwight Bliss. 1963.373

Edouard MANET (1832-1883), French: *The Guitarist.* Etching, $11\frac{11}{16}$ x $9\frac{9}{16}$ (29.6 x 24.3 cm). Gift of Mr. Charles A. Coffin h '22. 1923.76

James Abbott McNeill WHISTLER (1834-1903), American: *Black Lion Wharf.* Etching, $5\frac{15}{16}$ x $8\frac{13}{16}$ (15.1 x 22.4 cm). Gift of Mr. Charles A. Coffin h '22. 1923.57

James Abbott McNeill WHISTLER (1834-1903), American: *Little Lagoon.* Etching, $8\frac{7}{8}$ x $5\frac{7}{8}$ (22.5 x 15.0 cm). Gift of Miss Susan Dwight Bliss. 1956.24.169

James Abbott McNeill WHISTLER (1834-1903), American: *The Riva No. 2.* Etching, $8\frac{1}{4}$ x $11\frac{13}{16}$ (21.0 x 30.0 cm). Gift of Miss Susan Dwight Bliss. 1956.24.168

James Abbott McNeill WHISTLER (1834-1903), American: *Zaandam.* Etching, $5\frac{1}{8}$ x $8\frac{5}{8}$ (13.0 x 21.9 cm). Gift of Miss Susan Dwight Bliss. 1956.24.172

Ignace-Henri-Jean-Théodore FANTIN-LATOUR (1836-1904), French: *The Embroiderers.* Lithograph, $10\frac{1}{2}$ x 16 (26.8 x 40.7 cm). Gift of Miss Susan Dwight Bliss. 1963.302

Ignace-Henri-Jean-Théodore FANTIN-LATOUR (1836-1904), French: *Isolde Signalling to Tristan*. Lithograph, $9\frac{7}{8}$ x $14\frac{1}{4}$ (25.1 x 36.2 cm). Gift of Miss Susan Dwight Bliss. 1963.357

Jules CHÉRET (1836-1933), French: *Blazek Sisters*. Lithograph, $17\frac{3}{4}$ x $13\frac{1}{2}$ (45.1 x 34.3 cm). Museum purchase. 1971.37

Alphonse LEGROS (1837-1911), French: *Cottage on a Hill*. Etching, $5\frac{3}{4}$ x $8\frac{3}{4}$ (14.6 x 22.2 cm). Gift of Miss Susan Dwight Bliss. 1963.298

Alphonse LEGROS (1837-1911), French: *Head of a Man*. Etching, $6\frac{11}{16}$ x 4 (17.0 x 10.1 cm). Gift of Miss Susan Dwight Bliss. 1956.24.79

Alphonse LEGROS (1837-1911), French: *Remembrance of Italy*. Etching, $4\frac{13}{16}$ x 8 (12.2 x 20.3 cm). Gift of Miss Susan Dwight Bliss. 1956.24.78

Alphonse LEGROS (1837-1911), French: *The Wash House*. Etching, $6\frac{7}{16}$ x $4\frac{7}{8}$ (16.4 x 12.3 cm). Gift of Miss Susan Dwight Bliss. 1956.24.81

Thomas MORAN (1837-1926), American: *The Castle of San Juan de Ulua, Santa Cruz*. Etching, $11\frac{1}{2}$ x $10\frac{1}{16}$ (29.2 x 25.5 cm). Hamlin Fund. 1979.42

Mary Nimmo MORAN (1842-1899), American: *Along the Shore*. Etching, $11\frac{15}{16}$ x $7\frac{15}{16}$ (30.3 x 20.2 cm). Museum purchase. 1979.37

Félix-Hilaire BUHOT (1847-1898), French: *The Clock Tower, Westminster Bridge*. Etching, $11\frac{1}{8}$ x $15\frac{3}{4}$ (28.3 x 40.0 cm). Gift of Miss Susan Dwight Bliss. 1963.300

Eugène CARRIÈRE (1849-1906), French: *Portrait of Puvis de Chavannes*. Lithograph, $21\frac{1}{2}$ x $15\frac{5}{8}$ (54.7 x 39.7 cm). Gift of Miss Susan Dwight Bliss. 1956.24.285

William Merritt CHASE (1849-1916), American: *Self Portrait*. Monotype, $7\frac{7}{8}$ x $5\frac{15}{16}$ (20.0 x 15.2 cm). Museum purchase with anonymous gift. 1975.16

Auguste LEPÈRE (1849-1918), French: *The Cathedral at Rouen*. Wood engraving, 20 x $12\frac{1}{2}$ (50.8 x 31.8 cm). Gift of Mr. Charles A. Coffin h '22. 1923.46

Auguste LEPÈRE (1849-1918), French: *Notre Dame at Evening*. Wood engraving, $3\frac{5}{8}$ x $4\frac{1}{2}$ (9.2 x 11.4 cm). Gift of Miss Susan Dwight Bliss. 1956.24.91

Auguste LEPÈRE (1849-1918), French: *Parisians along the Seine on Sunday*. Etching, $3\frac{1}{2}$ x $3\frac{7}{8}$ (8.8 x 9.0 cm). Gift of Miss Susan Dwight Bliss. 1956.24.85

Auguste LEPÈRE (1849-1918), French: *Parisians on Sunday, Eating— A Table in the Hall*. Etching, $3\frac{3}{16}$ x $3\frac{5}{8}$ (8.7 x 9.2 cm). Gift of Miss Susan Dwight Bliss. 1956.24.86

Henry Wolf (1852-1916), American: *Winter in the Wood.* Wood engraving, 11 x 6⅛ (27.9 x 15.6 cm). Gift of the Achenbach Foundation for Graphic Arts. 1955.50.7

Max Klinger (1857-1920), German: *The Centaurs, III.* Etching and aquatint, 8 x 16 (20.3 x 40.6 cm). Museum purchase with the aid of the Helen Johnson Chase Fund. 1972.56

Fernand Khnopff (1858-1921), Belgian: *Untitled.* Lithograph, 7¾ x 5 15/16 (19.8 x 15.1 cm). Museum purchase. 1973.26

Lovis Corinth (1858-1925), German: *Portfolio of Ten Prints.* Etchings and drypoints, max. dim. 11¾ x 9½ (29.8 x 24.1). Museum purchase with the aid of the Helen Johnson Chase Fund. 1972.53. 1-.10

Lovis Corinth (1858-1925), German: *Self Portrait.* Lithograph, 12¾ x 9½ (32.2 x 24.2 cm). Museum purchase. 1957.101

Childe Hassam (1859-1935), American: *Dishabille.* Lithograph, 12 x 8⅞ (30.5 x 22.5 cm). Gift of Mrs. Maud Hassam. 1940.70

Childe Hassam (1859-1935), American: *Home Sweet Home Cottage.* Etching, 9⅞ x 11⅞ (25.1 x 30.2 cm). Gift of Mr. Charles A. Coffin h '22. 1923.83

Childe Hassam (1859-1935), American: *Joseph Pennell.* Lithograph, 15⅜ x 11¼ (39.1 x 28.6 cm). Gift of Mrs. Maud Hassam. 1940.75

Childe Hassam (1859-1935), American: *The Linden Tree.* Etching and drypoint, 6⅞ x 4⅞ (17.5 x 12.4 cm). Gift of Mrs. Maud Hassam. 1940.86

Childe Hassam (1859-1935), American: *Little Church around the Corner.* Etching and drypoint, 7⅞ x 11¼ (20.0 x 28.6 cm). Gift of Mrs. Maud Hassam. 1940.93

Childe Hassam (1859-1935), American: *Mrs. Hassam Knitting.* Lithograph, 12½ x 9⅛ (31.8 x 23.3 cm). Gift of Mrs. Maud Hassam. 1940.72

Childe Hassam (1859-1935), American: *Toby's Cos Cob.* Etching, 6⅞ x 8⅞ (17.5 x 22.5 cm). Gift of Mr. Charles A. Coffin h '22. 1923.78

Anders Zorn (1860-1920), Swedish: *Kesti, a Mora Peasant.* Etching, 6 3/16 x 4¾ (15.7 x 12.0 cm). Gift of Mr. Charles A. Coffin h '22. 1923.100

Anders Zorn (1860-1920), Swedish: *The Swan.* Etching, 9 13/16 x 7 13/16 (24.9 x 19.8 cm). Gift of Mr. and Mrs. John D. MacDonald. 1979.86

Anders Zorn (1860-1920), Swedish: *The Waltz.* Etching, 13¼ x 8 11/16 (33.7 x 22.1 cm). Gift of Mr. and Mrs. John D. MacDonald. 1979.84

Joseph Pennell (1860-1926), American: *James's Palace.* Etching,

8 x 11 (20.3 x 28.0 cm). Gift of Miss Susan Dwight Bliss. 1956.24.
133

James ENSOR (1860-1949), Belgian: *The Battle of the Golden Spur.*
Etching, $7\frac{3}{16}$ x $9\frac{7}{16}$ (18.0 x 24.0 cm). Museum purchase. 1960.59

James ENSOR (1860-1949), Belgian: *Portrait of Ernest Rousseau.*
Etching, $9\frac{1}{2}$ x $7\frac{1}{8}$ (24.0 x 18.2 cm). James Phinney Baxter Fund in
memory of Professor Henry Johnson h '14. 1963.486

James ENSOR (1860-1949), Belgian: *The Skaters.* Etching, $6\frac{5}{8}$ x 9
(17.7 x 23.7 cm). Museum purchase. 1963.487

Aristide MAILLOL (1861-1944), French: *Standing Nude.* Lithograph,
$11\frac{7}{8}$ x $4\frac{5}{8}$ (30.2 x 11.8 cm). Gift of Mme. Marguerite Yourcenar
h '68. 1980.5

Arthur B. DAVIES (1862-1928), American: *Angled Beauty.* Aquatint,
$7\frac{3}{4}$ x $11\frac{7}{8}$ (19.9 x 30.2 cm). Gift of Miss Susan Dwight Bliss. 1963.396

Arthur B. DAVIES (1862-1928), American: *Introspection.* Drypoint,
$4\frac{7}{8}$ x $3\frac{7}{16}$ (12.3 x 8.7 cm). Hamlin Fund. 1979.51

Edvard MUNCH (1863-1944), Norwegian: *The Children of the Archi-
tect Henry van de Velde.* Lithograph, $18\frac{7}{8}$ x $24\frac{1}{4}$ (48.0 x 66.7 cm).
Florence C. Quinby Fund in memory of Henry Cole Quinby h '16.
1969.73

Edvard MUNCH (1863-1944), Norwegian: *Portrait of Dr. Asch.* Drypoint, $10\frac{1}{2}$ x $7\frac{7}{8}$ (26.2 x 18.8 cm). Museum purchase. 1957.41

Henri DE TOULOUSE-LAUTREC (1864-1901), French: *Woman with a
Hat Box.* Lithograph, $8\frac{5}{8}$ x $6\frac{1}{2}$ (21.9 x 16.5 cm). Museum purchase.
1958.45

Félix VALLOTTON (1865-1925), Swiss: *Your Fifty Francs Will Be
Good. . . .* Lithograph, $11\frac{1}{4}$ x $7\frac{3}{4}$ (28.6 x 19.7 cm). Museum purchase.
1971.34

David Young CAMERON (1865-1945), Scottish: *Craigmillar Castle,
near Edinburgh.* Etching, $4\frac{1}{8}$ x $11\frac{7}{8}$ (10.6 x 30.2 cm). James Phinney
Baxter Fund in memory of Professor Henry Johnson h '14. 1931.1

David Young CAMERON (1865-1945), Scottish: *Golden House.*
Etching, 11 x 8 (27.9 x 20.3 cm). Gift of Mr. Charles A. Coffin h '22.
1923.101

Wassily KANDINSKY (1866-1944), Russian: *Small World, XII.* Etching, $9\frac{3}{8}$ x $7\frac{13}{16}$ (23.8 x 19.8 cm). Museum purchase. 1958.46

Käthe KOLLWITZ (1867-1945), German: *Head of a Woman.* Etching,
$9\frac{3}{16}$ x $5\frac{1}{2}$ (23.3 x 14.0 cm). Museum purchase. 1957.100

Käthe KOLLWITZ (1867-1945), German: *Memorial to Karl Lieb-
knecht.* Woodcut, $13\frac{3}{4}$ x $19\frac{5}{8}$ (34.8 x 49.8 cm). James Phinney
Baxter Fund in memory of Professor Henry Johnson h '14. 1952.11

Käthe Kollwitz (1867-1945), German: *Parents with Infant (Family, II)*. Lithograph, 9 x 12½ (22.9 x 31.8 cm). James Phinney Baxter Fund in memory of Professor Henry Johnson h '14. 1952.12

Käthe Kollwitz (1867-1945), German: *Self Portrait*. Aquatint, 5½ x 4 (14.0 x 10.2 cm). Museum purchase. 1957.99

Käthe Kollwitz (1867-1945), German: *The Unemployed*. Etching and aquatint, 17⅜ x 21 5/16 (44.1 x 54.3 cm). Florence C. Quinby Fund in memory of Henry Cole Quinby h '16. 1969.72

Emil Nolde (1867-1956), German: *Hamburg, Ship in Dock*. Etching, 11⅞ x 15¾ (30.2 x 40.2 cm). Museum purchase. 1957.42

Henri Matisse (1869-1954), French: *Head of a Woman with Kerchief*. Lithograph, 14 x 9½ (35.7 x 24.2 cm). Museum purchase. 1957.92

John Marin (1870-1953), American: *At the Window*. Etching, 7¾ x 5½ (19.7 x 13.8 cm). Gift of Miss Susan Dwight Bliss. 1963.420

John Marin (1870-1953), American: *Bal Bullier, Paris*. Etching, 5⅜ x 7⅝ (13.7 x 19.4 cm). Gift of Miss Susan Dwight Bliss. 1963.326

John Marin (1870-1953), American: *Brooklyn Bridge and Lower New York*. Etching, 6⅞ x 8⅞ (17.5 x 22.6 cm). Hamlin Fund. 1979.4

John Sloan (1871-1951), American: *Anschutz on Anatomy*. Etching, 7 7/16 x 8⅞ (18.9 x 22.6 cm). Gift of Mrs. John Sloan. 1962.9

John Sloan (1871-1951), American: *Charles Paul de Kock*. Etching, 15¾ x 12⅞ (40.2 x 32.8 cm). Bequest of Mr. George Otis Hamlin. 1961.69.172

John Sloan (1871-1951), American: *Cinder Path Tales*. Lithograph, 17 5/16 x 11 3/16 (43.8 x 28.3 cm). Hamlin Fund. 1973.18

John Sloan (1871-1951), American: *Connoisseurs of Prints*. Etching, 4⅞ x 6⅞ (12.4 x 17.3 cm). Bequest of Mr. George Otis Hamlin. 1961.69.65

John Sloan (1871-1951), American: *Crouching Nude and Press*. Etching, 7 x 5½ (17.8 x 14.0 cm). Bequest of Mr. George Otis Hamlin. 1961.69.51

John Sloan (1871-1951), American: *McSorley's Back Room*. Etching, 5¼ x 7 (13.3 x 17.8 cm). Bequest of Mr. George Otis Hamlin. 1961.69.117

John Sloan (1871-1951), American: *Night Windows*. Etching, 5⅛ x 6¾ (13.0 x 17.2 cm). Bequest of Mr. George Otis Hamlin. 1961.69.27

John Sloan (1871-1951), American: *Nude Reading*. Etching, 5 x 7 (12.7 x 17.8 cm). Gift of Mrs. John Sloan. 1962.12

John Sloan (1871-1951), American: *Saturday Afternoon on the Roof*. Lithograph, 11 7/16 x 14 (29.0 x 35.4 cm). Bequest of Mr. George Otis Hamlin. 1961.69.3

John SLOAN (1871-1951), American: *Sunbathers on the Roof*. Etching, $5\frac{7}{8}$ x $6\frac{15}{16}$ (15.0 x 17.6 cm). Bequest of Mr. George Otis Hamlin. 1961.69.26

John SLOAN (1871-1951), American: *Turning Out the Light*. Etching, $4\frac{7}{8}$ x $6\frac{3}{4}$ (12.2 x 17.1 cm). Bequest of Mr. George Otis Hamlin. 1961.69.149

John SLOAN (1871-1951), American: *Wake on the Ferry*. Etching, $4\frac{1}{4}$ x $5\frac{11}{16}$ (10.7 x 14.8 cm). Bequest of Mr. George Otis Hamlin. 1961.69.151

Lyonel FEININGER (1871-1956), American: *Steamer*. Woodcut, $3\frac{1}{4}$ x $4\frac{11}{16}$ (8.4 x 12.0 cm). Museum purchase with the aid of the Hamlin Fund and the James Phinney Baxter Fund in memory of Professor Henry Johnson h '14. 1971.8

Georges ROUAULT (1871-1958), French: *De Profundis*. Aquatint, $16\frac{7}{8}$ x $23\frac{1}{2}$ (43.0 x 59.8 cm). Museum purchase. 1957.3

Eugene HIGGINS (1874-1958), American: *Ever Shifting*. Monotype, $8\frac{1}{16}$ x $5\frac{1}{2}$ (20.5 x 13.9 cm). Gift of Mr. Charles A. Coffin h '22. 1923.63

Eugene HIGGINS (1874-1958), American: *Inhabitants of the Archway*. Etching, $3\frac{15}{16}$ x $5\frac{1}{8}$ (10.0 x 13.0 cm). Gift of Mr. Charles A. Coffin h '22. 1923.62

Jacques VILLON (1875-1963), French: *Portrait of Rimbaud*. Etching, $9\frac{1}{4}$ x 7 (23.5 x 17.8 cm). Museum purchase. 1967.46

Jacques VILLON (1875-1963), French: *Norman Woman*. Aquatint, $6\frac{11}{16}$ x $9\frac{11}{16}$ (17.0 x 24.6 cm). Florence C. Quinby Fund in memory of Henry Cole Quinby h '16. 1971.9

Ernest HASKELL (1876-1925), American: *Amelia*. Flick engraving, $5\frac{3}{8}$ x $3\frac{5}{16}$ (13.6 x 8.5 cm). Bequest of Mrs. Ernest Haskell, Sr. 1947.10.8

Ernest HASKELL (1876-1925), American: *Celestial Balcony*. Drypoint, 6 x 8 (15.2 x 20.3 cm). Bequest of Mr. Ernest Haskell, Jr. '42. 1974.20.19

Ernest HASKELL (1876-1925), American: *General Sherman*. Etching and engraving, $15\frac{3}{4}$ x $8\frac{15}{16}$ (40.1 x 22.7 cm). Gift of Mrs. Josephine Aldridge in memory of Mrs. Ernest Haskell, Sr. 1976.9.1

Ernest HASKELL (1876-1925), American: *Heavenly Hosts*. Etching, $7\frac{7}{8}$ x $9\frac{7}{8}$ (20.2 x 25.0 cm). Bequest of Mrs. Ernest Haskell, Sr. 1947.10.21

Ernest HASKELL (1876-1925), American: *Mirror of the Goddess*. Etching and engraving, 9 x 12 (22.9 x 30.5 cm). Bequest of Mr. Ernest Haskell, Jr. '42. 1974.20.57

Ernest Haskell (1876-1925), American: *Three Witches.* $7\frac{15}{16}$ x 6 (20.2 x 15.2 cm). Bequest of Mr. Ernest Haskell, Jr. '42. 1974.20.90

Ernest Haskell (1876-1925), American: *Twelve Etchings, (The Paris Set).* Etchings, max. dim. $3\frac{1}{2}$ x $2\frac{1}{4}$ (8.9 x 5.7 cm). Gift of Mrs. Ernest Haskell, Jr. 1975.9.1-.13

Kenneth Hayes Miller (1876-1952), American: *Leaving the Shop.* Etching, 8 x $9\frac{7}{8}$ (20.3 x 25.1 cm). Hamlin Fund. 1979.80

Muirhead Bone (1876-1953), Scottish: *Stirling Castle.* Etching, 10 x 7 (25.4 x 17.8 cm). Gift of Miss Susan Dwight Bliss. 1956.24.16

Marsden Hartley (1877-1943), American: *No. 6, Waxenstein.* Lithograph, $14\frac{3}{4}$ x $10\frac{1}{4}$ (37.5 x 26.0 cm). Gift of Mr. Lea A. Reiber '21 in memory of Mr. John G. Young '21. 1966.18

Paul Klee (1879-1940), Swiss: *A Spirit Serves a Small Breakfast.* Lithograph, $7\frac{7}{8}$ x $5\frac{3}{4}$ (20.0 x 14.6 cm). Florence C. Quinby Fund in memory of Henry Cole Quinby h '16. 1969.74

André Derain (1880-1954), French: *Head of a Woman.* Lithograph, $15\frac{3}{4}$ x $9\frac{1}{2}$ (40.0 x 24.2 cm). Gift of Miss Susan Dwight Bliss. 1963.397

Max Pechstein (1881-1955), German: *Rider with Donkeys.* Woodcut, $12\frac{1}{2}$ x $17\frac{3}{4}$ (32.0 x 45.2 cm). Florence C. Quinby Fund in memory of Henry Cole Quinby h '16. 1969.75

Pablo Picasso (1881-1973), Spanish: *The Dream and Lie of Franco.* Portfolio of etchings and aquatints, $12\frac{1}{2}$ x $16\frac{5}{8}$ (31.8 x 42.2 cm). Museum purchase. 1957.39.1-.2

Pablo Picasso (1881-1973), Spanish: *The Poor Ones.* Etching, $9\frac{3}{8}$ x $7\frac{1}{16}$ (23.8 x 17.9 cm). Gift of Miss Susan Dwight Bliss. 1963.372

Pablo Picasso (1881-1973), Spanish: *Two Sculptors before a Statue.* Etching, $8\frac{3}{4}$ x $12\frac{1}{4}$ (22.2 x 31.2 cm). Museum purchase. 1959.28

Edward Hopper (1882-1967), American: *The Railroad.* Etching, $7\frac{15}{16}$ x $9\frac{13}{16}$ (20.2 x 24.9 cm). Gift of Miss Susan Dwight Bliss. 1963.294

Rockwell Kent (1882-1971), American: *The Lovers.* Wood engraving, $6\frac{7}{16}$ x $9\frac{7}{8}$ (16.3 x 25.1 cm). Gift of Mr. and Mrs. Daniel B. Jones. 1979.25

Rockwell Kent (1882-1971), American: *Revisitation.* Lithograph, $8\frac{1}{2}$ x $13\frac{3}{4}$ (21.5 x 34.8 cm). Museum purchase with anonymous gift. 1975.12

Martin Lewis (1883-1962), American: *Arch, Midnight.* Drypoint, 8 x $11\frac{1}{2}$ (20.3 x 29.2 cm). Gift of Miss Susan Dwight Bliss. 1963.363

Martin Lewis (1883-1962), American: *The Orator, Madison Square.* Etching, $10\frac{13}{16}$ x $12\frac{9}{16}$ (27.5 x 31.9 cm). Gift of Miss Susan Dwight Bliss. 1956.24.93

Martin Lewis (1883-1962), American: *Stoops in Snow.* Drypoint, 9⅞ x 14⅞ (25.1 x 37.8 cm). Gift of Miss Susan Dwight Bliss. 1963.364

Erich Heckel (b. 1883), German: *Fjord Landscape.* Etching and aquatint, 10 x 13⅞ (25.4 x 35.2 cm). Museum purchase. 1957.40

Erich Heckel (b. 1883), German: *Portrait of Dangast Fischer.* Woodcut, 9½ x 7⅝ (24.3 x 19.4 cm). James Phinney Baxter Fund in memory of Professor Henry Johnson h '14. 1957.46

Max Beckmann (1884-1950), German: *Portrait of Frau H. M. (Naila).* Woodcut, 15¼ x 13¾ (38.7 x 35.0 cm). Museum purchase. 1957.95

Max Beckman (1884-1950), German: *Two Automobile Officers.* Etching, 4⅜ x 6⅞ (11.8 x 17.5 cm). Museum purchase. 1962.39

Karl Schmidt-Rottluff (1884-1976), German: *Crucifixion.* Woodcut, 14½ x 10 (36.8 x 25.4 cm). Museum purchase. 1968.1

John Taylor Arms (1887-1953), American: *Mont St. Michel.* Aquatint, 6⅜ x 7 9/16 (16.1 x 19.1 cm). Gift of Mr. Charles F. Adams '12. 1964.10

Alfred Kubin (1887-1959), Austrian: *Behemoth.* Lithograph, 9 x 14⅞ (22.9 x 37.8 cm). Museum purchase. 1967.48

Marc Chagall (b. 1887), French: *At the Town Gateway.* Drypoint and etching, 8½ x 10¾ (21.6 x 27.3 cm). Museum purchase. 1968.144

Ernst Barlach (1890-1938), German: *Jacob's Dream.* Woodcut, 10⅛ x 14⅛ (25.7 x 35.9 cm). Museum purchase. 1957.98

Otto Dix (1891-1969), German: *American Riding Act.* Drypoint, 13½ x 12⅜ (34.3 x 31.0 cm). Helen Johnson Chase Fund. 1968.117

George Grosz (1893-1959), German-American: *Illustration for "The Robbers" by Friedrich Schiller.* Lithograph, 19¾ x 14⅝ (50.0 x 37.0 cm). Museum purchase. 1957.51

Charles Burchfield (1893-1966), American: *Autumn.* Lithograph, 7½ x 13½ (19.0 x 34.3 cm). James Phinney Baxter Fund in memory of Professor Henry Johnson h '14. 1957.102

Charles Burchfield (1893-1966), American: *Spring.* Lithograph, 12 x 9⅛ (30.5 x 23.2 cm). James Phinney Baxter Fund in memory of Professor Henry Johnson h '14. 1957.96

Adolph Dehn (1895-1968), American: *North Country.* Lithograph, 10 3/16 x 13 15/16 (25.9 x 35.5 cm). Gift of Mr. Walter K. Gutman '24. 1936.2

Adolph Dehn (1895-1968), American: *Road to Gay Head.* Lithograph, 10⅝ x 14 5/16 (27.0 x 36.2 cm). Gift of Mr. Walter K. Gutman '24. 1936.1

Samuel CHAMBERLAIN (1895-1975), American: *Twelve Etchings of Yale*. Etchings, max. dim. 10 x $13\frac{1}{2}$ (25.4 x 34.3 cm). Gift of Yale University in memory of Mr. Charles A. Coffin h '22. 1940.353.1-.12

Peggy BACON (b. 1895), American: *Maine Problems*. Etching, $8\frac{7}{16}$ x 14 (21.5 x 35.5 cm). Hamlin Fund. 1979.43

John Stuart CURRY (1898-1946), American: *The Tornado*. Lithograph, $9\frac{7}{8}$ x $14\frac{1}{16}$ (25.1 x 35.7 cm). James Phinney Baxter Fund in memory of Professor Henry Johnson h '14. 1957.105

Reginald MARSH (1898-1954), American: *Penn Station*. Lithograph, $11\frac{3}{16}$ x $15\frac{3}{4}$ (28.4 x 40.0 cm). James Phinney Baxter Fund in memory of Professor Henry Johnson h '14. 1957.104

Reginald MARSH (1898-1954), American: *Switch Engines, Erie Yards, Jersey City*. Lithograph, 9 x $13\frac{3}{8}$ (22.9 x 33.8 cm). James Phinney Baxter Fund in memory of Professor Henry Johnson h '14. 1957.103

Alexander CALDER (1898-1976), American: *Balloons*. Lithograph, $39\frac{7}{8}$ x $28\frac{7}{16}$ (101.3 x 72.3 cm). Gift of Argosy Partners, Bond Street Partners, and Forstmann-Leff Associates. 1980.16

Raphael SOYER (b. 1899), American: *Artist's Brothers*. Etching, $5\frac{7}{8}$ x $4\frac{3}{8}$ (15.0 x 11.1 cm). Gift of the artist. 1964.26

Isabel BISHOP (b. 1902), American: *Two Girls*. Etching, $7\frac{1}{2}$ x $4\frac{1}{8}$ (19.0 x 10.3 cm). Museum purchase. 1968.40

Victor VASARELY (b. 1908), Hungarian: *Code*. Embossing and serigraph, $12\frac{1}{4}$ x $8\frac{3}{4}$ (31.1 x 22.3 cm). Florence C. Quinby Fund in memory of Henry Cole Quinby h '14. 1970.10

Victor VASARELY (b. 1908), Hungarian: *Untitled Composition*. Serigraph, $6\frac{1}{16}$ x $3\frac{1}{16}$ (15.4 x 7.8 cm). Susan Dwight Bliss Fund. 1969.12

Robert MOTHERWELL (b. 1915), American: *Untitled*. Lithograph, $26\frac{1}{16}$ x $19\frac{5}{8}$ (66.2 x 50.0 cm). Hamlin Fund. 1979.22

Gene DAVIS (b. 1920), American: *Alice Tully Hall Sampler/Lincoln Center for the Performing Arts*. Serigraph, 79 x $39\frac{7}{8}$ (200.8 x 104.0 cm). Gift of Mr. Austin List '45. 1971.39

Leonard BASKIN (b. 1922), American: *Torment*. Woodcut, 31 x 23 (78.9 x 58.5 cm). Museum purchase. 1960.56

Larry RIVERS (b. 1923), American: *Living at the Movies*. Silkscreen, $21\frac{9}{16}$ x $26\frac{3}{8}$ (57.3 x 67.0 cm). Argosy Partners, Bond Street Partners, and Forstmann-Leff Associates. 1980.8

Robert RAUSCHENBERG (b. 1925), American: *Support*. Lithograph, $29\frac{1}{2}$ x 22 (75.0 x 55.9 cm). Gift of Argosy Partners, Bond Street Partners, and Forstmann-Leff Associates. 1980.10

Paul WUNDERLICH (b. 1927), German: *Innocent?*. Lithograph, 12¼ x 18¼ (31.1 x 46.4 cm). Museum purchase with the aid of the James Phinney Baxter Fund in memory of Professor Henry Johnson h '14. 1968.18

Robert INDIANA (b. 1928), American: *Art*. Serigraph, 14⅛ x 11¾ (35.9 x 29.8 cm). Museum purchase. 1973.27

Sol LeWITT (b. 1928), American: *Lines and Color Straight, Not-Straight and Broken Lines Using All Combinations of Black, White, Yellow, Red, and Blue for Lines and Intervals*. Silkscreen, 29⅞ x 29⅞ (76.0 x 76.0 cm). Hamlin Fund. 1979.1

Horst JANSSEN (b. 1929), German: *Piffi I with Bones*. Etching, 11½ x 15⁷⁄₁₆ (29.2 x 39.2 cm). Museum purchase with the aid of the James Phinney Baxter Fund in memory of Professor Henry Johnson h '14. 1968.19

Claes OLDENBURG (b. 1929), American: *Lipstick (Ascending), on Caterpillar Track*. Lithograph, 19 x 14³⁄₁₆ (48.2 x 36.0 cm). Hamlin Fund. 1979.3

Richard ANUSZKIEWICZ (b. 1930), American: *"Anuszkiewicz Paintings."* Serigraph, 38⅞ x 29¼ (98.7 x 74.4 cm). Gift of Dartmouth College. 1967.65

Allan D'ARCANGELO (b. 1930), American: *Highway*. Silkscreen, 24 x 19¾ (61.0 x 50.2 cm). Hamlin Fund. 1967.45

Robert BIRMELIN (b. 1933), American: *Reflections—Underpass*. Etching, 13¾ x 20⅛ (34.9 x 51.1 cm). Susan Dwight Bliss Fund. 1970.71

James ROSENQUIST (b. 1933), American: *For Love*. Serigraph, 35¹⁄₁₆ x 26⅜ (89.0 x 66.9 cm). Hamlin Fund. 1967.50

Sigmund ABELES (b. 1934), American: *Untitled*. Etching, 11¹¹⁄₁₆ x 17⁷⁄₁₆ (30.0 x 44.3 cm). Hamlin Fund. 1965.50

Jim DINE (b. 1935), American: *Self-Portrait*. Etching, aquatint, and drypoint, 12¹¹⁄₁₆ x 10⁷⁄₁₆ (32.3 x 26.5 cm). Hamlin Fund. 1979.2

Michael MAZUR (b. 1935), American: *Closed Ward #9: The Occupant*. Etching and aquatint, 23⅝ x 17⅝ (60.2 x 44.7 cm). Museum purchase. 1968.129

Charles WELLS (b. 1935), American: *Portrait of Walt Whitman*. Etching, 17½ x 14¾ (44.5 x 37.5 cm). Hamlin Fund. 1964.48

Richard ESTES (b. 1936), American: *Seagram Building*. Silkscreen, 14 x 21¼ (35.5 x 54.0 cm). Anonymous gift. 1979.18

Friedrich MECKSEPER (b. 1936), German: *Sun Dial*. Drypoint and aquatint, 15⅛ x 19¼ (38.2 x 48.9 cm). Helen Johnson Chase Fund. 1967.41

Thomas Cornell (b. 1937), American: *Michaelangelo.* Etching, 19¼ x 14⅝ (45.9 x 37.2 cm). Gift of the artist. 1979.15

Gerard Haggerty (b. 1943), American: *Winter Conversation.* Monotype, 15⁹⁄₁₆ x 19¾ (39.5 x 50.1 cm). Anonymous gift. 1979.68

Watercolors

Edward Green Malbone (1777-1807), American: *Portrait of Elizabeth Bowdoin, Lady Temple.* Watercolor on ivory, 3³⁄₁₆ x 2⁷⁄₁₆ (8.1 x 6.2 cm). Gift of Mrs. Roscoe H. Hupper in honor of President Kenneth C. M. Sills '01 and Mrs. Sills h '52. 1951.8

Edward Green Malbone (1777-1807), American: *Portrait of James Bowdoin III.* Watercolor on ivory, 3¼ x 2½ (8.2 x 6.4 cm). Gift of Mrs. Roscoe H. Hupper in honor of President Kenneth C. M. Sills '01 and Mrs. Sills h '52. 1951.7

John Frederick Kensett (1816-1872), American: *Landscape.* Watercolor, 4¼ x 6⅝ (10.8 x 16.8 cm). Hamlin Fund. 1964.20

Augustus Abel Gibson (1819-1893), American: *Plowing, Maine.* Watercolor, 10¹⁄₁₆ x 13¹³⁄₁₆ (25.6 x 35.1 cm). Gift of Mr. Paul J. Newman '09. 1968.76

Augustus Abel Gibson (1819-1893), American: *Tree Study with Shed.* Watercolor, 14⅝ x 10¹³⁄₁₆ (37.1 x 27.5 cm). Gift of Mr. Paul J. Newman '09. 1968.80

John Ruskin (1819-1900), English: *Bellensona.* Watercolor, 8⁹⁄₁₆ x 6¹⁄₁₆ (21.7 x 15.4 cm). Gift of Miss Susan Dwight Bliss. 1956.24.257

John Ruskin (1819-1900), English: *Verona at Sunset.* Watercolor, 6½ x 9 (16.5 x 22.9 cm). Gift of Miss Susan Dwight Bliss. 1956.24.259

William Trost Richards (1833-1905), American: *An Italian Lake.* Watercolor, 5¼ x 8¾ (13.3 x 22.2 cm). Gift of Miss Susan Dwight Bliss. 1956.24.247

William Trost Richards (1833-1905), American: *Marine View.* Watercolor, 3¼ x 4¾ (8.3 x 12.1 cm). Gift of Miss Susan Dwight Bliss. 1956.24.243

John La Farge (1835-1910), American: *Meditation of Kuwannon.* Watercolor, 14¹⁵⁄₁₆ x 10¾ (37.9 x 27.3 cm). Gift of the Misses Harriet and Sophia Walker. 1904.18

John La Farge (1835-1910), American: *Peak of Mona Roa.* Watercolor, 19½ x 22¹⁄₁₆ (49.5 x 56.0 cm). Gift of the Misses Harriet and Sophia Walker. 1904.20

John La Farge (1835-1910), American: *Tokio Geisha, Dancing in the House of Our Neighbor the Priest.* Watercolor, 13⅛ x 8¾ (33.3 x 22.2 cm). Gift of the Misses Harriet and Sophia Walker. 1904.19

Oscar BLUEMNER (1867-1938), American: *Landscape with Arched Trees.* Gouache, $4\frac{13}{16}$ x $5\frac{7}{8}$ (12.2 x 14.9 cm). Hamlin Fund. 1979.47

Ernest HASKELL (1876-1925), American: *Green Valley Landscape.* Watercolor, $11\frac{13}{16}$ x $17\frac{3}{4}$ (30.0 x 45.1 cm). Gift of Mrs. Josephine Aldridge in memory of Mrs. Ernest Haskell, Sr. 1976.16.3

Ernest HASKELL (1876-1925), American: *The Oak.* Watercolor, $12\frac{11}{16}$ x $7\frac{11}{16}$ (32.2 x 19.5 cm). Gift of Mrs. Josephine Aldridge in memory of Mrs. Ernest Haskell, Sr. 1976.16.9

Daniel Putnam BRINLEY (1879-1963), American: *Landscape.* Watercolor, 15 x $9\frac{3}{4}$ (38.0 x 25.0 cm). Gift of Mr. and Mrs. Albert A. Loder, Jr. 1978.29.2

Daniel Putnam BRINLEY (1879-1963), American: *The Red House.* Watercolor, $9\frac{13}{16}$ x $7\frac{7}{16}$ (25.0 x 19.1 cm). Gift of Mr. and Mrs. Albert A. Loder, Jr. 1978.29.1

Rockwell KENT (1882-1971), American: *Greenland Home Interior.* Watercolor, 7 x 10 (17.8 x 25.4 cm). Anonymous gift. 1971.79.3

Rockwell KENT (1882-1971), American: *Greenland Landscape.* Watercolor, 9 x 6 (22.9 x 15.2 cm). Anonymous gift. 1971.79.5

Rockwell KENT (1882-1971), American: *Greenland Meadow and Mountain.* Watercolor, 6 x 9 (15.2 x 22.9 cm). Anonymous gift. 1971.79.6

Rockwell KENT (1882-1971), American: *Lobster Cove.* Watercolor, $9\frac{3}{4}$ x $13\frac{3}{4}$ (24.8 x 34.9 cm). Anonymous gift. 1971.79.1

Rockwell KENT (1882-1971), American: *Man in a Doorway.* Watercolor, $13\frac{15}{16}$ x $9\frac{7}{16}$ (35.4 x 24.0 cm). Anonymous gift. 1971.79.2

Rockwell KENT (1882-1971), American: *Two Greenland Figures.* Watercolor, $5\frac{13}{16}$ x $8\frac{5}{16}$ (14.9 x 21.3 cm). Anonymous gift. 1971.79.4

William ZORACH h '58 (1887-1966), American: *The Cove—View from the Knubble.* Watercolor, $15\frac{1}{8}$ x $21\frac{7}{8}$ (38.5 x 55.7 cm). Gift of the children of William Zorach. 1973.20

William ZORACH h '58 (1887-1966), American: *Untitled.* Watercolor with graphite, $13\frac{1}{2}$ x 10 (34.3 x 25.4 cm). Gift of Mrs. Dahlov Ipcar and Mr. Tessim Zorach. 1979.73

William ZORACH h '58 (1887-1966), American: *Untitled.* Watercolor with graphite, 10 x 12 (25.4 x 30.5 cm). Gift of Mrs. Dahlov Ipcar and Mr. Tessim Zorach. 1979.74

William ZORACH h '58 (1887-1966), American: *Fifteen Untitled Sketches.* Watercolor with graphite, max. dim. $8\frac{9}{16}$ x $11\frac{1}{16}$ (21.8 x 28.1 cm). Gift of Mrs. Dahlov Ipcar and Mr. Tessim Zorach. 1979.75.1-.11a & b

William ZORACH h '58 (1887-1966), American: *Weir—Robinhood*

Cove in Early Summer. Watercolor, 15¼ x 22⅛ (38.8 x 56.2). Gift of Mrs. Dahlov Ipcar and Mr. Tessim Zorach. 1979.76

Marguerite ZORACH (1887-1968), American: *Asleep in the Hills.* Watercolor with graphite, 13 x 17½ (33.0 x 44.4 cm). Hamlin Fund. 1979.46

Marguerite ZORACH (1887-1968), American: *Portrait of Harry Hathaway II.* Watercolor with graphite, 11½ x 9 1/16 (29.2 x 23.1 cm). Gift of Mrs. Dahlov Ipcar and Mr. Tessim Zorach. 1979.70

Reginald MARSH (1898-1954), American: *El Morro.* Watercolor with graphite, 13⅞ x 19⅞ (35.3 x 50.5 cm). Bequest of Mrs. Felicia Meyer Marsh. 1979.34

Reginald MARSH (1898-1954), American: *Untitled.* Watercolor with graphite, 13⅞ x 19⅞ (35.3 x 50.5 cm). Bequest of Mrs. Felicia Meyer Marsh. 1979.33

Ogden PLEISSNER (b. 1905), American: *Early Snow, Leadville.* Watercolor, 20⅞ x 29⅛ (53.0 x 74.0 cm). Gift of Mr. John D. MacDonald. 1972.67

Gene KLEBE (b. 1907), American: *Sea Shore Scene.* Watercolor, 7 x 11 (17.8 x 27.9 cm). Gift of Mr. William F. Bonner, Jr. 1976.51

Lawrence KUPFERMAN (b. 1909), American: *Exterior of a Victorian House.* Watercolor, 15⅝ x 21 (39.7 x 53.3 cm). Gift of Mr. and Mrs. John D. MacDonald. 1977.10

⌖Andrew WYETH (b. 1917), American: *Bermuda.* Watercolor, 21 7/16 x 29½ (54.5 x 74.9 cm). Gift of Mr. Stephen Etnier h '69 and Mrs. Etnier in memory of Mr. S. Foster Yancey '30. 1961.98

C. Ronald BECHTLE (b. 1924), American: *The Wind of No Allegiance.* Watercolor, 18 x 23⅞ (45.8 x 60.8 cm). Gift of the artist. 1974.11

Laurence SISSON (b. 1928), American: *Beach Scene with Boats.* Watercolor, 22⅜ x 30¾ (56.8 x 78.1 cm). Gift of Mr. William F. Bonner, Jr. 1976.72

Neil WELLIVER (b. 1929), American: *Moose Horn.* Watercolor, 33¾ x 29½ (85.8 x 74.9 cm). Museum purchase. 1978.37

Howard K. CLIFFORD, Jr. (b. 1950), American: *Dead Low Tide.* Watercolor, 21⅞ x 29⅝ (55.5 x 75.3 cm). Gift of the artist. 1976.19

Photographs

Edward WESTON (1886-1958), American: *Portfolio of Ten Photographs.* 9 black-and-white photographs, one color photograph, max. dim. 7 9/16 x 9 9/16 (19.2 x 24.3 cm). Anonymous gift. 1971.43.1-.10

Berenice ABBOTT (b. 1898), American: *Yuban Warehouse.* Black-and-white photograph, $15\frac{1}{8}$ x $17\frac{9}{16}$ (38.4 x 44.6 cm). Hamlin Fund. 1979.69

Alfred EISENSTAEDT (b. 1898), American: *Marilyn Monroe*. Black-and-white photograph, 11 x 14 (29.9 x 35.5 cm). Museum purchase. 1976.46

Ansel ADAMS (b. 1902), American: *Moonrise, Hernandez, New Mexico*. Black-and-white photograph, $10\frac{1}{2}$ x $13\frac{1}{2}$ (26.7 x 34.3 cm). Anonymous gift. 1973.7

Manuel Alvarez BRAVO (b. 1902), Mexican: *Portfolio of Fifteen Photographs*. Black-and-white photographs, max. dim. $9\frac{5}{8}$ x $7\frac{11}{16}$ (24.5 x 19.5 cm). Gift of Mr. Michael G. Frieze '60. 1979.81.1-.15

Brett WESTON (b. 1911), American: *Untitled*. Black-and-white photograph, $13\frac{1}{2}$ x $10\frac{1}{2}$ (34.2 x 26.6 cm). Museum purchase. 1969.30

Harry CALLAHAN (b. 1912), American: *Wisconsin*. Black-and-white photograph, $4\frac{1}{8}$ x $9\frac{5}{8}$ (10.5 x 24.5 cm). Anonymous gift. 1972.13

Mario GIACOMELLI (b. 1925), Italian: *Abandoned Land*. Black-and-white photograph, $15\frac{11}{16}$ x $11\frac{7}{16}$ (39.7 x 28.9 cm). Gift of the artist. 1978.2

David BATCHELDER (b. 1935), American: *Dead Bird*. Black-and-white photograph, 6 x $9\frac{1}{4}$ (15.2 x 23.5 cm). Museum purchase. 1968.147

John McKEE (b. 1936), American: *Katsurahama*. Black-and-white photograph, 8 x 12 (20.3 x 30.4 cm). Hamlin Fund with the aid of a matching grant from the National Endowment for the Arts in Washington, D. C., a federal agency. 1977.25

Harvey HIMELFARB (b. 1941), American: *Untitled*. Black-and-white photograph, $7\frac{1}{4}$ x $7\frac{1}{4}$ (18.5 x 18.5 cm). Hamlin Fund with the aid of a matching grant from the National Endowment for the Arts in Washington, D. C., a federal agency. 1977.24

Abelardo MORELL '71 (b. 1948), American: *Untitled*. Black-and-white photograph, $7\frac{1}{2}$ x $7\frac{1}{2}$ (19.0 x 19.0 cm). Museum purchase. 1975.2

FAR EASTERN ART

The museum's collections of oriental art include objects from China, Japan, Korea, and India. The holdings are for the most part in the decorative arts, including ceramic, jade, ivory, and lacquer objects.

The most extensive collection is a group of Chinese, Japanese, and Korean ceramics. In 1909 Mr. David S. Cowles donated several ceramic objects, including examples of Japanese Imari and Arita ware. The ceramic collection was greatly strengthened in 1940 through the gift of seventy-six objects from Mr. William Tudor Gardiner h '45 and Mrs. Gardiner. The Gardiner collection of Chinese and Korean pottery and porcelain dates from the Han dynasty (206 B.C.–A.D. 220) to recent times. Miss Elizabeth P. Martin's 1968 gift of ceramics, lacquers, and bronzes, including a bronze *hu* vessel dating from the twelfth century B.C., was a valuable addition to the existing collection. Also included in the Chinese collection is a double album of mounted calligraphy and watercolors by twentieth-century Taiwanese artists, given by the Honorable Karl Lott Rankin h '60 and Mrs. Rankin.

The museum's holdings in Japanese art include a variety of decorative objects in addition to ceramic examples. Japanese netsuke are small, intricately carved wooden or ivory toggles used to fasten a purse or other article to a kimono sash. Mr. Howard F. Moody '03 donated seventy-seven netsuke to the museum in 1958. In 1902 the Misses Harriet and Sophia Walker gave the museum many Japanese objects, including armour, swords and swordguards, and lacquer and jade objects. The museum also owns several Japanese prints, many through the bequest of Mr. Charles Potter Kling in 1935. Mrs. Philip Dana's 1954 gift of seven Japanese woodcuts strengthened the collections in this area.

The small Indian collection at the museum covers a wide geographic and cultural range. The Gandharan stone sculpture and the bronze from southern India not only come from the farthest corners of the Indian subcontinent, but they also represent opposite poles of Indian aesthetics. The paintings, on the other hand, are products of a totally different ambiance, and their secular themes depict the splendor of the great Mughals. All three of the major religions of India—Buddhism, Hinduism, and Islam—are represented by these objects in the collection. These few objects at Bowdoin cover almost fifteen centuries of Indian artistic tradition. Though far removed from their original context, they are messengers of a distant and diverse culture.   [K.A.O. & E.R.]

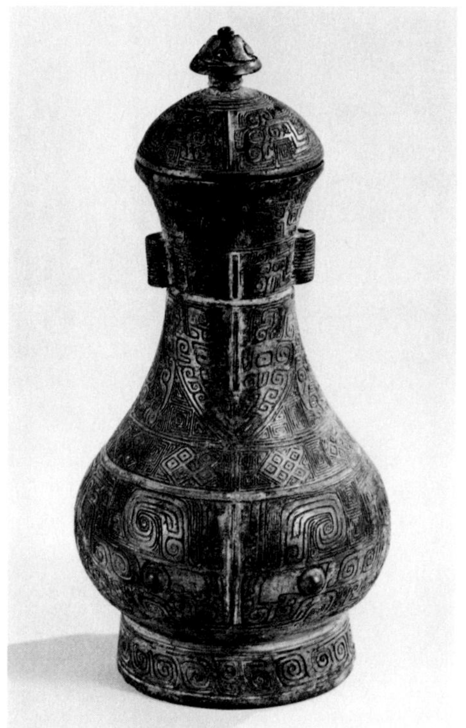

CHINESE

Hu, Shang dynasty (1523-1028 B.C.), 13th or 12th century B.C.
Bronze, 6½ x 3³⁄₁₆ (diam.) (16.5 x 8.1 cm)
Gift of Miss Elizabeth P. Martin. 1968.89

This piece is a fine example of a cast bronze ritual vessel from the earliest historical period in China. Such vessels, which vary in size from several inches to several feet, were the costliest and most technically complex of the period's man-made objects. While used in ritual, many of these works were also buried as offerings in the graves of the governing class. This interment, which insured that examples of the art would survive to the present, resulted in an alteration of the surface appearance. In this example, the original shiny, metallic finish has been muted and variegated in tone through an interaction with chemicals in the soil.

The casting of the vessels with their precise and intricate surface decoration has only been duplicated in the West with the help of the technical achievements of the Industrial Revolution. The technique used by the early Chinese in bronze manufacture has still to be determined. The piece-mold process, in which the design is carved in reverse on clay sections joined by keys before the metal is poured into the assembled mold, was possibly used; this technique has been suggested by the discovery of portions of such clay sections in excavations. However, the lost-wax method—casting in a mold built around a wax model—would have been easier and would better account for the perfection of detail. Possibly piece-molds were used to cast the wax models from which the final bronze vessels were realized.

Most of these cast bronze pieces were utilitarian in shape, suggestive of earlier pottery vessels. The shape of this *hu* is distinguished by its circular cross-section, a long neck with a flaring mouth at the top, and the cover. The lugs on either side of the neck allow for attaching a chain or braid handle.

Decoration of geometric and abstract zoomorphic forms such as that cast into the surface of the hu is an arresting feature of early Chinese bronzes. Like many vessels of this period, the hu exhibits a monster mask on its lower, swelling portion. This motif, called a *T'ao T'ieh,* is marked by protruding eyes on either side of a flange marking the middle of a nose, fangs in the outer corners of the mouth, and inverted C-shaped horns. Other standard elements are the square spiral that is used as a background pattern around the mask and the row of dragon shapes in the top band of relief. Attempts to assign symbolic meaning to these decorative motifs have so far been unsucccessful. Other features, such as the undulating profile of the lugs and the diamond-shaped patterns above the monster mask, are unusual and may suggest a provincial origin for this piece.

The decoration of a bronze vessel is also a key to its date. The presence of relief over the whole surface of the hu indicates that it was made in the latter part of the Shang dynasty; however, the rendering of such elements as the monster mask and the dragon band on the same level as the surrounding background pattern, rather than raised above it on another level of relief, suggests that the hu was not made at the very end of the period. [R.H. & S.W.]

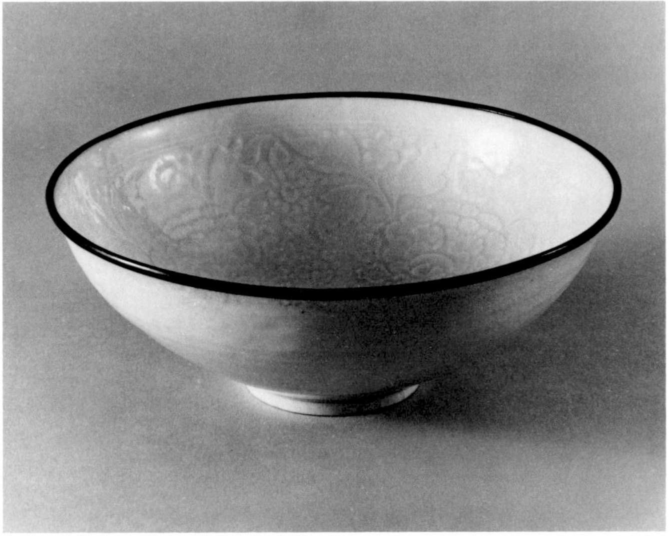

CHINESE

Bowl, Sung or Yüan dynasty (A.D. 960-1368), 13th or 14th century

Porcelain, $3\frac{3}{8}$ x $8\frac{1}{2}$ (diam.) (8.5 x 21.7 cm)

Gift of Mr. William Tudor Gardiner h '45 and Mrs. Gardiner. 1940.366

Deceptively simple in appearance, this white bowl is an excellent example of the monochrome porcelain style which dominated ceramic production from the tenth to the fourteenth century. Such wares ranged in color from brown through many shades of blue-green to white, hues treasured for their similarity to the colors of jade and other prized materials. The monochrome wares represent a dramatic shift from the colorful and exuberant forms and decoration popular in the preceding T'ang dynasty. This development was due to the disruption of communication with the Near East and to the emergence of a dominant scholar-official class in Chinese society in post-T'ang times.

With their simple shapes and lack of distinctive decoration, the wares disclose their artistic merits only when examined carefully. When struck, the porcelain rings; its surface is smooth and similar to jade. The thin clay body is translucent, with delicate combed, incised, or molded designs on the inside.

This particular bowl is an example of the white ware called Ch'ing-pai (bluish white), one of the earliest white wares to be produced in the Southern Chinese provinces of Kiangsi and Fukien. The characteristic bluish appearance of the white is due to feldspar in the glaze, and the tonality becomes deeper where the glaze is applied more thickly. Ch'ing-pai pieces were fired upside down so that the bottom of the bowl is also glazed. The resulting unglazed rim was covered with a metal strip. In this particular bowl the lotus and peony design on the interior resulted from the pressure of a mold on the buff-colored body before the glaze was applied. The use of a mold in rendering the design most strongly suggests a late-Sung or early-Yüan date for the piece.   [R.H. & S.W.]

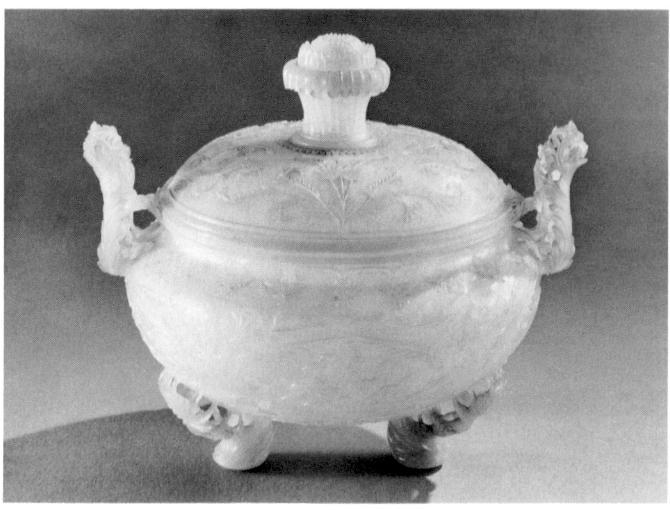

CHINESE

Incense Burner, Ch'ing dynasty (1644-1912), 1736-1795
  Jade, 6 x 5⅞ (diam.) (15.2 x 14.9 cm)
  Gift of Mrs. Elizabeth L. Power. 1960.51

An excellent example of oriental design and execution, this incense burner was rendered in the most "Chinese" of materials. Jade, varying in color from white to shades of green and brown, has been a prized material in China since prehistoric times. Early jade examples included insignia and symbols of power which were interred with the dead, for the material was believed to have life preserving qualities. Shaped into jewelry and display objects, jade later served a more purely decorative function.

Because it was not native to China, raw jade was imported from areas of southeastern and central Asia and Tibet. The Chinese accepted as jade both nephrite and jadeite, which have a dense structure and can be highly polished; because of their extreme hardness, both materials are also difficult to carve. The small size, pure color, and intricate decoration of this incense burner exemplify the high artistic achievement of many Chinese jade pieces. An inscription on the bottom of this incense burner dates the vessel to the reign of

Emperor Ch'ien Lung, the second outstanding era of jade production in Chinese history.

The incense burner is a religious utensil used on public and private altars. Its shape is derived from the earlier bronze *ting,* a three-legged bowl with handles near its rim. The bulging contour of the vessel, the outward curve of the handles and legs, and the emphasized juncture of the legs and body are elements found in tings of the late Chou period (480-222 B.C.).

The decoration on this incense burner does not reflect early bronzes. The lotus ornament on the cover, handles, and legs of the piece, here utilized in a purely decorative manner, is derived from the Indian use of the flower as a symbol of Buddha, introduced in the fourth and fifth centuries. The symmetrical foliate ornament appearing on the cover suggests eighteenth-century European decoration popularized in the Ch'ing dynasty by Jesuit missionaries working at court. The heavenly ladies mounted on auspicious animals appearing on the bowl of the vessel are derived from traditional Chinese subject matter; a deliberate archaism, the figures recall images of the fourth century.

[R.H. & S.W.]

CHINESE

Kuan Yin, Ch'ing dynasty (1644-1912), 18th century

Porcelain, $6\frac{1}{2}$ x $4\frac{13}{16}$ x $3\frac{1}{4}$ (16.5 x 12.3 x 8.2 cm)

Gift of Mr. William Tudor Gardiner h '45 and Mrs. Gardiner. 1940.385

This small statue of the Buddhist deity Kuan Yin is rendered in *blanc de Chine,* a white porcelain produced at Te-hua, Fukien province, on the south China coast. Blanc de Chine was greatly admired when first produced in the early Ming period (1368-1644). Considered a perfect marriage between glaze and paste, the porcelain is creamy white, is translucent where thin, and exhibits a soft-toned, smooth surface with no crackle. It rivaled the great white porcelain produced at Ching-te Chen, which was patronized by the Imperial Court.

The figure depicted in this statue, Kuan Yin, first appeared in India as one of the two major Bodhisattva at-

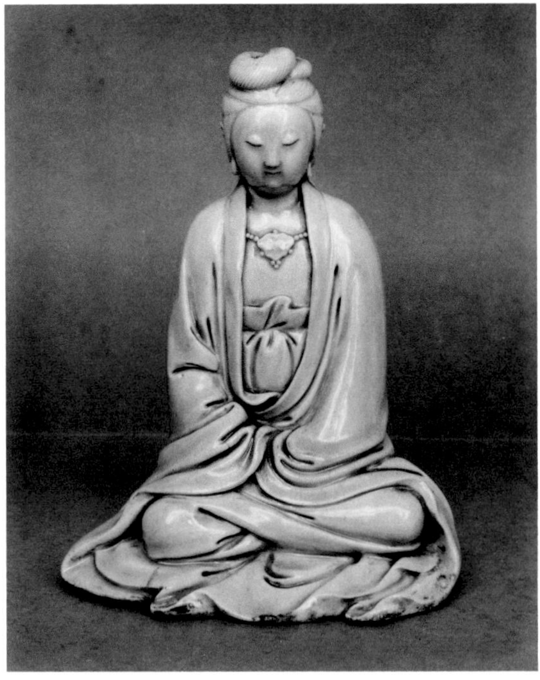

tendants of Amitabha Buddha, the Lord of the Western Paradise. In China, Kuan Yin gradually assumed a more prominent position and a more feminine guise, so that by the tenth century she was often worshipped as an individual deity. Another result of the Chinese repositioning of Kuan Yin in the Buddhist pantheon was her appearance in a number of specific roles that resulted from grafting native Chinese beliefs and practices onto her essentially Indian core.

One of the new depictions of the deity was the White-Robed Kuan Yin, suitably rendered here in blanc de Chine porcelain. This form of Kuan Yin was probably derived from a combination of the Tibetan Bodhisattva, the White Tara, and a Chinese Taoist goddess, Miao-shou. Moreover, it was thought that the White-Robed Kuan Yin had lived on the island of P'u-t'o where her shrine was located; this geographical consideration apparently led to the production of blanc de Chine porcelain figures of the deity at Te-hua, some three hundred miles to the south.

The pose of the Kuan Yin is the typical seated meditation position used for Buddha figures wherever the religion was practiced. The crossed legs, folded hands hidden under the robe, and downcast eyes contribute to the feeling of tranquility associated with meditation. Blanc de Chine figures of the White-Robed Kuan Yin were first produced in the seventeenth century. Some of the finest pieces bear the makers' names of Lin or Ho. Although it relates to examples in the Ho tradition, the timid handling of the material and the stiffness of the facial expression indicate that the piece probably dates from the latter part of the eighteenth century.

[R.H. & S.W.]

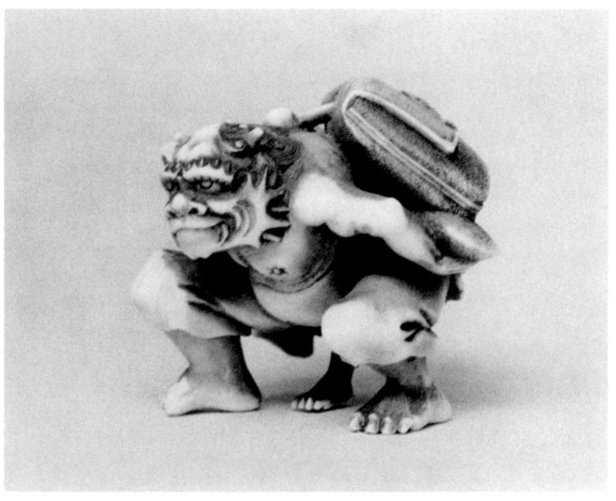

SHUN-PA, JAPANESE

Netsuke, Edo period (1615-1868), 19th century

Ivory, $1\frac{3}{16}$ x $1\frac{5}{16}$ x $1\frac{3}{16}$ (3.0 x 3.3 x 3.1 cm)

Gift of Miss Margaret Folger. 1966.56.1

This fine ivory netsuke exemplifies a popular Japanese decorative art form. Made from the mid-sixteenth to the mid-nineteenth century, netsuke are the equivalent of our grandparents' watch fobs, serving both a decorative and a practical purpose. Because the Japanese kimono was pocketless, a pouch was worn suspended from the belt (*obi*) on a silken cord; a netsuke functioned as a toggle, preventing the pouch from slipping to the ground. The prominent position of the toggle aroused the natural decorative interest of the Japanese; hence, netsuke were carved in a variety of intriguing shapes.

Netsuke were made in materials ranging from metal and lacquer to bamboo and semi-precious stones. Wood and ivory, from which this piece was carved, were the most popular materials. Ivory was particularly valued for its rich patina.

Since a number of early netsuke carvers also created religious images for temples and shrines, many netsuke depict figures from Buddhist, Shinto, and Taoist legend. This netsuke is composed of two supernatural, devilish figures, the Oni, with muscular, semi-clothed bodies, coarse and hairy facial features, and projecting horns. Netsuke makers also depicted animals, such as turtles, monkeys, and frogs; plants, such as mushrooms and chrysanthemums; and objects from everyday life, such as masks and sword guards. As is commonly the case, the carver of this netsuke signed his piece; his name, Shun-pa, does not appear in the standard lists of known artisans, indicating that his work is relatively unknown.   [R.H. & S.W.]

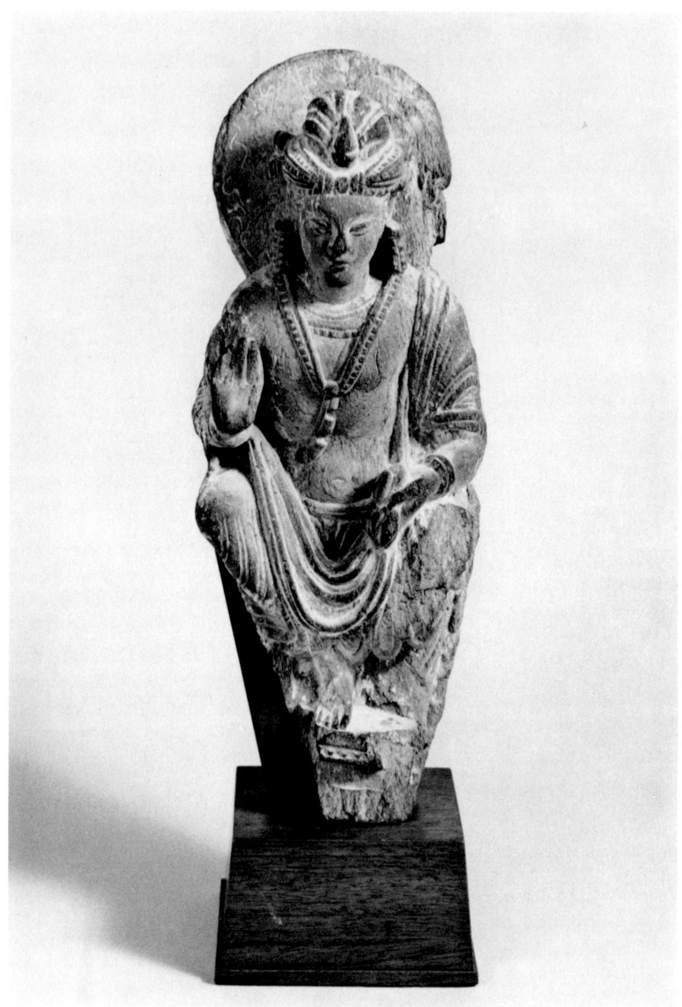

INDIAN

Bodhisattva, 3rd or 4th century

Schist, $13\frac{1}{4}$ x $4\frac{15}{16}$ x $3\frac{1}{8}$ (33.6 x 12.5 x 7.9 cm)

Gift of Miss Elizabeth P. Martin. 1968.84

This Bodhisattva of the Gandharan style is seated in the posture of leisure (*āsana*), with one leg partially drawn up and the other pendant, resting on a footstool. The lower garment (*dhoti*) covers both legs. The upper garment (*uttarīya*) is loosely draped, leaving the chest bare but covering the left shoulder and falling in broad arcs at the front. The ornaments are simple, consisting of a torque and a necklace. The string of amulet boxes, a common feature of Gandharan Bodhisattvas, is here abbreviated and attached to the necklace. The right hand is raised in the gesture of reassurance (*abhaya mudrā*) while the left hand appears to clasp a bunch of lotus buds. The slightly elongated face, with upturned schematic eyes, has a pleasant expression. The elaborate turban is typical of this period. The inscription on the rim of the damaged halo is extremely rare; the script is Kharosthi.

Gandhara was the name of the kingdom of the Kushans, who rose to great power in the first and second centuries. However, Gandharan art is usually considered to be that distinctive Indo-Classical school from the areas northwest of India, including present day Afghanistan and Pakistan. It flourished in the first four centuries. Although the style was hybrid with a strong classical accent, the content of this art was exclusively Buddhist, and the representations were often accurately based on religious texts.

The Kushan kings were earnest supporters of Buddhism, and many important alterations appeared in their religion at this time. The most significant change was the creation of the Buddha image (before this time, he was represented exclusively by symbols) and the growing popularity of the Bodhisattva. Bodhisattva is the divine being before he attains enlightenment and becomes Buddha (literally, the Enlightened One).

The Gandharan Bodhisattva images were based upon the prototype of Hindu princes, a direct reference to the royal lineage of the historical Bodhisattva, who was born in the Sākya dynasty as Prince Siddhārtha. [E.R.]

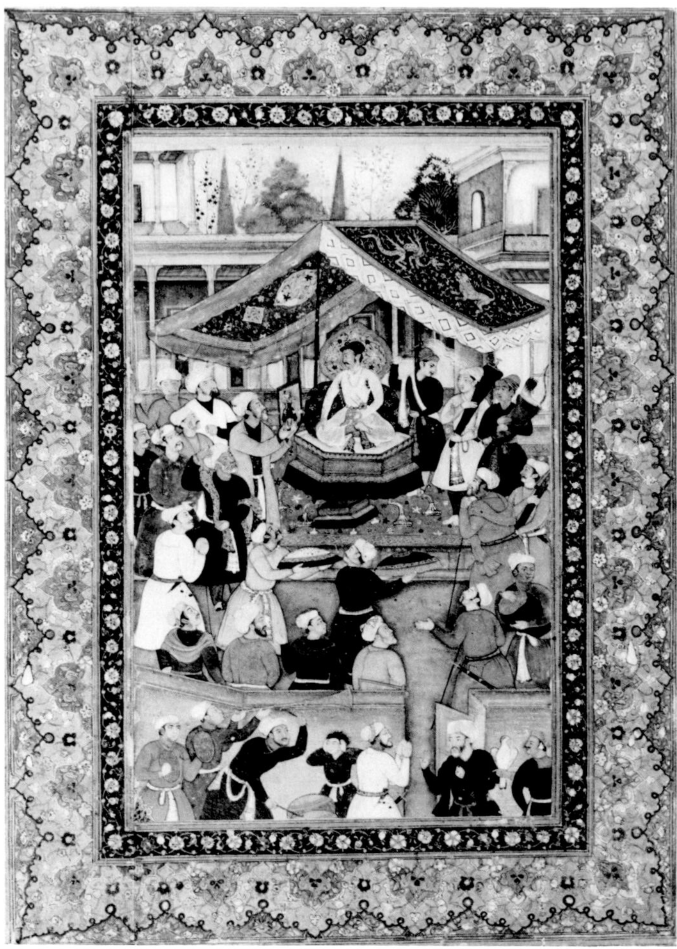

INDIAN

Page from an "Akbar-nameh" Manuscript, ca. 1600
   Tempera, 16¼ x 12¹³⁄₁₆ (41.3 x 32.5 cm)
   Gift of Miss Elizabeth P. Martin. 1968.25

In the center of the painting, the Mughal Emperor Akbar
is enthroned under an elaborate canopy. Encircled by attendants and visitors, he is giving audience in a palace court-
yard. On his right, a delegation presents him with a painting of a lady; two men carrying gifts on trays under
embroidered coverlets are also part of the entourage. To the

left of the emperor stands his retinue: one member swings a fly-whisk, and the others reverently carry the ruler's weapons. Musicians positioned outside the palace wall herald the arrival of other distinguished guests.

The *Akbar-nameh* (Akbar's memoirs), written by Abu-l-Fazl, is a historical documentation of the reign of this most remarkable emperor of India. At least three such illustrated manuscripts are known, and the most famous and complete set is housed in the Victoria and Albert Museum in London. Although it is one of the finest historical manuscripts of the Mughal period, the work has yet to be published in full. These manuscripts were painted toward the close of the emperor's reign and reflect the mature style of Mughal painting.

Although initially based on Persian style, Mughal painting in India quickly became a distinctive school under the vigorous patronage of the emperors. Akbar, the most gifted and powerful of the Mughal leaders, actively fostered an integration of Persian style with that of traditional India. Western influence, culled from the paintings presented by Jesuit missionaries, can also be identified. Commissioned works were painted in the royal atelier. Although several artists usually worked on each miniature, it was customary to attribute a painting to an outstanding artist if he completed the initial sketch.

Leaves such as the example illustrated here were bound in albums in which two paintings and two pages of calligraphy alternately face each other. This leaf is particularly similar to the scene of Akbar receiving Abd-ur-Rahim, signed by the well-known painter Anant, in the collection of the Victoria and Albert Museum. On the reverse is a quatrain written on a delicate arabesque ground and framed by a design of floral scroll intertwined with lion heads, a design typical of the early years of the seventeenth century.   [E.R.]

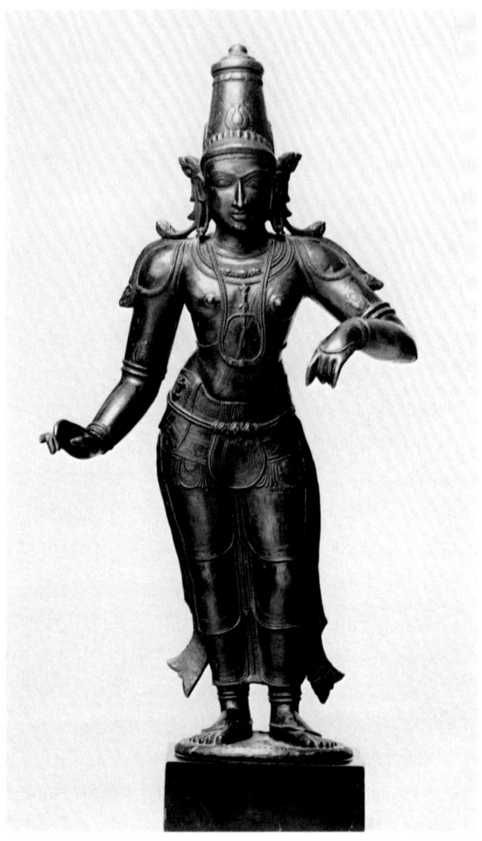

SOUTH INDIAN

Krishna, 17th or 18th century

Bronze, 22⅜ x 11¾ x 5⅝ (56.8 x 29.8 x 13.7 cm)

Gift of the Associates of the Bowdoin College Museum of Art. 1962.15

This large bronze image of Krishna, the most important incarnation (*avatār*) of Viṣṇu, is part of a two- or three-piece group. Such a figure would have been accompanied by an image of his consort Rukmiṇī, standing to his left, or it would have been flanked by the images of Rukmiṇī and Satyabhāma, his other consort. The bronze was cast in the round by the lost-wax method. In this process, the image was initially sculpted in wax by the artist. It was then encased in clay by the bronze-caster and fired, melting the wax and creating a terra cotta mould into which the liquid bronze could be poured. When the metal had cooled and hardened, the mould was broken to free the image, which was then polished. The four holes in the circular base were for anchoring the image to a larger platform so it could be carried in a procession.

The figure is gracefully posed, the curve of the hip balancing the slight bend at the left knee. The left arm is bent, as if resting on the shoulder of the now missing consort. The right arm is lowered and would have harmonized with the similarly lowered arm of the goddess.

The tall, cylindrical crown of the image indicates its *Vaiṣṇava* affiliation, as does the *Śrivatsa,* the symbol on the chest. An extremely popular divinity, Krishna is known and worshipped in three distinct forms: the mischievous but adorable child, the divine youth compelling the attention of the cowherds and their maidens, and the mature king, the narrator of the *Bhagavad Gītā*. It is the last form which is embodied in this sculpture, a direct counterpart of the familiar Viṣṇu image with his consorts Śridevī and Bhūdevī.

The smooth body and the tubular limbs are adorned with a variety of necklaces, bracelets, and armlets. The elaborate tie-strings of the crown are looped to frame the face, matching the loose ends of the waist sash which frame the legs. The modeling of the legs is revealed through the triple arcs of the lower garment (*dhoti*) in the well-established Indian sculptural tradition. The cloth panel around the hip is executed in great detail. Of particular interest is the hip belt, here supporting a dagger. Such double-banded belts with a central clasp are found on bronze images made centuries earlier, as well as on women today. The face is well defined, with arched brows, wide open eyes, a long, sharp nose, and a pointed chin, all characteristic of South Indian sculptures of the seventeenth and eighteenth centuries.

South Indian bronzes had reached perfection in the renowned Chola period (tenth and eleventh centuries). Though created a half millennium later, this large and graceful bronze is an honest embodiment of the same tradition.

[E.R.]

SELECTED WORKS FROM THE COLLECTION

[D. DEL G. M.]

In the notes which follow, each object is dated by dynasty and/or period. After that designation, some notes also include a closer approximation of the time the piece was created. Approximate dates for the Chinese, Japanese, and Korean dynasties and periods cited are below:

CHINESE

Neolithic period: 8th or 7th millennium B.C.-18th/16th century B.C.

Shang dynasty: 1523-1028 B.C.

Han dynasty: 206 B.C.-A.D. 221

Sui dynasty: A.D. 581-618

T'ang dynasty: A.D. 618-906

Northern Sung period: A.D. 960-1126

Chin dynasty: 1115-1234

Southern Sung period: 1127-1279

Yüan dynasty: 1260-1368

Ming dynasty: 1368-1644
Ch'eng-hua period: 1465-1487
Hung-chih period: 1488-1505
Wan-li period: 1573-1619

Ch'ing dynasty: 1644-1912
K'ang-hsi period: 1662-1722
Ch'ien-lung period: 1736-1795
Tao-kuang period: 1821-1850

JAPANESE

Edo period: 1615-1868

KOREAN

Koryŏ dynasty: 918-1392

Chinese Art

Chinese (Neolithic period): *Hand-formed Pot in the Shape of a Bronze Ting.* Earthenware, $4\frac{5}{16}$ x $5\frac{1}{16}$ (diam.) (10.9 x 12.8 cm). Gift of Miss Elizabeth P. Martin. 1968.29

✠Chinese (Shang dynasty, 13th or 12th century B.C.): *Hu.* Bronze, $6\frac{1}{2}$ x $3\frac{3}{16}$ (diam.) (16.5 x 8.1 cm). Gift of Miss Elizabeth P. Martin. 1968.89

Chinese (Han dynasty): *Dark Green Lead-glazed Storage Jar in the Shape of a Bronze Hu.* Earthenware, $13\frac{3}{4}$ x $11\frac{1}{4}$ (diam.) (35.0 x 28.5 cm). Gift of Mr. William Tudor Gardiner h '45 and Mrs. Gardiner. 1940.358

Chinese (Han dynasty): *Green and Amber Lead-glazed Jar in the Shape of a Bronze Hu.* Earthenware, $6\frac{1}{2}$ x $5\frac{13}{16}$ (diam.) (15.9 x 14.7 cm). Gift of Mr. William Tudor Gardiner h '45 and Mrs. Gardiner. 1940.359

Chinese (Sui dynasty or early T'ang dynasty, late 6th or 7th century): *Polychromed Standing Figurine of a Warrior.* Earthenware, $6\frac{11}{16}$ x $2\frac{3}{4}$ x $3\frac{3}{8}$ (17.0 x 6.9 x 8.5 cm). Gift of Miss Elizabeth P. Martin. 1968.35

Chinese (Sui dynasty or early T'ang dynasty, late 6th or 7th century): *Two Yellow Lead-glazed Figurines of Geese.* Earthenware, $4\frac{3}{16}$ x $1\frac{1}{2}$ x $3\frac{3}{4}$ (10.9 x 3.4 x 9.5 cm). Gift of Miss Elizabeth P. Martin. 1968.36.1-.2

Chinese (T'ang dynasty): *Pale Green Lead-glazed Globular Bowl.* Earthenware, $2\frac{1}{2}$ x $3\frac{9}{16}$ (diam.) (6.4 x 9.0 cm). Gift of Mr. William Tudor Gardiner h '45 and Mrs. Gardiner. 1940.360

Chinese (T'ang dynasty, probably late 7th or first half of the 8th century): *Polychrome (San-ts'ai) Lead-glazed Globular Bowl.* Earthenware, $3\frac{1}{16}$ x $3\frac{15}{16}$ (diam.) (7.7 x 10.0 cm). Gift of Mr. William Tudor Gardiner h '45 and Mrs. Gardiner. 1940.361

Chinese (T'ang dynasty, 8th or 9th century): *Black-glazed Ewer.* Stoneware, $4\frac{1}{4}$ x $3\frac{7}{8}$ (diam.) (10.9 x 9.9 cm). Gift of Miss Elizabeth P. Martin. 1968.32

Chinese (Northern Sung period, 10th or 11th century): *White-glazed Bowl with a Five-lobed Rim.* Stoneware, $2\frac{1}{8}$ x $6\frac{1}{4}$ (diam.) (5.3 x 15.9 cm). Gift of Mr. William Tudor Gardiner h '45 and Mrs. Gardiner. 1940.364

Chinese (Northern Sung period or Chin dynasty, 11th or 12th century): *Four Ting Plates with Incised Lotus Designs.* Porcelain, $\frac{3}{4}$ x $4\frac{9}{16}$ (diam.) (2.0 x 11.6 cm). Gift of Mr. William Tudor Gardiner h '45 and Mrs. Gardiner. 1940.363.1-.4

Chinese (Northern Sung period, 11th or early 12th century): *North-*

ern Celadon Bowl. Stoneware, 2 x 4½ (diam.) (5.1 x 11.4 cm). Gift of Miss Elizabeth P. Martin. 1968.90

Chinese (Chin dynasty, 12th or 13th century): *Chün Bowl.* Stoneware, 3⅛ x 7 9/16 (diam.) (8.0 x 19.2 cm). Gift of Mr. William Tudor Gardiner h '45 and Mrs. Gardiner. 1940.362

Chinese (Chin dynasty, 12th or 13th century): *Chün "Bubble" Bowl.* Stoneware, 1 11/16 x 3 3/16 (diam.) (4.3 x 9.1 cm). Gift of Mr. William Tudor Gardiner h '45 and Mrs. Gardiner. 1940.357

Chinese (Southern Sung period): *Black-glazed Chien Tea Bowl.* Stoneware, 2¾ x 5 (diam.) (7.1 x 12.7 cm). Gift of Mr. William Tudor Gardiner h '45 and Mrs. Gardiner. 1940.355

Chinese (Southern Sung period): *Hare's Fur-glazed Chien Tea Bowl.* Stoneware, 2 3/16 x 4⅞ (diam.) (5.5 x 12.5 cm). Gift of Mr. William Tudor Gardiner h '45 and Mrs. Gardiner. 1940.356

✠Chinese (Sung or Yüan dynasty, 13th or 14th century): *Bowl.* Porcelain, 3⅜ x 8½ (diam.) (8.5 x 21.7 cm). Gift of Mr. William Tudor Gardiner h '45 and Mrs. Gardiner. 1940.366

Chinese (late Chin dynasty or Yüan dynasty, 13th or early 14th century): *Ting Bowl with a Molded Floral Design in Six Panels.* Porcelain, 3⅛ x 8⅝ (diam.) (7.8 x 21.9 cm). Gift of Mr. William Tudor Gardiner h '45 and Mrs. Gardiner. 1940.365

Chinese (Ming dynasty, Hung-chih mark and period): *Shallow Dish with a Yellow Enamel Glaze.* Porcelain, 1 13/16 x 8½ (diam.) (4.6 x 21.5 cm). Gift of Mr. William Tudor Gardiner h '45 and Mrs. Gardiner. 1940.398

Chinese (Ming dynasty, Wan-li mark and period): *Covered Box with Underglaze Blue Decoration.* Porcelain, 4⅛ x 8¾ (diam.) (10.5 x 22.3 cm). Gift of Mr. William Tudor Gardiner h '45 and Mrs. Gardiner. 1940.388

Chinese (late Ming dynasty or early Ch'ing dynasty, second or third quarter of the 17th century): *Pair of Transitional Plates with Underglaze Blue Decoration.* Porcelain, 1 7/16 x 10⅜ (diam.) (3.7 x 26.4 cm). Gift of Mr. William Tudor Gardiner h '45 and Mrs. Gardiner. 1940.388.1-.2

Chinese (late Ming dynasty or early Ch'ing dynasty, second or third quarter of the 17th century): *Pair of Transitional Plates with Underglaze Blue Decoration.* Porcelain, 1 11/16 x 10⅜ (diam.) (4.3 x 26.3 cm). Gift of Mr. William Tudor Gardiner h '45 and Mrs. Gardiner. 1940.389.1-.2

Chinese (Ch'ing dynasty, K'ang-hsi mark and period): *Cup with Underglaze Blue and Overglaze Enamel Decoration.* Porcelain, 1⅞ x 2 9/16 (diam.) (4.9 x 6.5 cm). Gift of Mr. William Tudor Gardiner h '45 and Mrs. Gardiner. 1940.392

Chinese (Ch'ing dynasty, K'ang-hsi mark and period): *Water Pot with a Peachbloom Enamel Glaze and Incised Dragon Medallions.* Porcelain, $3\frac{5}{8}$ x $4\frac{15}{16}$ (diam.) (9.3 x 12.6 cm). Gift of Mrs. William Tudor Gardiner. 1962.17

Chinese (Ch'ing dynasty, K'ang-hsi period): *Baluster Vase with Underglaze Blue Decoration.* Porcelain, $18\frac{5}{16}$ x $7\frac{13}{16}$ (diam.) (46.5 x 19.9 cm). Gift of Mr. William Tudor Gardiner h '45 and Mrs. Gardiner. 1940.390

Chinese (Ch'ing dynasty, K'ang-hsi period): *Covered Box with Powder Blue Enamel and Gilt Decoration.* Porcelain, 3 x $3\frac{7}{16}$ (diam.) (7.8 x 8.8 cm). Gift of Mrs. William Tudor Gardiner. 1962.18

Chinese (Ch'ing dynasty, K'ang-hsi period): *Two Cups with Overglaze "Famille Verte" Enamel and Gilt Decoration.* Porcelain, $2\frac{1}{2}$ x $4\frac{5}{16}$ (diam.) (6.4 x 11.0 cm). Gift of Mr. William Tudor Gardiner h '45 and Mrs. Gardiner. 1940.391.1-.2

Chinese (Ch'ing dynasty, Ming Ch'eng-hua mark but probably K'ang-hsi period): *Cup with Underglaze Blue and Overglaze Enamel Decoration.* Porcelain, $1\frac{15}{16}$ x $2\frac{5}{8}$ (diam.) (5.0 x 6.6 cm). Gift of Mr. William Tudor Gardiner h '45 and Mrs. Gardiner. 1940.393

Chinese (Ch'ing dynasty, Ming Hung-chih mark but probably K'ang-hsi period): *Shallow Dish with a Yellow Enamel Glaze.* Porcelain, $1\frac{7}{8}$ x $8\frac{1}{2}$ (diam.) (4.7 x 21.5 cm). Gift of Mr. William Tudor Gardiner h '45 and Mrs. Gardiner. 1940.399

Chinese (Ch'ing dynasty, second half of the 17th or early 18th century): *"Blanc de Chine" Covered Box.* Porcelain, $2\frac{5}{16}$ x $4\frac{7}{8}$ (diam.) (5.9 x 12.4 cm). Gift of Mr. William Tudor Gardiner h '45 and Mrs. Gardiner. 1940.376

Chinese (Ch'ing dynasty, late 17th or 18th century): *"Blanc de Chine" Brush-holder with Openwork Floral Decoration.* Porcelain, $5\frac{7}{16}$ x $3\frac{5}{8}$ (diam.) (13.8 x 9.3 cm). Gift of Mr. William Tudor Gardiner h '45 and Mrs. Gardiner. 1940.381

Chinese (Ch'ing dynasty, late 17th or 18th century): *"Blanc de Chine" Figure of a Seated Kuan-yin Signed on the Back "Yün-shan i-ku chih."* Porcelain, $7\frac{1}{8}$ x $6\frac{5}{16}$ x $4\frac{5}{16}$ (20.1 x 16.0 x 11.0 cm). Gift of Mr. William Tudor Gardiner h '45 and Mrs. Gardiner. 1940.384

Chinese (Ch'ing dynasty, late 17th or 18th century): *"Blanc de Chine" Incense Burner in the Shape of a Bronze Lien.* Porcelain, $2\frac{11}{16}$ x $4\frac{7}{16}$ (diam.) (6.8 x 11.3 cm). Gift of Mr. William Tudor Gardiner h '45 and Mrs. Gardiner. 1940.383

Chinese (Ch'ing dynasty, late 17th or 18th century): *Set of Six "Blanc de Chine" Winecups.* Porcelain, $1\frac{13}{16}$ x $2\frac{7}{8}$ (diam.) (4.6 x 7.3 cm). Gift of Mr. William Tudor Gardiner h '45 and Mrs. Gardiner. 1940.379.1-.6

✠Chinese (Ch'ing dynasty, 18th century): *Kuan Yin*. Porcelain, $6\frac{1}{2}$ x $4\frac{13}{16}$ x $3\frac{1}{4}$ (16.5 x 12.3 x 8.2 cm). Gift of Mr. William Tudor Gardiner h '45 and Mrs. Gardiner. 1940.385

Chinese (Ch'ing dynasty, Ch'ien-lung mark and period): *Celadon Vase with Molded Decoration*. Porcelain, $8\frac{1}{2}$ x $3\frac{7}{8}$ (diam.) (21.5 x 9.8 cm). Gift of Mr. William Tudor Gardiner h '45 and Mrs. Gardiner. 1940.400

✠Chinese (Ch'ing dynasty, Ch'ien-lung period): *Incense Burner*. Jade, 6 x $5\frac{7}{8}$ (diam.) (15.2 x 14.9 cm). Gift of Mrs. Elizabeth L. Power. 1960.51

Chinese (Ch'ing dynasty, probably Ch'ien-lung period): *Bowl with Overglaze "Famille Rose" Enamel Decoration*. Porcelain, $3\frac{1}{16}$ x $7\frac{3}{8}$ (diam.) (7.8 x 18.8 cm). Gift of Mr. William Tudor Gardiner h '45 and Mrs. Gardiner. 1940.397

Chinese (Ch'ing dynasty, Ch'ien-lung mark but probably Tao-kuang period): *"Tou-ts'ai" Plate with Phoenix Decoration*. Porcelain, $1\frac{9}{16}$ x $7\frac{9}{16}$ (diam.) (4.0 x 19.2 cm). Museum collections. T1977.17

Chinese (Ch'ing dynasty, Tao-kuang mark and period): *Bowl with a Deep Blue Enamel Glaze and the Hallmark "Ts'ai hsiu-t'ang chih" on the Base*. Porcelain, $2\frac{1}{4}$ x $6\frac{7}{8}$ (diam.) (5.8 x 17.6 cm). Gift of Mr. William Tudor Gardiner h '45 and Mrs. Gardiner. 1940.402

Japanese Art

Japanese (Edo period): *Arita Dish with Underglaze Blue Floral Decoration*. Porcelain, $1\frac{1}{2}$ x $9\frac{13}{16}$ (diam.) (3.9 x 24.9 cm). Museum collections. T1977.19

Japanese (Edo period, second half of the 17th century): *Arita Plate with Underglaze Blue Floral Decoration*. Porcelain, $1\frac{9}{16}$ x $8\frac{11}{16}$ (diam.) (4.0 x 22.1 cm). Gift of Miss Gertrude H. Plaisted in memory of her mother, Mrs. Harris M. Plaisted. 1977.15

Japanese (Edo period, late 17th or early 18th century): *Arita Dish with Underglaze Blue Decoration*. Porcelain, $1\frac{5}{8}$ x $9\frac{1}{4}$ (diam.) (4.2 x 23.4 cm). Gift of Mr. David S. Cowles, Esq. 1909.14.3

Japanese (Edo period, late 17th or early 18th century): *Imari Bowl with Underglaze Blue and Overglaze Red Enamel and Gilt Decoration*. Porcelain, $2\frac{1}{2}$ x $7\frac{1}{2}$ (diam.) (6.3 x 19.1 cm). Gift of Mr. David S. Cowles, Esq. 1909.14.1

Japanese (Edo period, Chinese Ming Ch'eng-hua mark but 18th century): *Square Arita Plate with Underglaze Blue Decoration*. Porcelain, $1\frac{3}{8}$ x $6\frac{7}{8}$ (3.5 x 17.5 cm). Museum collections. T1977.18

✠Shun-pa, Japanese (Edo period, 19th century): *Netsuke*. Ivory, $1\frac{3}{16}$ x $1\frac{5}{16}$ x $1\frac{3}{16}$ (3.0 x 3.3 x 3.0 cm). Gift of Miss Margaret Folger. 1966.56.1

Korean Art

Korean (Koryŏ dynasty, 12th century): *Celadon Bowl with a Foliated Rim.* Stoneware, $1\frac{7}{8}$ x $4\frac{3}{8}$ (diam.) (4.8 x 11.1 cm). Gift of Mr. William Tudor Gardiner h '45 and Mrs. Gardiner. 1940.408

Korean (Koryŏ dynasty, 12th century): *Celadon Bowl with a Foliated Rim and an Incised Leaf Design.* Stoneware, $1\frac{3}{8}$ x $3\frac{3}{4}$ (diam.) (3.5 x 9.6 cm). Gift of Mr. William Tudor Gardiner h '45 and Mrs. Gardiner. 1940.409

Korean (Koryŏ dynasty, 12th century): *Celadon Bowl with an Overlapping Lotus Petal Design.* Stoneware, $3\frac{5}{16}$ x $6\frac{7}{8}$ (diam.) (8.4 x 17.4 cm). Gift of Mr. William Tudor Gardiner h '45 and Mrs. Gardiner. 1940.407

Korean (Koryŏ dynasty, 12th century): *Celadon Vase with an Incised Floral Design.* Stoneware, $13\frac{3}{8}$ x $6\frac{5}{8}$ (diam.) (33.9 x 16.9 cm). Gift of Mr. William Tudor Gardiner h '45 and Mrs. Gardiner. 1940.404

Korean (Koryŏ dynasty, 13th century): *Celadon Bowl with Inlaid Slip Decoration.* Stoneware, $3\frac{7}{16}$ x $7\frac{11}{16}$ (diam.) (8.8 x 19.5 cm). Gift of Mr. William Tudor Gardiner h '45 and Mrs. Gardiner. 1940.406

Korean (Koryŏ dynasty, 13th century): *Celadon Vase with Inlaid Slip Decoration.* Stoneware, $8\frac{11}{16}$ x $6\frac{1}{8}$ (diam.) (22.1 x 15.6 cm). Gift of Mr. William Tudor Gardiner h '45 and Mrs. Gardiner. 1945.405

Indian Art

✠Indian (3rd or 4th century): *Bodhisattva.* Schist, $13\frac{1}{4}$ x $4\frac{15}{16}$ x $3\frac{1}{8}$ (33.6 x 12.5 x 7.9 cm). Gift of Miss Elizabeth P. Martin. 1968.84

North East Indian (12th-13th century): *Plaque.* Terra cotta, $4\frac{13}{16}$ x $2\frac{15}{16}$ x $1\frac{9}{16}$ (12.2 x 7.5 x 4.0 cm). Museum collections. T1977.4

✠Indian (ca. 1600): *Page from an "Akbar-nameh" Manuscript.* Tempera, $16\frac{1}{4}$ x $12\frac{13}{16}$ (41.3 x 32.5 cm). Gift of Miss Elizabeth P. Martin. 1968.25

✠South Indian (17th or 18th century): *Krishna.* Bronze, $22\frac{3}{8}$ x $11\frac{3}{4}$ x $5\frac{5}{8}$ (56.8 x 29.8 x 13.7 cm). Gift of the Associates of the Bowdoin College Museum of Art. 1962.15

AFRICAN, NEW WORLD,
AND PACIFIC ART

While the museum's collections of African, New World, and Pacific art are small, they provide useful art historical, ethnological, and archaeological information and form a teaching collection which is a rich resource. The collections, which include objects from Africa, the United States, Canada, the Polynesian Islands, Mexico, Costa Rica, and Peru, are comprised of a variety of artifacts suggesting the many aspects of life-style and culture of these areas. Reliquary figures, masks, and funereal statuettes represent the ceremonial, ritual, and spiritual activities of the peoples; other objects of daily life bear carvings or decorations which refer to gods and heroes or elements of the spiritual world. Household utensils offer insight into daily activities, artisanry, and the integration of art and life through crafts; jars, bowls, baskets, and other cooking and serving utensils are included in the collections, as well as jewelry, weapons, and other tools, such as axes, boat paddles, and weaving pulleys.

A small but growing African collection includes ten weaving pulleys which were the gift of Mr. Raymond Myrer, and a cane and two walking sticks given by Mr. Barrett Parker.

The pre-Columbian collections from Mexico and Costa Rica are extensive, due in large part to the generosity of Mr. Henry H. Pierce, Jr., whose gift of Mexican artifacts included eighty-five objects, and Mr. John B. Chandler '37 and Mrs. Chandler, who donated large collections of pre-Columbian jade in 1976 and 1977.

Native North American art in the collections ranges from a Maine Passamaquoddy purse, the gift of Miss Virginia Dox in 1893, to an Eskimo soapstone sculpture, the gift of Mr. Robert W. Breed '35. Baskets made by the Tlingit Indians of the Northwest Coast were donated by Mrs. John R. Dunton in 1944. The Virginia Dox collection came to the museum in 1893 and includes fourteen examples of Pueblo pottery.

A small collection of decorative Peruvian pottery has been growing since 1906, when Mr. George Warren Hammond h '00 donated three examples. Recently, Mr. and Mrs. Brewster Doggett made a gift of two votive vessels; additional Peruvian artifacts were donated to the museum by Mr. John Moses, Jr. '60.

The museum's holdings of Pacific or Oceanic art were donated largely in the nineteenth century, soon after trading with the South Pacific islands was initiated. In 1850 a Sandwich Islands canoe paddle was donated by Mr. John C. Humphreys. Three years later Captain Weeks of Vassalboro presented two ceremonial axes to the museum; in 1898 a significant group of eight Malanggan ceremonial masks from New Ireland was the gift of Mr. Harold Sewall.

[K.A.O.]

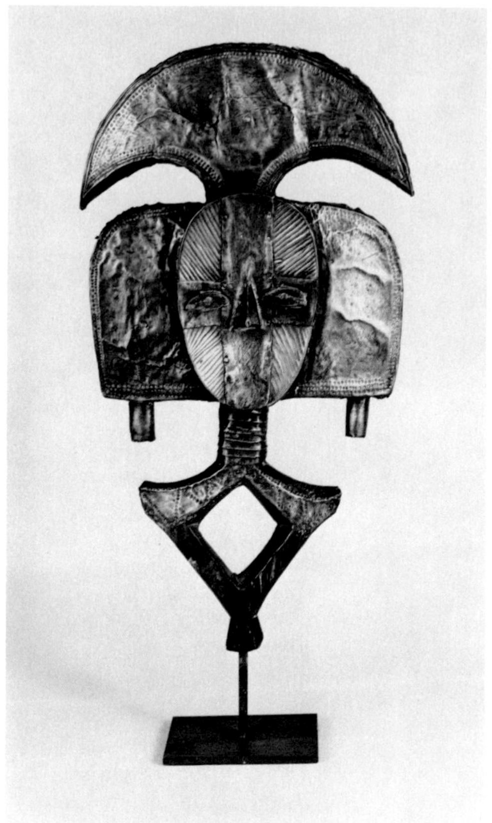

AFRICAN, ZAIRE, KOTA CULTURE
Reliquary Figure, late 19th century

Wood, brass, and copper, 20¾ x 11⅛ x 1¾ (52.8 x 28.2 x 4.4 cm)

Florence C. Quinby Fund in memory of Henry Cole Quinby h '16. 1969.69

An image of this type would be attached to a container holding the exhumed bones of a socially and politically important man. Regarded as a talisman, such an image was thought to aid and protect the family caring for it. The image was not intended as a specific portrait but was designed to suggest the spiritual power residing in the bones of the deceased. The basic form was carved from wood and covered with thin sheets of copper and brass. These metals, considered among the most valuable materials in that region of Africa, were decorated by the techniques of punching, scoring, and repoussé, a method of raising a design in relief through hammering.

Objects such as this are believed to have influenced several European avant-garde artists in the early twentieth century. The formal relationship can perhaps best be seen in the so-called African period of Pablo Picasso, especially in his studies for the famous *Les Demoiselles d'Avignon* of 1907.

[E.M.M.]

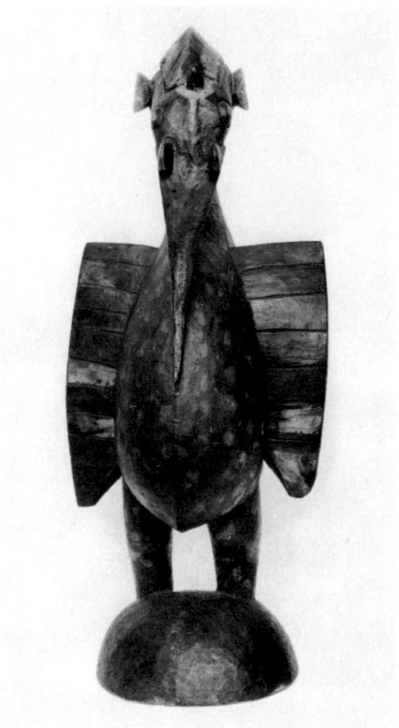

AFRICAN, MALI, SENUFO CULTURE

Figure of a Bird, ca. 1900

   Polychromed wood, 28 x 10⅜ x 8¾ (71.2 x 26.3 x 22.3 cm)

   Florence C. Quinby Fund in memory of Henry Cole Quinby h '16. 1969.71

This figure represents the hornbill, a bird which the Senufo believe was one of the first five creatures to inhabit the earth. The bird was called "Porpianong" or "Porparga," and its long beak and full stomach represent fertility and community continuance. These figures are often carried on the head in ceremonies of the Lô Society, a complex organization which helps structure the religious, social, and ancestral activities of the village.   [E.M.M.]

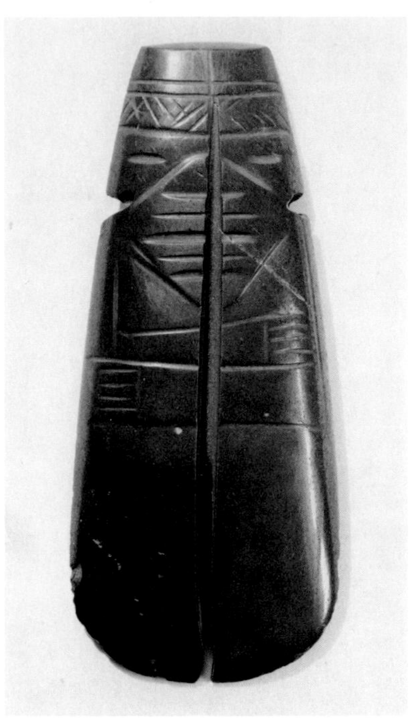

COSTA RICAN, NICOYA CULTURE

Pendant, ca. A.D. 800-1000

Jade, 5⅜ x 2 5/16 x 11/16 (13.7 x 5.8 x 1.7 cm)

Gift of Mr. John B. Chandler '37 and Mrs. Chandler. 1976.44.10

Jade was used throughout Middle and South America for the creation of sacred objects and valuable items of personal adornment. One of the most interesting varieties of jade sculpture, the so-called axe-god pendant of Costa Rica, is illustrated here. The jade was carved into the shape of a celt, a long, narrow axe blade common to most lithic cultures. In this case, the stylized design of a man with arms folded across his chest has been carved on the basic celt form, suggesting the name axe-god. This piece has been drilled through the top so that it could be suspended around the neck as a charm. An extremely hard substance, jade was worked by a variety of tools including strings and drills which used abrasives for their cutting power.   [E.M.M.]

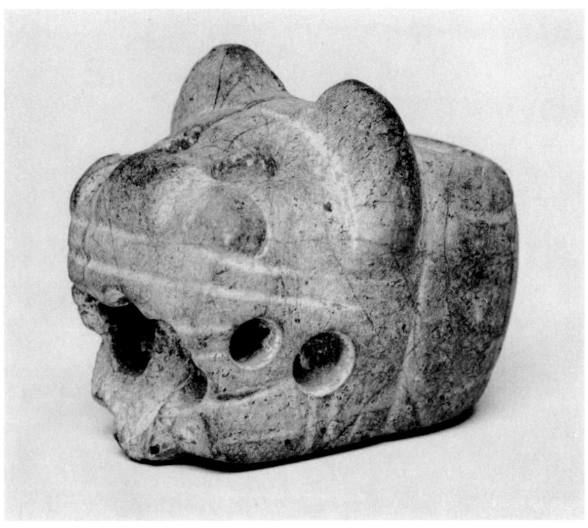

COSTA RICAN, NICOYA CULTURE

Mace Head, ca. A.D. 500-1000

Limestone, $2\frac{1}{2}$ x $2\frac{7}{16}$ x $3\frac{1}{8}$ (6.3 x 6.2 x 7.9 cm)
Gift of Mr. John B. Chandler '37 and Mrs. Chandler. 1976.44.25

A short, stone-headed club, the mace was used as a weapon and as a ceremonial object in many North and South American Indian cultures. This piece is similar to other examples discovered in Costa Rica. Made of a hard stone, the mace head has been carved into the general shape of a feline. Cats, along with birds, were the most prominent sacred animals represented in Costa Rican art. The deep, conical drill holes on the sides of the mace were used to secure the stone to the shaft.   [E.M.M.]

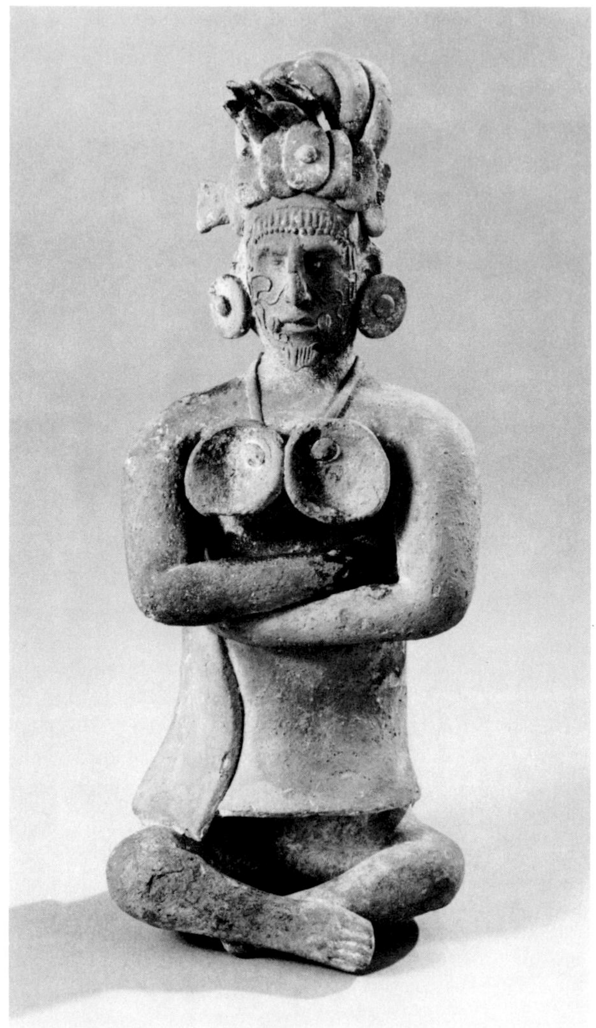

MEXICAN, MAYA INDIAN

Seated Male, ca. A.D. 600-800

Terra cotta, 7 x 3 1/16 x 2 1/2 (17.8 x 7.7 x 6.4 cm)

Florence C. Quinby Fund in memory of Henry Cole Quinby h '16.
1969.84

The small, clay figurine is a common form found in many
Mesoamerican cultures, but the most elegant and beautiful
of the type is the funerary terra cotta statuette of the classic

Maya. Although they were found in several sites, the large number of figurines which were located on the burial island of Jaina has led the whole group to be associated with that location. These realistically rendered figures were made from a fine-grained clay which enabled the pieces to be finished smoothly and with fine detail, as evidenced in this example. The surface also indicates that the figure was polychromed, although only traces of white and a deteriorated dark pigment remain. The man is seated with his arms folded across his chest, one of the most common Jaina poses. He is crowned with an elaborate headdress, a probable sign of his divinity. He also wears large, round spools in his ears and a necklace with two shell pendants. His face is embellished with a small, pointed beard and a tuft of mustache at each corner of his mouth. Finally, the broad area of his cheeks is covered with fine-line scarification. Contemporary scholarship has related these figures to Mayan epics of heroes and gods. [E.M.M.]

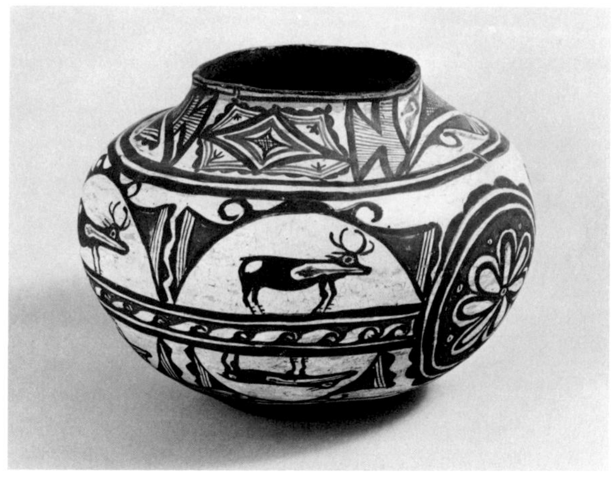

NORTH AMERICAN, ZUÑI INDIAN

Water Jar, ca. 1880

Terra cotta, 10⅛ x 13¾ (diam.) (25.7 x 34.9 cm)

Gift of Mrs. Herbert E. Hawkes. 1970.31

Although jars of this type were made well into the twentieth century, the squat profile and broad shoulder of this vessel suggest a date of circa 1880. Like all American Indian pottery, this piece was built by the coil method, for the wheel was never used by native craftsmen. After the pot was sundried, a slip of white clay was applied. This provided the background for the painted decoration consisting of a clay-based paint for the red and a vegetable-based paint for the black. Strongly architectonic in design, the four major areas of decoration emphasize the physical shape of the pot itself.

The decoration, such as the alternating geometric designs of the neck filled with fine-line notching, is typically Zuñi. The body of the vessel carries a symmetrically opposed double representation of the most prevalent Zuñi design, often referred to as the House of Deer pattern. Framed by an elaborate arch, each animal is embellished with a red line reaching from the interior of its body to its mouth. Nearly always found on these animals, this so-called heartline is a very common motif in American Indian art and is not restricted to the Southwest.   [E.M.M.]

NORTH AMERICAN, NORTHWEST COAST, TLINGIT INDIAN

Basket, ca. 1890

Spruce roots, grass, 9½ x 11½ (diam.) (24.1 x 29.2 cm)
Gift of Mrs. John R. Dunton. 1944.26.1

Since 1786, when the French explorer La Pérouse first encountered the tribe, the Tlingit have been considered the best basketmakers of the Northwest Coast. This fine example was constructed by the twining technique, using thinly split roots of the Sitka spruce. The four bands of geometric decoration were created with grasses applied in a false embroidery technique known as imbrication. While the rich brown color of the body was obtained from the natural, cured spruce root, the soft green, red, yellow, and black tones of the design were achieved by dyeing the grasses with various herbal and mineral compounds. Such baskets were used for the storage and serving of foods; some

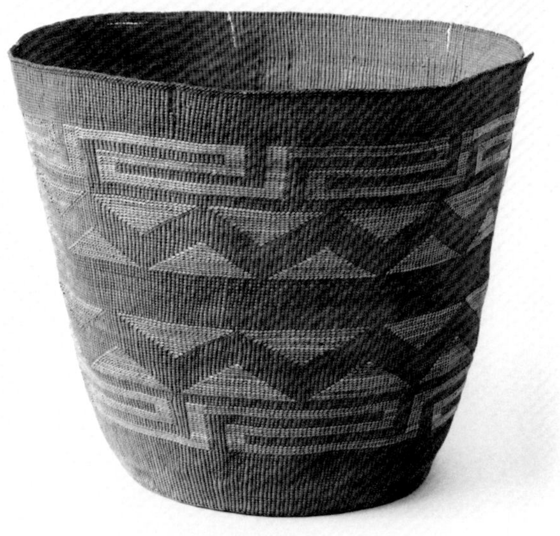

were so tightly woven that they could be used to hold liquids and, with hot stones placed in them, to boil food.

According to Tlingit mythology, the origin of basketry is attributed to the age when humans and spirits walked more freely together. The first basket was woven by the earthly wife of the Sun, and it was through her handiwork that the Tlingit women learned the art of basketmaking.

[E.M.M.]

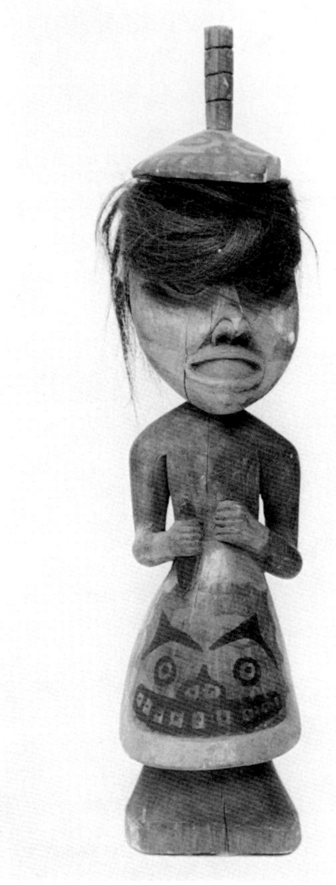

NORTH AMERICAN, NORTHWEST COAST, POSSIBLY NOOTKA INDIAN

Male Figure, probably 19th century

Polychromed wood, $15\frac{3}{8}$ x $3\frac{1}{4}$ x $3\frac{1}{4}$ (39.2 x 8.3 x 8.3 cm)
Anonymous gift. 1850.5

While small, free-standing carvings representing the full figure are not the most common sculptural type found among the tribes of the Northwest Coast, they were used in association with funereal, shamanic, and sometimes potlatch ceremonies. The artist's attention to plastic delineation and proportion on the face of the figure illustrated here attests to the more common tradition of mask carving which is prevalent throughout the area.

The figure is shown wearing an apron decorated with the painted representation of a totemic crest, probably a bear. In his right hand he holds one of the famous two-bladed fighting knives used by the warriors of the Northwest Coast. While first made from whalebone, these efficient weapons were later manufactured of both copper and iron. On his head is a clan hat which could have been made either of wood or twined spruce root and painted with the face of his clan totem. The vertical decoration, divided into four segments, represents basketry rings which are said to acknowledge the number of potlatches sponsored by the wearer of the hat. Since it is most common to find these rings in groups of three or less, the four on this figure mark a man of great wealth and social prestige.   [E.M.M.]

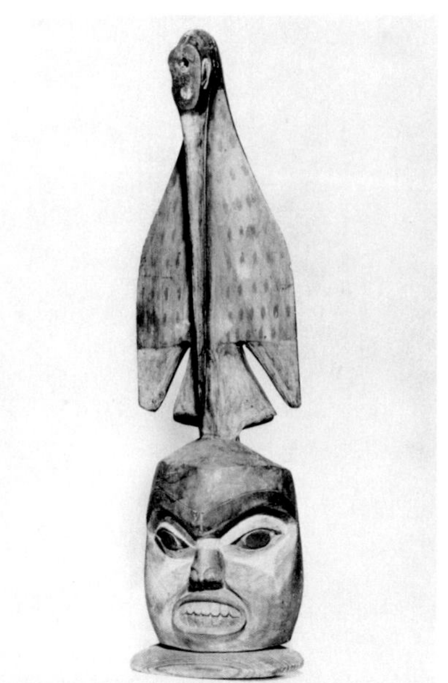

NORTH AMERICAN, NORTHWEST COAST,
POSSIBLY NOOTKA INDIAN

Mask, probably 19th century

Polychromed wood, 15$\frac{3}{16}$ x 4$\frac{1}{4}$ x 2$\frac{3}{16}$ (38.6 x 10.8 x 5.6 cm)
Anonymous gift. 1850.4

The Northwest Coast tribes have the greatest mask-carving tradition of any Indian cultures in America. While the bird is rather large in proportion to the face of this mask, the combination is not uncommon among the southern tribes of the region. With its long, thin, straight beak, the bird should probably be identified as a crane, the species most often represented in the Hamatsa ceremonies of the mainland Kwakiutl. In typical fashion, the mask has been painted to increase its visual effectiveness.   [E.M.M.]

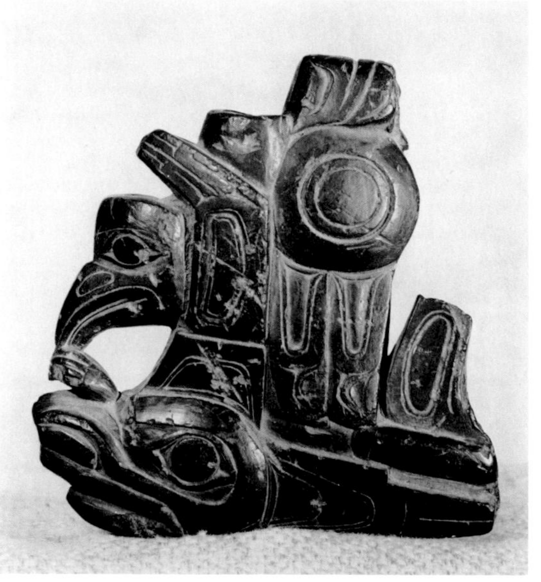

NORTH AMERICAN, QUEEN CHARLOTTE ISLANDS, HAIDA INDIAN

Ceremonial Pipe, ca. 1850

Argillite, $4\frac{3}{8}$ x $4\frac{3}{16}$ x $1\frac{1}{4}$ (11.2 x 10.7 x 3.2 cm)
Gift of Mr. Rufus K. Sewall 1837. 1896.8

The numerous fur-trading expeditions to the Northwest Coast introduced many aspects of Western culture to the native populations. Always regarded as astute traders themselves, many area tribes responded to the increased number of white visitors who desired to collect objects of Indian manufacture. Beginning around 1820, the Haida created a new industry to fill this market by carving various objects from argillite, a local carbonaceous shale. Although objects from this material were made expressly for sale to the white market, the carvers were traditional tribal artists who translated the motifs and styles of their ceremonial wood sculptures to the stone. Soft and easily workable when it is taken from the ground, the material gradually hardens when exposed to the air.

The killer whale forming the base of the pipe is the principal figure of this example. Design elements of other animals, such as the raven, are joined together with the base form to create the complex conglomeration of figures and motifs characterizing the Northwest Coast style.

[E.M.M.]

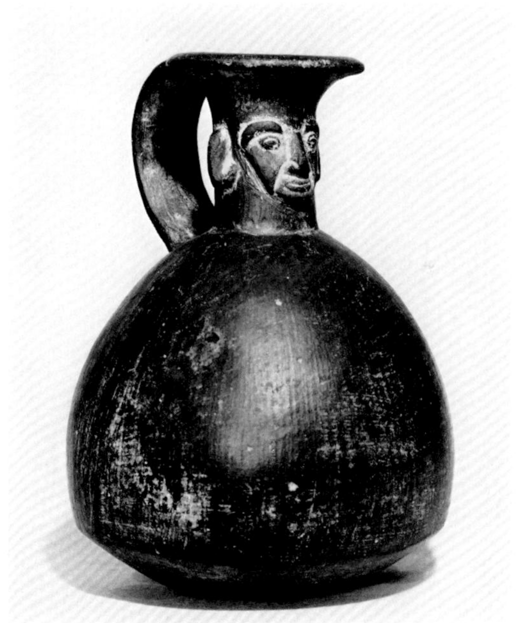

PERUVIAN, INCA INDIAN

Vase, ca. 1500

 Earthenware, 8¾ x 6¼ (diam.) (22.3 x 15.8 cm)
 Gift of Mr. George Warren Hammond h 1900. 1906.08

The marriage of a sculptural face to a long-necked jar with handle represents a vase type found in many ancient Peruvian cultures. This strong example was created by an Incan potter of the last great Indian empire flourishing before the European invasion. The emphasized structure of the face is reminiscent of the great sculptural traditions of the Chimu and Mochican cultures which preceded the Inca in Northern Peru. The surface of the vessel is also related to the earlier Moche work in its stone-polished body and rich black finish, the result of an oxygen-reduced atmosphere used in the final stages of firing. The articulated body and the strong but graceful flaring neck are more purely Incan in their origins and are derived from the common aryballos vase form which was made in many variations.   [E.M.M.]

MELANESIAN, NEW IRELAND

Mask, probably 19th century

Polychromed wood, plaster, and yarn, 19¾ x 8⅜ x 16⅛ (50.1 x 21.3 x 41.0 cm)

Gift of Mr. Harold M. Sewall. 1898.68

New Ireland sculpture has always been regarded as one of the most colorful and fascinating art forms in all of Oceania. Masks such as this represent just one of the many types of intricate sculpture produced on the island for the Malanggan ceremony. This complex and costly rite combined important ritual elements such as funerals and the recitation of ancestral lineage with totemic rites and the reenactment of the mythic cycle of rebirth. The helmetlike mask top was derived from the traditional hairstyle in which the sides of the skull were shaved, leaving a single crest of hair running down the middle of the head.   [E.M.M.]

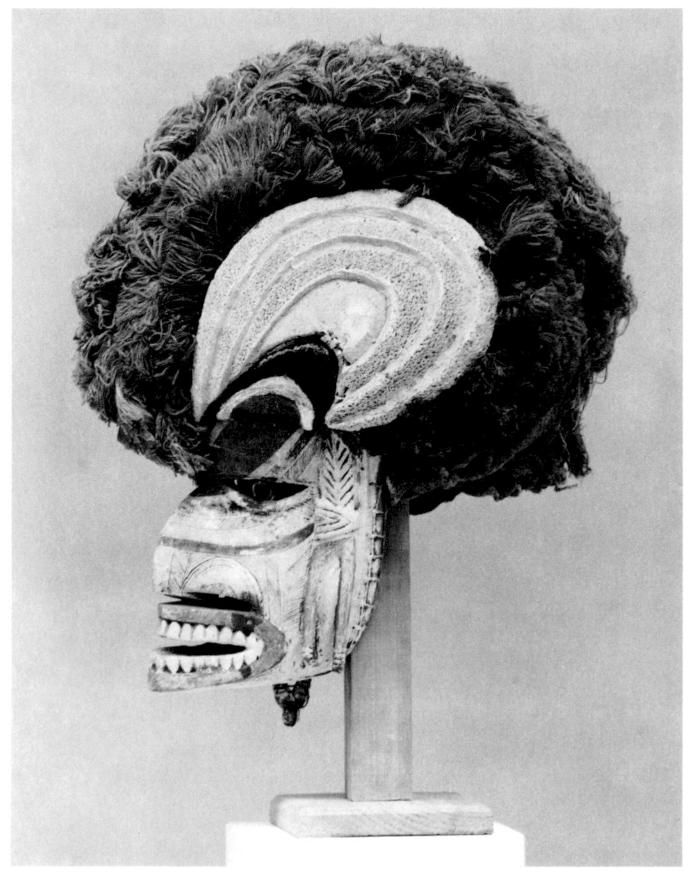

SELECTED WORKS FROM THE COLLECTION
[K.A.O.]

African Art

✠African, Zaire, Kota culture (late 19th century): *Reliquary Figure.* Wood, brass, and copper, 20¾ x 11⅛ x 1¾ (52.8 x 28.2 x 4.4 cm). Florence C. Quinby Fund in memory of Henry Cole Quinby h '16. 1969.69

✠African, Mali, Senufo culture (ca. 1900): *Figure of a Bird.* Polychromed wood, 28 x 10⅜ x 8¾ (71.2 x 26.3 x 22.3 cm). Florence C. Quinby Fund in memory of Henry Cole Quinby h '16. 1969.71

New World Art

COSTA RICAN

Costa Rican (pre-Columbian): *Anthropomorphic Axe God.* Jadeite and serpentine, 4 9/16 x 1¼ x 1⅛ (11.6 x 3.8 x 2.8 cm). Gift of Mr. John B. Chandler '37 and Mrs. Chandler. 1976.44.14

Costa Rican (pre-Columbian): *Anthropomorphic Axe God.* Stone, 9 7/16 x 1¾ x 15/16 (23.9 x 4.5 x 2.4 cm). Gift of Mr. John B. Chandler '37 and Mrs. Chandler. 1976.44.17

Costa Rican (pre-Columbian): *Bird Celt.* Stone, 3¾ x ⅝ x 11/16 (9.6 x 1.6 x 1.7 cm). Gift of Mr. John B. Chandler '37 and Mrs. Chandler. 1976.44.1

✠Costa Rican (pre-Columbian): *Mace Head.* Limestone, 2½ x 2 7/16 x 3⅛ (6.3 x 6.2 x 7.9 cm). Gift of Mr. John B. Chandler '37 and Mrs. Chandler. 1976.44.25

Costa Rican (pre-Columbian): *Monkey Pendant.* Serpentine, 1 x ⅞ x 2 1/16 (2.6 x 2.3 x 5.3 cm). Gift of Mr. John B. Chandler '37 and Mrs. Chandler. 1976.44.8

✠Costa Rican (pre-Columbian): *Pendant.* Jade, 5⅜ x 2 5/16 x 11/16 (13.7 x 5.8 x 1.7 cm). Gift of Mr. John B. Chandler '37 and Mrs. Chandler. 1976.44.10

MEXICAN

Mexican, Gulf Coast (800-300 B.C.): *Pottery Head.* Terra cotta, 1⅝ x 1⅛ x ⅞ (4.2 x 2.8 x 2.2 cm). Gift of Mr. Henry H. Pierce, Jr. 1976.41.26

Mexican, Oaxaca (1100-100 B.C.): *Head.* Terra cotta, 1 15/16 x 1 9/16 x 1 (4.9 x 4.0 x 2.6 cm). Gift of Mr. Henry H. Pierce, Jr. 1976.41.24

Mexican, Colima (ca. 100 B.C.-A.D. 100): *Two Fighting Shaman.* Terra cotta, 13⅛ x 9 x 5¾ (33.3 x 22.8 x 14.6 cm). Florence C. Quinby Fund in memory of Henry Cole Quinby h '16. 1969.83

Mexican, Valley of Mexico (A.D. 100-300): *Head.* Terra cotta, $1\frac{7}{16}$ x
1 x $1\frac{1}{8}$ (3.7 x 2.6 x 2.9 cm). Gift of Mr. Henry H. Pierce, Jr.
1976.41.32

Mexican, Valley of Mexico (A.D. 300-500): *Head.* Terra cotta, $1\frac{5}{16}$
x $1\frac{3}{8}$ x $\frac{11}{16}$ (3.3 x 3.5 x 1.8 cm). Gift of Mr. Henry H. Pierce, Jr.
1976.41.33

Mexican, Jaina Island (ca. A.D. 500-800): *Standing Personage with
Headdress.* Polychromed terra cotta, $7\frac{1}{8}$ x $4\frac{3}{4}$ x $2\frac{1}{4}$ (18.2 x 12.1 x 5.7
cm). Florence C. Quinby Fund in memory of Henry Cole Quinby
h '16. 1969.85

Mexican, Valley of Mexico (A.D. 500-1000): *Head.* Terra cotta, $1\frac{15}{16}$
x $1\frac{3}{4}$ x $\frac{7}{8}$ (4.9 x 4.5 x 2.2 cm). Gift of Mr. Henry H. Pierce, Jr.
1976.41.36

✠Mexican, Maya Indian (A.D. 600-800): *Seated Male.* Terra cotta, 7 x
$3\frac{1}{16}$ x $2\frac{1}{2}$ (17.8 x 7.7 x 6.4 cm). Florence C. Quinby Fund in memory
of Henry Cole Quinby h '16. 1969.84

Mexican, Cholula (A.D. 720-1500): *Head.* Terra cotta, $2\frac{7}{16}$ x $1\frac{1}{8}$ x $1\frac{1}{4}$
(6.2 x 2.9 x 3.2 cm). Gift of Mr. Henry H. Pierce, Jr. 1976.41.25

Mexican, Cempola (A.D. 900-1500): *Head of a Monkey.* Terra cotta,
$1\frac{13}{16}$ x $1\frac{5}{16}$ x $1\frac{1}{16}$ (4.6 x 3.4 x 2.8 cm). Gift of Mr. Henry H. Pierce,
Jr. 1976.41.29

Mexican, Oaxaca (1200-1400): *Head with Headdress.* Terra cotta,
$3\frac{11}{16}$ x $3\frac{3}{8}$ x $3\frac{5}{8}$ (9.4 x 8.6 x 9.3 cm). Gift of Mr. Henry H. Pierce, Jr.
1976.41.55

Mexican, Valley of Pueblo (1500-1600): *Head.* Terra cotta, $1\frac{5}{16}$ x
$1\frac{1}{16}$ x $\frac{11}{16}$ (3.4 x 2.8 x 1.8 cm). Gift of Mr. Henry H. Pierce, Jr.
1976.41.63

NORTH AMERICAN INDIAN

New Mexican, Santa Clara Indian (probably 19th century): *Jar.*
Terra cotta, $2\frac{1}{2}$ x $3\frac{3}{16}$ (diam.) (6.3 x 8.1 cm). Gift of Miss Virginia
Dox. 1893.12

North American, Northwest Coast, Nootka Indian (19th century):
Male Figure. Polychromed wood, $15\frac{1}{2}$ x $3\frac{5}{8}$ x $3\frac{1}{4}$ (39.3 x 8.2 x 6.7
cm). Anonymous gift. 1850.6

✠North American, Northwest Coast, possibly Nootka Indian (prob-
ably 19th century): *Male Figure.* Polychromed wood, $15\frac{3}{8}$ x $3\frac{1}{4}$ x $3\frac{1}{4}$
(39.2 x 8.3 x 8.3 cm). Anonymous gift. 1850.5

✠North American, Northwest Coast, possibly Nootka Indian (prob-
ably 19th century): *Mask.* Polychromed wood, $15\frac{3}{16}$ x $4\frac{1}{4}$ x $2\frac{3}{16}$
(38.6 x 10.8 x 5.6 cm). Anonymous gift. 1850.4

✠North American, Northwest Coast, Tlingit Indian (ca. 1890): *Basket.*

Spruce roots and grass, $9\frac{1}{2}$ x $11\frac{1}{2}$ (diam.) (24.1 x 29.2 cm). Gift of Mrs. John R. Dunton. 1944.26.1

North American, Northwest Coast, Tlingit Indian (probably 19th century): *Basket*. Grass, $6\frac{1}{2}$ x $7\frac{1}{8}$ (diam.) (16.5 x 18.1 cm). Gift of Mrs. John R. Dunton. 1944.26.2

North American, Northwest Coast, Tlingit Indian (probably 19th century): *Covered Basket*. Grass, 5 x $5\frac{3}{4}$ (diam.) (12.7 x 14.6 cm). Gift of Mrs. John R. Dunton. 1944.26.3

North American, Passamaquoddy Indian (probably 19th century): *Purse*. Chamois, textile, and beads, $7\frac{5}{8}$ x $7\frac{3}{4}$ (19.4 x 19.7 cm). Gift of Miss Virginia Dox. 1893.34

North American, Pueblo Indian (probably 19th century): *Bird*. Terra cotta, $3\frac{11}{16}$ x $5\frac{13}{16}$ x $3\frac{1}{8}$ (9.3 x 14.7 x 7.9 cm). Gift of Miss Virginia Dox. 1893.3

North American, Pueblo Indian (probably 19th century): *Bowl*. Terra cotta, 2 x 7 (diam.) (5.1 x 17.8 cm). Gift of Miss Virginia Dox. 1893.9

North American, Pueblo Indian (probably 19th century): *Jar*. Terra cotta, $2\frac{11}{16}$ x $2\frac{15}{16}$ (diam.) (6.8 x 7.5 cm). Gift of Miss Virginia Dox. 1893.7

North American, Pueblo Indian (probably 19th century): *Pitcher*. Terra cotta, $3\frac{5}{16}$ x $3\frac{3}{4}$ x $2\frac{13}{16}$ (8.4 x 9.5 x 7.2 cm). Gift of Miss Virginia Dox. 1893.4

North American, Pueblo Indian (probably 19th century): *Standing Bird*. Terra cotta, $3\frac{13}{16}$ x $3\frac{5}{8}$ x $3\frac{1}{16}$ (9.6 x 9.2 x 7.7 cm). Gift of Miss Virginia Dox. 1893.8

✠North American, Queen Charlotte Islands, Haida Indian (ca. 1850): *Ceremonial Pipe*. Argillite, $4\frac{3}{8}$ x $4\frac{3}{16}$ x $1\frac{1}{4}$ (11.2 x 10.7 x 3.2 cm). Gift of Mr. Rufus K. Sewall 1837. 1896.8

✠North American, Zuñi Indian (ca. 1880): *Water Jar*. Terra cotta, $10\frac{1}{8}$ x $13\frac{3}{4}$ (diam.) (25.7 x 34.9 cm). Gift of Mrs. Herbert E. Hawkes. 1970.31

PERUVIAN

Peruvian (pre-Columbian): *Bridge-Spout Vessel*. Earthenware, 8 x $6\frac{3}{4}$ (diam.) (20.3 x 17.2 cm). Florence C. Quinby Fund in memory of Henry Cole Quinby h '16. 1969.86

Peruvian (pre-Columbian): *Double Gourd Vase*. Earthenware, $5\frac{7}{8}$ x 6 x 4 (14.9 x 15.2 x 10.2 cm). Gift of Mr. George Warren Hammond h '00. 1906.10

Peruvian (pre-Columbian): *Double Gourd Vase*. Earthenware, $6\frac{1}{2}$ x $7\frac{3}{8}$ x $3\frac{7}{8}$ (16.5 x 18.7 x 9.8 cm). Gift of Mr. George Warren Hammond h '00. 1906.9

Peruvian (pre-Columbian): *Double Gourd Vessel*. Earthenware, $7\frac{1}{16}$ x 8 x $5\frac{1}{16}$ (18.0 x 20.3 x 12.8 cm). Gift of Mr. and Mrs. Brewster Doggett. 1976.36.2

Peruvian (pre-Columbian): *Vase*. Terra cotta, $8\frac{9}{16}$ x $5\frac{1}{8}$ x $3\frac{15}{16}$ (21.7 x 13.0 x 10.1 cm). Gift of Mr. John Moses, Jr. '60. 1962.116

Peruvian (pre-Columbian): *Votive Vessel*. Earthenware, $10\frac{9}{16}$ x 14 x $9\frac{5}{8}$ (26.8 x 35.6 x 24.3 cm). Gift of Mr. and Mrs. Brewster Doggett. 1976.36.1

✠Peruvian, Maya Indian (ca. 1500): *Vase*. Earthenware, $8\frac{3}{4}$ x $6\frac{1}{4}$ (diam.) (22.3 x 15.8 cm). Gift of Mr. George Warren Hammond h '00. 1906.08

Pacific Art

MELANESIAN

Melanesian, New Ireland (19th century): *Mask*. Wood, plaster, and textile, $18\frac{9}{16}$ x $11\frac{3}{4}$ x $8\frac{5}{8}$ (42.0 x 29.8 x 21.9 cm). Gift of Mr. Harold M. Sewall. 1898.67

Melanesian, New Ireland (19th century): *Mask*. Wood, plaster, and textile, $15\frac{1}{2}$ x $9\frac{7}{8}$ x $13\frac{9}{16}$ (39.4 x 25.1 x 34.4 cm). Gift of Mr. Harold M. Sewall. 1898.71

Melanesian, New Ireland (19th century): *Mask*. Wood, plaster, and textile, 17 x $10\frac{9}{16}$ x $11\frac{7}{8}$ (43.2 x 26.8 x 30.2 cm). Gift of Mr. Harold M. Sewall. 1898.72

Melanesian, New Ireland (19th century): *Mask*. Wood, plaster, and textile, $17\frac{1}{4}$ x $8\frac{1}{8}$ x $12\frac{1}{4}$ (43.8 x 20.6 x 31.1 cm). Gift of Mr. Harold M. Sewall. 1898.73

Melanesian, New Ireland (19th century): *Stylized Bird Carving*. Polychromed wood, $5\frac{1}{2}$ x $14\frac{5}{8}$ x $1\frac{3}{4}$ (14.0 x 37.2 x 4.4 cm). Gift of Mr. Arthur Sewall. 1898.75

✠Melanesian, New Ireland (probably 19th century): *Mask*. Polychromed wood, plaster, and yarn, $19\frac{3}{4}$ x $8\frac{3}{8}$ x $16\frac{1}{8}$ (50.1 x 21.3 x 41.0 cm). Gift of Mr. Harold M. Sewall. 1898.68

POLYNESIAN

Polynesian, Austral Islands (19th century): *Canoe Paddle*. Wood, $48\frac{1}{8}$ x $10\frac{15}{16}$ x $1\frac{1}{16}$ (122.3 x 27.8 x 2.7 cm). Gift of Mr. John C. Humphreys. 1850.8

Polynesian, Samoa (19th century): *War Club*. Wood, $42\frac{1}{8}$ x $5\frac{5}{8}$ x $2\frac{11}{16}$ (107.0 x 14.3 x 6.9 cm). Gift of Mr. Charles F. Adams '12. 1963.243

Polynesian, Tonga Islands (19th century): *Ceremonial Axe*. Wood, 39 x $7\frac{1}{2}$ x $3\frac{1}{8}$ (99.1 x 19.0 x 7.9 cm). Gift of Captain Weeks. 1853.5

Index